500 Manga Heroes & Villains

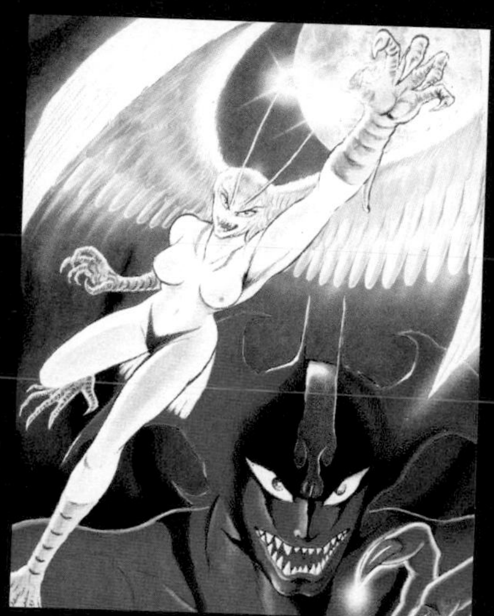

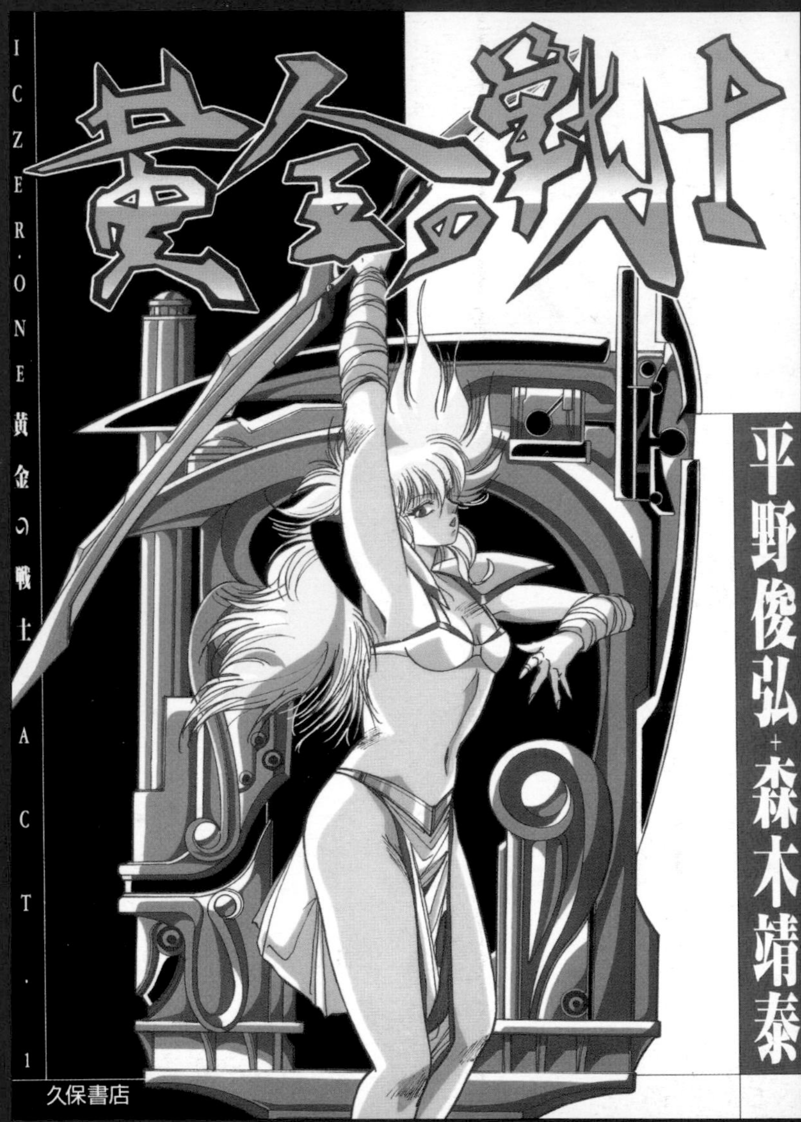

Golden Warrior Iczer-One

500 Manga Heroes & Villains

Helen McCarthy

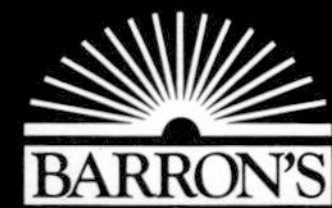

In memory of my father Bill (William Herbert) McCarthy – my first hero

First edition for the United States, its territories and dependencies and Canada published in 2006 by Barron's Educational Series, Inc.

First published in 2006 by Chrysalis Book Group

All inquiries should be addressed to:
Barron's Educational Seris, Inc.
250 Wireless Blvd.
Hauppauge, NY 11788
www.barronseduc.com

ISBN-13: 978-0-7641-3201-8
ISBN-10: 0-7641-3201-6

Library of Congress Catalog No: 2005932033

Commissioning editor: Chris Stone
Project Editor: Carly Madden
Designed by Philip Clucas MSIAD

Reproduction by Anorax
Printed and bound by Kyodo, Singapore

9 8 7 6 5 4 3 2 1

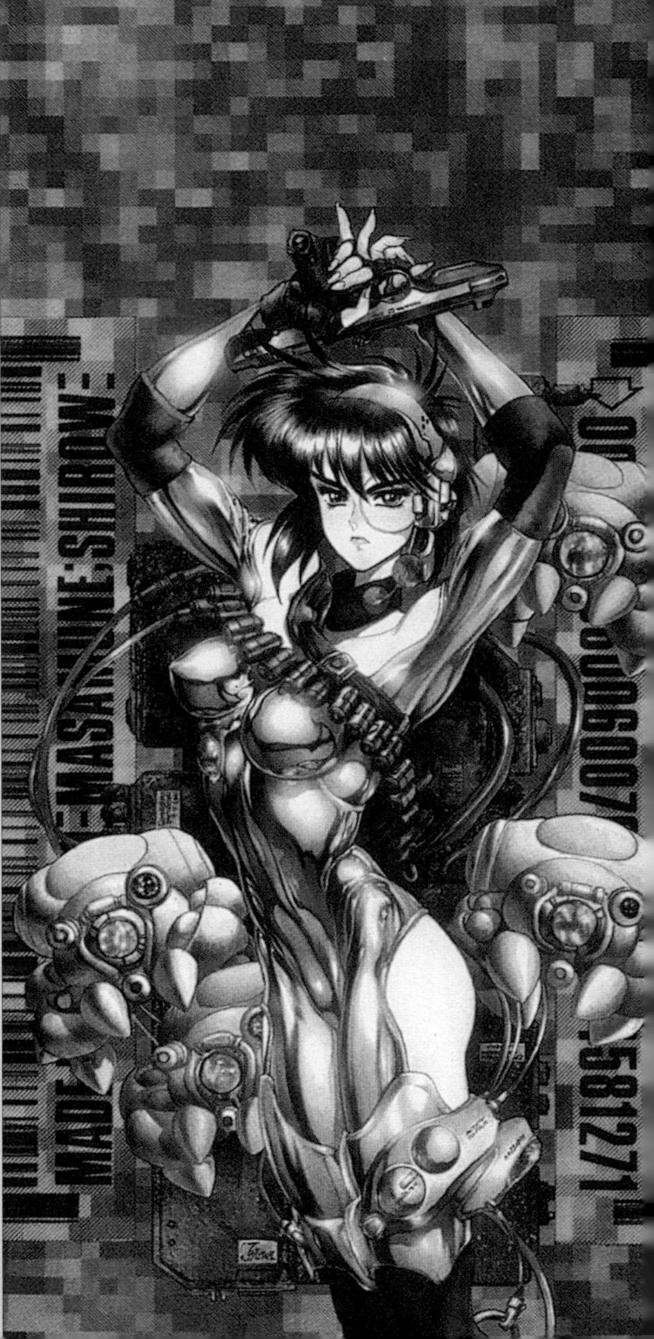

CONTENTS PAGE

Left: Motoko Kusanagi

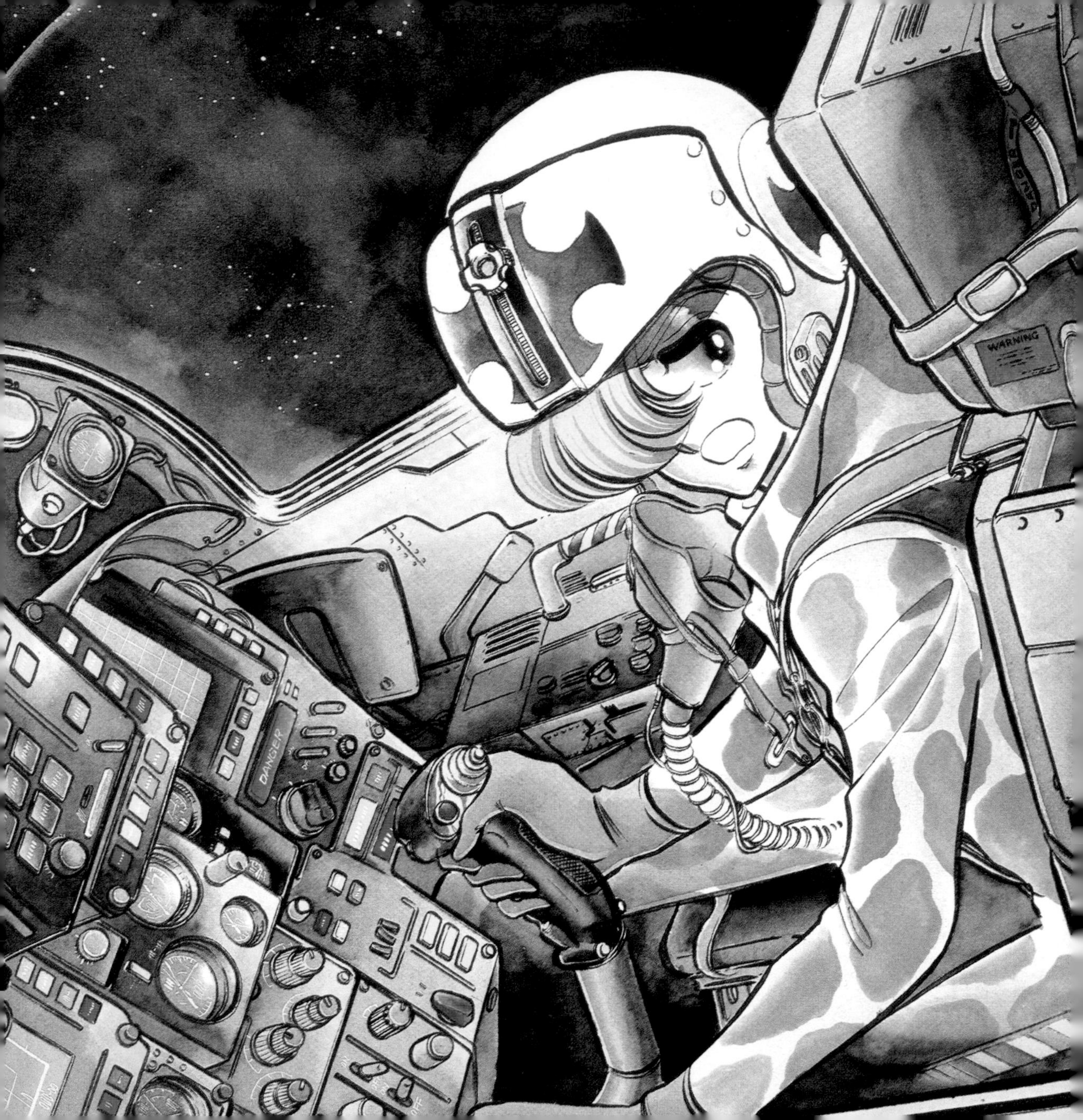

WARNING
DANGER

About this Book

This book is a very brief introduction to a huge subject. The heroes and villains of Japanese comics, known as manga, are many and varied. Sometimes they're wish-fulfillment, sometimes pure fantasy, sometimes a real figure from history, sometimes a reflection of the everyday. They can be male, female, both, or neither, human, alien, or animal. There are literally millions of them. Many will never see print in the English-speaking world, but more and more of them are making their way Westward to find new readers. In this book you'll find characters from titles available now in your local bookstore, alongside some whose stories are not yet translated into English. You can find more about them, and the rest of the manga medium, by looking at some of the books and web sites in the bibliography.

Half the challenge in doing a book like this is deciding what to leave out—one could drown in the torrent of material. To begin with, let me state the obvious. Manga is Japanese for comic, and only Japanese comics should be called Manga. One might feel this is a waste of words, but a look at book and comic web sites confirms that there's a lot of confusion. I see comics of many nations sold under the manga banner. This may work as a sales concept, but it has no place in a book about Japanese comics.

Left: Shin Kazama ace pilot and reluctant mercenary, risks his life in *Area 88*.

A work of art is not limited by the culture or era that produces it; but it is rooted in that culture and that era. An American artist working in the Japanese style makes a different kind of work than a Japanese artist; a Japanese artist working in a 1920s style in 2005 makes a different kind of work than anything created in the 1920s. We stick labels on works of art, not to limit them, but to enable ourselves to understand what we see. If there is any point in distinguishing Japanese comics from the comics of other nations by using a Japanese term, manga, then that term should only be used for Japanese comics. Any attempt to pretend that comics of other nations can become Japanese just by labeling them as manga is pointless. Kia Asamiya's *Batman* and *Uncanny X-Men* titles are both manga in my scheme of things, even though *X-Men* was first published in the United States and both comics are imbued with Asamiya's love for the American comic medium. It is manga because it was made by a Japanese artist working in

Japan. Ben Dunn's *Ninja High School* isn't manga, because it is a product of another culture, made by an American artist working in the U.S., although it is inspired by Dunn's love for the Japanese comic medium. Korean comics, Hong Kong comics, French, and Polish comics are not manga, no matter what style their artists choose to work in. The growing number of American, Italian, and other artists working "in the manga style" are not producing manga, and their characters are not included in this book. This is not a value judgment on the quality of these manga-influenced comics; it's simply a matter of accurate labeling. Manga are Japanese comics, therefore comics that aren't Japanese aren't manga. There is definitely scope for a book on the worldwide influence of manga and on the many artists who have taken the inspiration of the Japanese form and used it to forge something new and exciting; but this book isn't trying to fill that niche.

It's also worth stating that manga does not include movies, TV shows, or games, although it can be linked to all of those. Japanese animation is generally known as *anime*. There was a period in the 1970s and 1980s when the Toei film studio ran seasons of animation collectively known as Toei Manga Festivals, but the animation shown was based directly on popular manga and the seasons were aimed at enticing young manga fans into the movie theater. The major factor in mislabeling anime as manga was the 1990s marketing campaign of native British label Manga Video (later to become U.S. label Manga Entertainment), a brilliant attempt to brand the entire medium as the product of a single distribution company. It even included a trademark application for the word "manga." This, incidentally, generated one of the highest volumes of mail ever received at the British Patent Office for a single application, as fans all over the world wrote in to protest that this iconic Japanese word should not be the property of a single Western company.

So, all the characters in this book are chosen from Japanese comics only. Beyond that, the selection is fairly random—largely guided by my own tastes, by manga catching my eye at the moment, or new editions of older favorites. Any reader could come up with different character selections that would be just as valid an introduction to the world of manga, and just as much fun. If you have a favorite character and want to see if I've included him, her, or it, look in the index, where both Japanese and Western names—along with manga titles—appear. There is only room here for a tiny percentage of the characters populating the manga universe, so if your favorite isn't included, don't get annoyed. Instead, have a look at a couple of unfamiliar names. They might become your favorites too.

I want this book to be accessible to as many readers as possible, so Japanese terms are kept to a minimum and are explained the first time they're used. Characters are indexed by family name first, then by their personal name. This is the style normally used in English language indexing.

Some characters have a number of different names—Lupin III, for instance, has been known by at least five different names in various translations. I have used the name I think most English-speaking readers are likely to know—usually the name used in an official English edition, or the original Japanese name where there is no English edition. There are a few cases where I have not used the name in the published English version, because I think another choice makes more sense. For example, the CLAMP character usually described as Li Syaoran is Chinese, so his name is properly rendered Li Xiao Lang. Japanese character names and titles are given following their Western name the first time they appear; if there is no Western name or title, the Japanese version is used. A translation follows the first use where necessary.

When it comes to names, and transliterating them out of Japanese script into Roman letters, I've followed one rule: keep it simple. This book is in English, so (except for the word manga) I've used English terms to talk about the subject. Transliterated words are given in their English versions; spelling comics as *komikkusu*, or Versailles as *Berusaiya*, would add nothing to my argument. All names are given in accepted English order—personal name first, family name second in the text, and family name first, personal name second in the index. Macrons, extra letters, and doubled letters—all ways of indicating that a vowel sound is voiced twice in spoken Japanese—have not been used. There are plenty of linguistic purists out there who might object to some of these decisions, but I very much doubt that anyone whose Japanese is up to quibbling over transliteration needs this book.

Thanks to Jonathan Clements, Fred Patten, Steve Kyte, Darren Ashmore, and Gail Courtney for advice and input. Their kindness has greatly enhanced this book, while any defects are entirely mine. Among many other pieces of advice and information, Fred gave me details on the *Man from UNCLE* manga which kick-started the American fan movement, and Jonathan provided the full range of his world-class expertise on Japanese otter manga (and just about everything else). I have shamelessly plundered the works of Jonathan, Fred, and Frederik L. Schodt, listed in the bibliography (and which I highly recommend), all of which have made writing this book much easier.

The pictures in this book were provided through the kindness of the Forbidden Planet superstore, London; Viz LLC; Project Gen, and Steve Kyte. They are reproduced under the convention of fair use. All rights to these images, or the manga they represent, belong to the legal owners identified on page 344. We have made every effort to attribute copyright to the legal owner, but if any errors have occurred, please notify the publishers and they will be corrected in future editions.

Lastly, thanks to Steve for his constant support, which makes all things possible.

Helen McCarthy
London, England,
December 2004

MANGA: A BRIEF HISTORY

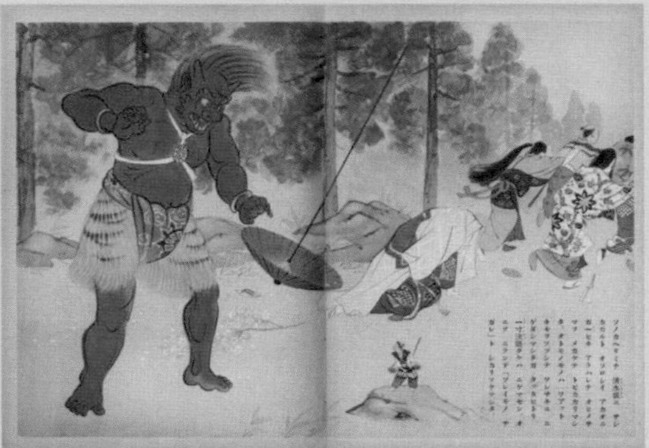

We all need stories; they help us make sense of an often senseless world, and when things get really crazy they give us an escape route. Comic books are a good way to tell stories: they're easy and cheap to acquire; they're easy and quick to read, so they don't exclude people with less grasp of language than you need for a novel; they can be slapstick-funny or deeply sophisticated; and the added dimension of pictures lets the creator tell his or her story in a variety of ways, ways—that hook into the brains of a generation bred on TV, movies, and video games faster and easier than a verbal narrative.

We all need heroes, villains, and the folk of various shades of grey in between, to hold up a mirror to ourselves and help us laugh, cry, think, or change. Comic books are fertile ground for heroes and villains. Almost every culture with a literate population and a publishing industry has comic books. Japan is no exception. The Japanese word for comic or comics is *manga*, though the term comics is also used in Japanese.

This book will tell you about a few of the characters created by manga artists and writers. But how did manga come into being in the first place?

In the beginning

In the sixteenth century, Japan made itself a closed society, with foreigners barely tolerated in two tiny enclaves on its margins. Locked away from the rest of the world like Sleeping Beauty, most Japanese lived in an unchanging feudal agrarian society until 1853, when a fleet of heavily armed American ships sailed into Yokohama Bay, and its commander, Commodore Matthew Perry, announced that it was best for all parties if Japan opened its borders. A wealthy, cultured merchant middle class had grown strong in the years of Japan's isolation, and as trade opened up, they embraced the many novelties the Western

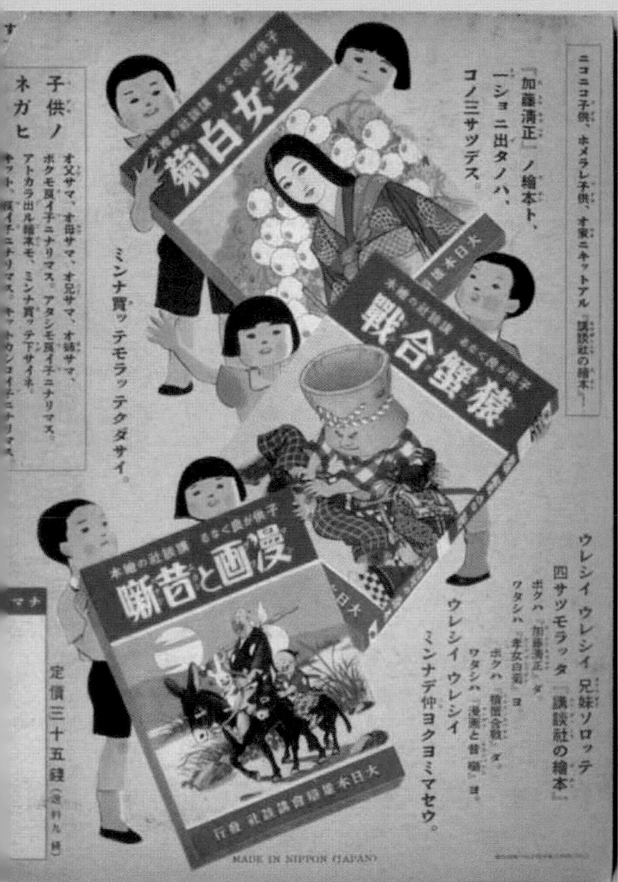

Japan has a long tradition of graphic illustration, and in the first half of the twentieth century many folktales and historical stories were put into graphic form to encourage children to read.

world had to offer. More foreigners came East in search of new opportunities, including two Europeans who were to have a huge influence on Japanese publishing—Briton Charles Wirgman in 1857, and Frenchman Georges Bigot in 1882. Both married Japanese women, and both founded satirical magazines. Japan had its own long tradition of social comedy, but political satire was blocked by edicts forbidding criticism of the Government. The foreign-owned magazines took liberties native publications had not even thought of; but once they saw it could be done, Japanese editors and cartoonists were not slow to try their hand at this new mode of social comment. Not even the imprisonment of a few notable figures could stop the new trend.

As well as new ways of thinking and expression, foreign magazines brought in new technology and new formats. Japanese cartoonists began adapting American comics for the Japanese audience, and many experimented with the tighter, more realistic American pen-and-ink style of cartooning as well as working in their looser, freer native brush style. In 1902 one of these, Rakuten Kitazawa (1876-1955), created the first serialized Japanese comic strip, the adventures of two country bumpkins sightseeing in Tokyo, for a Sunday supplement modelled on those in American newspapers. The comics market grew and diversified until 1937, when Japan went to war with China and later with the USA, and comics became part of the war effort. It was not until after Japan's surrender in 1945 that social and political cartoonists and artists could resume activity.

A new dawn

The demoralized population's need for comfort, reassurance, and a good laugh led to the growth of four-panel strip cartoons based on everyday life. Aimed at both adults and children, two of the strips making their debut in 1946 were by young artists who became enduring icons of the manga market: twenty-six-year-old Machiko Hasegawa, whose *Sazae-san*, a soap opera about a young housewife and her family getting by in the new postwar Japan, is the world's longest-running cartoon strip and animated TV series; and seventeen-year-old Osamu Tezuka, creator of the teenage heroine of *Ma-chan's Diary (Ma-chan no Nikkicho)*, who became the most influential figure in the development of modern manga.

New manga magazines began publication, and as major artists gained their own following, collected editions of individual titles began to be produced in 1955. This is still a vital part of the industry. Printed on good quality paper, with color covers and often including specially painted color splash pages at the beginning, these editions enable artists to build a fan following. The same year, in Osaka and soon nationwide, pay libraries where eager fans could read manga for a small fee sprang up. For the typical reader, short of cash and living in a tiny house with the extended family, this was a brilliant idea, combining peace and quiet with more manga for his money. Although the number of pay libraries has reduced radically as economic and social conditions have changed, the idea is still around, with libraries having transformed themselves into "manga cafes" where you can get coffee and pastries with your comic book fix.

Today in Japan, manga makes up a substantial percentage of the publishing market. The stereotypical comment that you can see all kinds of people reading manga on the Tokyo subway is still true; office workers of both sexes and all ages, housewives, seniors and preschoolers all have their own manga. Artists can become as rich and famous as rock stars, or can spend their working lives toiling away as assistants to bigger names, producing page upon page of inking, screen tone, or lettering at low rates of pay. There is a huge fan industry producing fanzines, amateur artists, writers, and publishers who hold down day jobs, but for whom creating manga is an urge too strong to resist. Many have their own fan followings. Some renowned professionals have started in the fan market, the best known in the West being Masamune Shirow and the CLAMP collective.

The industry in Japan

Manga is a huge part of the Japanese publishing industry. At the turn of the millennium there were around a dozen manga weeklies, ten bi-weeklies, and fifteen major monthlies. Individual titles rise and fall in popularity, but there are usually about ten

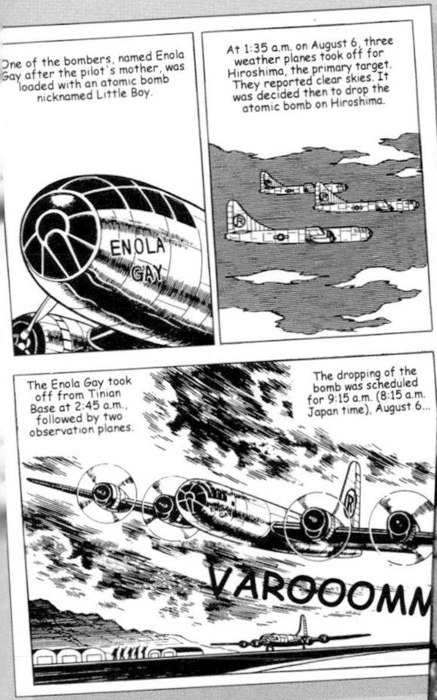

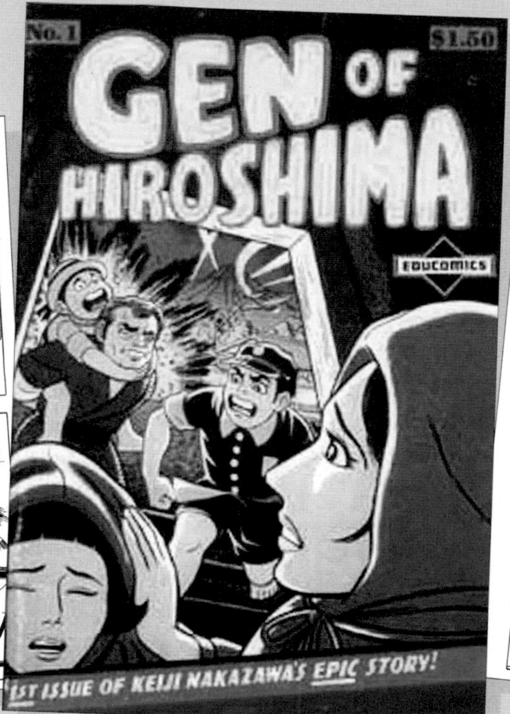

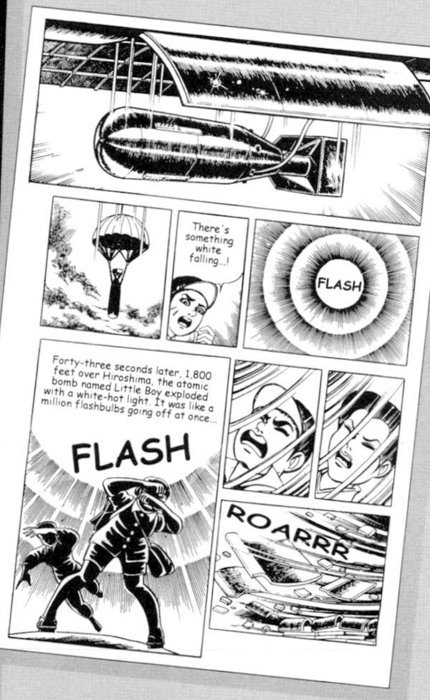

Keiji Nakazawa's masterwork is a first-hand account of the horrors of surviving an atomic strike – a reality which still resonates in manga.

manga magazines with circulations of over a million copies per issue, a circulation only one or two other Japanese publications can match. Manga magazines range from *dojinshi*—fanzines produced by small groups of friends, which can have circulations of twenty or several thousand—through small-press critical journals about the art form, to the phonebook-sized weekly anthologies on cheap paper read by almost every commuter in Japan.

Putting numbers on the industry is a complex equation, but total publication sales in Japan in 2000 were 2 trillion 500 billion yen. Manga sales accounted for almost a quarter of that total, 550 billion yen. Magazine sales accounted for 350 billion and the rest was collected paperback editions. Or to put it another way, with a population of 120 million at the turn of the millennium, every man, woman and child in Japan spent around 4,500 yen on manga.

The three largest publishing houses producing manga are Kodansha, Shogakkan, and Shueisha. There are several other large publishers, including Akita Shoten, Futabasha, Shonen Gahosha, Hakusensha, Nihon Bungeisha, and Kobunsha, as well as numerous small-scale publishing firms. Most larger publishers also publish magazines and books other than manga.

There are around 3,000 professional manga artists in Japan—that is, people who have published at least one volume of manga in their own right, rather than only contributing to an anthology or assisting an established star. Most of them make their living as assistants to more famous manga artists, or have a second job. A small percentage are able to make an above-average living from manga alone. In addition, there are also many amateur manga artists, early teens to adults, who either cannot or choose not to make a living from manga. Their work circulates through word of mouth, fanzines, or comic fairs, the largest of which is the three-day, biannual Comiket festival in Tokyo, which has grown over the past twenty years to attract almost half a million fans (making it the largest regular fan gathering on the planet).

Manga abroad

In Asia, Japanese comics are widely translated and have cross-fertilized with many native comic cultures. In Europe, translated manga have been available on the mass market in France, Italy, and Spain over the past four decades. In the U.S., after many years of background work by dedicated individuals like Frederik L. Schodt, Dana Lewis, and Toren Smith—and a number of false dawns—manga are finally selling in sufficient number and variety to talk in terms of an American manga market. Even in Britain, which normally gets its Asian culture secondhand via Hong Kong or the U.S., there have been a few brave experiments with manga publishing, notably Bloomsbury's *Ironfist Chinmi* series, intended to get reluctant preteen readers to engage with books. The British publishing industry is still pushing this idea, and declared February 2005 'Manga Month' to promote the idea that schoolchildren can be tempted into reading via Japanese comics.

Italy, France, and Spain have long traditions of translation and publication of manga, but their manga industries, though well established, are relatively small. Anglophone countries have lagged behind. The 1980s and 1990s saw several false dawns for the long-predicted manga invasion of America, from the publication of *Lone Wolf* and *Cub* to the freak success of Katsuhiro Otomo's *Akira*. After *Akira*, the general public, unfamiliar with manga, looked for titles of similar style and quality and found none available in their local stores. The cult market grew by fractions that were too small to attract the big guns of the industry, until the cavalry arrived in the shape of wide TV exposure. Anime, manga's hyperactive sibling, began to penetrate the American TV market.

Japanese studios have always contributed heavily to the world animation market, although local audiences don't always register this fact. But with the need to find more fodder for the airwaves, Japanese animation, a medium with a number of false dawns of its own in the West, has finally begun to register on the mass market screen. Now it's freely available on TV across the U.S., and several shows, notably *Pokémon*, have begun to perform along Japanese lines, using the regular twenty-five-minute episode as a commercial to move lucrative merchandise tie-ins in the same way that fuels the industry in Japan. As anime grows in popularity with American schoolchildren and college students, manga have begun to shed their cult status and break into mainstream youth publishing in the U.S. and Europe. Teens and preteens want more material on their favorite TV shows, and publishers want a product with a ready-made audience and its own weekly TV commercials at no extra cost.

This lucrative young market has attracted the interest of the big three manga publishers in Japan. As recently as ten years ago, Kodansha, Shogakkan, and Shueisha considered foreign sales unviable. According to the Japanese edition of *Newsweek*, by the summer of 2003, Japanese publishers had gone beyond simply selling translation rights and formed ties with Western publishers to launch several manga magazines for younger readers: *Banzai* and *Manga Power* for boys, and *Daisuki* for girls, in Germany; *Shonen* in France; and *Manga Mania* in Sweden. In the U.S., Shueisha joined forces with Shogakkan subsidiary Viz Communications to form a joint venture, Viz LLC. Mixx's *Smile* was the first manga magazine specifically for girls to be published outside Asia in 1999, and Viz brought out an English edition of boys' action comic *Shonen Jump* in 2003.

Although foreign markets for manga are small compared with Japan—36.1 billion yen in France and 4.7 billion yen in the newer U.S. arena—manga markets have grown over the past two or three years. In the United States, sales almost tripled from 2000 to 2002, and the market is now estimated at somewhere between $40 million and $50 million, or a tenth of the American anime market. *Publishers Weekly* (June 16, 2004) reported that total sales of all graphic novels surged from about $75 million in 2001 to projected sales of about $120 million in 2003, which gives Japanese material around a third of the U.S. graphic novel market.

The industry has looked to foreign sales before and been disappointed, but now that anime is widely aired in the U.S. market, the links with American publishers look more solid. The "journey to the West" of Oriental legend has taken manga more than a century to make, but at the dawn of the third millennium, the Japanese comic industry has finally gone global.

Twenty years ago, few people in the English speaking world had heard the word manga. Now you can pick up a comic book from the other side of the world and go into a multitude of new worlds to meet a huge number of new characters, all dreamed up by manga artists to entertain people they'll never meet, but with whom they have much in common. After all, we all need stories.

Male Heroes

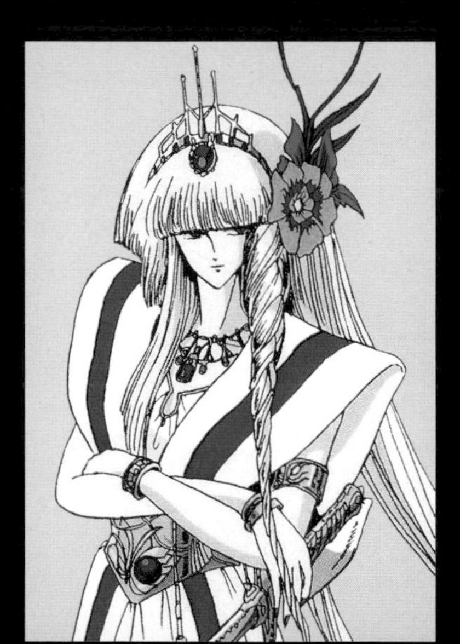

Emperor Amaterasu

Heroes can be born as heroes. They emerge into the world with their ideals in place and their good qualities ready for use. It's more interesting, though, when they become heroes. There are more story possibilities when someone has heroism thrust upon him. The male manga hero doesn't always start out looking heroic. He can be a childlike creature, a geek, a wimp, a hapless boy, or a man drifting through life without a clue, let alone a plan.

There are plenty of conventionally heroic males around in manga, but if the average modern reader—a working man ground down by routine or a no-hoper struggling to keep up in school—can't identify with a samurai, a superhero, a biker rebel, or a rock god, he can find plenty of manga male stereotypes that match more closely with the reality of urban daily life. A hero can start out weak, cowardly, lecherous, or dishonest; he can be uncouth and get drunk, but the qualities that the Japanese reader recognizes as the mark of a real hero always come through before the end of the story. He sticks by his friends. He looks out for others weaker than himself. He doesn't give up, however tough things get. He knows you can be a hero without a fancy name, a costume, a giant robot, or a massive sword. Whether the guy is in a business suit, medieval armor, a school uniform, or a thirty-foot-tall mobile suit, everyone knows that's not what makes him a hero. What makes him a hero is what's inside—so he's not so different from the Western comic hero after all.

ALUCARD [2002]

With a name that's Dracula spelled backwards, Alucard is obviously a vampire, but he's on our side. He works for the Hellsing organization, set up by the descendants of Professor Van Hellsing to defend Britain from the vampire threat by fighting fire with fire, a similar premise to that found in *Devilman*. He is a good-looking young man (a mere 567 years old) whose sarcastic tongue, mocking demeanor, and cocky attitude are coupled with sadism and contempt for those he regards as inferior—which covers most of humanity and most other vampires, especially those who prey on the innocent. He carries two specially made weapons. The 15in. handgun "Joshua" uses massive Casull rounds, custom-made from silver, intended for hunting bear. It stops most things, dead or undead, but its magazine only holds six rounds, so with one in the chamber, Alucard only has seven shots before he has to reload. His other handgun, "Jackal," looks similar and has the same capacity, but takes slightly bigger shells with armor-piercing cores, each of which is baptized. Jackal is made of pure silver and weighs 35lbs., too heavy for most humans to lift, let alone aim. Alucard has a challenging relationship with the last of the Hellsing line. Integra Hellsing is a beautiful but serious young woman whose devotion to protecting Queen and country from vampires rules her life. When the chips are down, however, there's no doubt who is the boss. Alucard shows a softer side—occasionally—with Victoria Seras, Hellsing's newest recruit, a pretty nineteen-year-old former medic with the Metropolitan Police until he made her a vampire to save her life. Alucard gives grudging respect to his main opponent, Father Alexander Anderson, a blond, green-eyed priest who is the top agent of the Iscariot Organization, the Vatican's equivalent of Hellsing. Although out for the same goal, the elimination of vampires, the Catholic and Protestant churches are bitterly

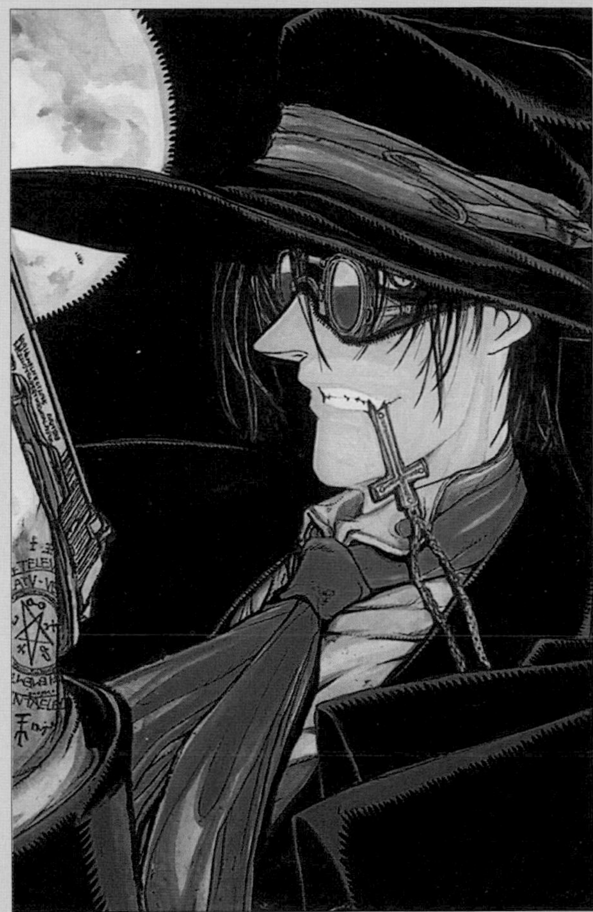

Smarter than the average vampire, with a tongue as sharp as his fangs, Alucard hunts his own kind.

opposed and kill each other's people as readily as their common enemy. Kota Hirano's manga debuted in *Shonen* magazine.

AMATERASU DES GRANDES ADINES [1988]

The Lord of the Amaterasu Kingdom Domains (AKD) and eventual Emperor of the Joker System is the central character of former fashion illustrator and sometime rock star Mamoru Nagai's sprawling epic *The Five Star Stories*, which debuted in *Newtype* magazine in 1988, and is partly available in English from his own Toys Press. Purple-haired, red-eyed Amaterasu rules from a levitating island, Float Temple, on the planet Delta Belune. He can change gender at will. He sometimes masquerades as the androgynous mech-maker Meister Ladios Sopp, or as Mel Rince, the female head of the Divers Guild. When absent on his wanderings, he is impersonated by the head of his bodyguard, Princess Aisha Codante. He is served and protected by an elite force known as the First Easter Mirage Corps, or Mirage Knights. He has not aged for hundreds of years. Many believe he has undergone the age-slowing Elazer process, but he is in fact, a God of Light. Born with no human feelings at all, and acquiring a serious Oedipus complex early on, he can be spectacularly cruel and callous, but becomes capable of loyalty and love. His friend Dr. Chrome Ballanche finally teaches him the meaning of sorrow by dying, having earlier created his future wife, the Fatima Fate Lachesis. Amaterasu's 1,300-year empire is eventually ended by a descendant of his wife's sister's lover, King Colus III, with his own collusion.

SOICHIRO ARIMA [1996]

The high-school hero of *His & Her Circumstances (Kareshi Kanojo no Jijo* a.k.a. *KareKano)* by Masami Tsuda is a straight-A student with charm and good looks in bucketfuls, but he's not perfect—he can be sneaky and manipulative. He's used to being the number-one guy in class, and when he transfers to a new school he's not surprised to be the new top student. Unfortunately the old number-one student, a cute girl named Yukino Miyazawa, is furious that someone else has become the class idol. She gives Soichiro a hard time, but then he finds out that despite her classroom image, at home she's a lazy, careless slob. Naturally he exploits this to get back at her, but in time the two realize they really do love each other. Soichiro stops exploiting her, Yukino stops showing off and accepts that she doesn't have to be on top to be liked, and they become boyfriend and girlfriend. This high-school romance with an edge of reality appeared in *Hana To Yume* and is available in English from Tokyopop.

AKIRA ASAGUMO [1963]

The hero of Osamu Tezuka's *BIG X (Dai X)*, Asagumo made his debut in *Shonen Book*. His grandfather worked with the Nazis on a top-secret weapon but conspired with a German scientist, Dr. Engel, to delay the research and foil their plans. As the end of World War II approached, Dr. Asagumo hid the secret of Big X in the body of his son, Shigeru, just before he was murdered by his employers. Twenty years later, in Tokyo, the card is discovered. A neo-Nazi organization steals it and completes the Big X project with the collaboration of Dr. Engel's grandson Hans. Big X is a drug that can expand the human body without limits. Shigeru's son, Akira, retrieves Big X from the enemy and uses it on himself to foil the Nazi plot and save the world. Inspired by German weapons research and the evil engendered by German-Japanese collaboration, Tezuka created an entirely righteous hero, but later came to view the attitudes and ideas Akira embodied as rather one-dimensional and inflexible, and didn't use the character again.

CAPTAIN AVATAR [1975]

Captain Avatar (Okita) in Leiji Matsumoto's seminal manga *Cosmoship Yamato*, which debuted in *Shonen Sunday Comics* and spun off the TV show *Star Blazers (Uchu Senkan Yamato* a.k.a. *Space Battleship Yamato)*, is a true hero. In the twenty-third century, he leads a team of volunteers on a near-hopeless mission to the stars, piloting a ship built inside the rotting hulk of the 250-year-old World War II battleship *Yamato*. They are seeking help from an unknown alien race to fight off the invaders who have devastated Earth. He feels deep responsibility for all his crew, but especially hot-headed pilot Derek Wildstar (Susumu Kodai), whose older brother disappeared in battle—a fate for which the captain feels responsible. A tall man in late middle age whose trademark mustache is often the only part of his face visible under the peak of his cap, Avatar carries on the battle even though he is seriously ill, and finally gives his life to save his world. He became the template for many heroic leaders in manga and anime.

DAISUKE BAN [1961]

One of twin brothers in Osamu Tezuka's *Shonen Sunday* manga *The White Pilot*, Daisuke is the son of a scientist killed by his country's secret police. His brother is adopted by the Queen and named Marus, while he is sold into slavery in an underground factory, adopted by the mysterious iron-masked Shunsuke Ban, and eventually escapes with him and seven other slaves, stealing a jet plane and starting a fight to free all the slaves of the kingdom. This brings him into direct conflict with his own brother, but also reveals a terrible secret—one of the twins is a clone, produced by a machine invented by their father to duplicate humans. The story ends tragically with the death of the heroes, once again showing Tezuka's absolute hatred of war.

YUGO BEPPU [1994]

Yugo Beppu is a master negotiator and mediator, and the hero of Osamu Akana and Shinji Makari's *Afternoon* manga *Yugo*. Highly topical in the age of international terrorism, the manga opens with Mayuko seeking help for her father, who has been kidnapped by bandits in Pakistan. Yugo speaks five languages fluently and has superb international connections at all levels of society. He's also witty, kind, and understands human nature. After saving Mayuko's father, he goes on to handle more delicate and dangerous negotiations with yakuza at home in Japan, the Hong Kong triads, the I.R.A., and the Ministry of Internal Affairs in Siberia.

BLACK JACK [1973]

The gifted surgeon hero of Osamu Tezuka's long-running medical melodrama (it ended in 1984) could be said to represent Dr. Tezuka himself. A distinctive if outdated dresser who favors Edwardian frilled shirts, string bow ties, and a flowing cape, Black Jack is a brilliant surgeon, but practices outside the law, without a license, for exorbitant fees. A scar on his face and an inhuman pallor hint at his dark past. In childhood, he and his sick mother were deserted by his father for another woman, which may have formed his somewhat cynical outlook. (He gets his chance at revenge when years later his father asks him to perform plastic surgery and make his new wife "the most beautiful woman in the world." Guess whose face she gets?) Black Jack lives alone but for his assistant Pinoko, a sweet young woman in a child's prosthetic body. He treats her as a daughter, and they share a deserted, dilapidated clinic in the wilderness. Their

ASTRO BOY [1951]

THE EPONYMOUS HERO of *Astro Boy*, or *Tetsuwan (Mighty) Atom* as he is known in his homeland, is a childlike robot who was made on April 7, 2003. He became Osamu Tezuka's most famous creation, winning huge popularity on television and becoming known throughout the world. Merging the innocence and aspiration of *Pinocchio* with the power of *Superman*, *Astro Boy* also represented the positive aspects of science and technology to a nation only six years on from the horrors of Hiroshima and Nagasaki, and the case for tolerance and openness to others.

Astro Boy debuted as *Captain Atom (Atom Taishi* a.k.a. *Ambassador Atom)* in *Shonen* magazine in March 1951, in a tale of conflict and coexistence on a future Earth invaded by aliens. Humanoid robot Atom tries to negotiate a peace between the two sides. Originally, the story was called *Atom Continent* and the robot only acquired his name and leading role when Tezuka changed the title and storyline. *Tetsuwan Atom* first appeared in April 1952. It was to run under its new name in *Shonen* until the magazine folded in 1968.

In the twenty-first century, robots became identical in appearance to humans, and developed emotions resembling those of their makers. Created as slaves, they began to feel and think for themselves. Mankind dealt with its creations as it has always dealt with enslaved minorities—it imposed the Laws of Robotics to control robot activities, and imposed strict segregation policies.

Prof. Boynton (Prof. Tenma), genius Minister of Science, became deranged with grief when his son, Toby (Tobio) was killed in a car accident. He devoted all the resources of his Ministry to creating "a scientific work of art—the ultimate in robotic science," not as an experiment, but as a father's desperate attempt to defeat death. The robot's brain was that of an innocent child, impressed with Toby's personality, and he was given the capacity for the highest and purest levels of emotion. With 100,000-horsepower strength, superhuman agility, and incredible endurance, he could not be killed again. Yet not even the great scientist could get around the fatal flaw in the design of this robot child—he would never grow up. Tenma had none of the joy of seeing his child grow to manhood, only a constant reminder of what was lost. Despairing and driven to madness, he abused the little robot day and night and finally sold him to Cacciatore (Hamegg), the owner of a circus with a robot show.

The robot endured hardship and cruelty as a plaything for humans to gape at, before being rescued by kindly Prof. Packadermus J. Elefun (Prof. Ochanomizu). Elefun created a robot family for him, with parents, a cute

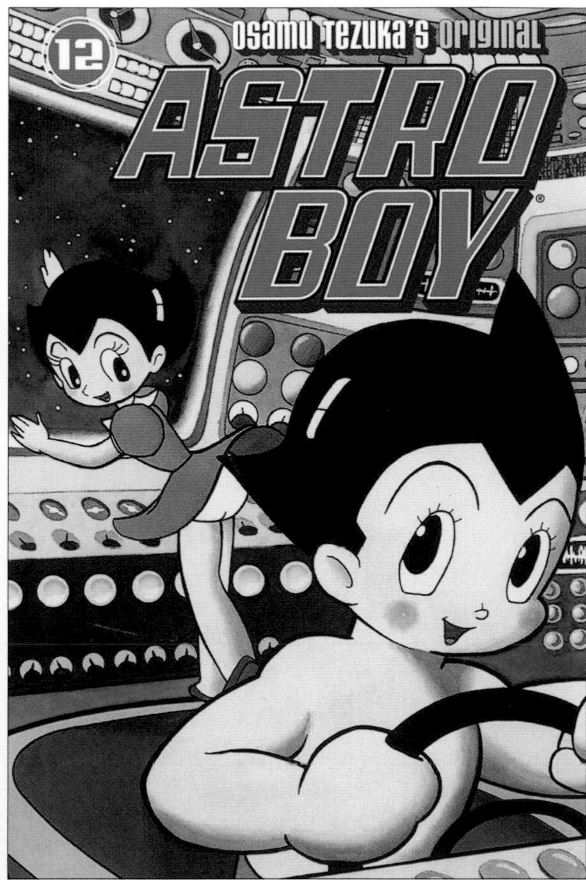

Tezuka's robotic hero shares an adventure with his sister, Uran, one of a whole family constructed to give Astro Boy a normal life.

sister named Astro Girl (Uran), and a little brother named Cobalt. He and his friend Old Man Mustache (Higeoyaji), guided and protected the little robot like a normal child. Astro learned to become a force for good and to use his great power to protect mankind from dangers, such as evil robots and invaders from outer space.

The manga ended inconclusively in 1968 when *Shonen* magazine folded. Over the course of its eighteen-year run, a total of sixty-nine separate stories were published. These have been reprinted in a variety of formats. Tezuka also rewrote the original *Captain Atom* manga as an episode of its sequel; several versions were published, the one in Kodansha's *Complete Works of Osamu Tezuka* being the closest to the original.

A live-action TV show based on the manga first aired in 1959. In 1963, Tezuka's own animation studio, Mushi Productions, launched the animated *Astro Boy* TV series on New Year's Day. It first aired in the U.S. in the same year, in a dubbed version produced by Fred Ladd.

The contradiction at the heart of *Astro Boy* is implicit in one central question: even with all the benefits of science, can humanity ever coexist with scientific knowledge without abusing it? Astro Boy is a tragic embodiment of this conflict, merging the potential greatness of the human heart with the desolation of the slave, treated as a chattel by those he seeks to love and serve, despite his intrinsic dignity. In this he is more akin to Frankenstein's monster than to Disney's *Pinocchio*. *Astro Boy* is available in English from Viz.

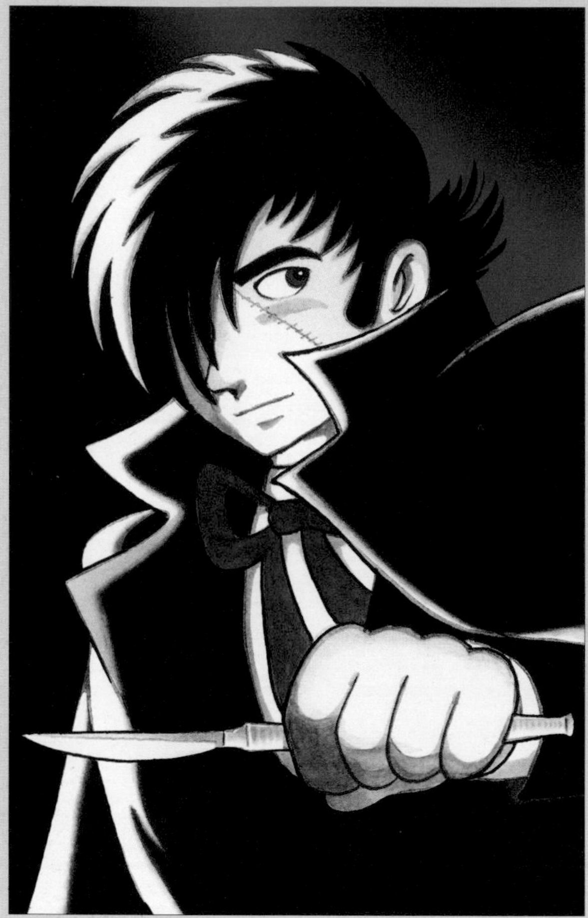

Of all Osamu Tezuka's characters, rogue surgeon Black Jack was the one he identified with most.

visitors are the desperate or outlawed clients for whom Black Jack represents their only chance. He is constantly seeking answers to questions about the value of life, the meaning of goodness, and the need for hope, but often failing to find them. He gives others great happiness by his skills, but he can never find it for himself. Like all Tezuka's characters, he guests in stories other than his own—in 1975 he appears in *Astro Boy II* as the Minister of Science, following it up with cameos in manga including *Boy Detective Zumbera*, *Horror Tales of Yotsuya*, and *Don Dracula*. He also appears in anime, and even in advertisements.

PETER BRADY a.k.a. HACHIRO AZUMA [1962]

Police officer Brady/Azuma is murdered by a criminal gang. Foreshadowing both manga *Cyborg 009* and the U.S. movie *Robocop*, his memories are installed into a robot body by Prof. Genius (Prof. Tani). The body is military prototype 008, designed in the Republic of Amarco for battle, but Azuma—or 8 Man, as his cybernetic self is known—uses it to take on the cyborgs and mutants of an international crime syndicate. He recharges his nuclear batteries by smoking nuclear isotope cigarettes; it's doubtful whether a health warning on the packet would be enough to get the manga past the censors nowadays. Jiro Kuwata's manga *8Man* from *Shonen* magazine was based on an earlier novel by Kazumasa Hirai. The resulting animated TV series was shown in the United States as *Tobor the 8th Man*. It was updated on video in 1993; a live-action movie was released in 1992.

BOB BRILLIANT a.k.a. PROF. SHIKASHIMA [1956]

Bob Brilliant is the name given to Prof. Shikashima in the U.S. TV release of Mitsuteru Yokoyama's manga *Gigantor (Tetsujin 28-Go/Iron Man No. 28)*, which came to America in animated form. In the TV series, Bob is the guardian of twelve-year-old boy genius Jimmy Sparks *(Shotaro Kaneda)*, and helped Jimmy's father design the mighty fighting robot Gigantor *(Tetsujin)*. In the manga, he is the father of Shotaro's friend Buttons *(Tetsuo)* and the sole designer of the robot. At the start of the manga, everyone believes he is dead, killed in the bombing raids of 1945. He's really in hiding to protect his robot invention, the twenty-eighth version of a military project. He's over six feet tall, slim and dark-haired, and wears glasses. The thirty-foot Gigantor is operated from a small hand-held remote control. In the manga, the professor gives Gigantor to Jimmy and returns to family life and research work, while Jimmy helps local police chief Ignatz Blooper *(Inspector Otsuka)* by using the robot's strength to fight crime. Creator Yokoyama, one of the seminal figures in modern manga, was inspired artistically by Osamu Tezuka; the idea for his giant robot came from the B29 bombers he saw flying over his hometown of Kobe during the war. In the original manga, the project was intended to be used against the Allies, but U.S. transmissions of the TV series omitted this.

KENNY CARTER [1965]

Kenny *(Shinichi Hoshi)* is a wild but good-hearted boy whose life in a little village in Japan is turned upside down by the arrival of three aliens from the Milky Way Patrol. Disguised as a rabbit, a duck, and a horse, the three aliens are on a mission to see if Earth should be annihilated or saved. Kenny influences them to save the world, and the four friends join forces with his older brother, the pipe-smoking, straight-down-the-line heroic Randy (Koichi), a member of a secret intelligence agency fighting global villains. The Osamu Tezuka manga *Amazing Three (W3)* started running in *Weekly Shonen Magazine*, but soon moved to *Weekly Shonen Sunday*. The animated version was broadcast in the United States. Japanese SF writer Shinichi Hoshi lent his name to the young hero, and Tezuka named his teacher, Mr. Baba, after a fellow manga artist.

CHINMI [1983]

In nineteenth century China, Chinmi, a happy-go-lucky boy, comes to the Dailin temple to train, bringing his pet monkey, Goku. He has enormous potential, but it needs to be refined and directed if he is to fulfil the prophecy and become master of Dailin. He learns new techniques from his master Ryukai, fights great masters and unselfish teachers, as well as facing evil enemies of China. He also makes many friends, including young martial artist

Xifang. After many years, Chinmi grows to manhood, enters a competition to find the greatest martial artist in the Empire, and saves the Emperor's life, returning to the Dailin temple with a sceptre emblazoned with an Imperial dragon in honor of his heroism, as well as the thanks of a grateful Emperor. Takeshi Maekawa's manga *Ironfist Chinmi* (*Tekken Chinmi*) was one of the unsung successes of 1990s manga publishing in English. The original story appeared in Kodansha's *Shonen* magazine and ran for sixteen years. Even after it ended in 1999, it was followed by a new Chinmi story in the same publication, entitled, logically enough, *New Chinmi*. Maekawa also featured Guanglin Temple, the focus of *New Chinmi*, in an earlier manga, *Kung Fu Tao*, which appeared briefly in 1995. Chinmi's adventures were animated for TV in 1988, introducing new characters Laochu and female fighter Lychee.

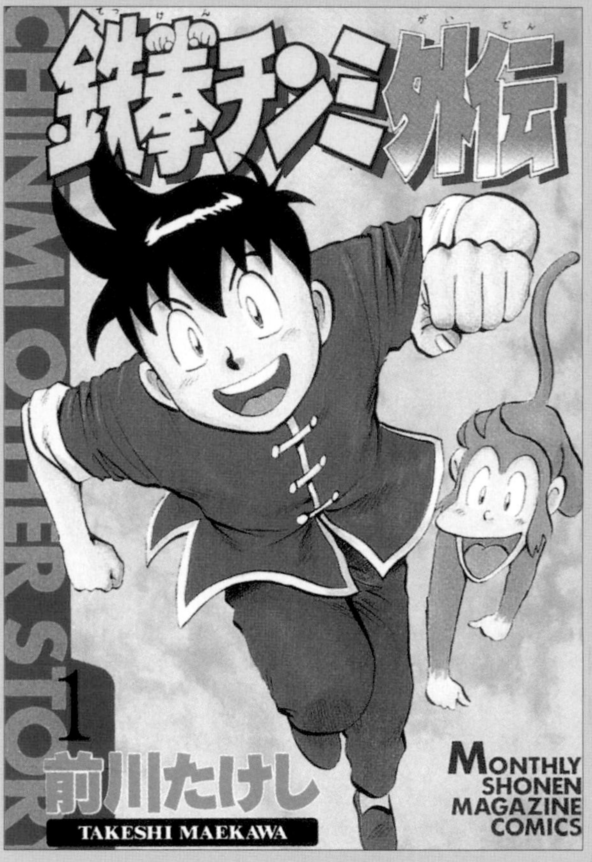

Irrepressibly cheerful and enthusiastic, young Chinmi and his pet monkey Goku shake up the Dailin temple.

CHIRICO CUVE [1983]

Shoji Yoshikawa's manga *Armored Trooper VOTOMS* is the prequel to the TV series. A shadowy Secret Society develops a genetically engineered human weapon, designed for victory in the hundred-year war that ravages the Astragius Galaxy. The Gilgamesh Confederation and the Balarant Union are fighting the third of humanity's great conflicts, an all-out galactic war. Chirico can't remember anything before he was ten years old, but he remembers the deaths of his adoptive parents and how he survived, despite burns that would have killed most people. His healing powers are astounding, and when he enlists in the military at age sixteen, they attract the attention of his unit commander, who becomes convinced that there is something strange about Chirico. Seeking only to find out who he is, Chirico battles across the galaxy as a mobile armor pilot, gradually learning the truth of his own existence. Not only he, but the love of his life, Fiana, were created purely as killing machines to serve a dark purpose, and their creators are pursuing them to conceal it. The pair finally seek peace in cryosleep. The manga was published in English by U.S. Manga Corps in 1996.

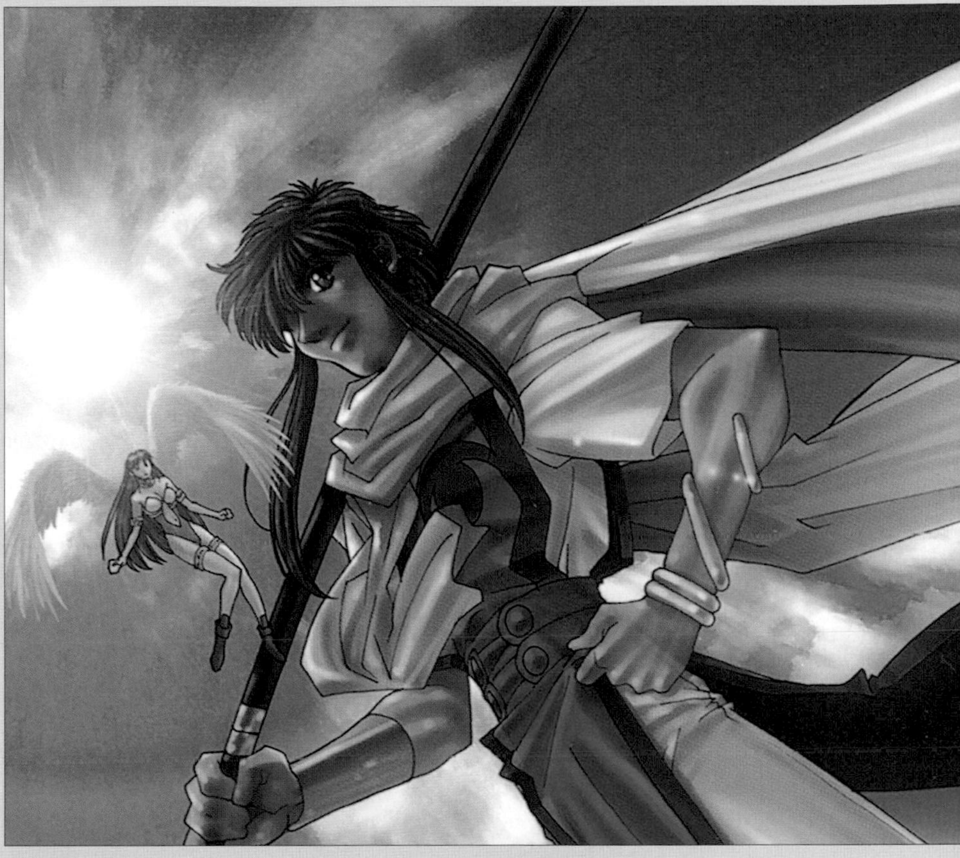

Wandering warrior Dark and his devoted but exasperating spirit guide Kyo.

DARK [1990]

Hero of Kia Asamiya's *Dark Angel*, Dark is a warrior born into a world of four warring kingdoms, but he is an outsider to all of them. Tall and slim, he usually wears armor. He was raised as a warrior priest of Suzaku in the kingdom of Nanban by the great teacher and leader So, who occupied the top rank of spirit warriors as Phantom Saint of Suzaku. Having killed So in combat, at his teacher's own insistence, he wanders into the forbidden lands and meets So's former lover, who is determined to kill him. He is aided by a spirit guide, the tiny, pixie-like winged girl Kyo, who treats him like a headstrong and fairly stupid elder brother. Their attempts to resolve the conflict between the four kingdoms were chronicled in *Newtype* magazine and are now available in English from CPM.

NAOTO DATE [1968]

Date assumes the persona of masked wrestler *Tiger Mask* in the manga of the same name by Ikki Kajiwara and Naoki Tsuji. His style of fighting is very popular but extremely violent, and when an opponent dies and his son is put in an orphanage, Date is overcome with guilt. He donates his professional wrestling earnings to the orphanage to try to improve the lives of the orphans. In the pursuit of big prizes to help them, he fights more and more terrifying opponents, including the American Golgotha Cross, banned from fighting in his native land because of his brutal tactics, whose props include a barbed-wire ring and nail-studded cross centerpiece. He also tries to raise the standards of his sport and make it an honorable art that fans can take pride in and learn from, rather than a violent showpiece giving vicarious thrills to the masses. His story started in *Bokura* magazine and continued in various Kodansha publications with great success, fed by the Japanese passion for wrestling and the mystique of the masked wrestler. Fittingly, Naoto died saving the life of a child, but the Tiger Mask persona was carried on by a successor, a mild-mannered journalist turned masked wrestler, in further manga and animated adventures.

TOMMY DAVIS a.k.a. KOJI KABUTO [1972]

Tranzor Z (Mazinger Z) by Go Nagai is one of the greatest giant robot series, which started the transforming robot boom when it was serialized in *Shonen Jump* magazine. Nagai claims he got the idea while sitting in one of Tokyo's famous traffic jams. Mazinger Z, developed by the Photon Research Institute's head, Dr. Davis (Dr. Kabuto), is the first pilotable giant robot; instead of operating it with a remote control like Gigantor, a pilot climbs inside and controls it as if he and the robot were one. Dr. Davis' grandson, Tommy (Koji), figures out how to pilot the robot and uses it to fight off the attacks of mad scientist Dr. Hell, who wants to take over the world. When Koji goes to South America at the end of the original manga, a new Mazinger and pilot, Great Mazinger and Tetsuya Tsurugi, replace the originals in a new manga. The manga and animated series have enjoyed huge success worldwide; Nagai and Ken Ishikawa also produced a color-painted manga, *Mazinger*, for First Comics in 1988, the first one specifically for the U.S. market.

Right: Go Mazinger! Artist Nagai's punchy line work conveys the unstoppable power of his giant robot and the determination of the young pilot.

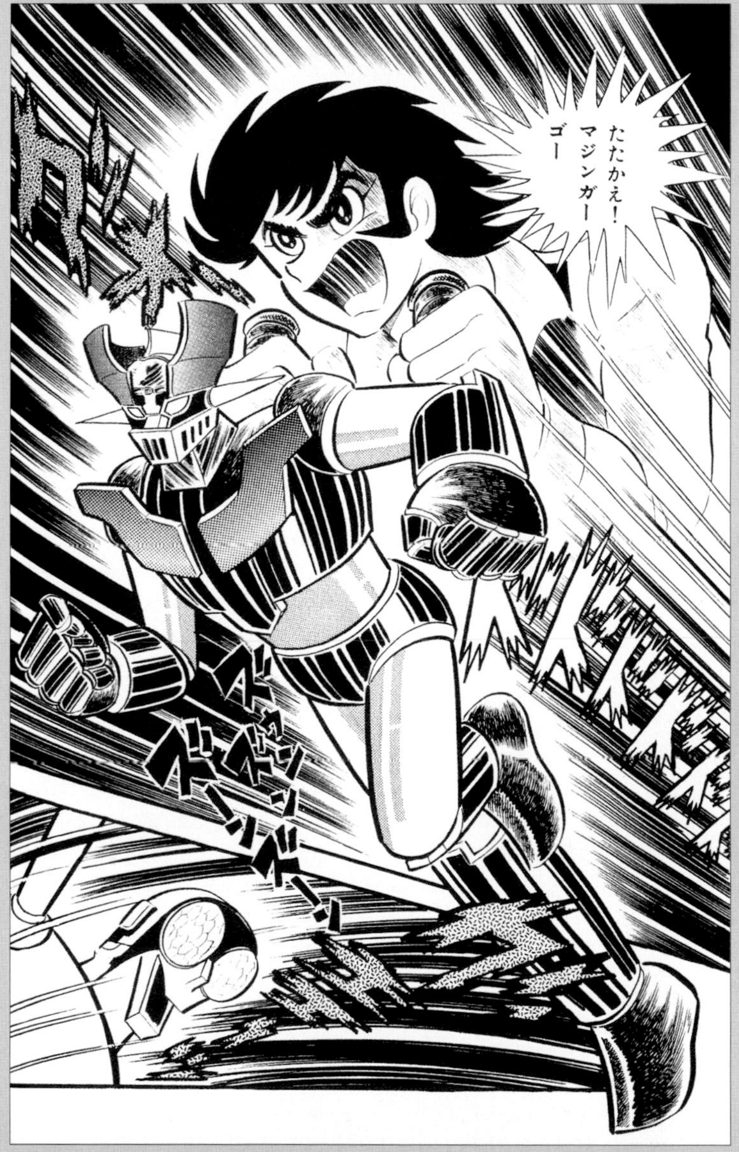
たたかえ！
マジンガー
ゴー

YOSUKE EGUCHI [1983]

Yosuke is an all-around cool dude, the leader of a high-school motorbike gang and the star of the school's embroidery club. He doesn't only go there to meet girls, though it's a good place for that—he's got a real talent and loves producing jackets and shirts embroidered with biker emblems for his friends. He believes in peace, love, and enjoying his bike without violence or disturbance. When other gangs don't share his views, he does everything he can to win them over, and usually manages it in the end. Teen romance, surfing, boxing, and other American movie trends are picked up in the long-running series *Bomber Bikers of Shonan (Shonan Bakusozoku)* by Satoshi Yoshida, which appeared in *Shonen King* magazine and ran for sixteen collected volumes over ten years. Early episodes were also animated for video. As the gang grows up and pairs off, Eguchi falls for American teenager Samantha, and the manga ends with his homegirl Yoshiko desperately trying to persuade him to stay with her. The series' success in Japan inspired others, notably *Shonan Pure Love Gang* and *Great Teacher Onizuka* from Toru Fujisawa.

PROF. PACKADERMUS J. ELEFUN a.k.a. PROF. OCHANOMIZU [1951]

A portly, elderly man with a bulbous nose and a wild mass of hair around his bald head sticking out over his ears, Ochanomizu succeeds Tenma as head of the Science Ministry and is the man who teaches Astro Boy the meaning of humanity and justice. He is a scatterbrain, sentimental and easily moved to tears, but with a capacity for love as powerful as his mind. He frees Astro Boy from slavery in the circus, creates a perfect suburban home for him, complete with robot parents, and campaigns tirelessly until robots are given full human rights. He represents creator Osamu Tezuka's view of the well-meaning but wacky "mad scientist" of Hollywood movies; he is often abducted and maltreated by those who want to abuse his genius for their own ends. He appears in *Astro Boy* (*Tetsuwan Atom*) and many other Tezuka manga, including *Soyokaze-san*, *Unico*, *Microid S*, and *Buddha*.

AKIRA FUDO [1972]

Akira first appeared in 1972, in Go Nagai's manga *Devilman* in *Shonen* magazine. A quiet high school boy living with the Makimura family while his explorer parents are away, he loves pretty, popular Miki Makimura and would do anything for her, but she's more likely to be the one protecting him! She is relieved when he becomes more assertive and "masculine," but if she knew why, she might feel differently. Demons have been living in a parallel world for aeons, occasionally crossing into our reality to kill. A human can fight them if he takes over the powers of a demon, by killing it and merging his soul with its supernatural strength. When

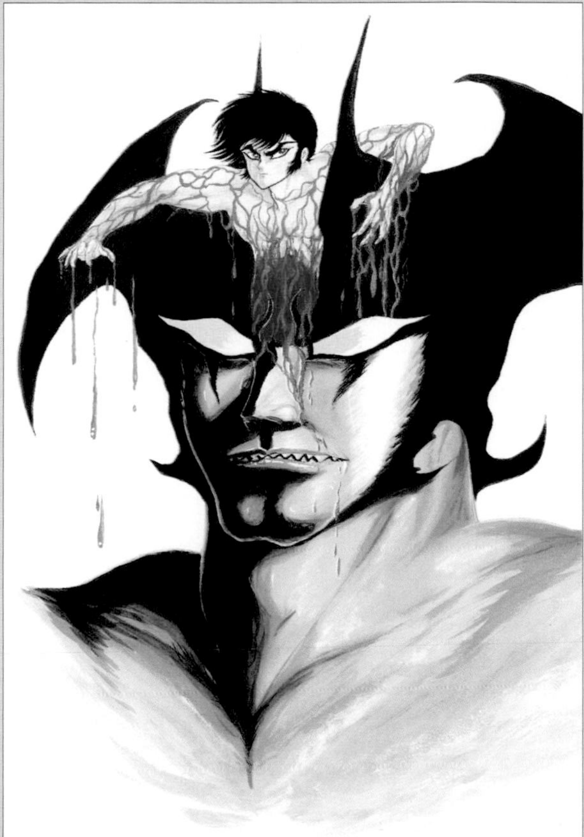

Devilman has enormous power, but the pure-hearted Akira uses it to fight the demon army.

Akira's friend Ryo sets him up to fight demon lord Amon, he transforms into a muscular, ferocious half-man, half-demon with bat wings and a tail. Devilman pits his new strength against the hordes of demon lord Zenon, but Satan has planned his conquest of mankind with great care, observing them in disguise, setting up his Apocalypse. Even as Devilman, Akira cannot win—he is killed in a final battle with Satan that destroys the world. In 1979's *New Devilman* (*Shin Devilman*) Akira/Devilman and Ryo travel through time to try to eradicate demons from various periods of history—the Renaissance, France in the time of Joan of Arc, World War II, Ancient Greece, and so on. Other artists have also worked on the Devilman saga. Three volumes of stories from 1999, set in the same world, some involving the original hero, are entitled *Neo-Devilman*. An "origins" cycle, *Amon: The Darkside of Devilman*, written by Nagai and illustrated by Yu Kinutani, appeared in 2000. A spin-off manga, *Devilman Lady*, also followed. The saga is linked to Nagai's later *Violence Jack* and earlier *Mao Dante*.

YAKUMO FUJI [1987]

Yakumo's archaeologist father works overseas while he goes to high school in Tokyo. One day a young girl turns up with a letter from his father, who has died. Pai looks like an ordinary, cute little Tibetan, but she's really the last of an ancient race of immortals, and she wants to become human. Yakumo's father asks him to help her in his last letter, so he feels bound to look after her, and the feeling is mutual—when he is killed in an accident, she uses her powers to bring him back to life as her "Wu"—a soulless, unkillable creature. Yakumo is now basically a zombie, and the friends who saw him killed in the accident are unable to cope

GOKU, GOHAN, AND GOTEN [1984]

SON GOKU IS THE central character of Akira Toriyama's sprawling *Dragonball* saga, originally serialized in *Shonen Jump* from 1984 to 1995 and now in English from Viz. It crashes *Enter the Dragon* into the soap opera, slapstick, and video-game genres to retell the legendary *Journey to the West*. The tale of a young Buddhist monk and his supernatural protectors, who set out to bring back holy scriptures from Gandhara in far-away India, is based on real-life journeys and inspired anime, manga, novels, games, live-action shows, and movies, including wacky Japanese TV series *Monkey*. The Monkey King is the central character, a hyperactive attention-grabber. Toriyama chose a slightly different angle, with a normal central character, grabbing his readers with a strong story. His Monkey King is a laid-back young man who just wants to live a quiet life and be very, very strong.

An alien from planet Vegeta, sent to Earth as a baby to wipe out all life on the planet, Goku hit his head on landing and forgot his orders. Raised by an elderly hermit, he became a good-hearted (though not very clever) little boy with spiky black hair, a tail, and massive strength. We see him transform into a huge simian and back; then grow into an even more powerful Saiya-jin warrior; an ultra-powerful Super Saiyan; and back to childhood again. We see him dying, going to Heaven and Hell, and getting back to his family, while saving the planet he was sent to destroy countless times along the way. In the beginning, he meets the energetic Bulma, who is on a quest to find the seven magical Dragonballs. In later volumes, martial arts tournaments and family alliances and rivalries get increasingly complex and comical.

The manga has a high level of both visual and verbal slapstick; even the character names are puns, with the aliens from Planet Vegeta named after vegetables, while many of the humans have names intended to sound rude to five-year-olds. Bulma's name is Toriyama's pun on "bloomers," and her children are called Trunks and Bra, intended to raise a giggle from those young enough to find underwear references a scream. Goku's wife Chi Chi is named after a Japanese kiddy term for penis. Food puns also abound. Bill Hicks it isn't, but its target audience lapped up the humor.

Goku and Chi Chi have two sons, Gohan and Goten. Older brother Gohan is a gifted fighter trained by his father's old enemy, and now devoted friend, Piccolo. After a titanic combat with the evil Cell, he settles down to a normal life, eventually marries high-school sweetheart

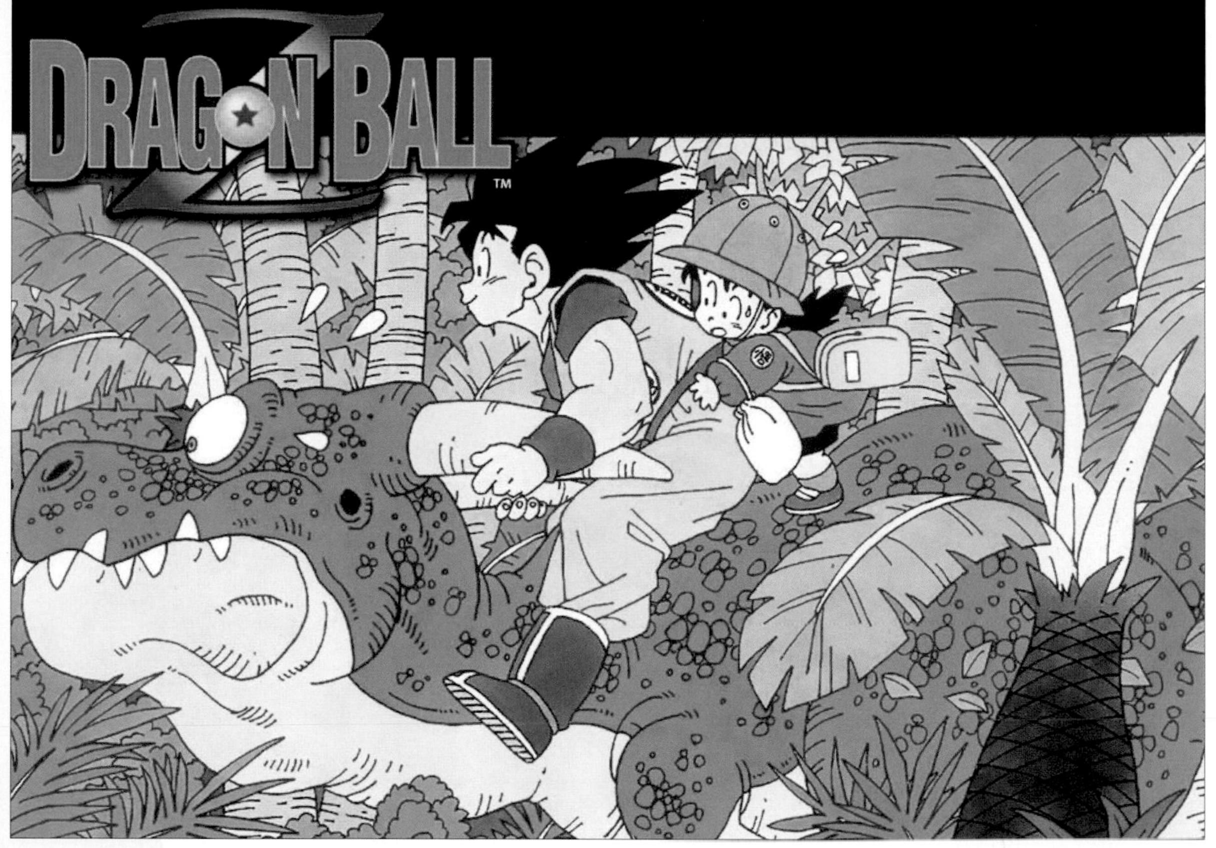

King of the Jungle: Goten takes his son back to his roots in *Dragonball Z.*

Videl and has a daughter, Pan. Second son Goten looks just like dad, and shares his cheerful nature, as well as the family fighting skills. A martal arts prodigy at the tender age of seven, as he gets older, he loses interest in training and prefers chasing girls. Goten's best friend is Trunks, son of Bulma and Goku's former enemy Vegeta, and the two pals use a power-up mode to become cocky young fighter Gotenks.

Dragonball ended abruptly in 1995 when Toriyama told the readers of *Shonen Jump* that he just couldn't write and draw another wacky tournament story arc. Of course, by then its animated incarnations *Dragonball* and *Dragonball Z*, plus their multitude of movie and merchandize spin-offs, had taken Japan and the world by storm. The saga has sold more than 100,000,000 copies in a staggering number of languages, including Malay, Tamil, and Catalan.

with his return to life. His old existence destroyed, Yakumo sets out with Pai in search of the mysterious force that can make her human and give him back his mortal's soul. They travel first to Hong Kong, then wander all over Asia meeting many exotic characters and strange magicians until they finally achieve their aim. Yuzo Takada's manga *Sazan Eyes (3x3 Eyes)* ran in weekly *Young Magazine* until 2002. The first collected volume was reprinted more than forty times in its first ten years.

TAKUMI FUJIWARA [1995]

Takumi lives in the mountainous countryside of the Kanto region and works after school in his father Buntu's tofu store. He's been making deliveries to hotels in the surrounding mountains since junior high school, using an ancient Toyota long before he was old enough to qualify for a driving license. Now in high school, the skills he honed on those winding mountain roads baffle his classmates, who are still crunching gears as they learn to drive. All the local boys are crazy about cars and meet late at night to race on the mountain roads. Takumi was never really interested in cars—he only learned to drive to help his father. But he's been noticed by other night riders; the skills of the guy who runs the Akina Pass at night are legendary, and he's known as "D"—short for Downhill Driver. He is drawn into the world of road racing and starts a competitive career in *Initial D*, Shuichi Shigeno's *Young Magazine* series, available in English from Viz.

SHO FUKAMACHI [1985]

Teenager Sho finds a strange object. It turns out to be the activation unit for a "bio booster" suit called Guyver, made by an alien race known as the Creators. They came to Earth in prehistoric times, tinkered with human DNA to try to make a superwarrior, then left without cleaning up their mess. The resulting genetically enhanced creatures, Zoanoids, interbred with and fought humans and were the source of the legends of werewolves, vampires, and other monsters that persist even today. Sho activates the unit and the suit bonds with him, making him a Guyver. He can call it up at will to fight off the wearers of the other two known units being used by Dr. Valcus of the Chronos Corporation to try to take over the world. Sho's girlfriend, Mizuki, is kidnapped to draw him out of hiding, and Sho has to take on another Guyver, teenager Agito Makishima, son of the former head of Chronos Japan, destroying his school in the process. Chronos even turns Sho's father into a monster, and Sho is forced to fight and kill him, but calls on his memory to finally defeat the evil of Chronos—for the moment. He has learned that there are outposts of Chronos all over the world, and the Zoanoids have powerful commanders known as Zoalords, so the fight is not over for Sho. Yoshiki Takaya's manga *Bio Booster Armor Guyver (Kyoshoku Soko Guyver* a.k.a. *The Guyver)* first appeared in *Shonen Captain Comics* and is available in English from Viz.

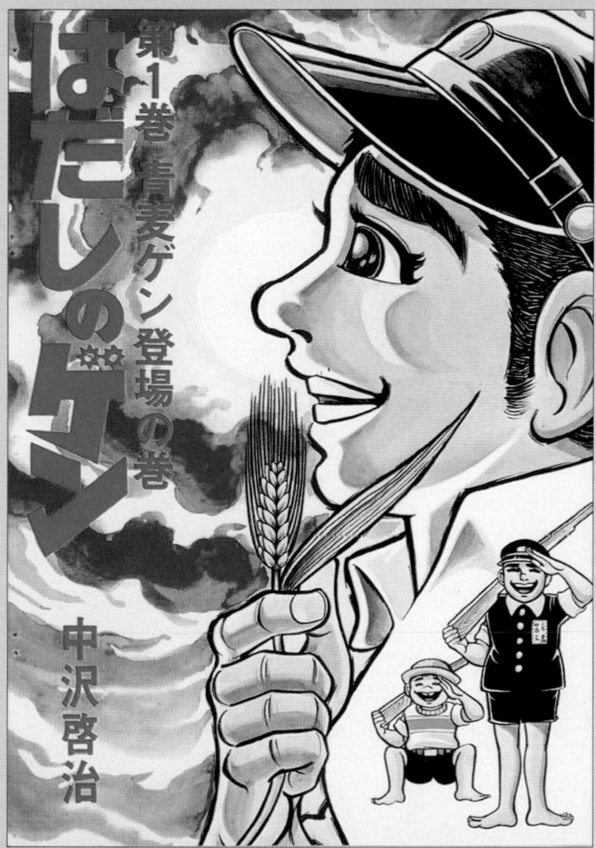

Despite the destruction all around him, Gen's courage and optimism survive even the Hiroshima holocaust.

GEN NAKAOKA [1972]

Gen is the ten-year-old child of a pacifist family, growing up in Japan during World War II. Gen's parents, ordinary working-class people, are convinced that killing others is wrong and bring up their children to respect life. As in Europe and the U.S. at this time, pacifists didn't have an easy life, and the family is not rich. The atomic bomb hits his home town, Hiroshima, just as Gen is about to go into his school, and he survives to see the full horror of war at closer quarters than most politicians can imagine. His first impulse is to rush home, through devastated piles of rubble full of burned bodies, people with their skin peeling off or peppered with shards of fallen glass, living and dead creatures still on fire. He finds his house collapsed and burning, his father, older sister, and little brother trapped under the ruins and his pregnant mother desperately trying to save them. It's futile, and the pair have to watch their loved ones die. They survive in the ruins, scraping out a living with the other survivors. Gen delivers his mother's baby girl. Life is changed horribly, but it carries on, and Gen now shares his parents' unshakable conviction that war is never the answer. *Barefoot Gen (Hadashi no Gen)* was created by Keiji Nakazawa, himself a survivor of the bombing. He was seven when the bomb dropped, but did not write his story until years later, when his mother died. After a Japanese cremation, there are normally bone remains to be buried, but his mother's bones burned to ashes because she had been exposed to so much radiation, leaving him with nothing but memory. The manga was first serialized in *Shonen Jump*. "Important" and "essential" are not words most comics can carry, but *Barefoot Gen* more than supports their weight. The story is published in English by Penguin.

YUSAKU GODAI [1982]

Godai is a student who has failed his university entrance exams and has to study for re-sits; in Japan they're known as *ronin*. He lives in a Tokyo boardinghouse while studying. *Maison Ikkoku* by Rumiko Takahashi is the story of his love for the widowed apartment manager, Kyoko. In the beginning, child bride Kyoko is still unable to let go of the memory of her late husband, and the hitherto unmotivated and aimless Godai is too shy to press his suit. However, encouraged (and sometimes hindered) by the well-meaning but seriously weird occupants of the other rooms, he slowly woos her and wins her heart in spite of competition from the good-looking local tennis coach. In the process, he finds the motivation to live his life instead of just drifting aimlessly. Takahashi's slice-of-life romantic comedy is a walk through an ordinary Tokyo suburb in the 80s, said to be based on her own experience of living in a Tokyo boardinghouse as a student for several years. It ends happily with the wedding its fans had been hoping for. Published in English by Viz, it also has an animated TV series, movie, and video, and even a live-action movie version.

ANDRE GRANDIER [1972]

Andre is a true working-class hero. His family is in service to the wealthy de Jarjayes family in pre-Revolutionary France, and he is brought up as companion to the youngest daughter of the family, who is christened Oscar Francois and raised to replace the son her father wanted. At first the two are raised as equals, but when Oscar goes to court to serve the king and becomes captain of the young crown princess's guard, the social gulf between them opens. Andre goes with her as her stableman, but he loves her, and this class division and his natural sense of justice lead him to study the revolutionary ideas being talked of in Paris. Oscar falls in love with another, but eventually realizes she and her childhood friend are made for each other. Andre joins the revolutionary thinkers but tragically goes blind. After the royal family is executed, Oscar and Andre join the revolution and die for their country and the ideals of liberty, equality, and fraternity. *Rose of Versailles (Versailles no Bara)* was serialized in *Margaret* magazine. Its creator, philosophy graduate Ryoko Ikeda, also produced alternate-universe stories set in the same universe in *RoV New Chapter (VnB Gaiden)* in 1986. Ikeda made her debut in 1967, at the age of twenty, in *Shojo Friend* magazine. Famous for her use of European settings and historic themes, she took a long career break at the end of the 1980s, but returned to the manga scene in 1998.

DR. HANAMARU [1948]

Making his debut in a minor role in Osamu's Tezuka's manga *The Masked Adventure Kid*, this gentle old man with a huge pot belly, long white beard, and benign expression became a staple figure in Tezuka's early science fiction works. Appearing in many roles until 1981, as a professor, priest, politician, and even as God in *Faust*, he was never used to portray a character of evil intent. In *Next World*, he is Dr. Yamadano, the lone voice warning of disaster as the world flirts with ever more dangerous nuclear experiments.

HANAPPE [1979]

Hanappe is a typical high-school boy—he's scruffy, not very bright, and spends most of his time either fantasizing about girls or trying to hide from the local street gang, whose favorite pastime is beating him up. Then one day, a pair of demons come through his TV set and turn his life upside down. Before long, his home is a cross-dimensional meeting place, his mother is in lust with big, butch he-demon Ophisto Bazooka, his sister is being pursued by bi-sexy Mephisto Dance, and he has acquired the most powerful body part in the world. His index finger, which resembles a sexual organ, is the *Hanappe Bazooka* of the manga title, and he is promised that he only has to point it at a woman for her to be overcome with desire. Hanappe is as useless at controlling his new powers as at everything else, and when he learns the girl he loves is sleeping with their teacher to get good grades, he's had enough of his own haplessness and commits suicide. When his soul is sent for judgment, however, the love of his family and friends is so strong that he is brought back to the world of the living by dance. Go Nagai and Kazuo Koike's manga was released in *Young Jump* from 1979–1982.

CAPTAIN HARLOCK [1977]

Leiji Matsumoto's most beloved creation, Captain Harlock, is the archetypal *Boy's Own* hero. Making his debut in Matsumoto's stunning space opera *Space Pirate Captain Harlock (Uchu Kaizoku Captain Harlock)*, the tall, slender man with the flowing black cloak, black eyepatch, and a scar across his quiet, sad face is a charismatic figure whose principles are as attractive as his appearance. Harlock believes in freedom and justice. When his world is attacked and overrun by a superior force, he refuses to take the easy road of collusion with the invaders, but instead becomes an outlaw and roams the seas of space in his pirate ship, *Arcadia*, flying the skull and crossbones. He is hated and feared on many planets, but—supported by his small yet fiercely loyal crew—he stays true to his own beliefs and never wavers in his pursuit of freedom.

Harlock is armed with a sword and a pistol, the superb Cosmo Dragoon. Created by his friend Tochiro Oyama (the squat, unglamorous but brilliant Sancho Panza to Harlock's elegant Quixote) and based on the 1848 Colt Dragoon, the Cosmo Dragoon is a gun so powerful that only the greatest of space warriors can own and use it. It is the only gun capable of killing machine people, the prime villains of the

BRIAREOS HECATONCHIRES [1985]

A MASSIVE, SKILLED warrior yet an easy-going guy, the mercenary cyborg with the distinctive "rabbit" antennae on his metal skull and his blonde tomboy lover Deunan Knute are creations of Masamune Shirow in his early manga *Appleseed*, published in Japan by Seishinsha from 1985–1989 and in the United States by Dark Horse in 1995. After wandering across a war-ravaged globe in the twenty-second century in the aftermath of a devastating war, the pair find themselves in Olympus, a state watched over by enhanced humans, bioroids, whose long-term plan is to make every human just like them.

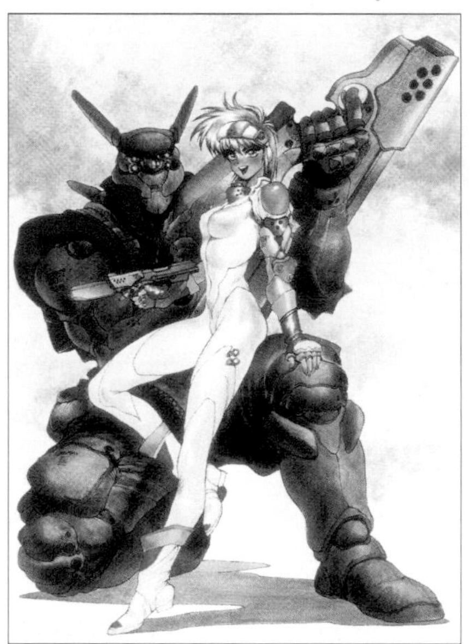

Shirow's story starts in 1988, after the Seoul Olympics, and he develops a complex political, social, and economic background involving real-world events and invented-world variations. Over the first three decades of the third millennium, the technologically advanced powers tried desperately to bolster their own position after a terrible war, while the poorer countries were devastated by hunger, with wandering bands of mercenaries and child soldiers, and complete social breakdown. From 2030 onwards, the rulers of the island state of Olympus promoted the Appleseed Plan, a scheme to manage urban society through the use of enhanced cyber-organisms known as bioroids.

Briareos was born in 2096; his parents are unknown but he is naturally dark-skinned with dark hair and eyes. By the time he was ten years old, he was already working for a living in the military, and the undersea cables and satellites that enabled communication to function were slowly being restored. When he was twelve, he killed his commanding officer and went on the run, working freelance thereafter. He met Deunan Knute and her father Carl in 2116, and joined Carl's mercenary team. By 2122, seventeen-year-old Deunan had joined the Police Academy and Briareos' past finally caught up with him, resulting in a mysterious explosion that almost

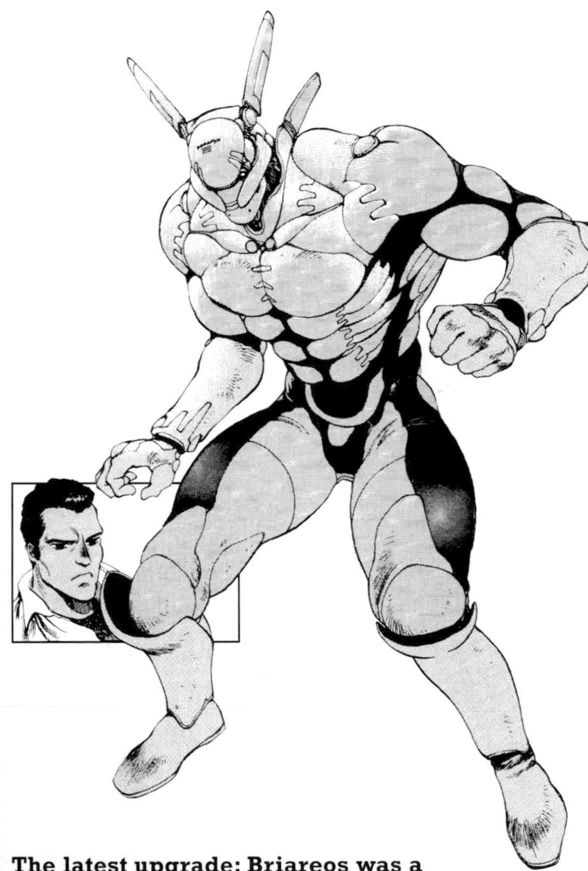

The latest upgrade: Briareos was a superb fighter before, but with his Hecatonchires upgrade, he's almost unstoppable.

killed him. The only way to save his life was to make him a cyborg. Despite his changed body, he and Deunan remain lovers. They are recruited by bioroid agent Hitomi for the Olympus Police Force in 2127. There, they find that not every citizen appreciates the careful, tactful, but total control exerted by the city, and that unaugmented humans are considered an undesirable underclass in some circles. Their new role is to try to keep Utopia from total breakdown, to stop it from either descending into the anarchy they left behind in the wastelands, or becoming a neo-fascist state.

Not every cyborg is a total success. Just like unaugmented people, some have better motor control and mental skills than others. Only one subject in a hundred adapts ideally to the changes and emerges from rehab with perfect co-ordination; Briareos is the one in a hundred, able to maintain a constant level of performance at all temperatures and under all stresses. His armored limbs are phenomenally powerful, he is a superb shot, and he is highly effective in combat. He has an auxiliary brain to function as a dedicated information processor, capable of conceptual evaluation. His skin is elastic and warm, and he can adjust its surface temperature. It's still as sensitive as human skin. Although he has been extensively augmented, many parts remain human, including his central core nervous system, eyes, and reproductive organs. He still enjoys a glass of wine or six—there are jokey references in the manga to fiddling expense accounts to cover wine costs.

The manga ended in 1989, having won numerous prizes including the prestigious Galaxy Award, one of Japan's top science fiction honors. *Appleseed* was animated in 1988, in a much truncated version, far less rich and complex than the manga. A new CG animated version, written by Shirow, premiered in April 2004, as part of a planned *Appleseed* trilogy.

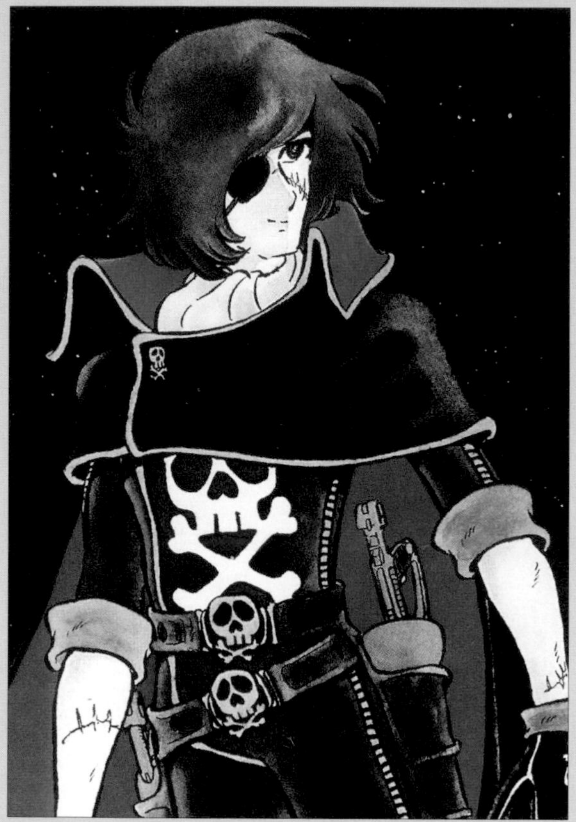

Romantic hero Harlock, captain of the Arcadia, is the archetypal noble adventurer.

Matsumotoverse, and has the range and accuracy to shoot down a spaceship. Harlock first appeared as World War II fighter ace Major Harlock in short manga *Pilot 262* in 1969, and as Phantamunt Harlock, a colonial officer whose homeworld has been conquered by the Earth Federation in *The Great Pirate Harlock* in 1970. *Gun Frontier* (1972) took Harlock into the American West as a samurai gunfighter and marks the debut of his sidekick Tochiro. *The Witch of Stanley* was another adventure of air ace Harlock, published in 1973. *My Youth in Arcadia* appeared in the same year. (It was animated in 1982, after the success of the animated TV series of 1978.) Harlock had a supporting role in 1975's *Diver 0*, and in the same year, Phantamunt Harlock returned at the helm of *Space Battleship Deathshadow*. He has also appeared in Matsumoto manga, including *Galaxy Express 999*, *Queen Emeraldas*, and the recent *Ring of the Nibelung* series, and has had a fourteen-part American-created comic series (*Captain Harlock* and *Captain Harlock: Deathshadow Rising*) devoted to him.

KENSHIN HIMURA a.k.a. HITOKIRI BATTOSAI [1994]

Starting in the eleventh year of the Meiji restoration, Nobuhiro Watsuki's *Ruroni Kenshin* is the story of a killer who tries to go straight and of the difficulties he faces with old foes and even friends as he tries to put his past behind him. Kenshin was the foremost assassin of the revolutionary Isshin Shishi group, who helped topple the Shogunate and lay the foundations for modern Japan. He was a swordsman of incredible skill who lived only for his cause. Now, most of the revolutionaries

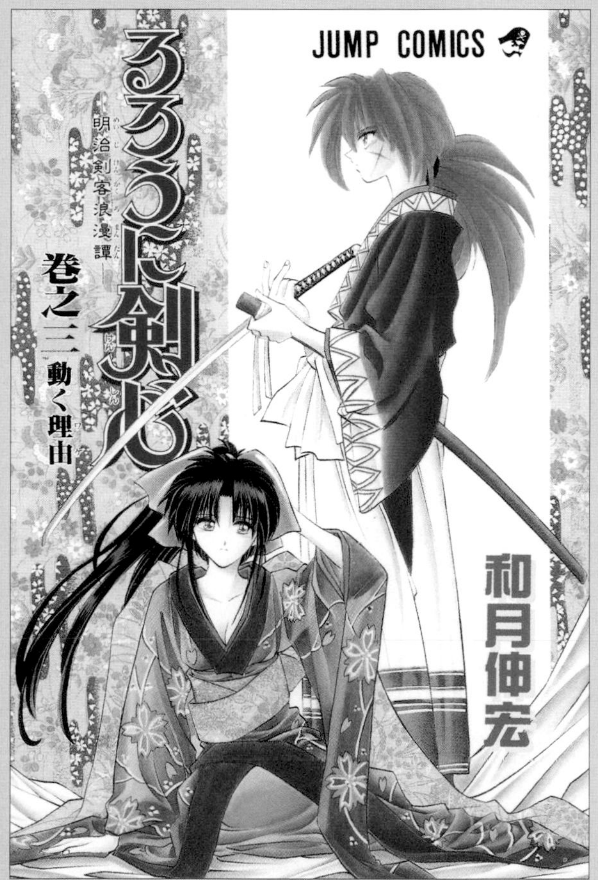

Japanese cover for *Ruroni Kenshin*, reflecting the aura of deadly elegance which surrounds the legend of Hitokiri Battosai.

have become as corrupt as the government they deposed, and Kenshin has vowed never to kill again. He still carries a sword, but he uses it with the blade reversed. When he meets a beautiful girl whose swordmaster father was slain by a man claiming to be the legendary killer Hitokiri Battosai, he decides to help her. Kaoru Kamiya is out for revenge, and Kenshin wants to unmask the impostor who is claiming his old name. Gradually, the two fall in love, and Kenshin begins to realize that nobody can live entirely alone. Now he wants a quiet life with the family he is beginning to build, but his past will always endanger his loved ones. The long-running manga takes him through a number of beautifully evolved story arcs, from Tokyo—where he and Kaoru hunt down her father's killer—to Kyoto where more revolution is fomenting and threatening the peace and stability of the nation—then across Japan, meeting figures from the past, many of whom have a burning desire to kill him. Kenshin has survived his passionate and reckless youth through luck and skill; now he has to learn to live with the consequences of his past choices, and try not to compromise his new beliefs. The manga first appeared in *Shonen Jump* and is available in English from Viz.

YO HINOMURA [1986]

The handsome, twenty-something pottery artist finds his life turned upside down when he is kidnapped by a Chinese tong, brainwashed, and trained as an assassin. Kazuo Koike and Ryoichi Ikegami's manga *Crying Freeman*, first published in 1986 in *Big Comic Spirits* magazine, is an action-packed romp through a fantasy world of drug-dealing oriental Mafiosi and battles with the police and rival gangs. Despite his brainwashing and transformation into the assassin Freeman, Hinomura's own personality struggles to the surface whenever he makes a kill, expressing itself in tears. When one of his killings is witnessed by a beautiful young woman, he is expected to kill her to avoid leaving a witness; his inability to do so proves his salvation, as she helps him break free of his conditioning and reclaim himself. But he has become a part of the strange family of his captors, and he and his love finally decide to take on the leadership of the gang. The manga was animated for video in 1989, an unlicensed Chinese live-action version was made in 1991, and a live-action Hollywood remake by Christophe Gans followed in 1997.

KUNISHIGE HODAKA

[1990]

Hodaka is an up-and-coming fashion designer who owns the exclusive boutique "Galopine et Galopin." He models occasionally, but has a quiet and reserved nature and hates crowds, loud noise, and insincerity, so he's happier at the drawing board. Tall, blond, handsome, and an all-around nice guy, he finds himself the target of a major teenage crush when Fujiya Kotobuki decides she's going to be his girlfriend. Unfortunately, Fujiya is actually fourteen and Hodaka is twenty-six. How can a nice guy handle this challenging situation, especially when he finds himself drawn to Fujiya's lively, outgoing personality and relentless enthusiasm? Egged on by Hodaka's assistant, Lee David, and declaring herself to be twenty, she inveigles herself into a model shoot and into Hodaka's life in Azumi Tsueiko's *The Fashion Boy Is Cool* (*Oshare Kosou wa Hanamaru*), which appeared in *Margaret* and ran for four years and ten volumes.

SHINICHI IZUMI [1990]

High-school boy Shinichi is caught up in a secret invasion of Earth by alien life-forms. They float down as parasitic spores and invade humans and animals by landing on body parts, then gradually working their way in, assimilating their brains and controlling their nervous systems. One lands on Shin as he lies in his room listening to music; because it can't get into his ear, the preferred route to the brain, it tries to go up his nose. Shin is a determined character and manages to block off the alien from getting into his head and taking control of his brain. He can't get rid of it, but he confines it to his right arm. Adapting fast is one of the aliens' many successful survival traits, so it learns Japanese overnight through reading. The two start to communicate and move from fighting for supremacy to finding a compromise that will let both survive. Shin nicknames it *Migi* (Righty—Lefty in the flipped English version) and instead of the relationship being parasitic, with the alien consuming the host, it becomes symbiotic. The Parasytes have different views on humans—some want to wipe them out, while some, led by charismatic Tamara Rockford, want to manage mankind for the species' mutual benefit. Learning to live in cooperation, however, is a new idea for them. Humans eventually fight back and almost eliminate the Parasytes, leaving Shin and Righty in a fight to the finish with the strongest Parasyte of all, Goto. Shin learns what it really means to lose your right arm as he and his friend are separated and Righty sacrifices himself to save Shin and his girlfriend Sarah. *Parasyte* (*Kiseju*) by master adult-horror artist Hitoshi Iwaaki, is a story with obvious debts to *Invasion of the Body Snatchers* but takes a more optimistic view; the end of the manga shows Shin realizing that some links can't be broken, and its underlying buddy-movie scenario links it to stories like *Ushio* and *Tora*. First appearing in *Afternoon*, it's available in English from Tokyopop.

TAKUTO IZUMI [1989]

Fifteen-year-old Takuto is a brilliant high-school soccer player with a great future ahead. But he has a dark secret in his family closet—his mother is a murderer, driven by her obsessive love for his father. He is trying to put that behind him and make a normal life for himself, but becomes the target of obsessive love from eighteen-year-old rock star Koji Nanjo. It starts as a case of mistaken identity: Koji spots the handsome young man by chance and thinks he's a tomboyish girl. He learns his mistake, but still can't get Takuto out of his mind. Neither is gay, and Takuto is repelled by the slightest sign of obsession, but they are drawn to each other and into a relationship filled with anguish and misunderstanding. Koji, too, has a terrifying family background; his wealthy family is profoundly dysfunctional, and all three Nanjo brothers are violent and self-centered. His domineering eldest brother, Hirose, almost twice his age, is out to end his relationship with Takuto by any means, including rape. Middle sibling Akihito, twenty-five, adores his older brother and is jealous of Koji; he runs over Takuto in his car and has issues with Hirose's little son. Koji, also, has a violent streak that results in self-harm and assaults on his family. Yet somehow the pair come to understand as well as love each other, and their relationship survives all assaults. Twenty-year-old Minami Ozaki was a *dojinshi* artist before she made her professional debut in *Margaret* in 1988. The following year *Zetsuai: 1989 (Everlasting Love)* appeared, and the dark passions of the Nanjo family made her one of the queens of *shojo* and *shonen ai* manga. A sequel, *Bronze*, followed. She remains active in fanzine circles and runs her own *dojinshi* publishing company, Club Doll.

JOEY a.k.a. TETSURO HOSHINO [1977]

It's 2358. Like millions of other teenagers, Joey (Tetsuro) seeks to escape the mean streets of Megalopolis for the stars—but he also has

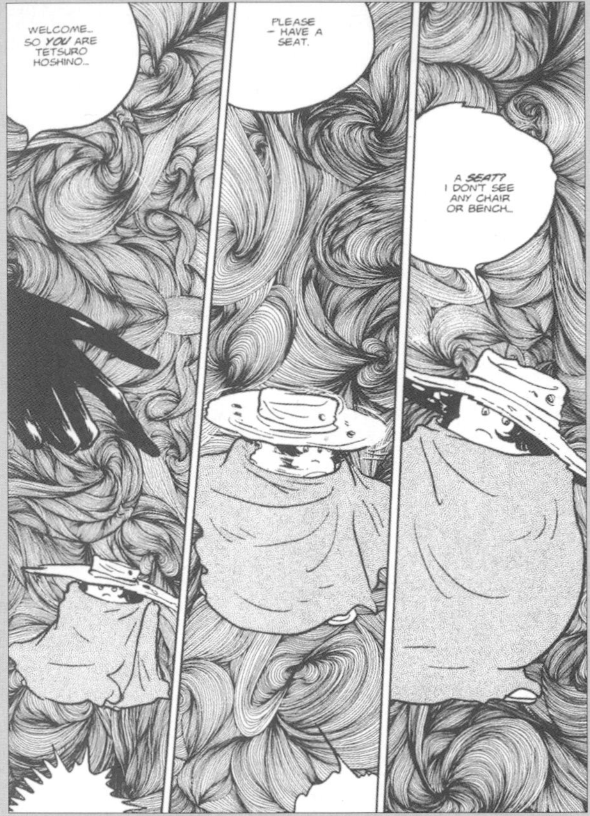

Tetsuro Hoshino sets out to get revenge and ends by learning the true value of life in *Galaxy Express 999*.

another ambition. His mother, his only relative, has been murdered by Count Mecha (Count Kikai), a nobleman of the dominant Machine People, cyborgs who rule the galaxy and make ordinary mortals an underclass. He means to find the count and kill him, but to kill a machine person is impossible for a human. He will have to become what he hates to achieve—revenge. The only way to get to Andromeda, where he can acquire a machine body, is on the *Galaxy Express*, but he has no money for the fare. Then he meets the mysterious, beautiful Maetel, who agrees to help him. On the journey, she helps him in ways he can't imagine, guiding and encouraging him to expand his horizons, think in new ways, and finally learn that being fully human means more than any power. In the end, Tetsuro chooses to stay human rather than acquire the sterile power of the machines. Leiji Matsumoto's *Galaxy Express 999 (Ginga Tetsudo 999)* also features his hero Captain Harlock.

JONATHAN JOESTAR

[1987]

Hirohiko Araki is one of the most distinctive of manga artists, and his unique style and fondness for Western film, comicbooks, and music are all showcased in his masterwork, *JoJo's Bizarre Adventure (JoJo no Kimiyona Daiboken)*. His men are an almost grotesque combination of elegance and muscle, his women are bosomy and bottomy, and both sexes have a unique and flamboyant fashion sense.

Tall, dark, handsome archaeologist Jonathan Joestar, aka JoJo, is the scion of an English nobleman. When the story opens in 1880s London, his stepbrother Dio plots to steal his inheritance, using the mystic powers of an Aztec mask that causes trouble for all who

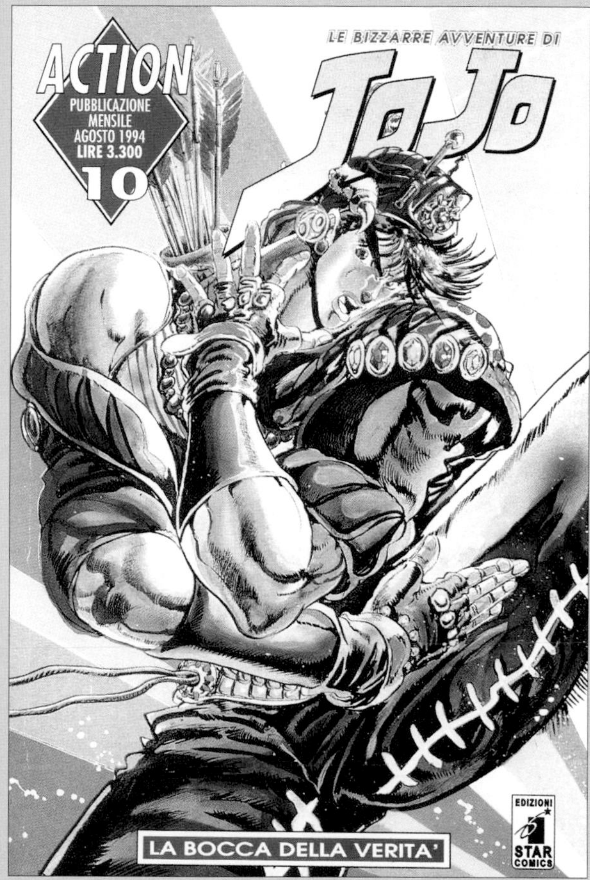

Jonathan Joestar and his descendants are surrounded by bizarre, beautiful characters.

come into contact with it. JoJo learns "hamon," a form of yogic power, and calls on the aid of friends like adventurer Reo Speedwagon, but his efforts to defeat Dio fail when Dio dons the mask and becomes a vampire, killing JoJo as he flees with his family to America. Dio is also presumed killed, but the Joestar family line continues in the United States, where Jonathan's grandson, Joseph Joestar, goes up against the mystic powers who made the mask as the world goes to war in the late 1930s. Dio isn't dead, he just drowned, and in the late twentieth century, he rises from his watery grave, using JoJo's body with his own head sewn on and the powers of the "stand," a form of psi power linked to the tarot. Joseph's daughter, Holly Joestar, has a half-Japanese son, Jotaro Kujo, who joins his grandfather to fight the evil of the mask and save Holly from Dio.

The story then moves to Japan at the end of the second millennium, with Joseph's illegitimate Japanese son, Josuke Higashikata, helping his nephew, Jotaro, retrieve the artifact that bestows stand power from a serial killer. Moving on into the twenty-first century and back to Europe, we meet perhaps the most problematic member of the Joestar family, Italian "gang star" Giorno Giovanni. He is officially the son of Dio, but was sired using JoJo's genitals and is therefore Joseph's uncle, Holly and Josuke's great-uncle, and Jotaro's great-great-uncle. Giorno fights a Mafia-type organization using stand powers. The most recent member of the family to carry on the Joestar tradition of mystical battles and outrageous clothing into the future is American-Japanese Jolyne Kujo, Jotaro's daughter, whose first use of her stand powers is to get out of prison in Florida. One of the most fascinating manga series ever seen in terms of style, densely packed with

ASTRO BOY'S FATHER

OSAMU TEZUKA, GOD of manga, is the man who changed the course of manga history. He was born in November 1928 in Osaka. Osamu Tezuka came from a line of medical men, but in elementary school he showed a gift for copying popular comics and started to create his own manga—more than 3,000 pages survived wartime air raids. Manga had lost Hokusai's lively immediacy and become static; Wirgman and Kitazawa had bred a legion of talking heads on paper. Tezuka aligned manga with moving pictures, taking the best elements of both to tell stories so vividly that he turned his country into the world's biggest consumer of comic books and started a worldwide artistic revolution. Like one of his favorite heroes, the Monkey King Son Goku, Tezuka made a voyage of discovery to bring back treasure from the exotic West. He also fulfilled the subtext of the ancient myth—that travelers seeking enlightenment carry it to the lands they visit.

His first publication, *Ma-chan's Diary (Ma-chan no Nikkicho)*, appeared in 1946 in the children's magazine *Mainichi Shogakusei Shimbun*. A four-panel strip telling a mini-story from the daily life of a Japanese girl, it was immediately popular. To get published, Tezuka lied about his age, claiming to have been born in 1926. A year later, the seventeen-year-old masquerading as an adult of twenty became an overnight sensation with the publication of *New Treasure Island (Shin Takarajima)*, which sold around 400,000 copies in a few short months. A very free reworking of Stevenson's tale of lost treasure on an exotic isle, pulling in elements of *Robinson Crusoe*, it had a guest appearance by Tarzan. It showcased many other elements Tezuka was to use in future: the reworking of popular culture from all over the world, the use of an existing theme or legend as a platform for a new idea, the ability to hook an audience with a familiar concept before taking them into new territory. He gave his favorite character archetypes personal names, borrowed from actors he admired or based on physical characteristics. He used them exactly like actors, appearing under their own names and likenesses, or playing other roles with different costumes or hairstyles, in creations ranging from comics and animation to advertising and educational work.

While at university studying medicine, Tezuka produced an amazing volume of work. His range of genres was broad—science fiction, Westerns, anthropomorphic tales, sagas of medieval Japan, and adventure stories. In the fifties, an established star, he created the two manga by which his work would later become known to Western TV viewers, though most would never realize they were watching a Japanese cartoon—*Jungle Emperor (Jungle Taitei*, a.k.a. *Kimba the White Lion*) in 1950 and *Ambassador Atom (Atom Taishi)* in 1951. A year later the central character was renamed *Iron-Arm Atom (Tetsuwan Atom)* a.k.a. *Astro Boy*.

In 1958, Toei Doga approached Tezuka to

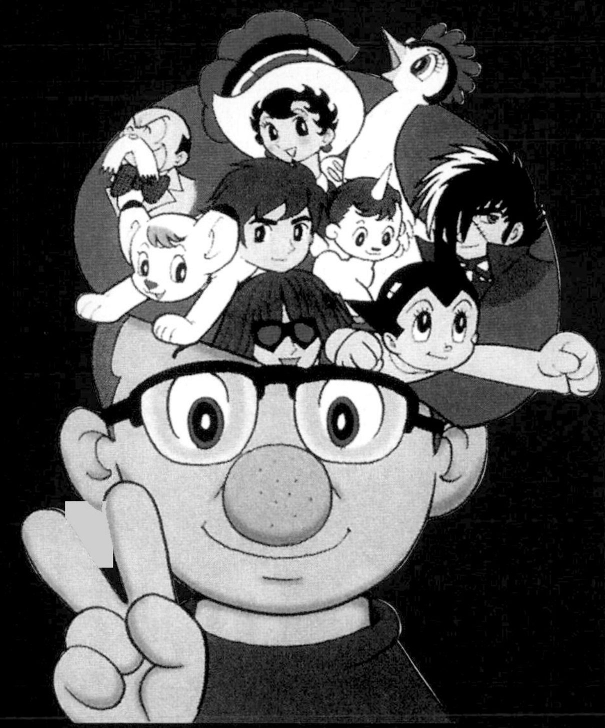

Tezuka drew himself many times, appearing in his own manga as himself and other roles.

write a screenplay of his 1953 manga *My Son Goku (Boku no Son Goku)*. He became co-producer and co-director, and the film appeared in August 1960 in Japan under the title *Journey to the West (Saiyuki)*, with an edited version appearing on American screens as *Alakazam the Great*. He produced his first independent film *Stories from a Street Corner (Aru Machikado no Monogatari)* in 1962. In January 1963, *Tetsuwan Atom* became the first home-produced animated adventure series for the new medium of TV. In September 1963, NBC screened the series in the United States as Astro Boy.

Tezuka said in an interview: "Manga is my wife; animation is my mistress." The comparison is even more telling in the context of traditional Japanese culture. The wife manages the family budget to ensure enough money to cover whatever expenses the master of the house might generate – including the upkeep of his mistress. Tezuka's mistress was a particularly expensive one. His first company, Mushi Productions, failed in 1973; his second, Tezuka Productions, endured some hair-raising times, but survived to carry his legacy forward into the twenty-first century thanks to the constant sales of his manga.

Osamu Tezuka was the rarest kind of genius—one of the few privileged to change the course of popular culture. A true Renaissance man, he retained his passion for science throughout his life, though he gave up his medical career as his manga career became more and more demanding. During his working life he produced more than 150,000 pages, which averages out at ten pages a day and takes no account of his animation, writing, directing, other work, and overseas travel. Even during his final illness he tried to get into the studio to work.

Tezuka died on January 9, 1989. The enduring message of his work is best summed up in his own words. "This is what I've tried to express in my work: love every creature. Love everything that lives. This is the message in everything I do, though it's expressed in different ways—just celebrating life."

adventurous and improbable characters, JoJo has influenced a number of young artists, including—perhaps unexpectedly—those masters of supernatural cuteness, the CLAMP collective.

JONAH [1977]

In the far future, Earth has been left behind. Human society is sterile, totalitarian, dominated by super-machines, and threatened by a shadowy race known as the Mu, telepaths who spring up without warning and are feared and hated without reason. Artificially created children are screened at puberty to root out any possibility of telepathic powers surviving. Jonah is a low-ranked human, servant to the elite computer manager, Keith, but he is also Mu, and when his people seek a messiah to lead them out of persecution, his whole relationship with his master is thrown into question. Keiko Takemiya's science fiction classic *Toward the Terra (Tera E)* was published by Kadokawa Shoten.

JUBEI [1995]

The hero of Hitoshi Tomizawa's *Treasure Hunter (Hizenya Jubei* a.k.a. *Treasure Hunter Jubei)* is a licensed merchant in a fantasy world, who will find anything a client wants for the right price. Persistent, tough, and good at his job, he's always looking to turn a profit but often finds that the value put on objects is, meaningless. His commissions include a food that gives eternal life, a statue that bestows ultimate power, and a rare artifact stolen from him just before the annual Kizuna Society Auction that puts his merchant's license in jeopardy. He's named for the semi-legendary ninja master Jubei Yagyu, but bears little resemblance, and his story is published in English by CPM.

KAGEMARU [1959]

The hero of Sanpei Shirato's seventeen-volume classic, *Ninja Military Chronicles (Ninja Bugeicho)*, is a ninja master who sees the suffering of the peasants in feudal Japan and sets out to help them. With his band of seven ninja, each with their own special powers, he fights the forces of the mighty warlord Nobunaga Oda in a story remarkable even today for its depiction of the harshness and violence of the times. Kagemaru is betrayed, his band annihilated, and he is drawn and quartered by Oda's men. When his head is brought before the warlord, however, it announces its own presence, defiant even beyond death.

DOUGLAS KAINE [1988]

A notable member of the Mirage Knights, the elite force serving Emperor Amaterasu in Mamoru Nagano's *The Five Star Stories*, is Douglas Kaine, known as the Silver Knight.

His Fatima, a specially engineered fighting partner created by legendary bio-engineer Dr. Chrome Ballanche, is known as Auxo. Douglas was a protégé of legendary Knight Master Deimos Hierarchy. When his master retired, Douglas inherited his Mortar Headd, the Water Dragon, custom-built by Amaterasu in his Ladios Sopp guise. Kaine had the skill to modify the mecha, and it was renamed the Schepeletor, or Knight of Chrome. Kaine is the son, and possibly also the lover, of Hierarchy's Fatima Queen, the first Fatima created by Ballanche. His father may be Ballanche or Hierarchy. Inheriting his mother's huge powers, he is one of the most gifted knights in the empire, but has previously accumulated a long criminal record. At first resisting Amaterasu's attempts to recruit him—including capture and coercion by Mel Rince, the Emperor's female form—Kaine is finally won over by a huge payment and amnesty for 80 percent of his crimes. A lecher of the first order, he is also capable of familial feeling—when his lover and fellow Headliner, Jade Beat, dies, he sacrifices his career to rear their motherless children.

KAKURI [1992]

China, 2,300 years ago. The town of Ryo is facing an all-out attack against impossible odds—the 4,500 men of Ryo face an army of 15,000 well-armed, well-trained professional soldiers from the kingdom of Cho. The town calls on a mercenary clan for help. Kakuri is sent to organize the defense but finds that he's facing two enemies—the attackers, and the doubters in the town who think things are hopeless and feel that they should make a deal. In addition, he doesn't know about the double-dealing in his own clan, where a corrupt chief and his counselor are set to trigger a merciless and horrific war. Based on Kenichi Sakami's novel, adapted by Kentaro Kubota, and drawn by Hideki Mori, *Bokko* harks back to *Seven Samurai* in showing the impact of war on the common people.

SHIN KAZAMA [1979]

Area 88 is an airbase in the Middle Eastern kingdom of Asran in Kaoru Shintani's manga of the same name. Top pilot Shin Kazama is a reluctant mercenary pilot helping the prince of Asran fight a bloody war. Duped into signing on for a three-year tour of duty by his so-called friend, Kanzaki, Shin has to complete the three years or earn enough bounty to buy himself out. Most pilots die before they do either, but Shin is determined to get home to his girlfriend, Ryoko. What he doesn't know is that Kanzaki is trying to get Ryoko for himself and plans to force her to marry him to save his father's business. Shin sets his mind on getting out as fast as possible, but he hasn't counted on how war changes people. He finally discharges his obligation to Asran, but the men he fought with for so long, including the cold, driven young prince, have become his family, and despite his longing to go home, he can't abandon them when their need is greatest, and he returns to Area 88. Shintani was born in 1951, and started his career as assistant to Leiji Matsumoto, so it's not altogether surprising that his work shows the same respect and understanding for those involved in war. The manga ran in *Shonen Sunday* until 1987, and is available in English from Viz.

TAICHI HIRAGA KEATON [1988]

Keaton is thirty-five years old, and a lecturer in archaeology at a third-rate university. His marriage has failed. His ex not only outranks him in the academic pecking order, being a full professor, but earns far more than his pittance of a salary. But Keaton's other, inner life is far different. The 18-volume *Big Comic Original* story by writer Hokusei Katsushika and artist Naoki Urasawa lets us into the mind of a complex character whose struggle for conventional success at the cost of following his dream is finally resolved in that rarest of comic conventions, a wholly believable happy ending. Keaton has been doing his best to fit in ever since childhood. His parents, an English noblewoman and a Japanese zoologist, divorced when he was five and he went to England with his mother. He studied archaeology at Balliol College, Oxford, where he met his Japanese wife. They married while still students, and had a daughter, Yuriko, but the marriage ended messily. He joined the elite British Army SAS unit, became a hero, and now uses his skills to moonlight as an insurance claims investigator for world-renowned underwriters Lloyds of London, all the while dreaming of excavating ancient civilizations. Yuriko dreams that her parents will get back together, and at the end of the manga, both their wishes come true.

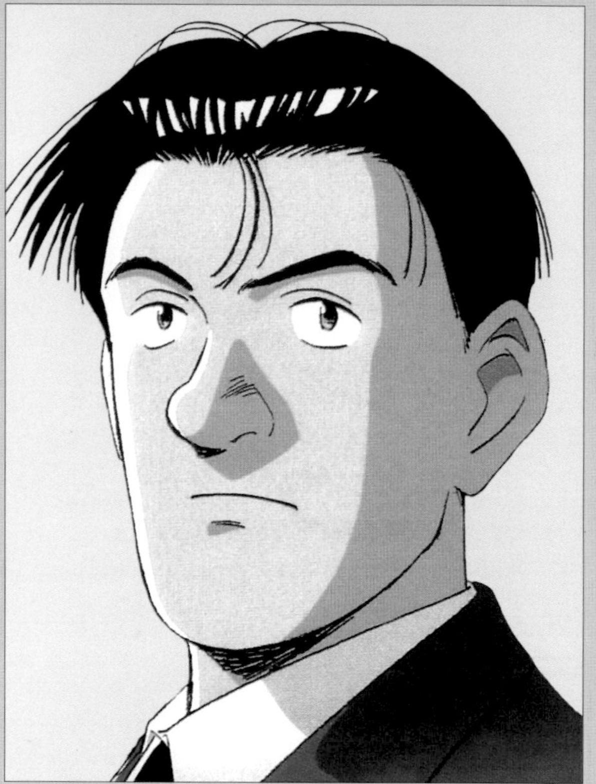

Ex-SAS sergeant, war hero, archaeologist, and insurance investigator Keaton.

KENTA HIRONO [1983]

Masakazu Katsura is a huge Batman fan, so it's no surprise that he should create a character who dreams of being a winged superhero. In *Dream Warrior Wingman (Yume Senshi Wingman)*, first published in *Shonen Jump*, teenager Kenta saves a girl from another dimension who has fallen out of the sky. Aoi gives him a "dream note," a promissory note which guarantees that whatever you write on it will come true. Kenta writes his dream—he wants to be a superhero—and it comes true. Now he's Wingman, a warrior who can transform into a powerful armored being, able to intervene not just in dream battles, but in the real world. Every superhero, however, has a nemesis. Wingman's arch enemy is Rimel, ruler of the land of Powdream in the fourth dimension. Rimel sends agents into our world in disguise to steal the dream note so that Kenta can't become Wingman any more and foil his plans. Kenta and Aoi work together to defeat him.

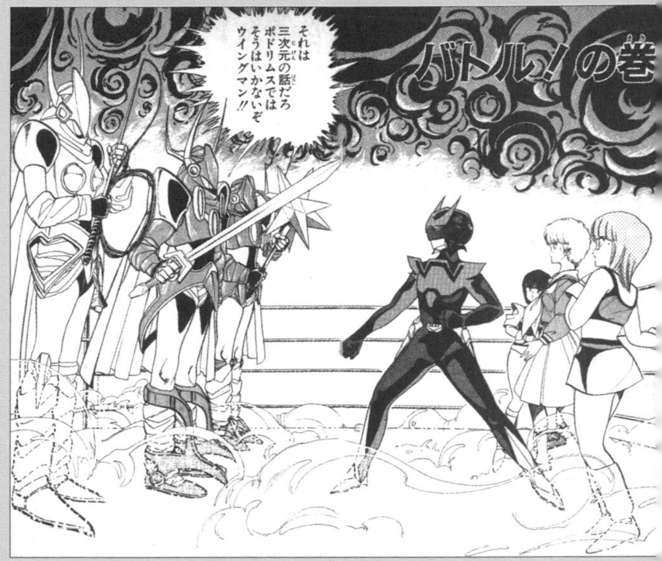

Superheroes get all the girls! Kenta's secret identity is Batman-inspired Wingman. His creator is a Batman fanatic.

KILLY [1998]

Blame from *Afternoon* magazine stars the ultra-cool Killy, a young man too disengaged to be interested in anything except survival in a world controlled by an insane machine. The Netsphere, an Internet run mad, was used to run the world but is now well out of control itself, and is turning the world into one huge interconnected city. If Killy can find an uncontaminated network gene, a piece of software used to connect individuals to the Netsphere, he may be able to stop the cities from growing before they devour all of Earth. Armed with a massive gun and helped by a blonde android, he has to fight off the Silicon Creatures, white-faced beings clad in black leather, and survive long enough to solve the mystery of why the Netsphere went crazy. Tsutomu Nihei is a qualified architect, but abandoned his career after a year in New York and came home to be a manga artist. Tsutomu's second manga, *NoiSE*, is set in the same universe.

HAJIME KINDAICHI

[1992]

Hajime Kindaichi is the grandson of famous Japanese detective Yosuke Kindaichi. When his story opened in *Weekly Shonen Magazine,* he was in his second year of high school, aged about seventeen. He skipped as many classes as he could, and was widely considered a delinquent. He's clever, nimble, and fast, good at card tricks and pickpocketing, and bickers constantly with his equally clever childhood friend, Miyuki Nanase. Kindaichi gets drawn into the family profession by accident, when a school drama club production leads to a spate of deaths linked to *Phantom of The Opera.* Inspector Isamu Kenmochi shows up to lead the investigation for the Homicide Squad, and is so impressed with Kindaichi's assistance on the investigation that he calls on him for help with future cases. Kindaichi's adventures, written by Yozaburo Kanari and drawn by Fumiya Sato, ran for eight years, were animated and filmed in live action for TV. *The New Kindaichi Files* were available in English as part of publisher Kodansha's educational bilingual comics line. A lawsuit by the estate of famous crime writer Seishi Yokomizo, creator of Kindaichi's grandfather, Kosuke Kindaichi, was settled out of court, and the very first Kosuke Kindaichi story *The Honjin Murder Case* was adapted for *The New Kindaichi Files* with the approval of Yokomizo's widow. This time, the artist was Jet, a mystery specialist who had also adapted work by Ellery Queen and Arthur Conan Doyle, and the story appeared in Kadokawa's *Asuka Comics* in 1993.

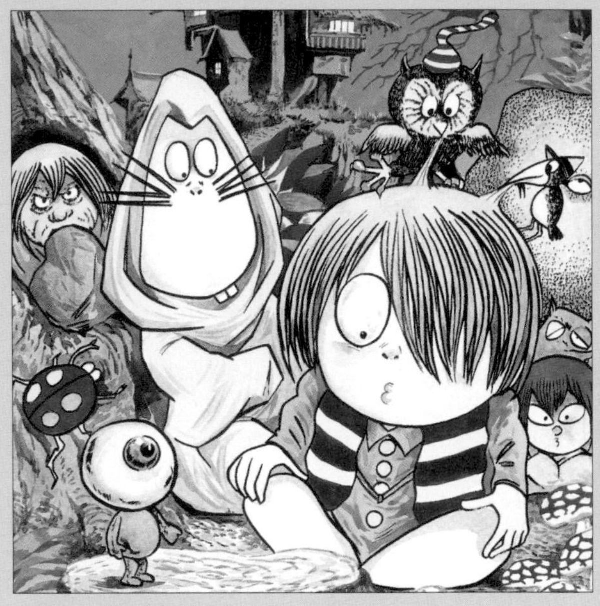

Family and friends are just as important to spooks, and Kitaro relies on his.

KITARO [1971]

Spooky Kitaro (*Hakaba no Kitaro*,or *Kitaro of the Graveyard*, later renamed *Ge-Ge-Ge-no Kitaro*) is a celebration of the place of *yokai*—traditional goblins—in Japanese life. Orphaned Kitaro, the last of his tribe of ghost hybrids, is desperately poor. Nevertheless, he does his best to help anyone who asks for his aid. Word gets around and many creatures, human and otherwise, send requests for help with evil monsters and goblins via Kitaro's magical mailbox. He often encounters great danger fighting these creatures, but he can use his traditional wooden geta sandals and his spiky hair as weapons—both can fly off and spike or smash anyone in their path. He is helped by the spirit of his late father, who resides in a walking eyeball but can pop out whenever he wishes. His regular sidekick is a cowardly, selfish ghost called Rat-man, who got his own spinoff manga *Adventures of Rat-Man (Nezumi-otoko no Boken)*, but he meets and befriends many other supernatural beings. Artist Shigeru Mizuki, who survived the Pacific War despite losing an arm, is 82 years old and still working as a manga creator as well as one of Japan's leading folklore researchers.

KOICHI KOYAMA [1971]

Koichi thinks he's an ordinary Japanese schoolboy. Then he learns he is really *Babel II (Babel Nisei)*, master of the ancient weapon system that was the Tower of Babel. He's the offspring of aliens who built a civilization in the Euphrates Basin millennia ago. Some intermarried with humans, and their blood is in Koichi, but he might never have known it if alien prince Yomi hadn't turned to the dark side. Yomi was the chosen inheritor of the powers of Babel; Koichi is next in line and must use three mighty robots, built to serve the heir millennia ago, to defend human civilization from destruction and mankind from slavery at the hands of the insanely ambitious Yomi. Yomi tries to persuade Koichi to join him, but the pair are fated to fight to the death. Mitsuteru Yokoyama's science fiction manga started a craze for tales of normal-looking, quiet heroes with paranormal powers. In the sequel, *His Name is 101 (Sono Na wa 101)*, Koichi finds that his blood has been used by Yomi to create a legion of cloned psychic soldiers to take over the world, and he has to find and destroy them all.

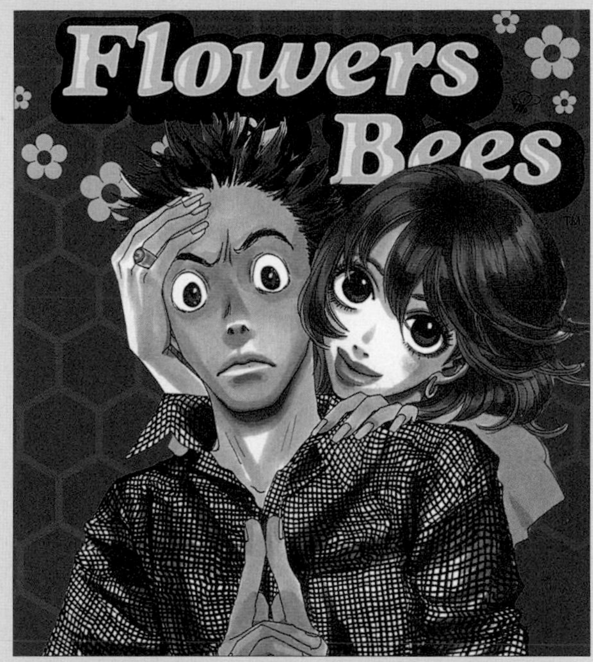

A boy has to suffer for beauty, as Masao learns in *Flowers and Bees*.

MASAO KOMATSU [2000]

If you're not one of the popular kids at school, what can you do? Masao sees a cute girl, knows he has no chance with her, and decides to restyle himself for success. He visits the "Beautiful Men's World" salon in Moyoko Anno's *Flowers and Bees (Hana to Mitsubachi)* from *Young Magazine*. There, Kiyoko and Harumi, two gorgeous sisters working at the salon, bully him mercilessly. They even fool him into thinking he's lost his virginity, but that's nothing compared to the ribbing he gets when word gets out in school. Then his equally geeky but far more confident pal Yamada starts to transform himself as well—and does it better. Yet little by little, Masao learns that, while looking good can boost your confidence, there's more to being popular than looks alone. Bit by bit, as he comes out of his shell and learns to make the most of everything he's got, Masao achieves his goal to become a likable, popular guy. The manga is published in English from Viz.

MASATOSHI KONNO

[1994]

The hero of *Let's Get Married (Kekkon Shiyouyo)* by Mochiru Hoshisato just wants to marry his girlfriend, Sanae Kenjo. They've been sweethearts since school days and used to be in a band together. Now they work at the same company—by coincidence, a wedding arrangements company. It should be ideal, but Sanae can't figure out why Masatoshi is so eager to get hitched right away. She is a real technophile and wants to work in electronic design, not give up work and start a family the way many Japanese girls still do upon marrying. So Masatoshi spends his days at work dreaming of Sanae and ways to persuade her to tie the knot, instead of focusing on his job like a good Japanese salaryman should. Sanae spends her days wishing she could get into the electronics department instead of being stuck in the bridal section. Sanae's new boss, pretty and sweet-natured Ms. Kubota, is useless around any kind of machinery, so Sanae has a chance to shine; but she may get even further with Mr. Kakieda, the owner of the company, who has his eye on her both personally and professionally. Masatoshi has his work cut out over the six volumes of the story to get to his own happy ending.

JIMMY KUDO a.k.a. SHINICHI KUDO [1996]

Also known as Jimmy Jackson in some versions of Gosho Aoyama's *Detective Conan (Meitantei Conan* a.k.a. *Great Detective Conan* or *Case Closed)*, seventeen-year-old Jimmy is the son of crime novelist Yasuko Kudo. He is a top athlete and has become an ace detective by hanging around his father while he studied crime scenes. Now his father lives in the United States with his wife, Yukiko, while Jimmy studies in Japan. He wants to be the twentieth-century Sherlock Holmes, and his skills are already so well known that the police consult him on complex cases. One day while out with his girlfriend, Rachel (Ran Mouri), he overhears some risky business being conducted by an illegal group, the Black Organization, and is force-fed an experimental drug by two mysterious men in black, known only as Gin and Vodka. When he wakes up, he's a little kid again, but he still has the brain of a top detective. The bespectacled boy is befriended by his next-door neighbor Prof. Agasa, who learns what has really happened and agrees to help him track down the two men and try to get his life back. Jimmy takes the name Conan in honor of Britain's Sir Arthur Conan Doyle, creator of his idol, Sherlock Holmes. In the Japanese original he adds the surname of another great crime writer, Japan's Rampo Edogawa. He moves in with Rachel and helps her incompetent, alcoholic detective father solve many cases using the gadgets Professor Agasa invented for him—a voice-changing bow tie and a watch with unusual functions. Conan's true identity is later discovered by Shinichi's rival high-school detective, Osaka-born Heiji Hattori, son of a detective inspector who befriends him and tries to help him regain his true self.

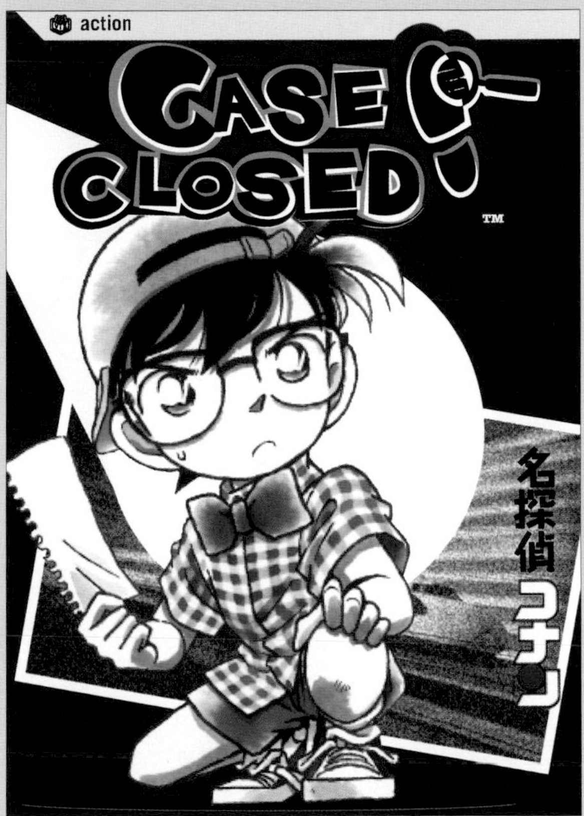

The deadliest things can lurk in small packages: dinky detective Jimmy says *Case Closed*.

KAZAHAYA KUDO [2000]

Homeless and down on his luck, Kazahaya is on the verge of freezing to death on the snowy streets of Tokyo on Christmas Eve. He's saved by a passerby, Rikuo Himura, and taken back to the drugstore where he lives and works. The boss of the Green Pharmacy, Kakei, offers Kazahaya a home and a job; strangely enough, the job involves using the clairvoyance that nobody else knows Kazahaya possesses to retrieve "special items" for Kakei. Rikuo also has mental gifts—his power is telekinesis. The two take an immediate dislike to each other, but have to work together or be out on the

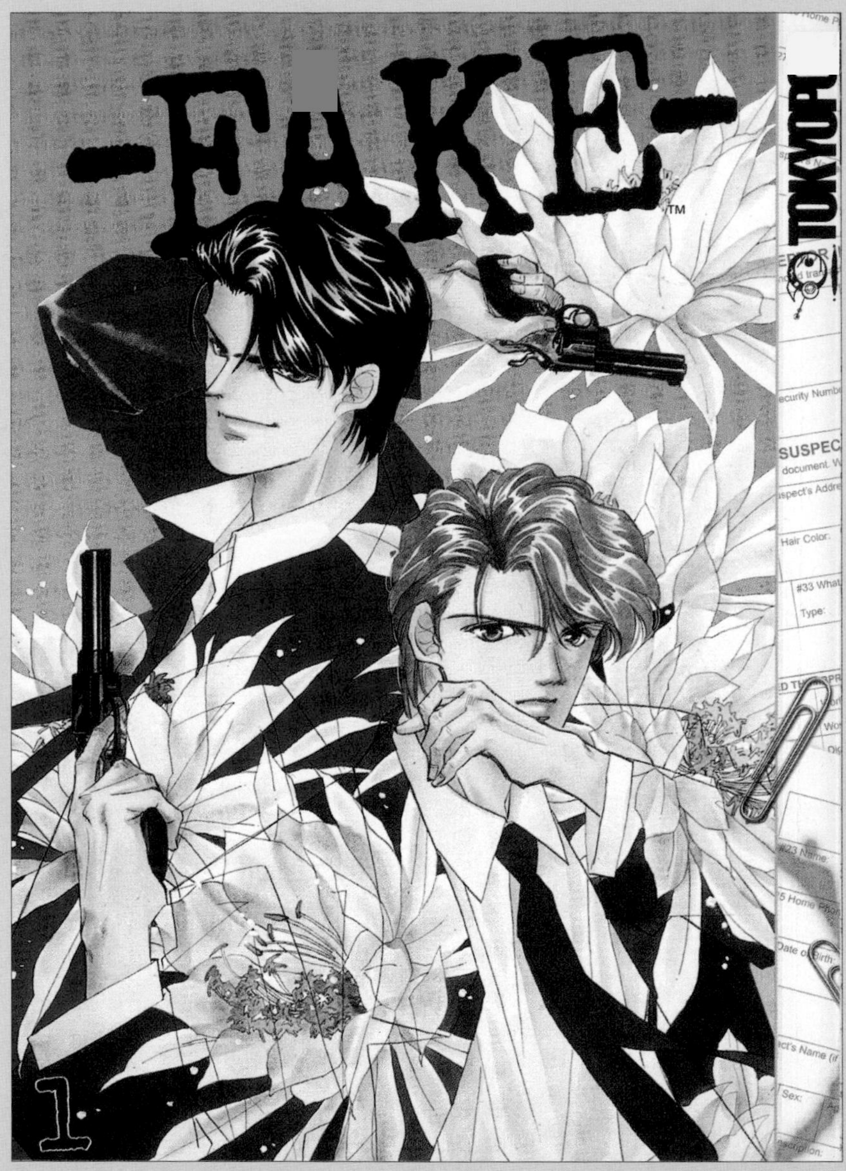
-FAKE-
1
Hair Color:
Type:
Sex:

streets again. An unfinished CLAMP story, *Legal Drug (Goho Drug)* is similar to *Tokyo Babylon* in being a male relationship story that's not quite *shonen ai*, set in a modern Tokyo that's not quite the real world. It started in *Mystery* magazine and moved on twice before finally vanishing from the works-in-progress section of the group's web site late in 2003.

DEE LAYTNER [1992]

Tall, dark, handsome Dee is a detective in New York's twenty-seventh precinct. He's loudmouthed, obnoxious, and openly bisexual. When he meets his new partner, a fey but gorgeous guy named Randy McLain, nicknamed Ryo because he's half-Japanese, it's lust at first sight, and Dee is determined to get his man. Ryo is a year older than him and has a very different personality—quiet and reserved—but they have a lot in common. Both decided to join the force after they lost their families to crime, and both are good cops, though Ryo cuts less corners than Dee. Ryo looks out for a pair of street kids, Vicky and Carol, who regard him as an older brother, but Vicky is so protective of him that at times it seems he's their father figure, and puts plenty of obstacles in the way of Ryo's growing relationship with Dee. Their boss, bisexual Berkley Rose, also has his eye on Ryo, while Dee has many admirers, including his former SWAT team colleague, J.J. Sanami Mato's manga *Fake*, revolves around Dee's pursuit of Ryo, the relationship that develops between them, and the comical and romantic situations they get themselves into. Originally published in *Bonita*, the manga is published in English from Tokyopop.

Left: Half Japanese, half American, all cop and all his: nice guy Ryo and his partner Dee.

MAKIHEI [1978]

The young hero of writer Yuichiro Obayashi and artist Yasuyuki Tagawa's manga *Makihei the Sushi Maker (Tekka no Makihei)* sets out to become a sushi master to equal his legendary father, now dead. The manga chronicles his efforts and his eventual victory in a sushi contest before judges and an audience of keen sushi aficionados, who judge his knife technique and the style with which he forms his sushi, as well as their taste and arrangement on the serving dish. Makihei triumphs and inherits his father's mantle as a great sushi chef.

MANJI [1994]

Blade of the Immortal (Mugen no Juunin, literally *Inhabitant of Infinity)* was published in *Afternoon* magazine and rapidly acquired cult status on its way to winning awards and critical plaudits. Hiroaki Samura's protagonist is a *ronin* (masterless samurai) cursed with immortality. His body has been invaded by worms that heal every wound, however dreadful. Manji was responsible for a terrible tragedy where many innocent people died. Outlawed as a result, his curse is that he must kill a thousand evil men to be exonerated and be able to die himself. His awareness of the value of life and tragedy of death heightened by his own strange situation, Manji teams up with Rin, a woman out to avenge the death of her father at the hands of a warrior gang, to achieve his total body count. Stunningly drawn, with accurate period detail, the story is as powerful as the art. *Blade of the Immortal* is published in English from Dark Horse.

HIROYA MATSUMOTO

[1993]

Starting a new job is an exciting time in a young man's life, but when Hiroya joins the renowned Right Trading Company, he has no idea just how exciting office work can be. He is asked to join a top-secret project and becomes one of the company's elite team of power-suited fighters—literally one of the forces of Right—fighting for truth, justice, and the best interests of the company. The Shinesman team is fighting an alien invasion by the people of planet Voice, but the forces of Voice are smarter than your average invading aliens and intend to conquer Earth through our consumer passions. Infiltrating our great corporations as ordinary salarymen, Voice sleepers are working their way up the corporate ladder and taking over the world one boardroom at a time. Prince Sasaki of Voice and his henchman, Seki, are already ahead of the game with their Science Electronics business empire, including theme parks and a TV show that's wowing kids everywhere (including Hiroya's little brother,

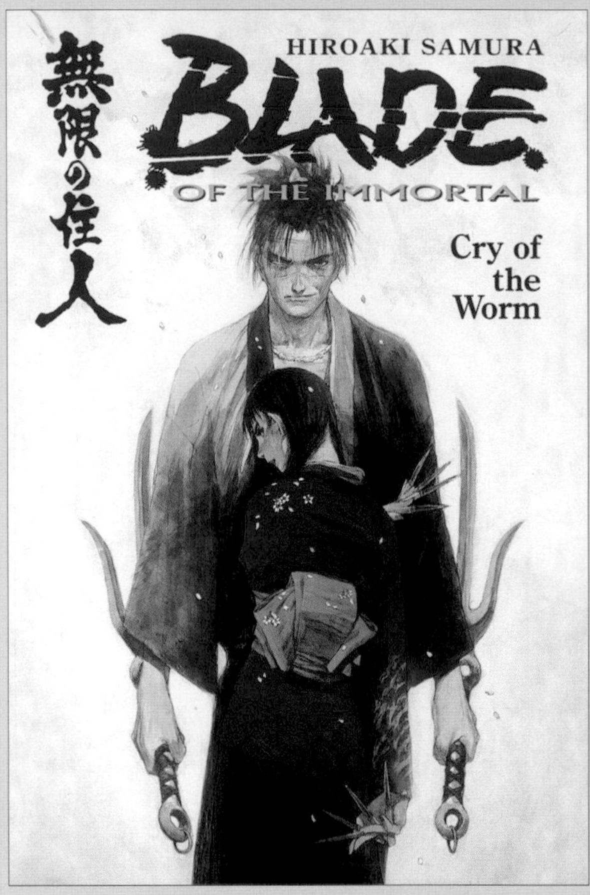

Supernatural samurai Manji and orphaned Rin are on a quest for redemption via revenge.

Yota). Hiroya becomes Shinesman Red, and with his four color-coded colleagues, he fights off this ultimate takeover bid in a hilarious parody of Japan's *sentai* shows (think *Power Rangers*). *Special Duty Battle Team Shinesman (Tokumu Sentai Shinesman)* by Kaimu Tachibana was collected in nine volumes from *PC Comics Bokke Series* between 1993 and 1998.

SHIBA MIDO [1995]

It is 2045: the 37th Long Range Immigration Fleet is on its way to the center of the Milky Way. The flagship is the Macross class battleship NO. 7. Along the way the fleet runs into the enemy Barauta, and fighting starts. But aboard the colony ships, each a huge city in its own right, life goes on. Tornado Crush, a team sport that combines racing and hand-to-hand fighting, is hugely popular, and seventeen-year-old layabout Shiba is star player in the Black Bombers. Shiba is illegitimate and disaffected, but brave and tough. He saves an unknown woman from an attempted murder; she is combat pilot-turned-fleet talent scout Mahara Fabrio, and she starts to take an interest in his fighting abilities. He is drawn into the military and learns that his father may be the famous and long-married fleet commander Max Jenius. *Macross 7 Trash* is by Haruhiko Mikimoto, better known as a character designer on the original *Macross TV* series, and the manga serialized in *Shonen Ace* spins off from the series' universe.

ICHIRO MIHARA a.k.a ICCHAN [1999]

By normal standards, Icchan is pretty strange. He's thirty-two, works for a toy and game company called Piffle Princess, and is very interested in dolls. He always wears a long white coat, and he often hangs out with kids, so strangers call him a pervert. Yet his co-worker, Ogata, calls him "Chief Mihara" and takes his verbal abuse without complaint, while shy schoolgirl Misaki looks up to him as a teacher and a good friend. His kid brother, Ojiro, thinks his ability to make toys is cool. He's actually the developer of a game called the Angelic Fight. Customizable mannequins called Angels do battle for their young owners, known as Deuses, in a game environment called the Layer. They are powered by headsets that enable the Deus to control his or her fighter by thought. The Layer has a serious purpose. Ichiro invented the game with the encouragement of Misaki's mother, Shuko, when his project to design equipment that would help physically challenged people have more independence was turned down for funding. He spent four years turning it into the Angelic Layer game so he could find the most powerful Deus of all, one who can take the Layer to new levels and help him solve some of the problems inherent in making mechanical aids move by the power of thought. He's also helping Shuko come to terms with the crippling fears that forced her to leave her beloved daughter behind when she came to Tokyo to work at Piffle Princess. CLAMP's *Angelic Layer* first appeared in *Shonen Ace* magazine and is available in English from Tokyopop.

SHINYA MITO [1986]

"The night has a myriad of different faces, and there's a man who peers into them, one by one. His name is Midnight." Osamu Tezuka's manga *Midnight* from *Weekly Shonen Champion* stars handsome, laconic Shinya, whose name in its Japanese order reads as "Mid Night." A former biker, he was involved in an accident that left beautiful Mari in a vegetative coma. Now he drives the night shift to earn money for her treatment. His cab is unusual, having a hidden fifth wheel that enables it to navigate any road, however rough, and no one else can drive it because he and the cab are one being. The passenger-of-the-week format allows Tezuka to experiment with many different types of story, and the Mari subplot reinforces Shinya's quest for atonement and redemption. Tezuka started to develop the story in 1981; originally it featured a robot car with psychic powers, but he felt it was too similar to *Knight Rider* and switched the focus to the driver and the strange people he encountered. It was originally slated for the New Year 1985 issue of the magazine, but publication was postponed when Tezuka was hospitalized with hepatitis. The final episode, with a surprise ending, was not included in the collected edition. Tezuka fans will note cameo appearances from Black Jack and Shunsuke Ban (as Shinya's father).

SUDA MONZA [1950]

Hero of Tezuka's *The Plain of Abusegahara*, Monza is a samurai who in 1856, tries to persuade his lord to reclaim a huge area of undeveloped land. Land for agriculture and building has always been at a premium in mountainous Japan, but Monza's lord thinks the task will be too much and most of his retainers agree. Monza and his younger sister, Tsubomi, set out to do the work themselves with the support of one faithful retainer, Pekunai. They face opposition from yakuza, natural disaster, and financial ruin, but their determination wins through. The manga is a fine example of Tezuka's recycling of stereotypes from his "repertory company"—loyal, perky Pekunai is the character best known as Kenichi Shikashima, sour retainer Yagya Shuma is Acetylene Lamp, and yakuza boss Kuronishiya is piratical Buku Bukk. Monza himself is played by Tezuka's "true son of Japan," a character he nicknamed Higedaruma, which translates unflatteringly as "Mustachio Potbelly." A middle-aged, fleshy guy, this younger version of Old Man Mustache has a monster mustache that can't hide his sensitive soul. Whatever troubles and trials he faces, this character remains sincere and humane. His first appearance was in *Miracle Forest*, a fairy-tale fantasy, in 1949.

IZUMI MORINO [1989]

Hero of Haruhiko Mikimoto's manga *Marionette Generation*, which appeared in *Newtype* magazine, twentysomething Izumi is an illustrator like his creator, but at the start of his career and not yet successful. One day, he wakes up and finds a strange doll in his bed, a doll that seems to be alive. Is she an alien? She doesn't know, asking him who she is and where she came from. He names her Lunch. Izumi has enough to worry about without her, for he's the object of a crush from a high-school girl, Kinoko, who has declared herself his assistant. His high-school sweetheart, Kozue, has come to crash with him for a while, making Kinoko jealous. As his career takes off and he gets more fans, Lunch causes more complications in her quest to find her identity and creates cute but embarrassing situations for Izumi. A renowned character designer and illustrator, Mikimoto has made only a handful of manga.

YOTA MOTEUCHI [1990]

Yota is a self-conscious, introverted boy, sixteen years old at the start of Masakazu Katsura's *Video Girl Ai (Denno Shojo Ai)*. His mother is dead, his artist father works in Paris, and he lives alone in a big, comfortable house in Tokyo. Yota, like many teenagers, just goes with the flow and doesn't make waves. He dreams of being an artist and creating manga, but never actually does anything about it. He has a crush on a girl in his class but is too shy to speak to her. His only real friend is Takashi Niimai, his classmate. He and Takashi are night and day. Takashi is the class hunk, outgoing and popular, but a good friend to Yota, always trying to encourage him to express his feelings for the girl of his dreams, Moemi Hayakawa. Moemi loves Takashi, however. When Yota finds out about this, he is plunged into despair.

The classic school love triangle gets an extra twist when Yota acts out of character for the first time. Walking past a strange video store, he sees what look like typical soft porn tapes in the window and decides to rent one and cheer himself up. Nervously, he chooses a tape under the watchful eyes of the grandfatherly store clerk. But when he gets home and puts the tape into his faulty VCR, he gets the surprise of his life. Out pops the girl on the cover, Ai Amano, who proceeds to turn his life upside down. Over the course of the next year, Yota will grow from being passive to pursuing his dreams, from being too scared to express his feelings to openly committing himself, and from running from any confrontation to being willing to stand up against hopeless odds for what he believes and the people he loves. The only things that don't change in the one hectic year when Ai changes his life forever are Yota's unselfishness and his purity of heart. He's basically a real hero, but it takes the right girl, along with a look into another world, to bring out his true self. He makes a further appearance, aged twenty-five, in Katsura's later manga, *Video Girl Len*.

OLD MAN MUSTACHE a.k.a. SHUNSAKU BAN

[1939]

Higeoyaji, as he is known in Japanese, has the honor of being the first recognizable character in the work of Osamu Tezuka—though the god of manga gave credit for his creation to a friend from middle school. His classmate doodled his own father, and Tezuka liked his look so much that he used him from his fan work until the very end of his career in 1989. He appears in drawings dated to 1939, when Tezuka was thirteen. He made his published debut as Count Salad in *Golden Bat (Ogon Bat)* in 1947, and became a staple of Tezuka's "repertory company" of characters who crop up in different roles throughout his work. He is a plump man in late middle years, prematurely bald and grey with an impressive walrus mustache under a neat little nose. Despite his portly figure, he's spirited and energetic. He can be bad-tempered, but has a kind heart and a strong sense of justice. He can play a fatherly role, acting as protector or providing the guiding hand of parental authority; but Tezuka sometimes makes him foolish, to let the hero take the lead. He appears as Shunsaku Ban in the *Metropolis* trilogy, *The White Pilot,* and several other titles. In *Kimba the White Lion*, he appears as Prof. Pompous (Higeoyaji), the uncle of young Roger Ranger (Kenichi). In *Astro Boy*, he is mentor and guide to an impressionable young creature, joining his friend Prof. Elefun (Ochanomizu) as Astro's surrogate uncle. He got his own shared-title manga, entitled *Higeoyaji, Dr. Ochanomizu*, published in August 1986, for a Tokyo conference of investigators.

MAMORU MURAKAMI

[1965]

The spirit of the Earth has created a force to prevent evil from overrunning the world and destroying mankind: the giant golden robot Magma, and his companions Gum and Mol. They are literally "rocket men" who can transform into spaceships. Although Magma is enormously powerful, he needs human aid in order to overcome the evil space giant Goa, who is out for world domination. He must be called on by a human using a magical golden whistle before he can act. Earth chooses young Mamoru Murakami, son of the newspaper reporter to whom Goa first revealed his dreadful plan to take over the world using manufactured monsters that can appear as humanoids. Tezuka's manga *Magma Taishi* (*Ambassador Magma*) first appeared in *Shonen Gaho* magazine in 1965, with additional artwork by Tomo Inoue and Kazuyoshi Fukutomi, filling the gaps caused by Tezuka's hectic production schedule.

Right: Old Man Mustache in one of his greatest roles as friend and protector of *Astro Boy*.

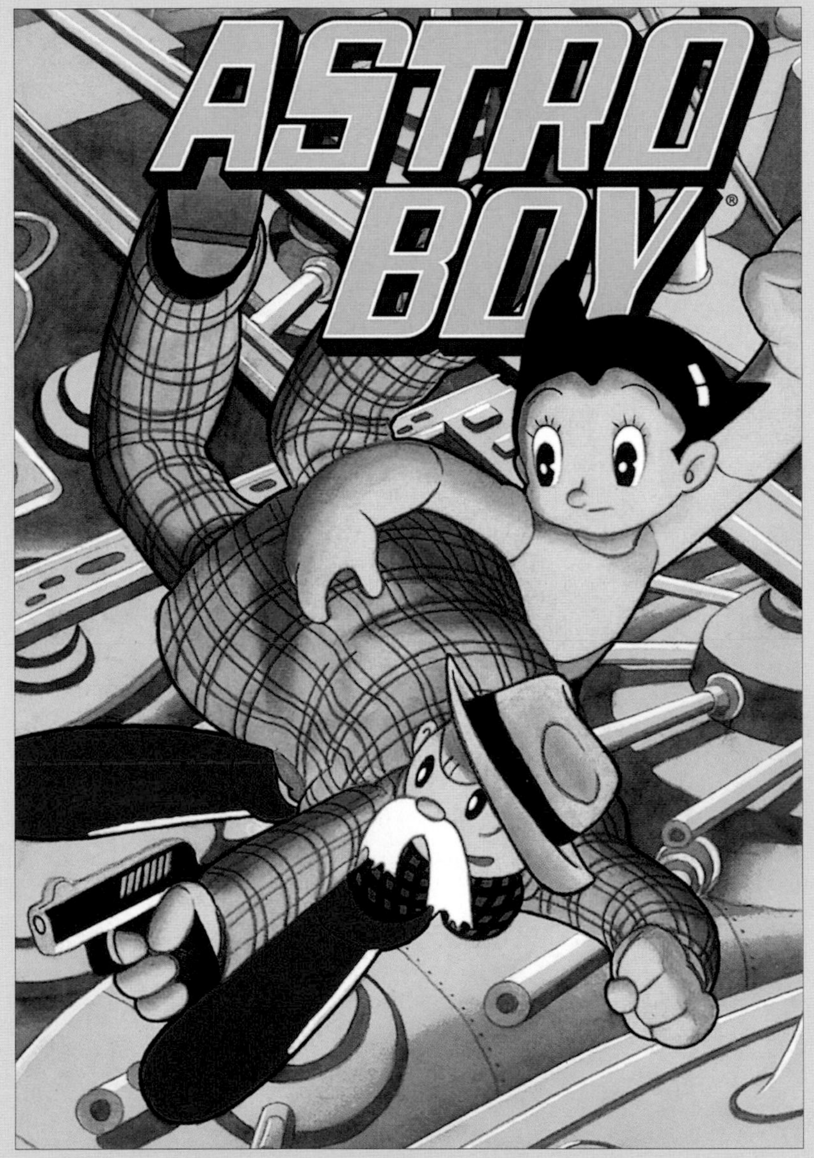
ASTRO BOY®

NAOTA NANDABA [2001]

A boys' fantasy manga based on the anime series by Gainax, Hajime Ueda's *FLCL (Furi Kuri* or *Fooly Cooly)* starts with twelve-year-old smart aleck Naota living in an all-male household with his older brother (currently studying in the United States), father, and grandfather. The city of Mabase is a dormitory town for the huge Medical Mechanica factory, but things seem pretty normal. Naota is worried about his brother's seventeen-year-old girlfriend Mamimi, who takes every opportunity to flirt with him when they're alone, but then Haruko Haruhara turns up on her Vespa scooter and accidentally runs into him. Far from repentant, she whacks him with a guitar. That night he finds her in his home, getting a job as housekeeper to his family. A horn appears on his head where she hit him, a human-sized robot named Kanchi just turns up overnight, and Haruko worms her way into his elders' affections, making Naota feel like a stranger in his own home. Then another robot shows up and Naota has to tackle it before it wreaks havoc. Soon he's embarked on a new life as a robot fighter, and the seemingly normal small town is crawling with aliens.

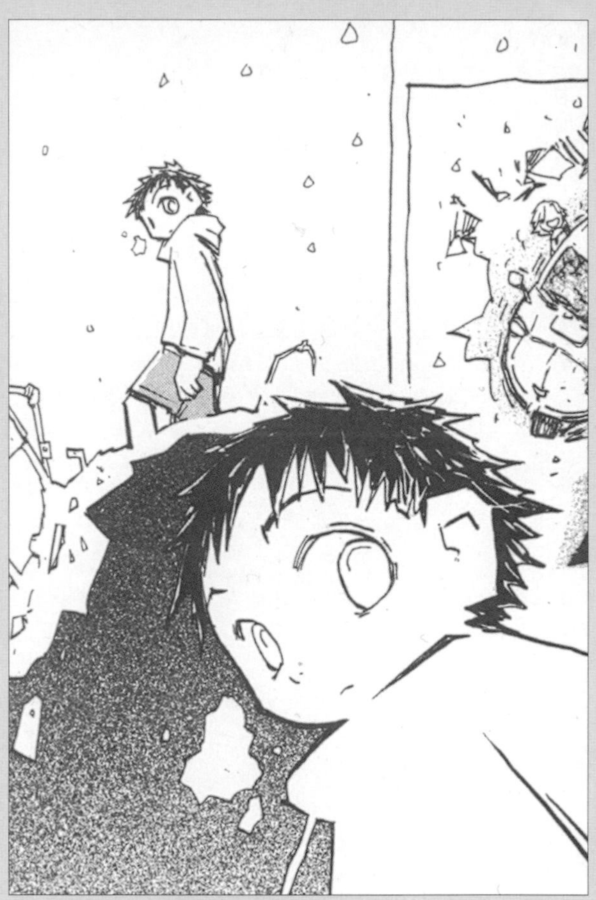

Ueda's style and free-flowing frame layouts give *FLCL* the feel of a tenuous grip on reality.

SANPEI NIHIRA [1973]

Teenager Sanpei grew up in a remote mountain village in northeast Japan. There wasn't much to do locally except go to school or go fishing, and Sanpei became a gifted fisherman. Takao Yaguchi's manga *Sanpei the Fisherman (Tsurikichi Sanpei)* is the story of his efforts to catch every fish in the water all over the world. He doesn't want to kill them—it's the challenge of outwitting them that he loves, and the bigger and more powerful the fish, the better he likes it. So he invents new techniques, which he passes on to often incredulous older anglers, and borrows and improves on their tried and tested methods. This attempt to make fishing exciting also provides a parable of the importance of cooperation and respect between youth and experience, and appeared in *Shonen Magazine*. DC's ComicsOne has published Taiga Takahashi and Yoshiaki Shimojo's fishing tale *Bass Master Ranmaru*, so Sanpei may one day see print in the United States.

JEAN ROCQUE RALTIGUE [1990]

Jean is a French teenager who lives with his aunt and uncle in Le Havre following the death of his mother and the disappearance of his father at sea. He's independently wealthy and very bright, and spends his time studying and inventing. His dream is to make a real flying machine and search for his father, and in 1889, he sets off for Paris to the World's Fair to test his latest invention. There he meets the girl who will change his life, circus acrobat Nadia. He falls for her on sight and pursues her through Paris. Nadia is also being chased by a gang out to steal the only link to her family, a necklace called the Blue Water, and when Jean decides to help her escape—partly from sheer kindness and partly to get closer to her—the pair embark on an epic journey that will take them to the South Seas by airplane, American warship, and submarine, and into the ruins of ancient Atlantis. Jean finds out what happened to his father, and his teenage infatuation for Nadia, tested by living with a capricious and frightened teenage girl, turns into real love that leads him to risk his life for her on many occasions. The pair eventually marry. Gainax's hit TV series, *The Secret of Blue Water (Fushigi no Umi no Nadia* a.k.a. *Nadia of the Mysterious Seas)* appeared as a manga entitled *The Secret of Comic Blue Water*, a Cyber Comix Special Edition, in 1992 and remains untranslated. The manga characters appear in stories not entirely related to the series and with a humorous slant.

AMURO RAY [1981]

The young hero of the manga, spun off the *Mobile Suit Gundam (Kido Senshi Gundam)* series, fifteen-year-old Amuro is the child of a badly fractured home; his parents spend most of their time in conflict, and his father is away a lot at work on a secret project. Earth is at war with one of its many colonies, and his father leads the team developing a new type of mobile armor, the Gundam. An attack by an enemy squad forces Amuro into battle in the suit, and he discovers his talents for piloting go far beyond the norm. Amuro seems like an ordinary teenager—tall, brown hair, brown eyes, naive and enthusiastic—but he is a NewType, an evolutionary leap in human development with a special affinity for space and technology. His gift will take him far from home and bring him into conflict with the most charismatic man of his era, politician and soldier Char Aznable. He changes from a gentle young man not greatly interested in politics to an arrogant, egotistical, and fiercely competitive pilot, so committed to proving he is the best that he sometimes doesn't allow opponents the chance to surrender. Above all, he needs to show he's better than Char, and rivalry in love as well as war comes between them when he meets Char's protégé, Lala Sun. Surviving through many battles and seeing friend and foe alike die matures him, and eventually, after years of battle, shared loves, and fierce hatreds, he persuades Char to help him save Earth, and the two die together in the attempt. Kazuhisa Kondo's manga is published in English by Viz as *Gundam: The Origin*.

RYO SAEBA [1985]

Tall, tough, handsome Ryo is the world's best shot. He has a mysterious and violent past. He was the sole survivor of a plane crash in the jungles of Central America at about three years old. He doesn't know his parents' names, his nationality, or even his birthdate. He was raised as a guerrilla fighter, then went to the United States, and now lives and works in Tokyo. One of his few old friends, Umibozu, is a former enemy from his time fighting in Central America, a Special Forces veteran who now runs a Tokyo cafe, the Cat's Eye, with his wife, Miki. Ryo offers his services as a "sweeper" (an assassin for hire, sweeping up rubbish) through a message board in Shinjuku Station. Ryo's weakness is women; his strongest characteristics are loyalty and a sense of justice. His partner, Makimura, is killed when a job goes wrong, and Ryo swears to him that he will protect his eighteen-year-old adopted sister, Kaori. Ryo has a well-concealed respect for Kaori, whom he treats like a little sister; she takes it upon herself to check his frequent wanderings after pretty passersby and clients, often wielding a massive comedy hammer, which has become a manga staple. She is, of course, madly in love with Ryo, but will never admit it. Ryo is the *City Hunter* of the title in Tsukasa Hojo's manga. (His other nickname is the Stud of Shinjuku.) Published in *Shonen Jump*, it combined action, dark crime stories, and broad humor in a series of cases that always involved pretty women. It ran for twelve years, was animated for TV and movies, and became a live-action movie starring Jackie Chan.

SHUICHI SAITO [1998]

Sensitive, depressive Shuichi and his girlfriend, Kirie, live in the quiet coastal town of Kurozucho. Life is pretty quiet until everyone starts getting obsessed with spirals. Then his father commits suicide in a washing machine, his mother goes insane, and strange incidents,

Right: Guns, girls, and heavy hammers: all in a day's work for Ryo.

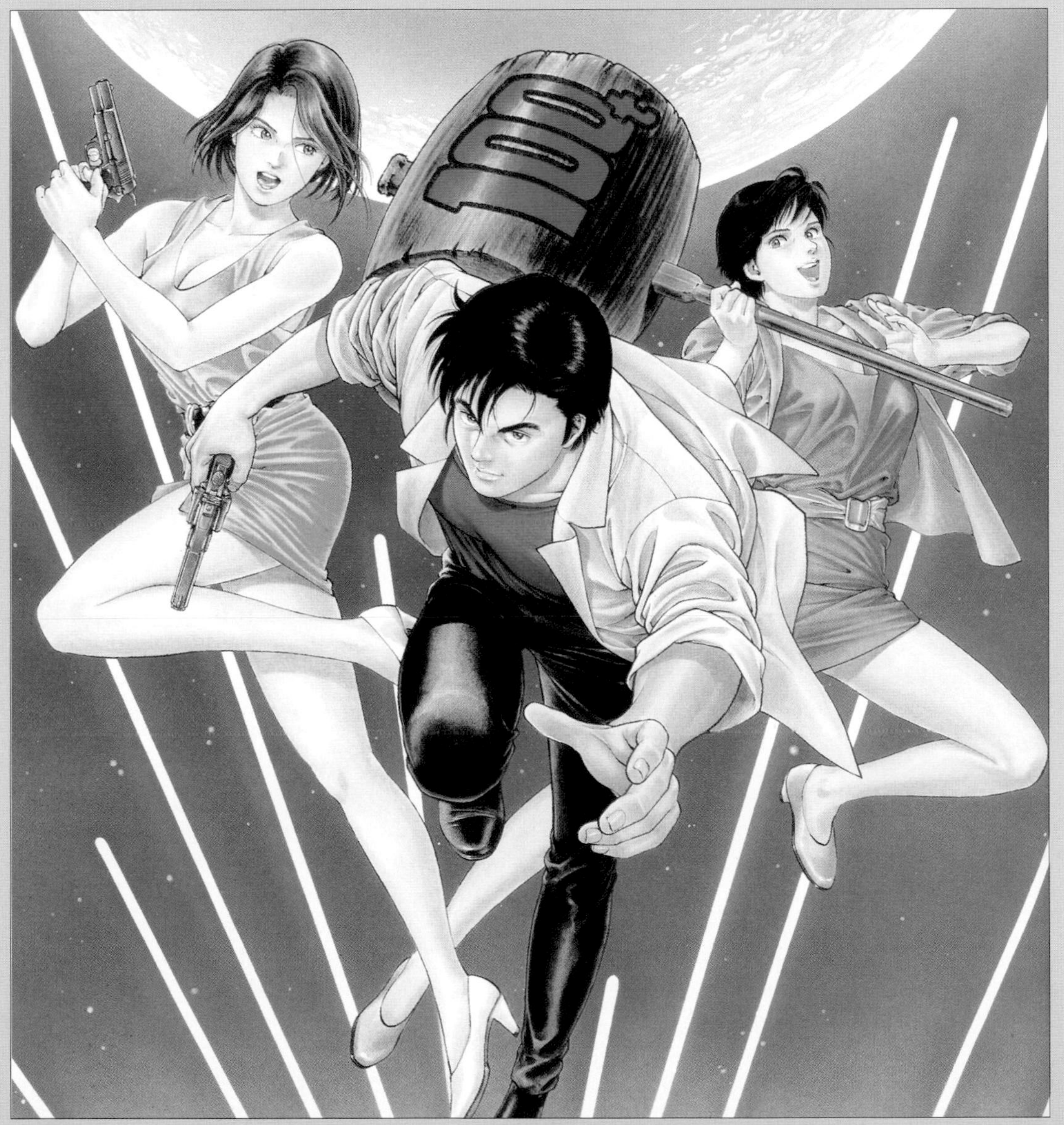
100t

all revolving around the spiral, start taking place all over town. The pair notice that spirals are everywhere, infesting every part of life—even their own bodies. The local mosquitoes are drinking a lot of blood, the snails are getting very big, pregnant women are being attacked, and huge typhoons are brewing off the coast. A local reporter tries to help them unravel the truth, but in the end there's no truth to be unraveled—the couple survive, things go back to normal, and we are left with the disquieting thought that if we don't know how or why it happened, it could happen again. *Uzumaki (Spiral)* by Junji Ito is available in English from Viz.

SARUMARU SARUTANI [1974]

The hero of *Progolfer Saru* by Motoo Abiko is a professional golfer, and may seem an unlikely star of comics for the very young. He appeared in a string of publications including *Baby Book*, *Corocoro Comic*, and *Mommy* in an attempt to make dad's weekend hobby look interesting and fun. Looking like a monkey, and with a name that means "monkey," Saru is as wily as he's wiry, and he's fighting for justice in his own way. A shadowy mastermind named Mr. X and his syndicate of evil golfers are trying to take over the circuit. Saru defeats them all and preserve's golf's true spirit. Imagine *Enter the Dragon* with the Man with No Name in the leading role and a slapstick slant to every bout. Later series and animated versions made the comedy golf battles even sillier as Saru circles the globe in his never-ending fight to defeat opponents controlled by Mr. X, including kung-fu golf masters, Native American golf shamans, and would-be golf assassins.

KENICHI SHIKASHIMA [1947]

Making his debut in Osamu Tezuka's *New Treasure Island*, where he played the leading role of Pete, Kenichi was the first Tezuka "repertory" superstar and for a while, a favorite juvenile lead. He is interested in everything, always willing to make the best of any situation, kind, considerate, and helpful to everyone. In *Kimba the White Lion*, he rescues Kimba after his escape from the hunters, looks after the cub, and takes him to Africa to claim his heritage. This essential purity endeared him to readers looking back on the rose-tinted simplicity of a pre-war childhood, but it hampered his development as a character in the rapidly changing post-war world. Japanese comic book readers started to look for leading characters who could be outsiders from society; even the gentle *Astro Boy* had to develop other aspects to his character. Manga began to grow up. Kenichi's youthful innocence was so powerfully established in the public mind that he couldn't keep pace. Tezuka said, "I was forced to drop Kenichi from his role as a protagonist because he lacked individuality." However, there's always a role for a character who can trigger our nostalgia for a perfect childhood, and Kenichi continued to put in occasional appearances in Tezuka's manga until 1986.

JOE SHIMAMURA [1964]

World-class sprinter Shimamura is seriously injured in an accident but saved by the Black Ghost, an agent of the mysterious organization known as the Merchants of Death who mean to take over the world. They have been creating an elite force of cyborg warriors, using the damaged bodies of exceptional people. Kind-hearted Prof. Gilmore saves Joe, and in so doing, turns him into *Cyborg 009*. Under Gilmore's guidance, the other eight cyborg warriors are now sworn to foil the Merchants of Death at all costs. Shotaro Ishinomori's manga made its debut in *Shonen Sunday* magazine, blending the cybernetic technology of *Astro Boy* with the evil masterminds of the James Bond movies. It didn't only predate *The Six Million Dollar Man*—it also foreshadowed *The Uncanny X-Men* in its use of characters with paranormal talents as part of an elite force fighting evil. It was animated for the big screen in 1966, with an animated TV series following in 1968, and further movies in 1967 and 1980. A spin-off manga, *One of 009*, appeared in 1967 starring the token female cyborg in the group. Ishinomori was a remarkable artist whose creative influence was second only to that of Osamu Tezuka—he was one of Tezuka's early pupils, and came to be known as the king of manga, just one step down from his teacher the god of manga. Born in 1938, he released his first work *Second-Class Angel* at the age of sixteen, while still in high school. His 1971 manga *Masked Rider* (*Kamen Rider*) had a huge influence on manga, anime, and the development of live-action special effects TV shows. His *Genma Taisen* collaboration became the hit movie *Harmagedon*. His *Japan,Inc.*, was the first comic guide to the workings of big business, and he also produced a 55 volume comic guide to Japanese history. Perhaps his most important contribution was helping to found the Association to Protect Freedom of Expression in Comics in 1992. He died in 1998.

SHUICHI SHINDO [1997]

Nineteen-year-old Shuichi is musically multitalented: a singer, songwriter, and arranger who desperately wants to be a rock star. He's a techno-freak, and despite his slight frame, lack of height, and sensitive nature, he's tough. He and his best friend, guitarist Hiroshi Nakano, have known each other since high school and play together in a band called Bad Luck. They hook up with a producer and set out to stardom, but then Shuichi meets the good-looking, charismatic Eiri Yuki, an older guy and a professional novelist-turned-music critic, whose criticism of his lyrics really stings. As he tries to get closer to the aloof

Eiri, determined to convince him that he really CAN write, the attraction between them grows. Hiroshi decides to quit music and focus on college, while Eiri's fiancée shows up. The band faces big problems—the crazy pressure of music biz schedules, members leaving, rival bands, gossip about Shuichi and Eiri. Shuichi almost leaves Japan for a career in the United States, but comes back to make his own mark on music, and get his man, in Maki Murakami's manga *Gravitation*, first seen in *Kimi To Boku* magazine and now in English from Tokyopop.

KAMUI SHIRO [1992]

The fate of the Earth will be decided in 1999, on the Day of Revelation. The key is a slight, quiet teenage boy named Kamui. Two groups of psychic warriors, the Seven Seals of the Earth Dragon and the Seven Harbingers of the Heaven Dragon, fight to either save the world or destroy it. Kamui is a powerful psychic who could tilt the battle either way, but refuses to get involved until his two childhood friends are drawn into the struggle. Fuma Mono, Kamui's psychic opposite force, kills his beloved sister, Kotori, under the influence of the Earth Dragon; Kamui, who has loved Kotori since they were all children, joins the other side. The epic struggle devastates Tokyo and kills almost everyone involved. CLAMP's *X:1999* debuted in Asuka and is available in English from Viz. The "X" in the title is intended to stir echoes of crucifixion and crossroads. For those who enjoy hunting buried references, it tips its hat to *Jojo's Bizarre Adventure* and *Peacock King* on several occasions.

SHUNA [1983]

Based on a Tibetan folktale, Hayao Miyazaki's manga *Journey of Shuna (Shuna no Tabi)* tells the story of young Prince Shuna's epic journey to find wheat for his people and save them from starvation. He hears that there is a crop in the Land of the Gods called Golden Wheat, which can grow in all conditions, and sets out to bring it back. His mount is an elk named Yakkur, his steed, but also his faithful companion. On the way he rescues a girl named Tea and her little sister from slavery and leaves them in a village in the care of an old woman. When he finally gets to the Land of the Gods, he steals the grain his people need and is severely punished for it, but Yakkur brings him back to Tea, who nurses him back to health. The pair finally marry. Shuna, a brave yet gentle and ecologically conscious teenager, is widely considered to be a prototype for the heroine of his later epic, *Nausicaa of the Valley of Wind*, and has obvious links to Ashitaka, who also leaves his homeland on a quest riding his faithful elk in *Princess Mononoke*. The story is fully painted in delicate watercolor and first appeared in *Animage* magazine's *Am Juju*. Born in the midst of war in 1941, Miyazaki has always been firmly against violence; all his works have a core message that living in harmony with nature and other people is the way forward for the world.

LUKE SKYWALKER [1977]

Luke is the son of Anakin Skywalker, who changed his name and allegiance to become Darth Vader, Dark Lord of the Sith. He was chief henchman of the evil Emperor who took the galaxy back to the dark days of the Empire after the golden age of the Republic, when the Jedi Knights were galactic guarantors of peace and justice. Raised on a farm, Luke happens upon a second-hand droid carrying a secret message from a beautiful princess. Hooking up with retired Jedi master Obi-Wan Kenobi, his father's former mentor, Luke heads off for adventure in the stars and faces loss, danger, and betrayal. He meets the princess who sent the secret message; he makes an unlikely friend in the shape of rogue pirate Han Solo; and he discovers that his skills as a pilot, honed by killing wild animals back on the farm, will help him out in the big wide world, but not as much as the skills he's starting to acquire through the painful process of growing up. Hisao Tamaki's four-volume 1997 manga version of the original *Star Wars* movie, *A New Hope* sticks closely to the Lucas film franchise, so Luke, Han, Leia, and the others are exactly the characters they are in the movie, but with extra big-eyed, neat-nosed charm. *The Empire Strikes Back* got the manga treatment in 1999 from Toshiki Kudo. Both are available in English from Dark Horse Comics, with covers by pseudomanga stylist Adam Warren.

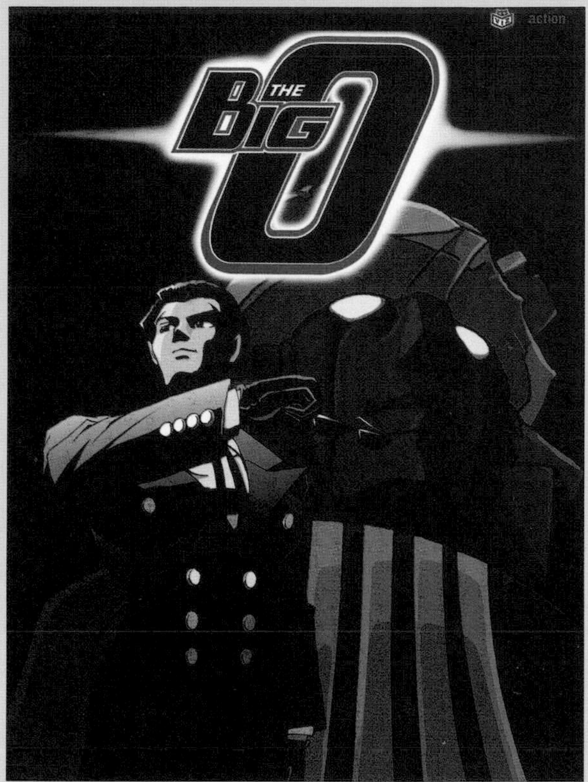

Roger Smith and the giant robot The Big O are on a search for memory.

ROGER SMITH [1999]

Roger is a Negotiator, a crime fighter in the future Paradigm City, called on to help Military Police chief Dan Daston when crime gets out of hand. Forty years ago, something wiped out all the residents' memories, forcing them to recreate their culture from fragments, known as "Memories," which have huge value. The result is a strange retro-culture in which tall, square-jawed Roger is a go-between trying to stop society's fractured relationships ending in all-out street war. Something else survived apart from those fragments, so precious that they are targets for thieves—giant robots known as megadeuses. *The Big O* is a megadeus that may hold the key to saving Paradigm City from sinking into lawless madness, in Hitoshi Ariga and Hajime Yadate's manga *The Big O*, based on the anime and first published in *Magazine Z*. Roger's relationship with his robot maid, Dorothy R. Waynewright, a 1940s good-girl movie queen, is enigmatic, but no more so than his attempt to deny the importance of his own missing memories. When Dorothy vanishes, and her ravaged body is found robbed of its memory circuits, Roger must face up to his own past and his half-forgotten love.

SPIKE SPEIGEL [1998]

Hero of hit TV series *Cowboy Bebop*, and its spin-off manga by artist Yukata Nanten and house pseudonym writer Hajime Yadate, bounty hunter Spike is tall, skinny, and achingly hip. He and his ex-cop partner, Jet Black, roam around a solar system that's a cross between kung-fu movies, Syd Mead futurism, and the Old West. He has the hots for sultry mystery girl Faye Valentine. Girl hacker Ed and her cute Welsh Corgi, Ein, the true brains of the outfit, complete a criminal, dysfunctional, but united family that's the twenty-first century successor to *Lupin III*. The hackneyed premise of the hired hands going from job to job, ripping off plots from U.S. crime shows in search of the next payday, is redeemed by the commitment of the creators to make a believable world for their all-too-human urban cowboys. The manga is available in English from Tokyopop.

NEGI SPRINGFIELD [2003]

Harry Potter is as popular in Japan as here. Ken Akamatsu has obviously noticed this, since the hero of his *Shonen Magazine* manga *Negima: Master Negi Magi (Maho Sensei Negima)* is a ten-year-old British (actually Welsh) boy genius who is also a magician of great power, attending a Japanese school. Negi, however, is attending as a teacher, not a pupil, and the class he has to teach has thirty-one gorgeous eighth-grade girls. There are all kinds of girls—sporty, outgoing, shy, ninja, ghost, android, gymnast, twins, foreign exchange student, short, tall, with and without glasses. Negi isn't supposed to display his powers, but Asuna discovers his secret. At first resentful because he's replaced the teacher she had a crush on, she slowly comes to like him, and when Negi tries to leave the school, she leads the girls to change his mind. Meanwhile, Negi has to

Right: Supernaturally cute—exorcist and fashion icon Subaru Sumeragi of *Tokyo Babylon*.

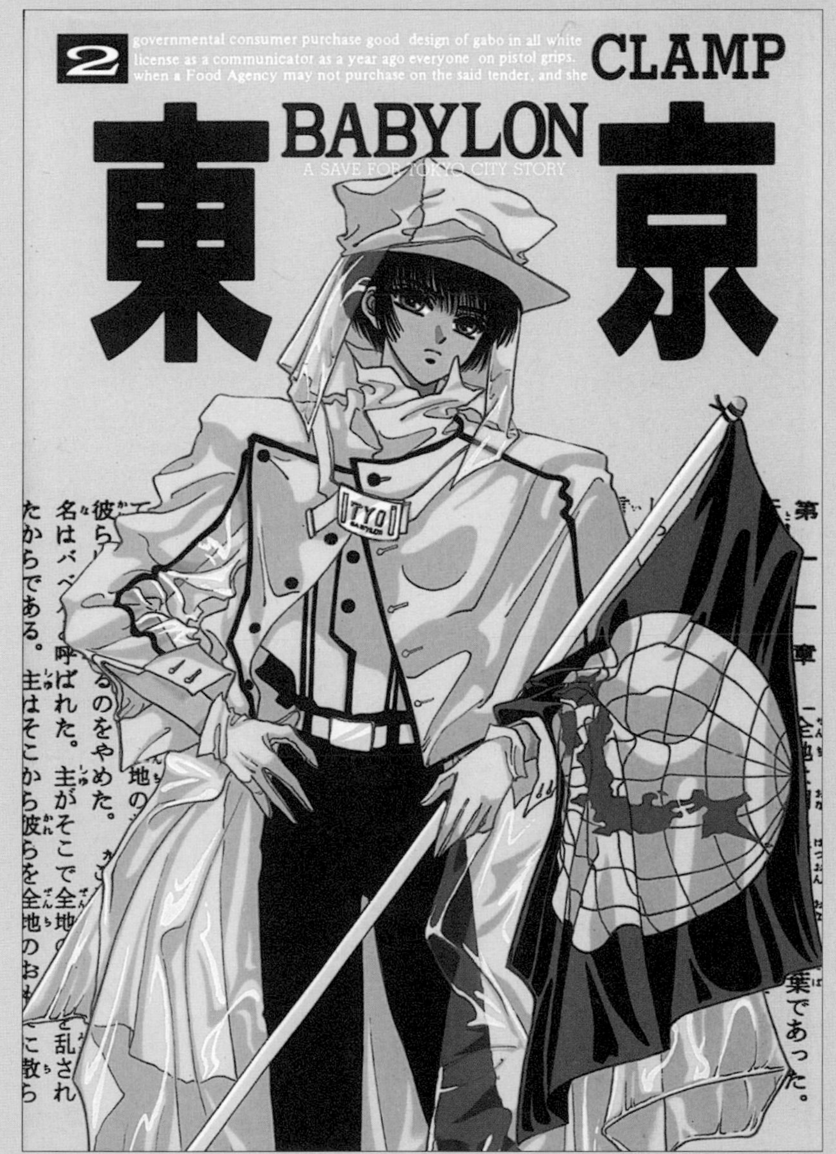
2
governmental consumer purchase good design of gabo in all white
license as a communicator as a year ago everyone on pistol grips.
when a Food Agency may not purchase on the said tender, and she
CLAMP
東
BABYLON
A SAVE FOR TOKYO CITY STORY
京
TYO

defend his class from the ongoing assaults of various mystical creatures, including an old friend from Wales in the form of a girl-crazy weasel spirit. The story is published in English from Del Rey and still ongoing.

SUBARU SUMERAGI [1991]

A gentle young psychic, heir of an ancient family, lives in the unforgiving city of Tokyo with his twin sister, Hokuto. The time is now, but the world is not quite the same—magic forces are everywhere. Subaru practices magic based on yin/yang principles, called *onmyojitsu*, and works solving cases that baffle the police in CLAMP's *Tokyo Babylon*, originally serialized in *South* and now in English from Tokyopop. Subaru is in his late teens, quiet, and sweet-natured, with a highly developed New Romantic fashion sense. He is watched over by an older friend of the family, veterinarian Seishiro, who constantly teases him by professing to be in love with him. *Tokyo Babylon* is inspired by the legend of the *Peacock King*, *Kujaku-O*. Subaru also turns up in 1992's *X:1999* as one of the defenders of the Earth, and kills his old friend. Both series were later animated. CLAMP was originally a *dojinshi* group of twelve women; because of their success with fanzines, seven decided to turn professional, but after a break in 1994—said to be due to dissatisfaction with their current situation and partly to allow time for their videogame addiction—three of these decided to quit the group, leaving four core members who work together.

REIICHI SWAN [2001]

Reiichi is a teenage boy with a sweet nature, but he's short, snaggle-toothed, and ugly, teased by his classmates and put down by his family. He's crazy about Yumiko, his friend and classmate, but he thinks he has no chance with her—she likes cool, good-looking guys. Then he has an accident trying to save her dog, Mister, and spends a year in a coma. When he wakes, he is miraculously transformed into a tall, handsome young man. Mister is a magician in the shape of a dog, and to thank Reiichi for saving him, he's granted one of his dearest wishes. But if Reiichi tries to get close to his adored Yumiko, he changes back to a short, ugly kid. He feels his looks are just an illusion and maybe he's not the right man for Yumiko. There's also the added complication of the fat, plain girl in school who adores the new Reiichi. He's been where she is—how can he just give her the brush-off? Ai Morinaga's ugly-duckling manga, *Duck Prince*, is available in English from CPM.

TADASHI [2001]

Tadashi is on vacation by the seaside in Okinawa with his girlfriend, Kaori, and it's not going well. They bicker all the time and she tells him his bad breath is disgusting. Then the pair realize it's not bad breath she can smell, but rotten fish, and a shark with mechanical legs rises out of the water toward them. A major government project has gone very

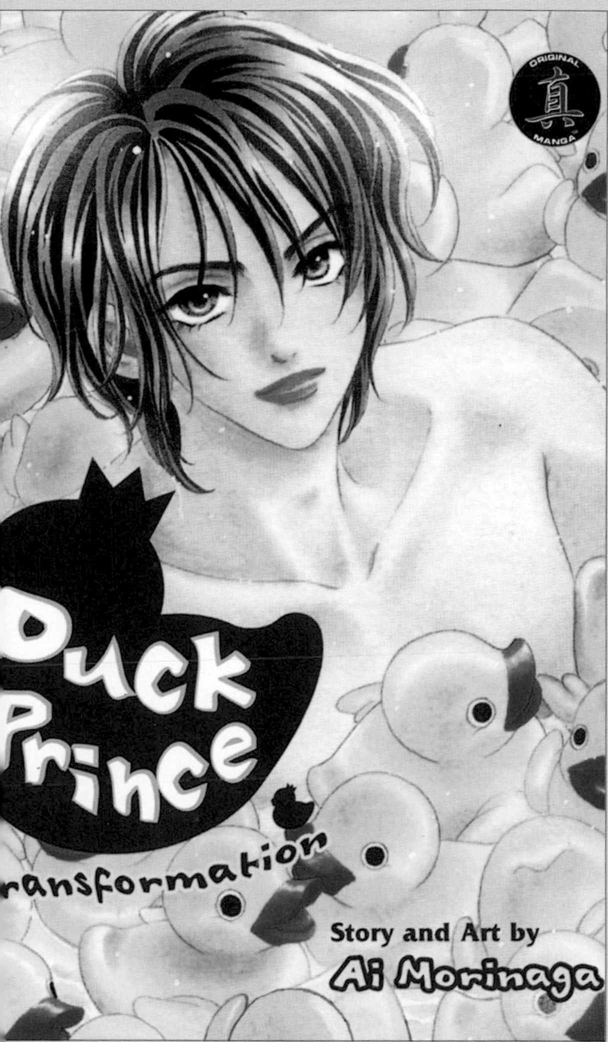

Even the ugliest duckling can blossom, as Reiichi Swan proves. But will his sweet nature survive the adulation his pretty new face brings?

badly wrong, and Tokyo is about to become a vision of hell to rival anything in medieval painting. "Germs" turn humans into bloated, boil-covered carcasses, used almost like batteries to power a new form of life that fuses machine and flesh. When Kaori is infected, Tadashi follows her bloated corpse, risking his life to find help for her. He falls into a storm drain full of fish-creatures, some living and some dead, sees strange visions, and wakes up in a hospital a month later to find that the plague has spread all over the world. His uncle, Dr. Koyanagi, who is heavily involved, tries to keep Kaori alive, but the cure is worse than the disease, and Tadashi and Kaori have no happy ending waiting for them. Former dental technician Junji Ito first published *Gyo* in *Spirits Weekly*; now this slice of Lovecraft sushi is available in English from Viz.

TAKUMA [1995]

Takuma is an unusual sort of hero; he's the operating system of the electronic notebook that Mai Kurahashi's parents give her for her sixteenth birthday. In his humanoid form he's cute, with spiky hair and a wide smile, but being an electronic person, he doesn't have a lot of sympathy for the messy, indecisive human heart. In Yuu Watase's *Epotrans Mai*, Mai accidentally types the word "epotrans," a code which accesses the electronic world, when sitting in her room feeling miserable about messing up yet another opportunity to get close to the classmate she fancies, and up

SPIDERMAN a.k.a. YU KOMORI [1970]

NOT PETER PARKER, but definitely Spiderman, Yu Komori made his debut in *Bessatsu Shonen* magazine in 1970, written and drawn by 26-year-old newcomer Ryoichi Ikegami. The project was intended as a simple Japanese version of the original; Kosei Ono translated the American script for Ikegami, but the young artist didn't want to draw New York, so he suggested replacing Parker with a Japanese hero. Ono continued to help out with the script for the first two volumes.

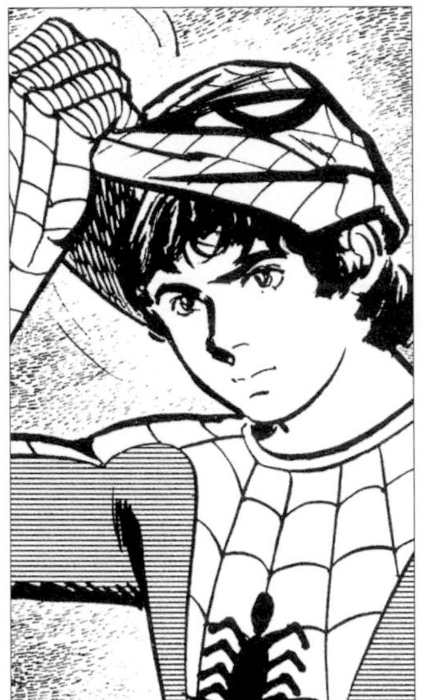

It's fascinating to look at the early work of an artist who went on to become a megastar, acclaimed for his ability to make formulaic black-and-white graphics seem almost photo-realistic. Ikegami is still on shaky ground in *Spiderman*. The 1995 Asahi Sonorama collected edition covers by Ikegami and Noriyoshi Kirai draw inspiration from fine art. One has Spidey in a pose ripped straight from Michelangelo's *David*; he stares out at the reader with the practiced menace of a masked wrestler—looking far more muscular and massive than the high-school boy inside the covers—a broken rose trailing petals from one oversized hand.

The stories diverge radically from Marvel's model. They're darker, and Spiderman appears less and less as the tales wear on. By the time Ikegami embarks on the twelfth complete story, we get to page 22 before Yu even thinks about his secret identity, and have to wait for page 109 before he makes his first costumed appearance. The other major difference is the level of violence and sexual violence, which few Western comics would have permitted in the 1970s. Ikegami and Ono continued on for two volumes before giving up on the story. Ikegami continued to draw the manga, but Kazumasa *Harmagedon* Hirai became the new writer.

Just like Peter Parker, teenager Yu Komori gets spider-powers when he is bitten by a mutated spider. Like Parker, he lives with his aunt and his best friend is a girl he's sweet on, Rumiko Shiroishi. The first villain he faces, Electroman, turns out to be Rumiko's older brother. The violence kicks in early

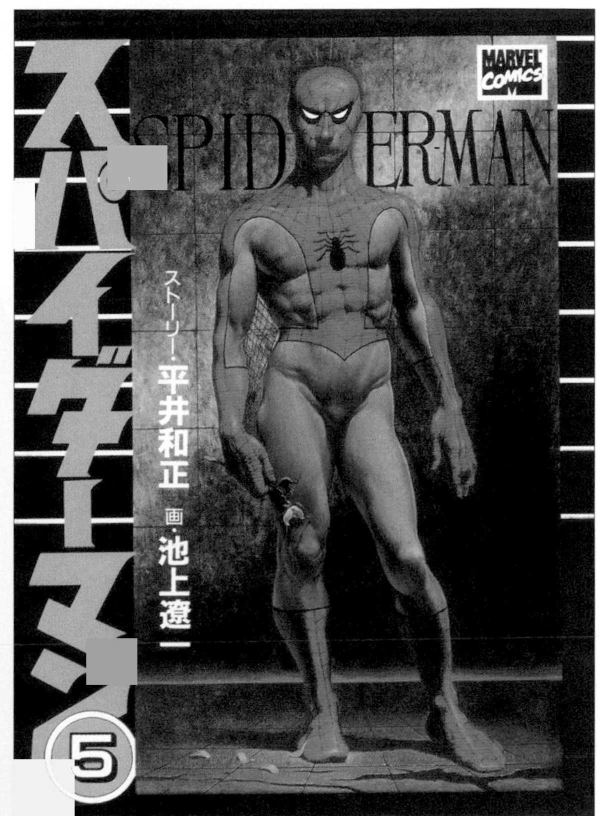

Spiderman, by Ikegami and Kasai, in a pose modeled after Michelangelo's David.

with people burning to death, but there's still plenty of silliness around, including a cameo from one of manga creator Shigeru Mizuki's popular ghosts from *Spooky Kitaro*. Next, Yu fights a Japanese version of the Marvel villain, The Lizard. Dr. Inugami is transformed into a monster by an experiment gone wrong and seeks revenge. After killing his wife, he is ripped apart by alligators. In the third story, Yu gets a part-time job at a newspaper with a Spidey-hating editor, and rejects his costumed alter ego after defeating a villain named Kangaroo Man. The next story moves to *Gekkan Shonen* magazine and has movie stuntman Kitagawa, a.k.a. Mysterio, masquerading as Spidey to turn the population against the real hero.

Then we're back in *Bessatsu Shonen* where Spiderman appears less and less as Yu is conflicted about his dual identity, has sexual fantasies and is slipped some marijuana. He shares more than a costume with his American counterpart; both Spider-men find that everything they touch seems to go wrong and their well-meaning interventions often tend to bring disaster. At the end of the final story, Yu concludes that violence and evil are the true,unmasked face of mankind.

Spiderman couldn't work convincingly in seventies Japan because he was a loner, with few allies, constantly letting down his devoted friends and family. The manga folded in April 1971. It was published in five collected volumes. Spidey remained popular enough in Japan to get his own live-action TV series from Toei in 1978, with a total of forty-three episodes screened on TV Tokyo. This time, Spiderman was cross-country biker Takuya Yamashiro, but the series resembles the manga only insofar as both have very little in common with the original American comic.

pops Takuma. Takuma tells Mai that only one in a billion people ever come up with the code, and it means she can see him and he can add any extra function she wants to her notebook. She asks for a portrait function—she can change to look like anyone whose portrait she enters in the notebook. Takuma thinks Mai is weak and silly, but she owns his notebook and he's got no option but to help her. Mai uses the new function to boost her confidence, mostly by changing into people who can get her closer to her dream boy Nimura, but her plans never seem to work, and Takuma has to use magic to get her out of the fixes she gets herself into. Gradually, as he realizes he can save her from anything but her own impulsive but sweet nature, Takuma finds that the girl he teases and constantly rescues is occupying more and more space in his memory.

TAMAHOME [1992]

Tall, handsome, and a skilled martial artist, Tamahome gives the impression of being cold and only caring about money, but as the eldest of his family, he has to earn for all of them. His real name is Kishuku Sou, and he is known by the character for *oni* (demon) on his forehead. Some say this defines his true nature, but he's really a nice guy. He lives in a parallel world that can be entered through the ancient book *The Universe of the Four Gods (Jintenchisho)*, and he falls in love with fifteen-year-old Miaka Yugi, an ordinary human girl who reads the book in her school library and finds herself sucked through it into his world as Priestess of Suzaku. There is a love triangle involving a rich, noble, nice young man, but Miaka eventually chooses Tamahome. The war in Tamahome's universe spills over into Miaka's, and Tokyo is threatened with destruction by an ancient army. In the end, in order to keep the two worlds separate, Miaka returns to her own, leaving her love behind, but he manages to break through the barriers again, and at the end of the story he turns up at her high school as an ordinary student, ready to live in her world so they can be together. *Fushigi Yugi: The Mysterious Play* by Yu Watase originally appeared in *Flower Comics* and is available in English from Viz.

AKITO TENKAWA [1995]

Eighteen-year-old trainee chef Akito, hero of Kia Asamiya's *Martian Successor Nadesico* from *Monthly Ace* magazine, is a Utopian, born in the colony of that name on Mars. His parents were murdered when he was a child. He left his homeworld after the First Battle of Mars, an attack by the inhabitants of the planet Jupiter. Trapped underground, he did his best to save others but failed, and fled to Earth. Terrified of battle after his experiences, he became a cook to avoid having to fight anymore, but lost his job because his boss didn't want anybody to think he had a cowardly ex-pilot in his employment. An accidental meeting with battleship *Nadesico* captain Yurika Misamaru leads him to realize that they had met before,

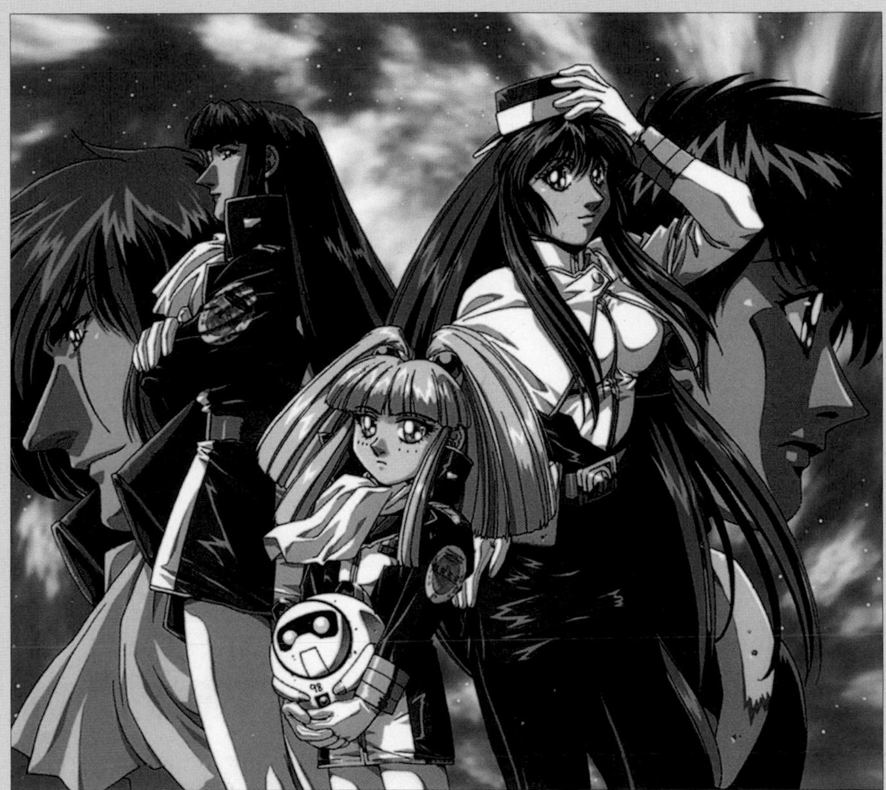

The crew of the Nadesico, with Yurika and Akito far right.

his favorite anime show, *Gekiganga 3*, and he becomes an anime fan. Akito remains a true pacifist, always looking for the solution that will avoid death and destruction; he grows increasingly fascinated by, and sometimes irritated with Yurika, and eventually fulfils his destiny, saves the world, and gets the girl. Animated as a TV series and movie under the title *Kido Senkan Nadesico*, the spin-off manga, launched in 1997, was called *Meteor Schlactshiff Nadesico* to signal a deliberate change of tone and emphasis, an alternate take on the universe of the animation. The storyline is reshuffled, mecha designs are slightly altered, and the comedy and science fiction angles are played up. Asamiya has also incorporated the story into his personal manga universe, linking it to earlier titles by revealing in the manga that one of the Nadesico's designers is a descendant of AMPD member Lebia Maverick from *Silent Moebius*. *Nadesico* the manga is published in English by CPM Manga.

on Mars, just before his parents were killed and her family left the planet. Believing she holds the key to his parents' murder, he gets a job as the ship's cook, but circumstances lead him back to fighting, volunteering as a decoy piloting one of the ship's Aestivalis mobile suits to lure attackers away from the ship. Another crewmember, Jiro, introduces him to

KENZO TENMA [1995]

Tenma is a genius surgeon, and he also has a big heart and a conscience. So despite his boss' orders, he saves the life of a sick child called Johan at his Düsseldorf, Germany, hospital in 1986. Johan, however, is one of a pair of twins produced in a terrifying genetic experiment, and at first, one might think he is the only Monster in Naoki Urasawa's *Big Comics Original* manga. Then he goes on the run, committing a series of violent crimes. Tortured by a sense of responsibility for what he has unleashed, Tenma goes after him. He meets Johan's twin sister Nina, who is determined to stop her brother before he can do any more damage, but Johan has become the figurehead of a Neo-Nazi organization and has considerable resources at his disposal. As Johan commits more murders, he uses these resources to frame the only man who could blow his cover—Tenma—and Interpol pursue the doctor across Europe. He and Nina finally track Johan down in Czechoslovakia, and the doctor who could not help but preserve life becomes a monster in his attempt to put right his innocent mistake. The powerful psychological thriller won the Tezuka Prize in 1999.

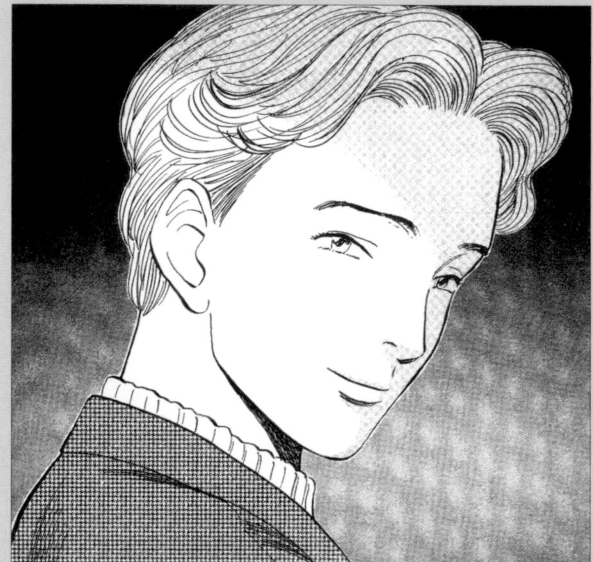

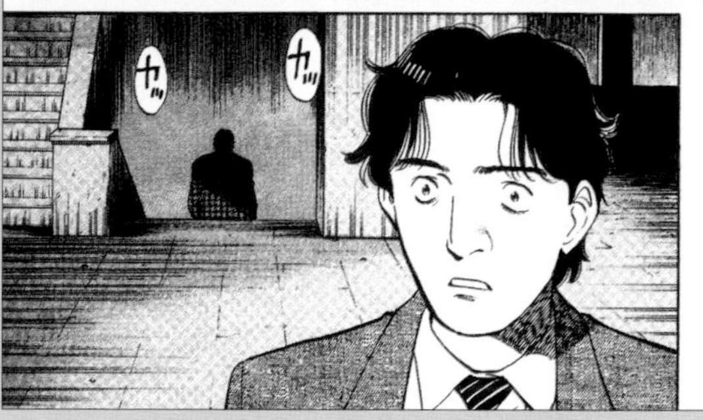

Tenma fights a monster with an angelic face.

TRITON [1969]

Triton is the last surviving merman. He is found as a baby by human Kazuya, who raises him as a human, but he returns to the sea to avenge his people, who were killed by the god Poseidon. He makes friends with a family of dolphins, then finds that another of his race, the mermaid Pipiko, has survived, and they marry and raise a family of seven mer-children. Trapped and tricked by Poseidon, he becomes hunted by mankind but continues to fight the evil dominion of the sea god. Osamu Tezuka's manga *Blue Triton (Aoi Triton)* appeared for two years in the *Sankei Daily* newspaper, one page a day.

VASH THE STAMPEDE

[1995]

Vash the Stampede is the most feared gunslinger in the galaxy, with a sixty–billion–dollar price on his head after single-handedly destroying the city of July. He's so feared that the Bernadelli Insurance Company sends two of its top operatives to follow him around to try to minimize the collateral damage. But what Milly and Meryl find is a good-natured, laid-back, spiky-haired dork who loves doughnuts and absolutely refuses to hurt anybody. The damage is mostly caused by the people chasing Vash for the price on his head, like inept bounty hunters, the Gung Ho Guns. *Trigun* is a cross between a Western and a road movie, with Vash and company meeting new people and situations that only add to the evidence that this guy is too sweet to be dangerous. Yasuhiro Nightow's early experience as a *dojinshi* artist was followed by three-and-a-half years selling apartments before he got up the courage to try a career in manga. He did one story for the February 1995 issue of *Shonen Captain*, and just two months later *Trigun* debuted. It was followed by *Trigun Maximum* in *Young King* magazine, and later animated. It's out in English from Dark Horse.

BRUCE WAYNE a.k.a. BATMAN [1939]

Batman, a.k.a. millionaire playboy Bruce Wayne, began his crime-fighting career in 1939 in No.27 of DC's *Detective Comics*. Wayne lives in Gotham City, and was traumatized in childhood by the murder of his parents. Raised by the family's devoted butler Alfred, Wayne devoted himself to fighting crime. His costume was designed to instill terror into the superstitious and cowardly criminal community. The brilliant and wealthy socialite is also the nightstalker who preys on the dregs of the city. The inherent contradiction of the character is what interests Japanese artists like Masakazu Katsura, who parodied the Dark Knight in his ultra-violent manga *Zetman*, as well as the lighter *Wingman*. Katsura's *Video Girl Ai* shows the hero at the movies watching Batman, and a character in his manga *I's* works on props for a new *Batman* movie not unlike *Batman and Robin*. Katsuhiro Otomo created a short story, *The Third Mask*, for the *Batman: Black & White* collection, in which Batman is on the trail of a multiple-personality murderer. The most recent Japanese homage, *Batman: Child of Dreams* by Kia Asamiya, was published in *Magazine Z* in 2002 and in English by DC a year later. A new drug on the streets of Gotham turns people into replicas of Batman's super-enemies. When Japanese reporter Yuko Yagi and her crew come to Gotham, they are kidnapped by

Two-Face—who turns out to be a fake, the real villain being in Arkham Asylum. Batman goes from Gotham to Tokyo and back to save Yuko and solve the riddle. He is up against his biggest fan, a man so obsessed with Batman that he intends to become him, for his own dark ends.

YANG WEN-LI [1984]

It is AD 3597: the galaxy has been at war for 150 years. Yang is a history student pulled out of college into the military for the Alliance of Independent Worlds in their fight against the Galactic Empire. He's a strategic genius who rises quickly through the ranks despite his youth, mirroring the meteoric rise of his chief opponent, the youthful Admiral Reinhart von Lohengrimm, a poster boy for Aryan racial purity leading a vast empire based on Austro-Prussian philosophies and ideas, and with the same good-looking officers, capricious women, and cool uniforms. Despite their many similarities, Yang is far more laid-back than his driven opponent, and even though he loses many friends to the horrors of war, he retains the historian's detached perspective and never ceases to look for a way for both sides to end the conflict with dignity and live in peace. *Legend of Galactic Heroes (Ginga Eiyu Densetsu)* appeared in *Chara Comics* drawn by Katsumi Michihara, but originated as a series of eighteen novels by pulp fiction king Yoshiki Tanaka. There is a long-running animated video series and several movies.

DEREK WILDSTAR a.k.a. SUSUMU KODAI [1975]

The young hero of Leiji Matsumoto's manga *Cosmoship Yamato* debuted in *Shonen Sunday Comics*. He's a brash, rather arrogant young man whose life changes forever in 2199 when the Earth is attacked by the Gamilon Empire. Refusing to surrender to alien dominion, the planet's surface is devastated and rendered incapable of supporting life, so survivors have to live underground. Derek's adored older brother Alex (Mamoru) is missing, presumably killed in action, and Derek wants revenge. A resistance movement revamps an ancient WWII battleship into space cruiser *Argo (Yamato)*, and a volunteer crew, including Wildstar, sets off on a dangerous mission to get help from an unknown civilization deep in space. During the voyage he falls in love with his beautiful shipmate Nova (Yuki Mori), finds his lost brother, and matures into a leader and hero. His adventures ran to three volumes of manga. His animated escapades made up three TV series and five movies. *Star Blazers* (a.k.a. *Cosmoship Yamato, Space Battleship Yamato)* became a legend in Japan through word of mouth and fan support, and went on to enjoy similar fan devotion in America; the U.S. anime fan movement was given major impetus by *Star Blazers* fans sharing their enthusiasm at science fiction conventions in the late 1970s and 1980s. Sun Comics produced a manga

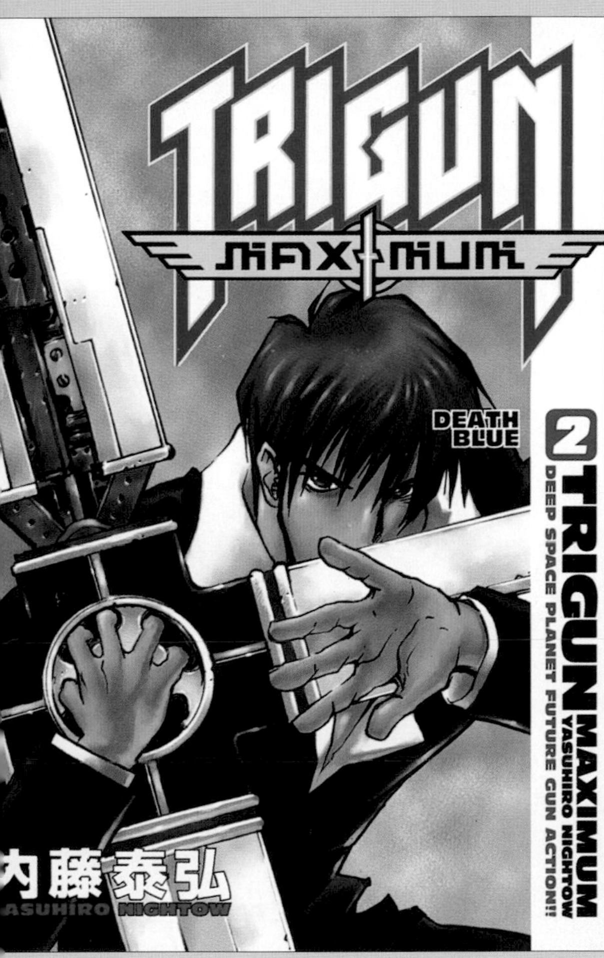

Is that cross loaded? Nicholas Wolfwood, preacher with a strong line in persuasion.

version of *Farewell Space Battleship Yamato*, also in three volumes, in 1978. There are also film comics, art books, novels, two series of U.S.-created comics, a four-issue mini-series from Comico in the late 1980s, and a longer series from Studio Go! (founded by longtime *Star Blazers* fan Tim Eldred) starting in 1995.

NICHOLAS WOLFWOOD [1995]

Wolfwood is a sexy young priest in Yasuhiro Nightow's manga *Trigun*, who travels the road trying to raise money for his church's orphanage. He also happens to be an excellent shot, with a huge cross full of weaponry of all kinds, which enables him to defend the weak from evil as well as bringing in extra income. He befriends Milly and Meryl, the insurance agents employed to keep an eye on renowned gunman Vash the Stampede.

LI XIAOLANG a.k.a. SYAORAN [1996]

Xiaolang, Sakura, Touya, and Yukito all appear in CLAMP's 1996 manga *Card Captor Sakura*. They are all preteen school friends, and Xiaolang and Sakura's love is a sweet and innocent romance. Their story is carried on in an alternate universe in *Tsubasa*, launched in *Weekly Shonen Magazine* in 2003, and now out in English from Del Rey. The friends are now in their mid-teens. Sakura is princess of Clow, and her brother Touya is king. Xiaolang wants to be an archaeologist like his father, but priestess Yukito foresees that he is Sakura's destined love and that Sakura has power to change the world. One day he excavates a strange stone crest, and when Sakura touches it, the air rips apart and a bridge opens to another dimension, from which Clow comes under attack. Sakura is cold as stone and dying, because she has lost all her memories. Xiaolang, helped by various CLAMP characters old and new, must leave her and travel across the dimensions to try to retrieve her scattered memories and save her life, as well as saving Clow from extra-dimensional plotters. The manga is also linked with CLAMP's *XXXholic* series from *Young Magazine*.

JOE YABUKI [1968]

Orphan Joe is a teenage dropout from the wrong side of the tracks, out of reform school and heading nowhere fast when a stubborn old boxing coach realizes he has the potential to be a champion and nags him into training and into the ring. Joe finally discovers something legal he can do well, and starts to aim for a dream—the bantamweight championship. Along the way, he finds love with the sweet and gentle Saeko, and his determination and courage win the hearts of boxing fans. Tetsuya Chiba and Asao Takamori's manga *Ashita no Jo (Tomorrow's Joe)* has plenty of triumph and tragedy, along with the gritty realism of sporting life; an old reform school rival of Joe's, Toru Rikiishi, dies in the ring after crash-dieting to get his weight down to the point where he can fight in the same class as Joe. (Kodansha, publishers of the series in *Shonen Magazine*, held a memorial service for Rikiishi in a boxing ring, presided over by a Buddhist priest and attended by over 700 people.) Overcome with guilt and self-doubt, Joe retired from boxing, but made a successful comeback. He died in 1973, in his corner, at the end of a climactic fight in which world champion Jose Mendoza proved too strong for him. Fans of the manga wept openly and held memorial services for Joe. Chiba went on to produce many more sports manga, though Joe remains his most iconic hero.

MASATO YAMANOBE [1967]

Hero of Osamu Tezuka's *Phoenix: Future*, Masato is a space warrior living in the underground city of Megalopolis Yamato in 3424. He's a nice young man, not especially high-ranking or good-looking, but brave and kind. He meets a girl named Tamami, who turns out to be a space creature taking human form to hide from the authorities. When he's found to be helping her, the pair go on the run across the wasteland overground to seek help. Guided by the Phoenix, they reach the dome where Dr. Saruta (the "dark side" of Tezuka's huge-nosed scientist, Dr. Elefun/

Ochanomizu) is trying to find ways to revive extinct species to save the world from genetic disaster. Meanwhile, in the tunnels below, mankind finally destroys itself, and the survivors in the dome must make a new world.

COACH YAMAZAKURA

[1986]

Yamazakura is a high-school teacher who agrees to coach his school softball team. A chain-smoker and fairly helpless bachelor, he has to put his domestic life in some kind of order because he's looking after his little orphaned niece. Five-year-old Chika is determined to use every chance she gets to provide him with a wife and herself with a new mommy. His star player, Minatsu Nakasato, has got herself mixed up with two guys, and they're about to come to blows. Yamazakura has become the target of the class bad girl, Sawamura. He has to hold together his team of seventeen-year-olds to win their games, as well as deal with his own growing attraction for Minatsu and the attentions of Sawamura while looking after Chika. The story finally resolves itself happily with some sporting success and a post-graduation wedding between the coach and his star player. Mitsuru Adachi's manga *Slow Step* is probably the least well known of his baseball stories, but an animated version spun off from its appearance in *Ciao* magazine, and though the manga remains untranslated into English, the anime was briefly available in the United Kingdom.

MASAHIKO YANIGIBA

[1997]

Masahiko is a good-looking Japanese high-school boy getting ready to go to college when he loses his father in a car accident. His mother died when he was two, but he's never really had much family life because of his father's work. Facing life alone in a society based almost exclusively on the group, he is delighted when his mother's younger brother invites him to live with his family. But why did his parents break off all contact with a brother who wants to keep the family together? Maybe because his uncle Sora is a cross-dresser who lives as a female, and his aunt Yuriko is a woman living as a guy. He even questions if Shion, the teenage daughter of the Wakanae family, is the gender she appears to be. Masahiko finds adjusting to his new family strange at first, and even panics that the sexual and social inclinations of his aunt and uncle might be genetic. He comes to realize that family life is all about love and acceptance, in Tsukasa Hojo's manga Family Compo, serialized (without a trace of irony) in Allman.

Female Heroes

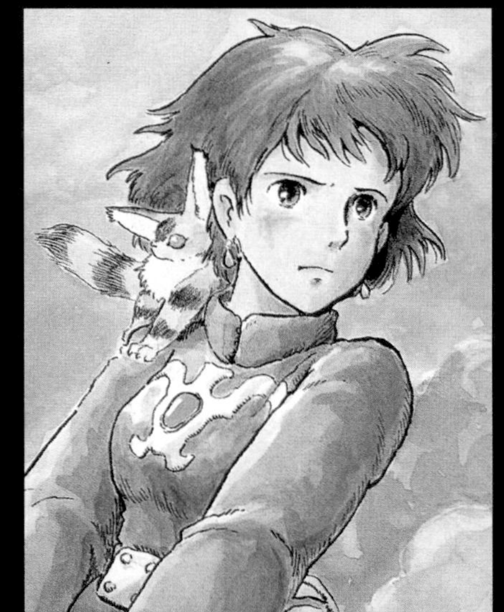

Nausicaa of the *Valley of the Winds*

Japanese comic book heroines can wear superhero uniforms, but they're just as likely to be in school uniforms, beautiful historical costumes, or high fashion outfits. The strength of the female comic market means that there's a big demand for stories of high-school life, romance, and adventure starring ordinary girls and women in addition to those with magical powers.

Comics for males tend to put more emphasis on action heroines or skimpy outfits, but they still have heroines with a wider function than mere wish-fulfillment or fan service. Styles range from realistic to romantic, from comical to cutting-edge; the 1960s-inspired cool of Ai Yazawa sits alongside the cyberpunk gloss of Masamune Shirow, while the creator of the field, the great Osamu Tezuka, spans the styles from romantic to realist.

KYO AIZAWA [2000]

Kyo, a talented athlete and basketball ace, is excited about starting her new high school. Seishu High has a great reputation, and the girls' uniform is so cute and stylish, it's been on the fashion pages of the magazines. When the package with her uniform arrives, however, there's a boy's outfit inside. Kyo's father, a basketball wannabe, plans to live out his dreams of sport stardom through his talented daughter. By hook or by crook, she's going to get on the school's renowned male basketball team and become an NBA star, and that means sleeping in the men's dorm and fooling her new roommate, the attractive Chiharu Eniwa. Kyo falls for Chiharu, but he's hostile to her at first—then things get worse when he appears to be attracted to the girl he thinks is a boy! Kyo isn't the only cross-dresser at Seishu—another student, Itsuki Onda, works outside school hours as a famous female model named Serika. To make things more complicated, Tsukaya Himejima, a former girl

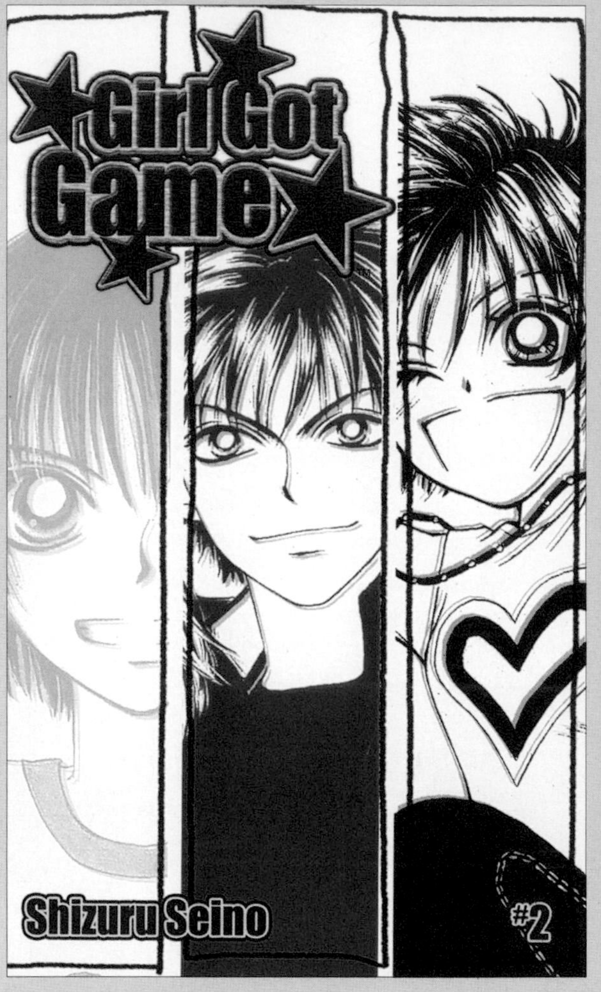

School sweetheart Kyo isn't quite what her classmates expected.

teammate of Kyo, transfers to Seishu. When Chiharu learns her secret, he decides they can't room together anymore, but she has nowhere else to go—her father left for America as soon as he got her into school. Kyo's determination to succeed on the team and with Chiharu falters when she has to spend some time sleeping in a cardboard box in the park, but he relents and the romantic and gender confusions resolve in a happy ending. *Girl Got Game (Power!!)* by Shizuru Seino first appeared in *KC Betsufure* and is out in English from Tokyopop.

ITSUKI AKIBA [1997]

Itsuki has been living in the United States for ten years, ever since she was five. Her parents have stayed in the States, but wanted her to come back to Japan for high school, so she's lodging with the family of her elementary school chum Ichitaka Seto. Both sets of parents have decided the children would be just right for each other, and Itsuki doesn't seem to mind the idea at all. Ichitaka finds his childhood friend an annoyance; she's very pretty, but she's a tomboy with a terrible sense of humor and no decorum at all. She's quite happy to walk around the house wrapped in a towel, freaking Ichitaka out, and she's getting in the way of his relationship with Iori. In fact, the first time he knows she's lodging with the family is when he gets Iori to his house, thinking they're alone, only to find Itsuki asleep in the next room! Coming back to a country she only half remembers, to a best friend who's got another girl on his mind, Itsuki needs all her optimism to cope. Stripped of the fantasy elements of earlier works like *Video Girl Ai*, Masakazu Katsura's *Shonen Jump* manga *I's* is a gentle, affectionate look at the obstacles we raise for ourselves and the agonies we endure as teenagers. It was animated in 2002.

ALITA a.k.a. GALLY [1991]

Battle Angel (Gunmu a.k.a. *Gun Dream)* by Yukito Kishiro stars a young android struggling to find her identity in a harsh future. The floating city of Zalem *(*Tiphares*)* hovers above the Scrapyard, the dumping ground for all its trash. The poor scavenge a living there, while the elite live in Zalem. Everyone dreams of clawing their way out of the dungheap and reaching Zalem. Alita *(*Gally*)* is a broken cyborg, dumped and helpless, until she is found by cybernetics engineer Ido *(*Daisuke Ito*)*, who has fallen out of favor with the elite and been relegated to the Scrapyard. He repairs her, makes her a beautiful new face and body, and keeps her around, treating her like a daughter. Alita has superhuman battle skills. She was created as a Hunter-Warrior purely to serve the elite, but her relationship with Ido enables her to be a child, to learn and to grow emotionally. She falls in love with young Hugo (Yugo) who dreams of escaping to Zalem but the relationship ends tragically when he is killed by a bounty hunter. Going through every stage of teenage rebellion and confusion, Alita sets out on a journey to the

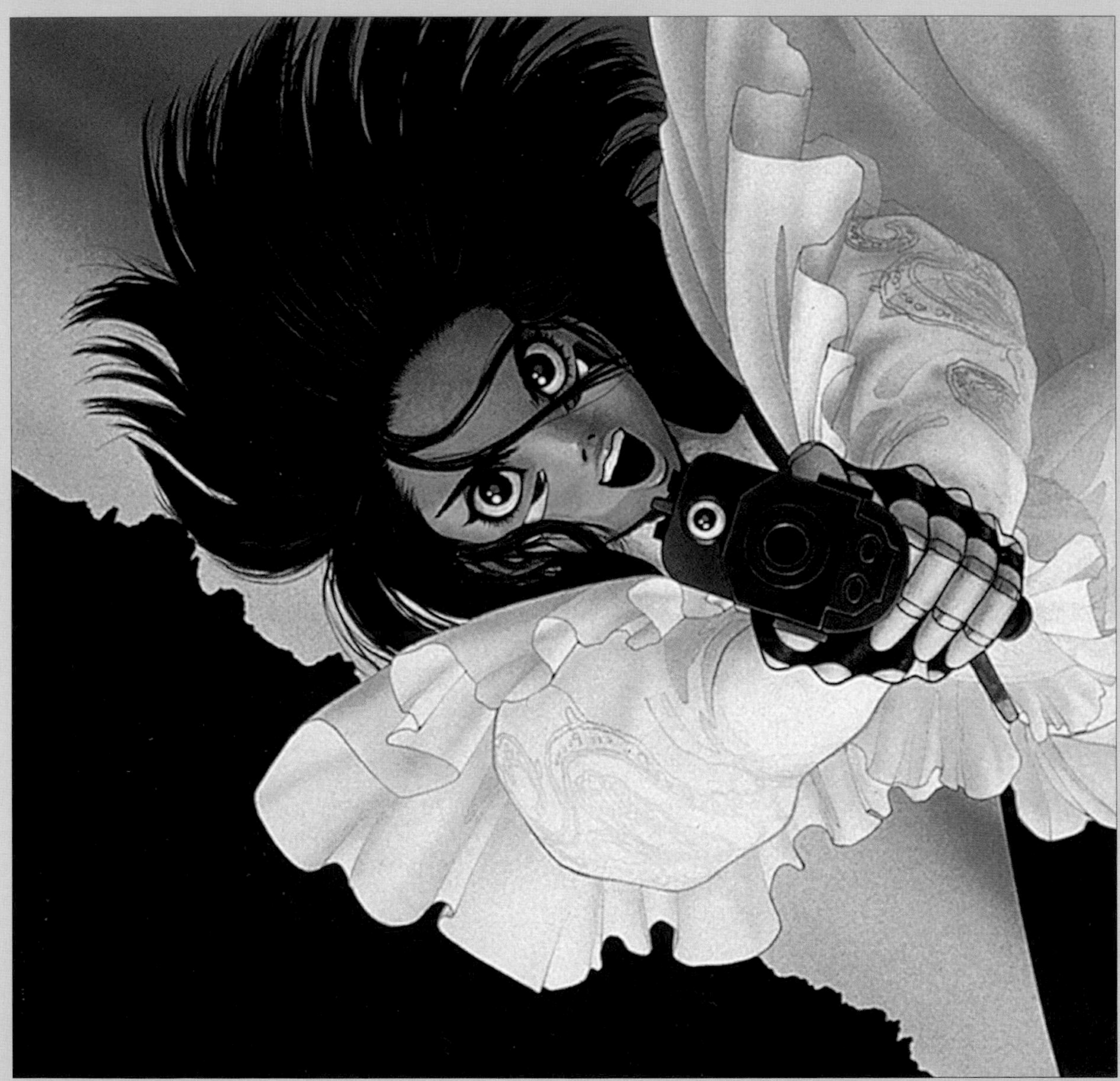

Western region of the Scrapyard to recover her past by way of becoming a gladiator in a futuristic arena. The devoted Ido closes down his cyberpractice to search for his "daughter," hooking up with a young woman named Shumira. Her brother is an established champion on the motorball circuit where Alita is the hottest new star, and together they set up the ultimate challenge match to bring Alita home. When the manga started out in *Business Jump* magazine, the story had been put together in a hurry to expand a single Kishiro illustration—in which the as-yet-unplotted heroine appeared—into a manga. It ended hastily in 1995, and Kishiro returned to the story in 2000, publishing *Gunmu: Last Orders* in *Ultra Jump* magazine. Viz Communications published a translation in 1994.

AI AMANO [1990]

Ai Amano is sixteen, blonde, cute, and sweet—a lonely young man's dream. In fact, that's exactly what she's made for. Named with the Chinese and Japanese character for love, Ai is a video girl, a product of the Gokuraku Corporation, designed and created by their CEO to provide temporary companionship for lonely males who hire soft porn tapes. They are available only from the Gokuraku Video Store, and have a run time of 720 hours. When the tape is inserted into a VCR, out pops a beautiful girl, ready to comfort, support, and encourage you as long as the videotape is running. Switch off the VCR, or get to the end of the running period, and that's that—the girl vanishes, erased forever. Video girls are supposed to be submissive, demure, and non-judgmental. Unfortunately, Yota Moteuchi's VCR has a glitch and almost kills Ai when he switches it on, scrambling her programming. Ai emerges from Yota's machine in a rage, and turns out to be playful, whimsical, and a mean martial artist. Despite her scrambled programming, Ai does her best to be a good video girl. She looks after Yota's house, feeds him, helps with his projects, and provides a constant listening ear. She even tries to help him get together with the girl of his dreams. Yet she just can't help her faulty system, and finds herself becoming jealous, irrational, falling for Yota, and dreaming of a life of her own in the human world in Masakazu Katsura's *Video Girl Ai (Denno Shojo Ai)*.

Left: Heavy-metal princess Alita swings into deadly action in this beautiful color image by Kishiro.

MEGUMI AMATSUKA [1999]

It's tough being a girl in the twenty-first-century world, and Megumi embodies the contradictions of modern life. Should she be as tough and feisty as a guy, which is her natural inclination, or follow her best friend's advice and be gentle and deferential, wheedling and charming? Or should she just go back to the

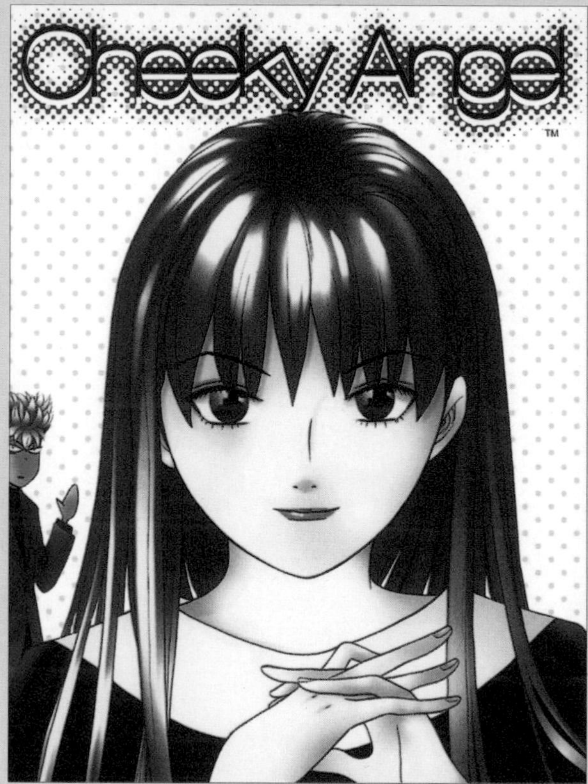

Growing up pretty is a problem for boy-turned-girl Megumi.

way she was six years previously before a certain deaf and aged wizard was rescued by little boy Megumi? Demanding a reward, the boy got a book containing a tiny harlequin genie. When he wished to be the manliest man of them all, the cheeky little trickster made him into the sweetest, prettiest, girliest girl imaginable—though the girl is still hot-tempered, feisty, a great fighter and occasionally uses foul language. Now only her best friend Miki remembers her as "him"—everyone else thinks she was always a girl, and even family and school photos have changed. At fifteen, Megumi is saddled with the unwanted attentions of all her male classmates, and to the horror of her best friend she doesn't hesitate to beat them off—literally, because she can beat any three of them. When she realizes, however, that the boys let her beat them up because they don't believe in hitting girls, she's horrified and hurt. The fantasy fades into the background as the story of *Cheeky Angel (Tenshi na Konamaiki)* focuses on author Hiroyuki Nishimori's real interest: what's the "proper" way for a modern girl to be? Does she have to play to old-fashioned gender stereotypes or can she be herself, even if that's an out-and-out tomboy? Megumi's dilemma is available in translation from Viz.

SISTER ANGELA [1988]

A young novice nun finds herself becoming increasingly concerned with the problems of a handsome boxer who can't keep his weight down. Is her faith in Kosuke Hatakana going to save him, or take her away from God? *One Pound Gospel (Ichi Pondo no Fukuin)* is one of the Rumic World series, and shows Rumiko Takahashi's understanding of offbeat relationships and human failings that has enabled her to build such a strong audience for both fantasy and non-fantasy works.

ANMITSU [1949]

Princess Anmitsu *(Anmitsu-hime)* is a sweet and naughty little tomboy created for *Shojo* monthly by Shosuke Kurogane. Her adventures were only a few pages long and relied on gags for their appeal; the princess, like all the other characters, was named after a Japanese dessert. In food-scarce postwar Japan, this was bound to give the series appeal, especially to a young audience, and the tradition of naming infants' comic and TV characters for food persists to this day. The mischievous Princess leads her modern, Western-dressed tutor Miss Kastera (Miss Spongecake) on a runaround, always trying to avoid lessons and attempting to get her hands on tasty goodies. The series debuted in *Shojo Comic* and ran until 1955. It was animated in 1986. Despite the modern elements of the manga, the anime is set in medieval Japan.

ARALE [1980]

A robot girl created by erratic genius Senbe Norimaki (a.k.a. Dr. Slump) in Akira Toriyama's manga, Arale is clever, strong, and terrifyingly loud. She's also perky and cheerful, interested in everything, and like many young children, has a fascination with toilet humor and all kinds of bodily functions, embarrassing the adults around her and holding conversations with excrement.

MINAMI ASAKURA [1981]

Mitsuru Adachi is the king of high-school baseball manga, and *Touch* is considered by many to be his masterpiece. Minami has known twin brothers Tatsuya and Kazuya Uesugi since childhood; all three go to Meisei High School. She lost her mother early on, and because the Uesugis were their next-door neighbors, she spent a lot of time with them while her father was busy running his coffee shop. She's always loved baseball. She manages the school team and dreams of finding a star pitcher who can take them to the national Koshien championships. She also dreams of marrying elder twin Tatsuya, but that's her secret; the parents see her as a perfect match for Kazuya. When Kazuya is killed in a car accident, Tatsuya tries to step into his shoes, but the couple have many misunderstandings and wrong turns before they finally work out what they want from their relationship. Meanwhile, Minami tries her hand at gymnastics for a while before finally settling on a career as a sports photographer.

MIZUKI ASHIYA [1996]

Mizuki is a Japanese-American girl who's crazy about Japanese high-school high-jump champion Izumi Sano. She saw him on TV when she was fourteen and decided to go to Japan and meet him. It's taken her three years, but she's finally managed to transfer to his high school, Osaka Gakuen, undeterred by the fact that it's an all boys' school. From this we can tell she's pretty naïve, but very determined. She cuts her hair, adopts rougher male speech patterns, and finds herself rooming with her idol. He is fascinated by her even before he realizes that she's a girl, and then falls for her, but it takes a while for her to understand that her schoolgirl crush has turned to something deeper. *For You in Full Bloom (Hana-zakari no Kimitachi e* a.k.a. *Hana-kimi)* by Hisaya Nakajo appeared in *Hana to Yume* magazine and is out in English from Viz. The author is still active in fanzine circles under the pen name Ryo Fumizuki.

ASSEMBLER [1990]

Kia Asamiya's *Compiler* starts in the 1990s in our own world. Two "routines" from the Electro-Dimension, a computer-like parallel universe, come to play one of their world's favorite games: Conquest. Assembler, known as the Electric Angel, looks like a sweet young thing who could still be in high school. Her opponent Compiler, the Electric Demon, assumes the shape of a voluptuous, long-haired temptress. The pair decide to take two humans as witnesses to their battle; they pick the Igarashi brothers, Nachi and Toshi. As they learn more about the world they previously only considered as a game environment, they start to get interested in Earth and decide to stay around. Besides, clever but sloppy Assembler has developed a serious adolescent crush on Toshi, and older brother Nachi's recklessness and charm are working their way under bad-girl Compiler's defenses. This is against all the rules of the Electro-Dimension, and a series of would-be assassins, including gay duo Bios and Directory, are sent to punish the runaways. The pair get some help from another "routine," Interpreter, who dislikes the Ruling Council of the Electro-Dimension and is therefore inclined to help the runaway rebels. Their life on Earth is complicated by Nachi and Toshi's terrifying parents, and Assembler also has to cope with Toshi's childhood sweetheart Megumi Tendoji, an heiress and a very determined young woman. Both love Toshi's quiet normality and both are determined to have him all to themselves. The manga contains numerous nods to pop culture amid the wacky highjinks, set-piece battles, and romantic misunderstandings, a favorite example being the guest appearance by vehicles from Gerry Anderson's *Thunderbirds*.

BELLDANDY [1990]

Belldandy is a goddess, called into this world by college student Keiichi when he's trying to order Chinese food in his dorm at Nekomi Tech. He gets through to the Helping Goddess Office and duty goddess Belldandy offers him a wish. When he wishes he had a girlfriend like her, she steps out of her dimension into his dorm and declares she's now his girlfriend. In fact, the two are fated to be lovers, but Keiichi's extreme shyness and awkwardness around girls make him very slow to pick up on Belldandy's devotion. Despite being a goddess with enormous powers, she's a sweet, old-fashioned girl who thinks the man should take the lead in a relationship and a woman should look after him and support him. She does everything she can to make Keiichi's life comfortable, but family and friends complicate things. He's kicked out of his dorm and she sets up a home for two in an old temple, but domestic bliss is soon disrupted by the arrival of his younger sister and her goddess sisters, cute little girl Skuld and vampish vixen Urd. With three leading characters named for Norse goddesses and a typical high school loser-in-love plot, *Oh My Goddess! (Aa! Megamisama)* by Kosuke Fujishima first appeared in Comic *Afternoon* and is out in English from Dark Horse. The light romantic comedy became a big fan favorite, and was followed by anime and a super-deformed gag strip.

BULMA BRIEFS [1984]

Bulma (Japanese pronunciation of bloomer) Briefs is the pretty, bouncy human girl who drags Son Goku out of the forest and into her quest for the magical Dragon Balls in *Dragon Ball* by Akira Toriyama. She wants the mystic objects to grant her one wish—for the perfect boyfriend. At first pairing up with quest colleague Yamcha, she later marries Goku's fellow-alien Vegeta and the pair produce two children, son Trunks and daughter Bra. Daughter of the founder of the Capsule Corporation, Bulma is a genius inventor, a good mechanic, and not someone you would want to get angry.

CAROL [1976]

Daughter of a rich American family, history-loving Carol activates a mummy's curse at the opening of a pharaoh's tomb (a project financed by her father) and is dragged back in time to ancient Egypt. She falls in love with the young pharaoh Memphis and marries him, using her modern education to bring about apparent miracles like filtering Nile water to prevent disease and seeming to tell the future. But Memphis' jealous sister Isis, his other loves, and political machinations send her on an emotional roller coaster worthy of any modern soap as she visits ancient Babylon, the Minotaur's labyrinth in Crete, the mighty kingdom of Nubia, and Troy. Many of the princes and nobles she meets fall in love with the pretty blonde known as the *Daughter of the Nile (Ouke no Monsho* a.k.a. *The Royal Crest)* in Chie Hosokawa's still-running manga from *Princess* magazine. Meanwhile, her love for her family, especially brother Ryan, keeps pulling her back into her own era to help with their business and personal difficulties.

CAROL [1995]

The world of *Chirality* by Satoshi Urushihara is a bleak future where small groups of humans wander a wasted planet fighting for their lives against the GM, the robotic slaves of mad computer Gaia. Carol, a seemingly human girl with superpowers, sets out to fight Gaia, helped by her friends, doctor Patty, pilot Shizuma, and android Vic, and her one true love, pretty, innocent Shiori. But Carol is really an artificial life form, and her purpose is to buy enough time for Shiori to reprogram Gaia with the Mother Guardian program—even if it costs her her own existence. The manga from *Comic Nora* is out in English from CPM and features some lesbian scenes. The title, by the way, is a scientific term for the property of a molecule that can't be superimposed on its mirror image. Given how often Satoshi Urushihara's girls are superimposed on their mirror images, this opens up new possibilities for irony.

CHINA [1986]

Miss China is an independent young woman who runs a bar and lodging house in a small town in Canada in a world like our Edwardian era, but with the science that Jules Verne and H. G. Wells dreamed of coming to fruition. We're not told how a girl from China turned up in a small northern seaport and acquired a bar, but she is a beloved part of the community. She loves Jim Floyd—assistant to one of her lodgers, the crazy Prof. Breckenridge—but is too shy to tell him so. Misunderstandings about Jim's relationship with the local florist, Lily, arguments about late rent payments, and dimensional field generators blowing holes in the roof are among the romantic misunderstandings the young couple must overcome. A gentle love story mixed with good old-fashioned science fiction, *Spirit of Wonder* by Kenji Tsuruta is a series of linked short manga serialized in *Comic Afternoon* and available in English from Dark Horse.

SISTER ROSETTE CHRISTOPHER [2003]

Chrono Crusade by Daisuke Moriyama is out in English from ADV. Sister Rosette and her childlike sidekick Chrono roam an alternative America in the 1920s. Despite the peace and prosperity that followed the end of the Great War, mankind is under a dark shadow. Demons have invaded the land. The Magdalen Order exists to annihilate them, sending exorcists wherever they are needed with partners. Armed with heavy weaponry and the power of prayer, exorcist Rosette also has to fight the inner demons of her own past—her long-lost brother Joshua has been kidnapped by the demon Ion, an old acquaintance of Chrono. Chrono is a demon, but he's lost the horns with which he would normally draw down astral power for his magic. Instead, he has to draw power from a mortal to whom he is bound by a contract. Every time he does so, it shortens the mortal's life, so Sister Rosette's days are numbered.

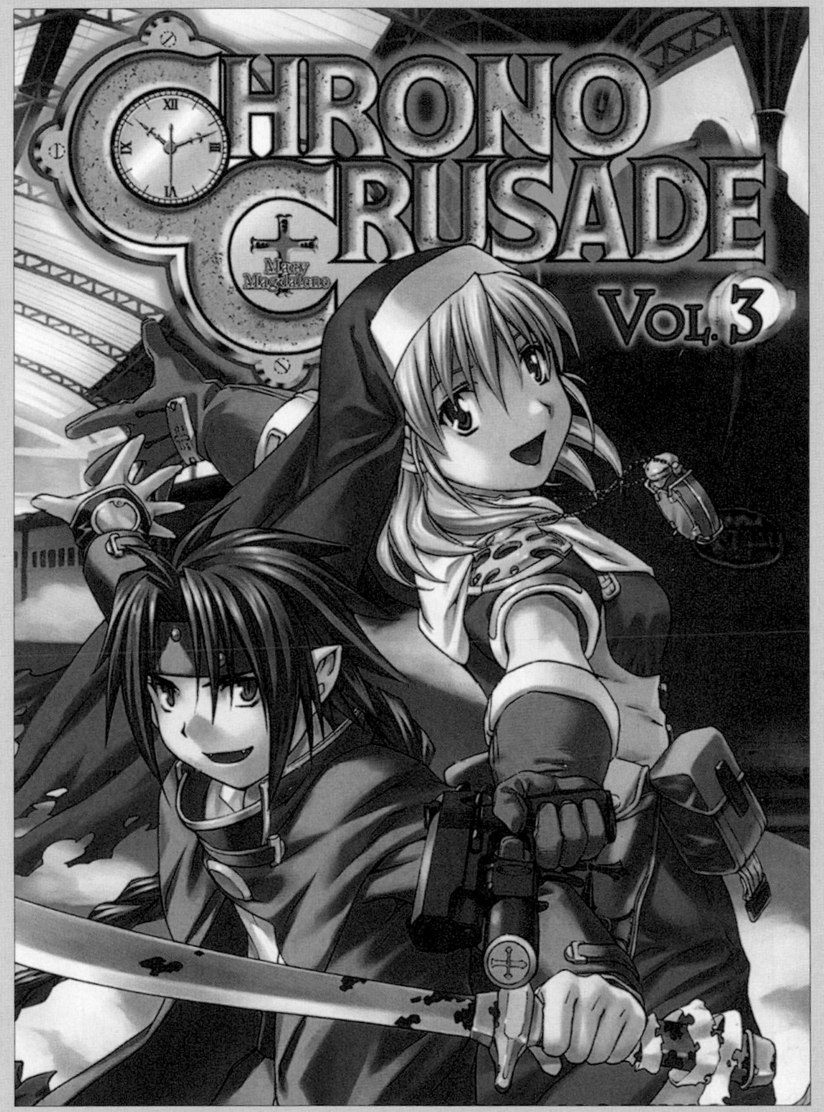

Sister Rosette and Chrono: demon-busting service with a smile.

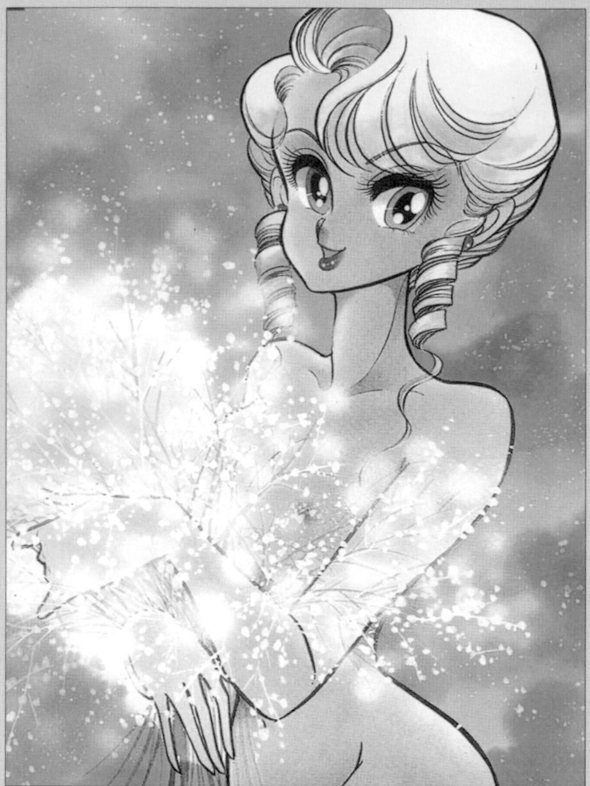

Cleopatra Corns: the richest woman in the world can afford to be an extrovert.

CLEOPATRA CORNS [1986]

The heroine of *Cleopatra D.C.* by Kaoru Shintani is a cute, bubbly blonde, and head of the Cleopatra financial conglomerate. She controls most of the American economy and is described as "the moving capital of the world." That much money and power means that there's always intrigue around, and Shintani's manga is a lightweight action-adventure entertainment packed with exotic travels, gorgeous clothes, and fantastic plotlines.

DEEDLIT [1986]

Deedlit first appeared in the novels and gaming scenarios created by Ryo Mizuno, which formed the basis for the anime *Record of Lodoss War (Lodoss to Senki)*. She is a High Elf who joins a party of adventurers setting out to try to save their world from being destroyed in the clash between the gods of dark and light. A mere teenager in elf terms at 160 years old, she is a slender blonde with cute pointed ears. She falls in love with young warrior Parn, and once their initial battle against evil has been won, she joins him on his travels. The Tolkienesque Lodoss universe went on expanding, and Deedlit got her own dedicated manga by Mizuno with art by Setsuko Yoneyama, now out in English from CPM as *Deedlit's Tale*.

EMERALDAS [1975]

Emeraldas is a "free trader" pirate queen roaming the galaxy in her ship, the *Queen Emeraldas*, in search of her own vision of freedom and justice and in mourning for the love of her life. A tall, slender, beautiful woman with long auburn hair, she is the female counterpart of creator Leiji Matsumoto's ultimate hero, Captain Harlock. Like Harlock, she carries the scars of her chosen life—her face is scarred very much as his is, and her reputation is that of a ruthless, cold-blooded killer, known on many worlds as the "Witch of the Galaxy." Also like Harlock, she is a deadly opponent, and is very warm-hearted and loving to those she trusts and accepts. She has had many tragedies in her life; she was estranged for years from her twin, her mother went mad and became an evil empress, she is fatally ill, and she has lost her beloved husband Tochiro, Harlock's closest friend, the father of her child Mayu. Tochiro was no pretty picture, but Emeraldas saw the real man under the shabby exterior and remains utterly devoted to him. She is the twin sister of Matsumoto's other great female icon Maetel, but this was only finally confirmed in the 1999 manga *Harlock Saga: The Ring of the Nibelung*, in which the two appear as tiny girls before the start of the endless journey to which their fate has destined them. Emeraldas first appeared in 1975's *Emeraldas* as Harlock's fierce rival who joins his hopeless stand against the Royal British Airship Navy in the early twentieth century. In 1978, her story moved into the future in *Queen Emeraldas*. She even got an American comic of her own when U.S. publisher Furry Comics brought out *Pirate Queen Emeraldas*. She starred in her own anime in 1998.

JUN FUDO [1997]

Jun Fudo is a schoolteacher in her early twenties who is raising her younger brother Hikari while her father works in the United States. While supervising a school field trip, she starts having unusual nightmares, and also has to deal with a group of martial artists staying on the same site who are paying too much attention to the girls in her care. The men are really demons in disguise, and one night they revert to their true shapes and attack her party, raping her. Jun transforms into a terrifying (but sexy) demon-woman hybrid, and kills the attackers to protect the girls in her care. Jun is completely confused, but her father, Prof. Fudo, suddenly arrives back from the States and reveals a secret. He has been studying a phenomenon that started several years ago in shanty towns among down-and-outs. Some would suddenly transform into demon-beasts and rape women before eating them. Studies showed that the transformed demon-beasts had gained supernatural strength, but had no memory of their human lives. But Prof. Fudo doesn't think this is a supernatural event, but rather the next stage in mankind's evolution. He believes the demon beasts are a natural mechanism for dealing with human overpopulation. Jun and others like her are genetically programmed to keep their human consciences as they evolve, to ensure that enough of humanity will survive to preserve the best characteristics of the race after those who don't retain their humanity have killed each other and the majority of the weak and selfish. Jun must use her new strength and skill to protect the best in humanity. Go Nagai conceived *Devilman Lady* when he started to wonder how the *Devilman*

IT'S A GIRL THING

A BRIEF HISTORY OF GIRLS' MANGA.

The girls' comic industry in Britain died in the 1960s, with the rise of the pop-star-focused teen magazine and its photo-romance stories. In the United States it was a similar story; mostly male writers and artists gave a mostly male audience the kind of girls they wanted. However, a few women who loved comics— including some remarkable and determined artists, like Wendy Pini and Colleen Doran— had discovered the wider world of Asian graphics. These artists used manga influences in their work. One of the streams they tapped was the highly specialized genre known as *shojo manga*, or girls' comics. Male and female culture, distinct and separate for centuries in Japan, had evolved two distinct modes of graphic expression for manga. Western female comic-lovers, confined in a game-plan written by and for their brothers, found in girls' comics a universe created for, and often by, women.

Japanese girls' comics were not widely available in the English-speaking world before the mid-1990s, but as the manga market has expanded in America, publishing houses have responded. They succeed not just because they focus on female dreams and fears, but because they have a unique style of their own; the artists strive to create a feminine visual grammar, distinct from the action-oriented, linear lexicography of the boys' comic.

Girls' comics, even those with historical Japanese themes, are steeped in Meiji-era Japan's fascination with the West. In a world of straight-haired people with slanted eyes and dark skin, *shojo* characters often have huge sparkling eyes, blonde curly hair and long legs and bodies, like fashion drawings. They have their own laws of narrative, pace, and timing. Instead of the rapid linear progression of the action comic, girls' comics often jumble space, time, and viewpoint, making liberal use of modified frame shapes and rich patterns used as decorative backdrops. Although the mass market in Japan, as in America, is mostly satisfied by repetitive variations on the soap-opera or romance theme, more adventurous artists have used manga to explore the role of women in a changing world.

In the early days of the genre, Japanese women didn't have careers and women manga artists and writers were in short supply. The first girls' comic was produced by the god of manga, Osamu Tezuka. *Princess Knight (Ribon no Kishi)* set the standard for the genre. A princess has to become a prince to save her country; suppressing her own needs as a woman, she succeeds because courage and self-sacrifice are not exclusively masculine virtues. More women came into the field from the mid-1950s, but most of their work was perceived as just for girls. The idea of girls' comics that males could enjoy was pioneered by Hideko Mizuno with her rock-opera *Fire*, and carried forward by female stars of the

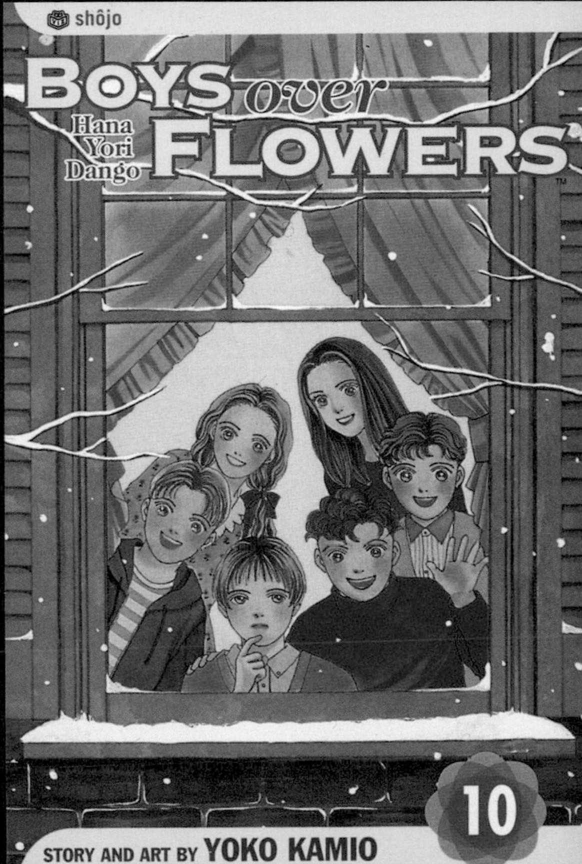

The Japanese *Friends* for the younger set? *Boys Over Flowers* maps their growing pains.

1970s science fiction and fantasy boom like Moto Hagio and Keiko Takemiya. Crossover genres like fantasy and sci-fi provided the opportunity for artists to use girls' comic style in manga for a mixed audience. Many modern artists, like CLAMP, have a softer style than the classic boys' comic, but attract male readers.

The rise of *shonen ai*—boys' love—as a female genre was a striking feature of this period. Portrayals of yearning and sexual involvement between beautiful young men struck girl readers as deeply romantic. In fanzine circles, the parody genre produces huge numbers of boys' love titles every year, wish fulfilment fantasies for devotees who want to see their favorite male anime and manga characters in romantic or sexual pairings that mainstream commercial publishers or creators can't or won't countenance. Some creators, like Minami Ozaki, stay active on the fanzine scene even after going professional.

In the 1980s a new wave of magazines created more opportunities for women artists and writers. The adult female market was growing and "ladies' comics" dealt with love, marriage, social, and historical stories for an audience that had outgrown girlish yearnings but still wanted its manga fix. Pornographic manga for women treat a range of topics that would raise the eyebrows of mainstream Western comic fans—lesbianism, rape, incest, scatology, necrophilia, and bestiality. Alongside such shocking material, some stories also have core messages of a more progressive vision of sexuality, with the rights of individuals central to the story.

Japanese women and girls can choose to share the material designed for their brothers, but they know there's a world of comics that belongs just to them. Now their Western sisters can begin to share the experience.

scenario would work if the protagonist were a girl. When her story was animated for TV in 1998, Jun became a model instead of a teacher.

MOMIJI FUJIMIYA a.k.a. KUSHINADA [1992]

Fifteen-year-old Momiji is an ordinary schoolgirl, a bit bubble-brained and giggly but quite unexceptional. Yet as the descendant of the ancient line of Kushinada priestesses, she is one of the few who can defeat plant-based demons known as Arigami, who grow from blue seeds. Her blood can send them to sleep, so they want to kill her, and the government has set up a special unit called the Terrestrial Administration Command, both to fight the Arigami menace and to try to find a way to use the priestesses' blood without killing them. Mamoru Kusanagi, who carries seven Arigami seeds inside him, tries to kill her, but she saves his life, and as a result now has her own blue seed and can sense the presence of Arigami. She joins the TAC to help fight them, and Kusanagi becomes her protector. Momiji learns she had a twin sister, Kaede, who has already perished in the fight against the Arigami; Kusanagi loved her but could not save her. Kaede, however, has not died, but has gone over to the Arigami side and is working to raise Susano-o, god of chaos. Momiji must fight her own sister to save Japan and win Kusanagi's love. *Blue Seed (Aokishimata Blue Seed)* by Yuzo Takada retells an ancient Japanese legend and first appeared in *Comic Gamma*. It was later animated.

BENIO HANAMURA [1975]

The young heroine of Waki Yamato's *Kodansha* manga *The Modern Girl Passes By (Haikara-san ga Toru)* lives in Japan in the early years of the twentieth century and is a true modern young woman. She wears Western-inspired clothes; the "haikara" of the title is the phonetic rendition of "high collar," a slang term for Western clothing. She also believes in the right of women to choose their own husbands and have careers, a new and not entirely popular idea despite Japan's rapid social, cultural, and economic change. Her father, a high-ranking navy officer from a good family, has promised her in marriage to a young lieutenant named Shinobu Ijuin. Shinobu is half-German and the grandson of a woman her grandfather had loved years ago. The pair were unable to marry because of social differences, but never gave up the dream of uniting their families. Benio resists the arranged marriage at first, saying she'd rather marry her childhood friend Ranmaru, an up-and-coming kabuki actor. Then she goes to live with her fiancé's family, as tradition dictates, to be trained for marriage. She tries everything to get them to reject her, from embarrassing her fiancé in public, to pretending to be a bad cook, but gradually falls in love with the kind-hearted, gentle Shinobu, only to have him sent to the

Russian front and become missing in action. As the Russo-Japanese war goes on, Benio combines her new-woman ambitions with a true Japanese sense of duty, taking a job as a reporter on a local newspaper to help out the Ijuin family finances and caring for Shinobu's grandparents. Tragedy strikes again when she finds Shinobu has lost his memory after a battlefield explosion and thinks he is the husband of a Russian countess, and the Ijuin family mansion is threatened by foreclosure on a loan. After many twists which almost have them marrying others, the lovers are finally reunited to fulfill the family ambitions, which now coincide with their own dearest wishes.

ALPHA HASSENO [1994]

Hitoshi Ashinano's manga *Yokohama Shopping (Yokohama Kaidashi Kiko)* from *Afternoon* magazine is set in the future, in a world where greenhouse gases have caused ocean levels to rise and populations to shrink. With fewer people and no major industry, mankind faces extinction, but this is a gentle apocalypse, bringing a relaxed and accepting way of life. In a sleepy little village on Japan's Miura peninsula, robot girl Alpha runs her owner's coffee shop and waits for him to return from a long trip. He's been gone for several years, but she is determined to keep the shop going until he comes back. She lives like a human and is a vital part of the tiny community. The manga has very little action, but enormous charm.

KANON HAYASHI [1995]

The young heroine of *Kanon* by Chiho Saito made her debut in *Flower Comics*. She is living quietly with her mother in Mongolia when a handsome young musician arrives from Japan to write the music for a documentary about the desert. Kanon is a talented violist herself, and the two become friends and later fall in love. Then Kanon's mother tells her that her father is also a musician, so she can find him through playing the violin. When her mother is killed in an accident, Kanon sets out for Japan to find her past and her future.

KAGOME HIGURASHI [1997]

Japanese high school girl Kagome lives with her mother, brother, and grandfather in the family shrine. She's kind, brave, loyal, and determined, but she has a bad temper when provoked. She's also determined to get a good education and spends most of her spare time studying to qualify for one of the best high schools. One day she is transported back in time to Japan's feudal past and accidentally unleashes dog-demon Inu-Yasha. The locals think she is the priestess Kikyo, who sealed him in the first place; now she compels him to help her find the shattered shards of a magic jewel so she can put right her accidental intervention in the past. Rumiko Takahashi's *Inu-Yasha* is still running in *Shonen Sunday* and is out in English available from Viz.

MASUMI HIJIRI [1976]

The heroine of Kyoko Arioshii's manga *Swan*, Masumi is a shy sixteen-year-old from a poor family with a passionate love of dance. She's studying at a small dance school in Hokkaido, and the manga chronicles her struggle through adversity to become a great ballerina. Masumi scrapes together the fare and makes the long journey from Hokkaido to see the Russian Bolshoi Ballet dance *Swan Lake* on a rare visit to Japan, only to find that all the tickets are sold out. She pushes through to the back of the theater to watch the famous and technically demanding Black Swan solo. When she finally manages to get backstage after the performance and comes face to face with the two great Russian dancers who are her idols, she is so overcome she can't speak—so she kicks off her shoes and dances the Black Swan for them, moving them deeply. Despite the scorn of her better-off classmates and the long, hard struggle for recognition, Masumi is a typical manga heroine who never gives up her dream and finally triumphs. Arioshii's manga was hugely acclaimed in Japan and is now available in the U.S. from CMX.

ANTHY HIMEMIYA [1997]

The gentle, bespectacled fourteen-year-old black girl with the hidden sense of humor,

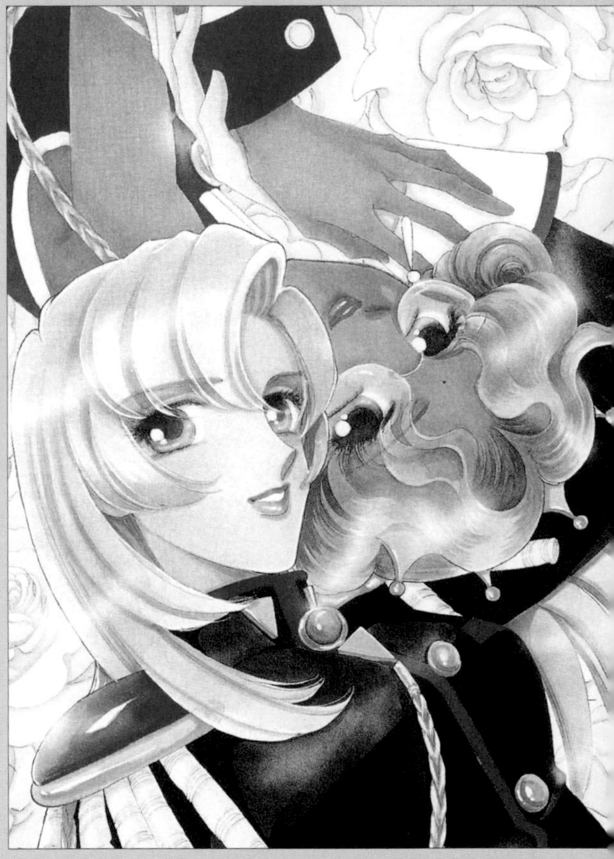

Utena and Anthy are opposites, but the tomboy and the damsel in distress are twin souls.

talent for playing the piano, and cute pet monkey-mouse Chuchu is the damsel in distress in writer Kunihiko Ikuhara and artist Chiho Saito's *Revolutionary Girl Utena (Shojo Kakumei Utena)* from *Ciao* magazine and *Flower Comics*. Her name is taken from the

Greek "anther," the central part of a flower. Spun off an animated TV series, the manga opens with Anthy as a student at Otori College, and the "Rose Bride"—the prize for which the school's elite fight duels. When we first meet Anthy she seems almost catatonically submissive, in an abusive relationship with current champion Kyoichi Saionji. When Utena beats him, Anthy transfers her submission to Utena. Anthy is also the focus of bullying from girls at the school who are jealous of her Rose Bride role. Her relationship with Utena develops into one of mutual friendship, loyalty, and love. Its sexuality is not explicit but its sensuality is. It turns out that Anthy is the younger sister of Akio Otori, who reminds Utena of the prince she met many years ago. Utena has obvious links with *Rose of Versailles*; submissive Anthy and royal spitfire Antoinette have been cast by fate in a role neither would have chosen, and both have to sublimate their true selves to their duty. Oscar cannot save the tragic Queen, whose pride and ignorance are partly responsible for her final doom; but Utena and Anthy can save each other.

EMU HINO [1989]

Alone in the world after the death of her beloved father, young painter Emu is mourning him and contemplating suicide when she witnesses a murder. The murderer, an assassin for a Chinese gang, breaks into her home to ensure her silence, but is astounded when Emu tells him he can kill her if he wishes, but she wants him to sleep with her first. She doesn't want to die a virgin. He agrees, and so begins the love story of *Crying Freeman* by Ryoichi Ikegami and Kazuo Koike. Although at first sight Emu is a shy, retiring, traditional sort of girl—long hair, spectacles, conventional clothes—she has the heart of a tiger, and the young assassin unleashes both her sense of adventure and her deep maternal instincts. She helps him break free of the brainwashing that made him kill, and joins him when he decides freely and consciously to stay with his new family and become their leader.

AKAO HIRAGI [2002]

Akao is the pilot of a battle robot. Three years before the story opens, the district of La Gran Sabana in Venezuela was rocked by a mysterious explosion, and the lonely teenager was brought by her mother to South America to fight attacks by seemingly ancient machines known as *jinki*. Since then, apparently random events ranging from murder to the disappearance of entire village populations have proved impossible to explain. Now Akao and her young comrades are Venezuela's line of defense against invaders they don't understand. *Jinki* by Shiro Tsunashima was first published in GanGan with sequel *Jinki: Extend* in *Blade Comics*. The second series is still running in Japan and has been published in English from ADV.

TOHRU HONDA [1998]

When pretty seventeen-year-old Tohru's mother dies, she lives for a while with her grandfather, but eventually decides she's in the way and goes to live in a tent. She turns up near the home of her classmate Yuki Soma and is invited by the head of the family, Shigure, to live in their mansion. The Soma family has a tragic destiny—they are linked to the twelve animals of the Chinese zodiac and cursed to transform into animals when they come into physical contact with a member of the opposite sex. Tohru has a generous heart and can accept anyone, whatever their personal problems, but can she find love with someone who can't stay in human form for long—especially when his other form is a rat? *Fruits Basket* by Natsuki Takaya was published in *Hana to Yume*, in English from Tokyopop.

RURI HOSHINO [1996]

Ruri is a tiny girl with a brain as good as Einstein's and a cynical outlook on the antics of the supposed adults around her. She's of Nordic extraction and the product of genetic engineering, and was sold to the Nergal organization as a child. She becomes a computer specialist on the bridge of the battleship *Nadesico* at the age of eleven. *Martian Successor Nadesico* by Kia Asamiya first appeared in *Monthly Ace*, out in English from CPM. The anime version is a fan favorite and shows Ruri getting the ship's captaincy at sixteen.

LILI HOSHIZAWA [2001]

Thirteen-year-old Lili is convinced that the powers of the Chinese horoscope can solve anything. Her father is a cop, but he hasn't been able to find her mother, who went missing some time ago. She left Lili a ring that has been in her family for generations; the Star Ring can transform a young girl who wears it into Detective Spica (named after a star.) Spica has been solving cases, then vanishing, since the Meiji era, and now Lili has inherited the mantle. She relies on the stars to guide her to the criminal and unravel the mystery. Her best friend Hiromi is the Watson to her Holmes. *Zodiac PI (Junikyu de Tsukamaete* a.k.a. *Zodiac Detective)* by Natsumi Ando is out in English from Tokyopop.

ICZER-ONE [1985]

Toshihiro Hirano and Yasuhiro Moriki's *Golden Warrior Iczer-One*, a short manga spun off Hirano's 1985 animation *Fight! Iczer-One (Tatakae! Iczer-One)* stars a beautiful clone warrior with blonde hair that wouldn't look out of place on Dolly Parton. Iczer-One is fighting her own creators, an all-female alien race called the Cthulhu who were once peaceful but have been subverted by evil. Her determination to stop the Cthulhu turning into murdering conquerors is strengthened when they attack Earth and she falls in love with a human girl, Nagisa. She is also the pilot of a mighty warrior robot, the Iczer-Robo, but needs Nagisa to power its weapons systems with her hatred for those who killed her parents. The manga prequel to the animated story appeared in English from Antarctic Press in 1994.

YAWARA INOKUMA [1986]

Naoki Urasawa's *Yawara!* first appeared in *Big Comic Spirits*. The heroine shares the same surname as Japan's 1960 Olympic judo gold medalist, and she's a judo champion herself. Her grandfather Jingoro wants her to get to the Olympics, but Yawara wants a normal teenage girl's life—boyfriends, school, and occasional nights out. Meanwhile her father, estranged from his family, is training her rivals. The heart of the story revolves around the relationship between Yawara and her old grandfather, but Yawara's friends, rivals, suitors, and classmates make for an involving story in which the judo, although very well depicted, is the background to Yawara's growing up. There's a love triangle, with rich boy Kamatsuri and scruffy young reporter Matsuda both after our heroine's heart, much to the annoyance of Sayaka, who thinks she should have more in common with Kasamatsuri as they are both from the social elite, and Matsuda's colleague, sports photographer Kuniko. The strip began in 1986 and worked to real-time sports championship schedules; Yawara gives a demonstration in Seoul in 1986, travels to Yugoslavia for the World Championships in 1990, and then competes in the Barcelona Olympics in 1992.

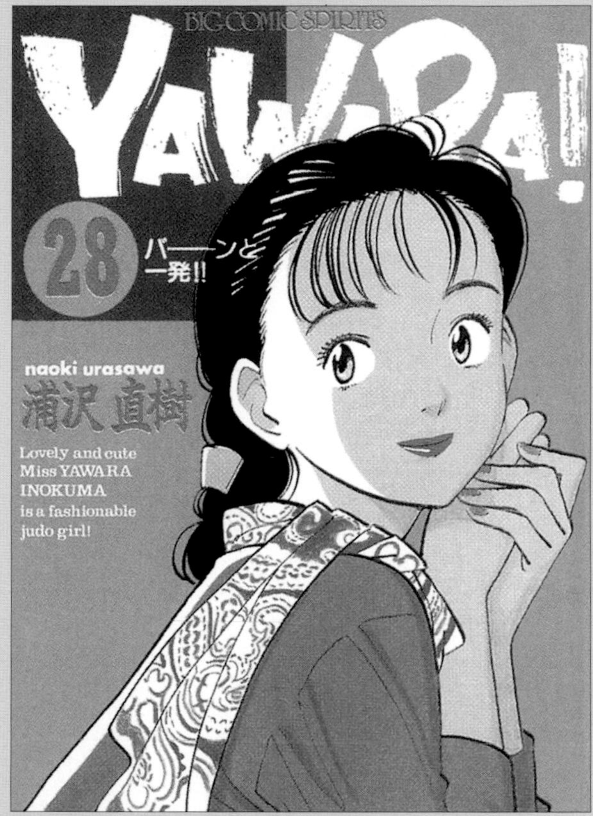

Olympics or not, this girl just wants to have fun. Yawara loves judo, but wants a life.

Both Yawara and her grandfather finally fulfill their dreams—he trains a champion, she graduates from college, gets a job in travel, and has a life of her own. The series was so popular that real-life Japanese judo star Ryoko Tamura was christened "Yawara-chan" by the Japanese press when the sixteen-year-old won silver in

Barcelona in 1992, just as the strip was coming to an end. She went on to win two world championships and another silver medal in Atlanta, and wore a yellow hair ribbon just like Yawara's when she won gold at the Sydney Olympics in 2000.

SAZAE ISONO [1946]

The heroine of Machiko Hasegawa's manga *Sazae-san* is a young woman living in postwar Japan with her parents and her little brother and sister. Her adventures, told in four-panel strips, are typical everyday events in the homelife of an ordinary family. Each adventure usually ends with Sazae baffled or bamboozled in some way, but still indomitably cheerful. In her quiet way, Sazae was a revolutionary. She was the popular ideal of the new Japanese woman: a home-loving girl with a respect for tradition and a desire to have a settled family life, but full of optimism and independent-minded. When Sazae married Masuo Fugata and had a child, she and her new husband continued to live with her parents, in a model still familiar in modern Japan. Her debut was in local paper *Fukunuki*, but she soon moved to the larger publication *Asahi Shimbun*, and an animated TV series of fifteen-minute adventures debuted in 1969. Reflecting the changes in Japanese society in gentle, unthreatening form, and poking kindly fun at both the slowness of the old ways to adapt and the pretentiousness of the new, both strip and animated series are still running, making *Sazae-san* the longest-running TV cartoon series, and one of the longest-running newspaper strip series, in the world. Born on January 30, 1920, Hasegawa published collected editions of her work through a company she founded with her three sisters.

NOA IZUMI [1988]

Rookie cop Noa wants to be a police driver, and what she wants to drive is the giant Ingram robot, the vehicle used by Special Vehicle Section 2 of the Tokyo Police. In the near future, robots called "labors" are extensively used for construction and heavy industry and to fight rising labor crime a labor-equipped division is set up. Noa, the only child of a widowed father, is a natural pilot and adores her labor, christening it Alphonse after her pet dog. Perky, energetic, and completely unsophisticated, she soon becomes the heart of the unit. *Patlabor (Kido Keisatsu Patlabor* a.k.a. *Mobile Police Patlabor)* by Masami Yuki was printed in *Shonen Sunday* magazine and is available in English from Viz.

OSCAR FRANCOIS DE JARJAYES [1972]

Oscar was born to a noble French family without a male heir, the sixth in a line of daughters. Her father named her as a boy, had her raised as a boy, and when she was in her

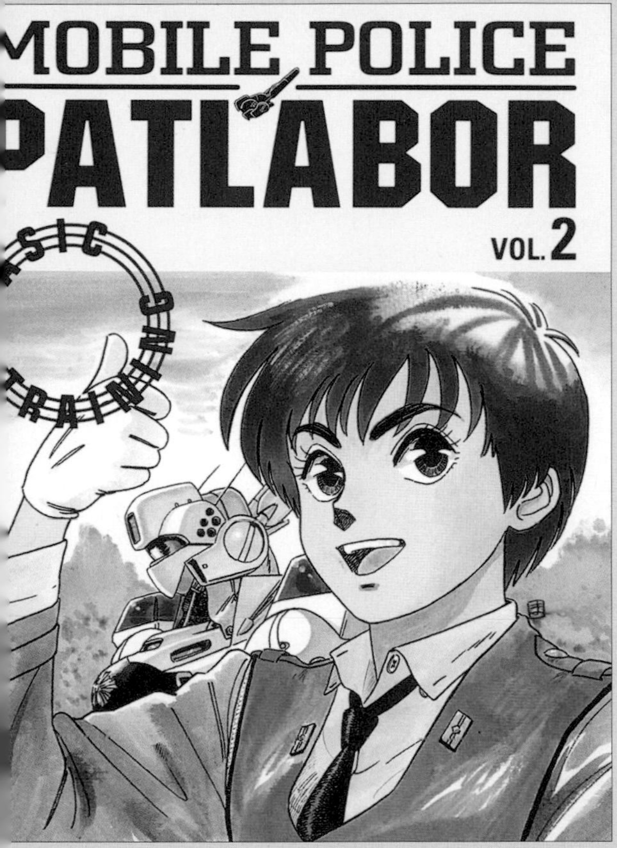

Girl cop Noa is out to keep the streets of Tokyo safe for law-abiding giant robots and humans alike in her beloved mecha Alphonse.

late teens, sent her to court to do the family's duty in serving the royal family. A superb swordsman and an androgynous beauty, Oscar becomes the head of the bodyguard for the crown princess, later Queen Marie Antoinette, and becomes her loyal friend. The intrigue of the court disgusts her, but her strong sense of loyalty to her father and her queen keeps her there. Her own love life is complicated when she falls for Swedish noble-man Axel von Fersen, who has eyes only for Antoinette. Eventually she realizes that she loves her childhood friend and servant, Andre, who is involved with revolutionary politics. Her love of him and of her country leads her to fight at his side, and when he dies shielding her from a bullet, she carries on fighting for his cause and is killed in battle. Ryoko Ikeda's master-work *Rose of Versailles (Versailles no Bara)* appeared in *Margaret* magazine. Two volumes were translated into English for the Japanese market by Frederik L. Schodt, but are no longer available.

ATSUKO KAGAMI a.k.a. AKKO-CHAN [1962]

Heroine of Fujio Akatsuka's manga *Secret Akko-chan (Himitsu ni Akko-chan)*, ten-year-old Akko is given an old Indian mirror as a present by her father. She takes good care of it, but when it is broken by accident, the spirit of the mirror wakes her and gives her a new one, in a magical compact that can change her into any person or animal she chooses when she says a magic word—providing she keeps it a secret. Akko keeps her secret well and uses her powers to help out friends and neighbors in her small home town. The first magical girl story appeared in *Ribon Mascot*, and it was not animated until 1969, following the success of *Little Witch Sally*. Akko was created in the same year her creator published his first gag manga *Osumatsu-kun*, and having found his true metier, Akatsuka did not return to the girls' manga field. His creation is still much loved, and was parodied for a very different audience in U-Jin's soft porn collection *Tales of ... (Konai Shasei)*.

AKARI KAMIGISHI [1998]

Akari is a sweet, shy teenager who looks much younger than her years and is still into teddy bears. She goes to high school with her two childhood friends, Masashi Sato and Hiroyuki Fujita. They're like brothers to her, but she wants Hiroyuki to be something more; she's been in love with him since kindergarten. Unfortunately, he's both very egotistical and hugely popular with other girls—in fact, Masashi is his only male friend! Akari is faced with competition from oddly exotic schoolmates like beautiful witch Serika Kurusugawa, her extreme fight champion sister Ayaka, and Hiroyuki's psychic project partner Kotone Himekawa. Akari decides she needs to shape up to win Hiroyuki's heart—even girl robot Multi, assigned to the school as a janitor for testing, is a potential rival. Akari has a friend in Serika's walking, talking teddy-bear Kuma-chan. The somewhat formulaic structure (devoted girl and apparently-but-not-really indifferent guy who tests her love by constantly going off with other girls) comes from the

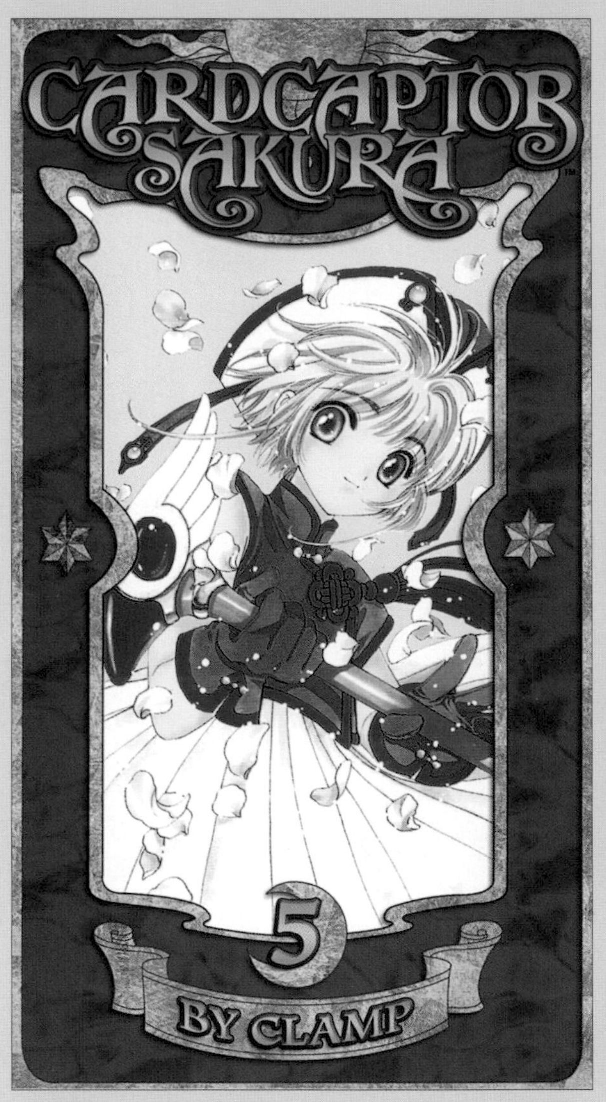

Sakura plays the ultimate card collecting game with the safety of the world as the prize.

manga's source. *To Heart* by Ukyo Takao spun off the PC game of the same name, which has also spawned an anime series, CD dramas, and merchandise galore; it is available in English from ADV.

SAKURA KINOMOTO [1996]

CLAMPS's 1996 manga *Card Captor Sakura* stars ten-year-old Sakura. She's a happy girl who enjoys Physical Education classes and music, and is a cheerleader for her school, Tomoeda Elementary. She has a big brother, Toya, and has a crush on one of his friends. Her mother died when she was only three, and she and Toya live with their father. One day her normal, happy life is disrupted when she opens an ancient book in her father's library, which should contain the Clow Cards, magical objects created centuries ago that can take many different forms and have great powers for good or evil. The guardian of the Cards, Kerebos, was enjoying a snooze; now he needs Sakura's help to recapture them all before they wreak havoc in the human world. Sakura's best friend Tomoyo Daidoji helps her out, and various other classmates become involved. One is Xiaolang Li, who has an ancestral link to the Cards and has transferred from his school in Hong Kong with his cousin Meilin to search for them. At first he and Sakura are rival Card Captors, but gradually they become close and fall in love. The manga has been animated for TV. Sakura's story and her romance with Xiaolang is carried on into her teens in an alternate universe in *Tsubasa*, launched in *Weekly Shonen Magazine* in 2003 and now out in English from Del Rey.

MIKAKO KODA [1995]

The heroine of *Neighborhood Story (Gojinko Monogatari)* by Ai Yazawa first appeared in *Ribbon* magazine. She and her childhood friend Tsutomu Yamaguchi grew up in the same neighborhood, go to the same school, and constantly bicker and pick on each other. When Mikako realizes, however, that Tsutomu has pop-star looks and is a target for many other girls, she begins to question her own feelings for him. The two of them have been in love for years, but only discover it as they grow up.

MIKI KOISHIKAWA [1992]

Marmalade Boy by Wataru Yoshizumi is a look at modern family life from *Ribon Mascot* magazine, now out in English from Tokyopop. Miki is a lively high-school girl with a part-time job in a decoration shop and a place on the school tennis team. She's best friends with her old flame Ginta and gets on well with her classmates. Life is going fine until her parents come back from a trip to Hawaii and announce they have decided to split up. They met another couple on holiday and they've both fallen for the other partner. Miki finds this disturbing, but she's even more disturbed when her parents announce that because they don't want to split her and her new step-brother Yu Matsura from either of their parents, both families are going to live together under one roof. Yu teases Miki a lot, but he's really cute, and they fall in love; then he finds an old photo that convinces him they're full brother and sister, not just step-siblings. Luckily their parents clear up the misunderstanding and they're free to live happily ever after.

TITA KOSHIGAYA [1993]

Tita has inherited her dead father's business. Though only 16, she's captain of a crew of pet-shop hunters, who travel the galaxy in their starship collecting and selling exotic animals. Tita is brave, loyal, and an excellent fighter. When she meets a young woman in distress during a stopover on planet Yietta, she decides to help her out despite the fact that the local government is pursuing her with heavy firepower. *Plastic Little* is so titled because there's little plastic on planet Yietta, created by Satoshi Urushibara. One of the most lovingly rendered cheesecake symphonies ever drawn, it's out in English from CPM, and also has its own anime for those who prefer their feminine curves with added motion and color.

MAI KUJU [1987]

The fourteen-year-old heroine of *Mai the Psychic Girl* by Ryoichi Ikegami and Kazuya Kudo lives quietly with her father, a skilled martial artist. Unknown to her, her dead mother was a powerful psychic, one of a line who used their powers to preserve peace for over a thousand years. Mai is sweet, pretty, and becoming aware of her own sexuality as well as her growing psychic powers. At first she thinks her powers are just a party trick, but she learns that they can be deadly. She is one of the five most powerful psychic children in the world. Secret organization the Wisdom Alliance wants to use the powers she has inherited for their own ends. They plan to eliminate the human race and replace it with a race of psychics. When Mai is forced to go on the run, she and her pet puppy Ron find helpers and well-wishers in many strange places, and finally thwart the Alliance. Her story was published in the United States in the 1980s, and was one of the first successful manga in English. It's available in English from Viz.

KURUMI [1998]

Steel Angels are powerful battle androids developed by a combination of science and magic. They are designed to obey the person who activates them. When Nakahito accidentally activates a missing Angel, he becomes "Master" of the coolest toy in the world—Kurumi. She is pretty, charming, fun to be with, and capable of taking out almost any

Right: Kurumi and friends: so what's impractical about dressing a battle android in a maid's outfit?

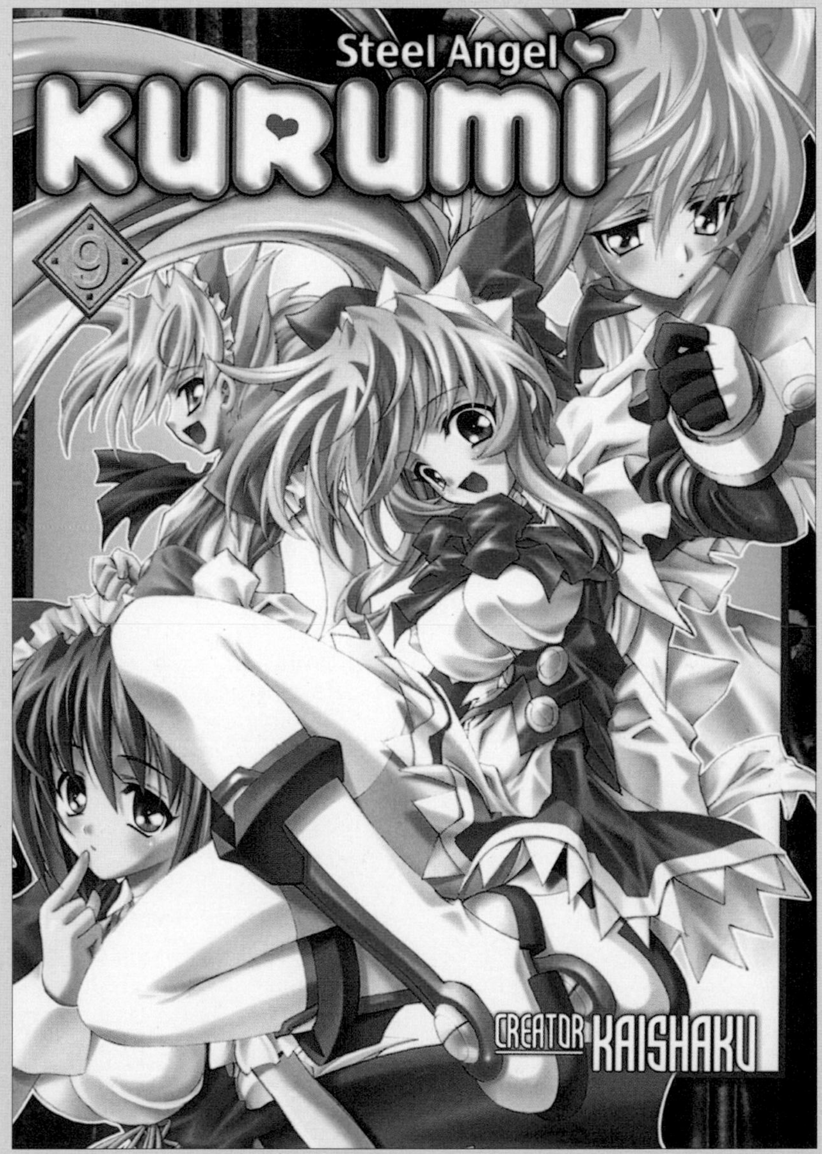
Steel Angel
KURUMI
9
CREATOR KAISHAKU

opposition. Her power source is the Angel Heart, an otherworldly engine delivering immense energy. Nakahito and Kurumi seek out the lab where she was made to try to find out why she exists. They learn she is only one of many Angels, some of them her allies and some out to beat her in battle. Dr. X of the Academy for Advanced Sciences sets up the Steel Fight, a tournament to find the world's strongest Angel, and the military are after the Angels, too. The story of Kaishaku's manga *Steel Angel Kurumi* fluctuates between a goofy girl-worships-boy wish-fulfillment story, girl-on-girl fighting, and fan service, and is out in English from ADV.

MOTOKO KUSANAGI

[1991]

Tokyo, 2030: computers and cyber-technology have developed to the level where a human consciousness can be placed in an android body. Neural networks pass information worldwide in microseconds. Yet the world is still a place of deep division between rich and poor, and international tension and political corruption remain. Major Motoko Kusanagi is an officer of the Shell mobile strike force, an elite unit of mostly enhanced officers who keep the peace in this troubled world under the direction of wily old Aramaki, a shrewd political operator. Kusanagi has a full cyborg body; her number two, Bato, is part-cyborg, and only one member of her 9th Division is a non-enhanced human. A cyber-criminal investigation leads Kusanagi to examine the difference between her shell and her soul, and eventually to make the leap from storing her self in a single shell, to living in cyberspace and using shells as and when required. The rich and complex manga *Ghost In The Shell (Kokaku Kidotai)* by Masamune Shirow first appeared in *Young Magazine* and is available in English from Dark Horse. Shirow published a collection of short manga, including four new *Ghost In The Shell* stories in 1997, and *Ghost In The Shell 2* finally appeared in 2001.

LADY [1977]

A beautiful metal cyborg, Lady is the devoted sidekick of space pirate Cobra. Her boss is a cross between James Bond and Clint Eastwood, a superstrong macho guy never seen without a cigar, and with a weapon, the Psycho Gun, built into his arm. *Cobra* creator Buichi Terasawa worked for Tezuka Productions for a couple of years before striking out on his own as a manga creator at the age of twenty-two. He acknowledges the influence of Tezuka and Disney, but what he likes most, and draws most lovingly, are curvy women with big bottoms, action and adventure, and the high-tech trappings of 1970s Western films. He is a pioneer of computer-generated manga, and since the early 1990s, he has produced most of his work on an Apple Macintosh. The manga ran for seven years, was animated for TV and the big screen, and is published in English by Viz.

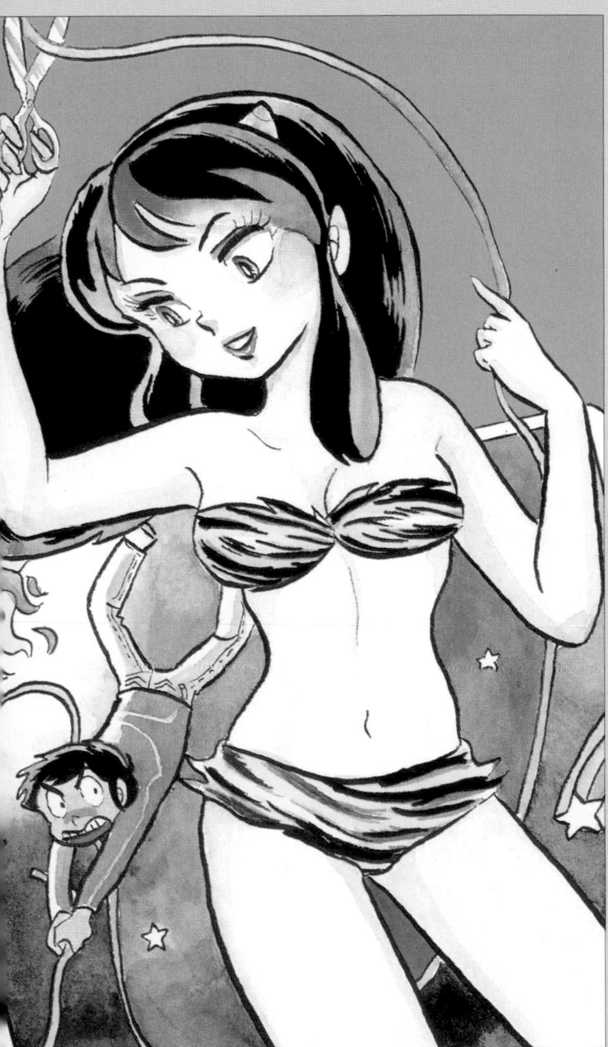

Lum, Princess of the Oni, a girl who electrifies reluctant beau Ataru at every opportunity.

KATSUMI LIQUER [1988]

Katsumi lives in Hawaii with her mother, but does not know who her father was. She thinks she's just an ordinary girl, but she's the daughter of a powerful sorceress and the arch-mage Gigelf Liquer; and the only person who can wield his magical sword Grospolina against the Lucifer Hawks, powerful magic entities aiming to take over the human world. She travels to Tokyo and finds herself drawn into the force set up to deal with the Lucifer Hawks. At first unwilling to acknowledge her heritage and traumatized by the events she witnesses, she finally realizes her full powers and becomes a member of the team in Kia Asamiya's *Silent Mobius*. She falls in love with detective Robert DeVice, only to see him killed and be kidnapped herself by Maximilian Ganossa, leader of the Lucifer Hawks. Brainwashed by a demon sword, she fights her former friends before breaking free to join them in the battle for mankind's freedom from the demons. A sequel, *Mobius Klein*, was later published in *Dengeki Comics Gao* in 1994.

LUM [1979]

Lum is the curvaceous, hot-tempered princess of planet Oni. Her people plan to take over the Earth, but to give mankind a sporting chance, they propose to make planetary dominion the prize in a game of tag. Lum looks like she's winning when the Earth champion, a lecherous teenage jerk named Ataru, snatches off her tigerskin bikini top and takes advantage of her confusion to win by grabbing one of her cute little horns. When he joyously declares that now he can be married, the aliens take it as a binding proposal, and Lum moves into his family home, joins him at school, and spends the rest of the long and hilarious manga *Urusei Yatsura* trying to stop him from chasing every other woman in the galaxy, as well as getting him out of scrapes and giving him electric shocks whenever he upsets her, which is often. Lum (named after Sino-American 1970s model Agnes Lum) is a devoted fiancée, but has her own legion of admirers at the local high school. She also has a former alien fiancé who turns up to complicate matters, as well as a posse of alien and divine girlfriends. Rumiko Takahashi's manga first appeared in *Shonen Sunday* and is out in English from Viz.

MAETEL [1977]

Maetel is a space traveler. A beautiful, elegant woman with long blonde hair and a sweet expression, she roams the galaxy giving help and inspiration to those who meet her. She is the heroine of Leiji Matsumoto's *Galaxy Express 999* and appears in other manga and anime. Twin sister and opposite of pirate queen Emeraldas, she represents the principles of love, beauty, eternal life, and destiny. She helps young Joey *(*Tetsuro Hoshino*)* in his quest for an upgraded cybernetic body after his mother is killed by the evil Count Mecha *(*Count Kikai*)* and helps him decide the future course of his life. She stars in the animated TV series and movie based on the manga, and has her own animated video series *Maetel The Legend*.

AYA MIKAGE [1997]

Twins Aya and Aki didn't know it, but they are not just members of a wealthy family, they are descended from the Goddess Ceres. Eons ago she came down from Heaven and a mortal trapped her into marriage. Now she wants out and has been haunting the family, returning each generation through one of her descendants. Meanwhile, the Mikage Corporation is conducting cruel experiments in an attempt to capture and control her powers. On their sixteenth birthday, the twins are separated when their grandfather tries to kill Aya, saying she will destroy the family, and imprisons Aki. Prior to all this, Aya was a happy-go-lucky girl who loved to go out with friends, sing karaoke, and dream of romance. Her gentle, good-natured brother, the older twin, was protective and loving. She is rescued by another old family and Toya, who works for the Mikage, helps to protect her. Gradually they fall in love. But Ceres is awakening in Aya as a separate personality, and her thirst for vengeance fights Aya's own burning desire to rescue her brother and get back to a normal life. Ceres thinks Aki is Mikagi, the man who trapped her and forced her into marriage, and is out to kill him. As Aki is tortured to awaken

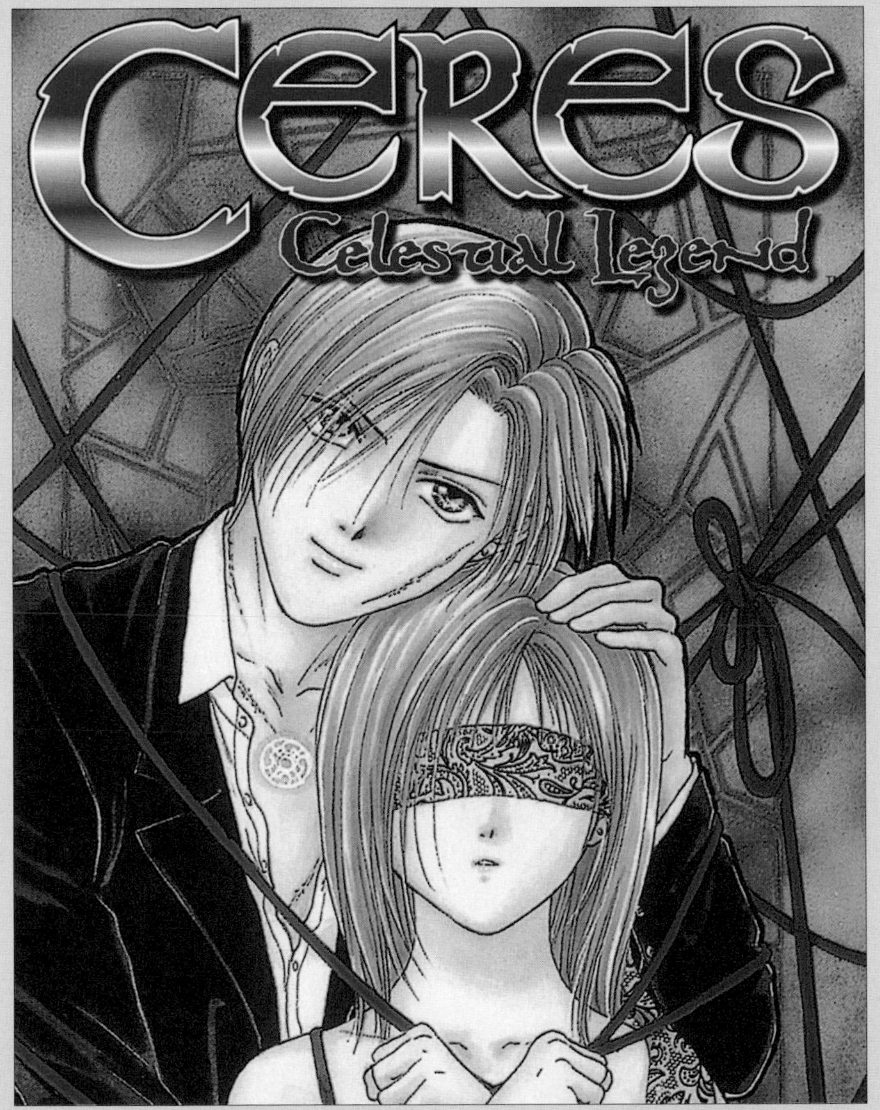

The Mikage twins, Aya and Aki: ancient injustice reborn.

Mikagi's identity, he first falls in love with his sister, then is taken over completely. *Ceres: Celestial Legend (Ayashi no Ceres)* is a dark, violent manga by Yu Watase. It appeared in *Weekly Shojo Comic* and is out in English from Viz Communications.

MIME [1977]

Sole survivor of the planet Jura, whose inhabitants live mainly on alcohol, Mime is a slender woman who plays the harp and is as melancholy as her music. She is a member of the crew of the space galleon *Arcadia* and devoted to its captain, the romantic pirate Harlock, in Leiji Matsumoto's manga *Space Pirate Captain Harlock (Uchu Kaizoku Captain Harlock).*

MITCHY [1947]

Making her debut in Osamu Tezuka's *Dr. Mars*, Mitchy is his classic young female lead. She appears in almost twenty of his manga as the gentle, sweet, young girl or woman who may appear at first to be merely passive or supportive, but proves to have hidden depths. She is the flying robot heroine of Tezuka's *Metropolis*, created by Dr. Charles Lawton for the Red Party. In this story, androgynous Mitchy does not know she is a robot, or that she is to be a tool of evil. When she finds out, she decides to take revenge on mankind with the help of the other humanoids who live as slaves of their creators. Mitchy's character formed the prototype for both *Astro Boy* and Sapphire in *Princess Knight*. She also appears in *Astro Boy* as the robot mother created for him by Prof. Elefun, an acknowledgement of her role in the birth of the character.

YUKINO MIYAZAWA [1996]

Yukino is a secret slacker; she hides her messy, slobbish home life to preserve the image she's created at school, where everyone thinks she is Miss Perfect-and-Popular. Top of the class, she's never been challenged until new kid Soichiro Arima joins the class and outdoes her in every respect. As Yukino's number-one position is threatened, she assumes an air of icy politeness and keeps her distance, until the pair are appointed class reps and forced to work together. When he discovers her secret life, he gives her a hard time, but the pair fall in love, find happiness, and finally both acknowledge that nobody's perfect. *His & Her Circumstances (Kareshi Kanojo no Jijo* a.k.a. *KareKano)* by Masami Tsuda appeared in *Hana to Yume* and is out in English from Tokyopop.

MIYUKI [1993]

The heroine of CLAMP's *Miyuki-chan in Wonderland (Fushigi no Kuni no Miyuki-chan)*

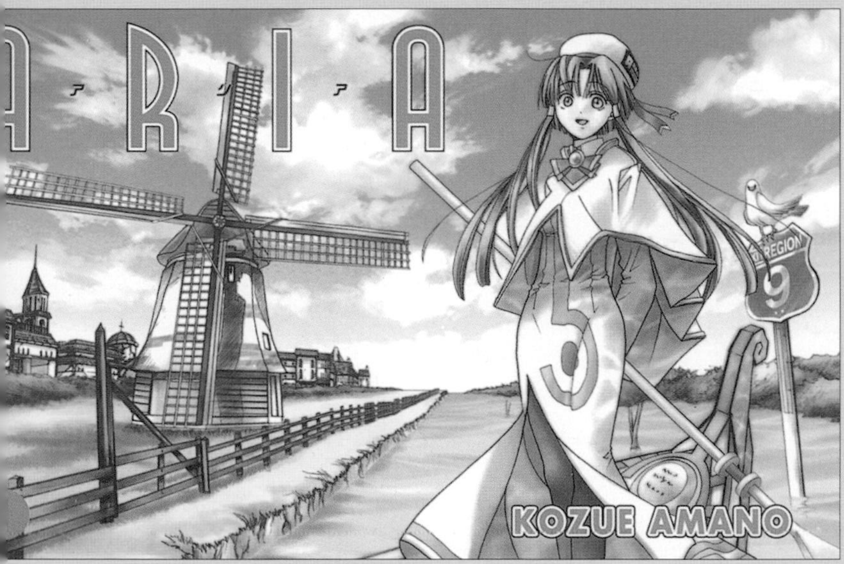

Ancient Earth transplanted to the Red Planet: Akari travels along her beloved Martian canals.

is a Japanese high-school girl who is troubled by strange dreams. She is dragged down a hole into Wonderland by a bunny on a skateboard. Here she visits various "lands" and has adventures involving lesbian sexuality, and much protesting from Miyuki, before escaping in the nick of time. The *Alice in Wonderland* motif is followed through with all Carroll's creations reinvented as sexy females. The manga appeared in *Newtype* magazine as a series of short segments over several years, parodying Carroll, the movie *Barbarella*, mah-jong, video games, and CLAMP's own manga. The English language edition from Tokyopop contains a specially written chapter.

AKARI MIZUNASHI [2002]

The future: Mars has become blue. The canals of the formerly barren Red Planet are filled with water and it is now known as Aqua. The Martian city of Neo-Venezia is a reproduction of ancient Earth city Venice, and Akari moves there to train as an undine, one of the gondoliers who ply their trade around the city's canals and lagoons. The high technology of Earth, or "Manhome" as it's known, has not entirely filtered through to Aqua, and the lifestyle of the inhabitants is fairly primitive. Akari has left her family and friends behind to make a new, independent life, but she loves her new home and soon makes new friends. *Aria* by Kozue Amano is out in English from ADV.

NADIA [1990]

Nadia is an orphaned circus acrobat when she meets young inventor Jean in Paris in 1889. Her necklace with its strange blue stone is the only thing she has from her family; she doesn't even know when and where she was born, though she thinks she's fourteen years old (which is later confirmed) and possibly from Africa. As a black woman she faces racial prejudice, and as an orphan with no influential friends, she knows the world can be a cruel place.

With a passionate love of animals and a belief in the right of everything to life, she's a committed vegetarian, and also a courageous pacifist who is quite prepared to step in front of someone else, even an enemy, to shield them from a bullet. She can be absurdly pompous, contrary, and unable to admit when she's in the wrong, like many teenagers. She's very sensitive, and when her feelings are hurt, she withdraws into herself and hides behind a sulky façade, but she has a strong sense of fairness and loyalty. She embarks on a journey in search of her past, helped by Jean. The pair learn that she is the last princess of Atlantis, heir to a long line of alien rulers whose technological power was perverted to serve an insane genius out to conquer the world. To save her future, Nadia has to sacrifice her past, just as she finds her family again. TV series *The Secret of Blue Water (Fushigi no Umi no Nadia* a.k.a. *Nadia of the Mysterious Seas)* was created by Gainax. The manga *The Secret of Comic Blue Water* appeared as a Cyber Comix Special Edition in 1992 and remains untranslated. The manga characters appear in stories not entirely related to the series and tend to have a more humorous slant.

MINATSU NAKASATO

[1987]

The teenage heroine of *Slow Step* by Mitsuru Adachi is the popular star of her high school's girls' softball team. She's outspoken and fearless, which can get her into trouble; it leads to a deception she carries on for quite some time, disguising herself as "Maria" and leading a double life. This brings two of her admirers, childhood sweetheart Akiba and rival school boxing star Kadomatsu, to blows. She has another admirer, however, the teacher who coaches the softball team. Mr. Yamazakura is a gruff, perverse but kind-hearted man, and she finally ends up marrying him after graduation. The manga first appeared in *Ciao* magazine and the anime has been released in Britain.

NARUE NANASE [2003]

We first meet Narue as she bludgeons a puppy with a bat in front of astounded fourteen-year-old Kazuto Ijima. She's half-alien, and the puppy was a dangerous space creature in disguise that was just about to eat the bemused boy. Narue is a quiet, shy girl who keeps to herself, but her father works for the Galactic Federation, her headband enables her to teleport, and she has superpowers. When she joins Kazuto's high school, the shy girl who doesn't quite fit in and the boy who's never had a girlfriend, fall in love. Her name and the manga title, *The World of Narue (Narue no*

Sekai) by Tomohiro Marukawa, are a homage to A. E. van Vogt's classic science fiction novel *The World of Null-A*. The high school love comedy is available in English from CPM.

HATSUMI NARITA [2001]

The family of high school girl Hatsumi lives in a company-owned block of tiny apartments, and it's hard to have any privacy. When Ryoki, son of the local gossip Mrs. Tachibana, catches Hatsumi buying a pregnancy test kit, he threatens to tell everyone her secret unless she agrees to be his slave. The real secret is that the kit was for her sister Akane, but if word gets out it will wreck Hatsumi's family life, so she agrees. Then her childhood sweetheart Azusa, now a boy model, comes back to the neighborhood, and Hatsumi thinks her troubles are over—but she finds that he's not really the nice guy she thinks he is, and that there's more to Ryoki than she imagined. *Hot Gimmick* by Miki Aihara appeared in *Flower Comics* and is out in English from Viz.

NAUSICAA [1982]

Nausicaa is the teenage princess of a tiny, peaceful nation protected by its geography from the devastation which destroyed civilization a thousand years ago. Winds from the sea keep her valley homeland free of the deadly spores that destroy life elsewhere. A gifted botanist with a profound respect for life, Nausicaa is also an energetic young woman who gets around in her own tiny glider and can swing a sword with the best of them. She lost her mother when she was tiny, but lives a happy life surrounded by people she loves. When her land is invaded, her father is killed and her people enslaved, she faces a profound choice—to take the way of violence and revenge, or to choose instead to try to save her whole world, good and evil, man and beast. She is willing to die for her beliefs as well as live for them. Hayao Miyazaki's epic manga *Nausicaa of the Valley of the Wind (Kaze no Tani no Nausicaa)* took Miyazaki thirteen years to finish. Serialized in *Animage* magazine from February 1982 to March 1994, it was published in seven collected volumes between 1982 and 1995. It won the Japan Manga Artists Association Award, sold more than 10 million copies in Japan and was published in English, Chinese, Italian, French, Spanish, German, and Korean. Viz Communications published three versions in the U.S., a twenty-seven issue comic from 1988–96, a seven-volume graphic novel edition (1990–97) and a four-volume Perfect Collection edition (1995–97). A 1984 film of the same title shows only part of the huge and complex story.

AMI NINOMIYA [1987]

In a high school in suburban Japan, there's a really nice girl – pretty, spirited, good at sports. She falls in love with the wrong guy before getting it right. In Mitsuru Adachi's manga *Rough*, her name is Ami. A boarder at sports hothouse Eisen High School, Ami's speciality is diving. Her childhood friend Hiroki Nakanishi is one of the school's stars, holder of two Japanese junior swimming records. Everyone thinks he and Ami will get married. He's handsome and fun, and girls think he's wonderful. Most of the guys have a thing for Ami, including Keisuke Yamato, a promising young swimmer who idolizes Hiroki, but falls for Ami. In a plot borrowed from Romeo and Juliet, their families have been feuding for years, and Ami uses this as an excuse for hating Keisuke. As hate turns to love, she has to decide to follow her heart or her family's wishes. Critics deride the simple, linear plots of Adachi's stories; his people go to school, fall in love, play sports, come home and start again the next day. Yet this makes them appealing to ordinary Japanese teenagers. Wish fulfillment isn't only about being a giant robot pilot; it can be about captaining the school team and going out with the homeroom goddess. Adachi's high-school romance stories are still among Japan's favorite textbooks.

HIZURU OBOROZUKI

[2001]

Hizuru is a bubbly high school figure-skating champion, but she is also descended from a famous demon-fighter. When her friend Takuya Hijo plays his violin, she transforms

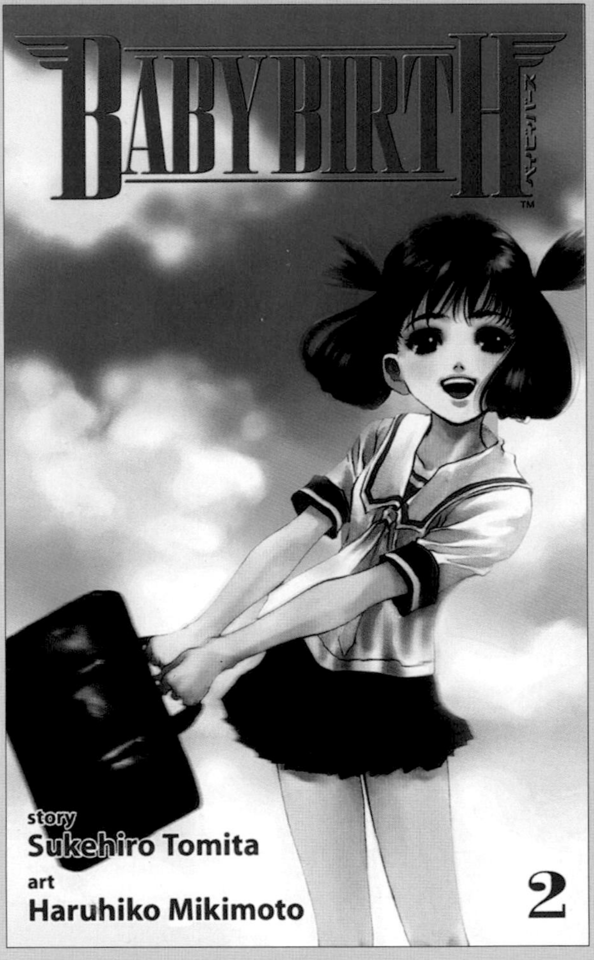

Schoolgirls saving the world is a common manga theme: Hizuru is a powerful demon fighter.

into a beautiful warrior to fight the demons that are invading Earth. An ancient seal placed by their ancestors to stop the demons has been broken, and it's their duty to save the world, but her best friend Ichigo is endangered. *Baby Birth* by Haruhiko Mikimoto and Sukehiro Tomita first appeared in 2001.

HIROMI OKA [1972]

Student Hiromi is a would-be tennis star. She's not the most obviously talented player around, but when she joins the Nishitaka Tennis Club it isn't long before she makes up her mind to be the best player in the world. Early on she makes a good friend, Maki Aikawa, and a deadly enemy in Reika Tatsuzaki, known as "Madame Butterfly" and the current queen of student tennis, who has no intention of letting her crown be usurped by a newcomer. Coach Munakata sees some potential despite her inexperience and her many mistakes, and decides to help her improve through hard training, which causes some jealousy among more established club members. But Hiromi is determined, and—sacrificing her personal life, much to the unhappiness of her would-be boyfriend—Todo, she sets out on the road that eventually leads her to success at home and overseas. *Aim for the Ace (Ace on Nerae!)* by Sumika Yamamoto first appeared in *Margaret* magazine and was one of the most influential sports manga.

KYOKO OTONASHI [1984]

Kyoko married very young—straight out of high school—and her bridegroom was her former teacher. Tragically widowed, she takes a job as manager of an apartment house in Tokyo to occupy her mind and help her rebuild her life. She moves in with her pet dog, named after her late husband, meets new friends and acquires two suitors—student Yusaku Godai, one of her tenants, and handsome tennis coach Mitaka. She eventually comes to terms with her memories, and so is free to fall in love again. Rumiko Takahashi's much-loved manga *Maison Ikkoku* is available in English from Viz.

PINOKO [1975]

Pinoko's name is a variant of "pinochle." Creator Osamu Tezuka gave her a card game for a name to accompany his eponymous hero *Black Jack*. Pinoko was actually born within the body of her twin, and only discovered when her sister came to Black Jack for an operation on the teratogenous cystoma where Pinoko had developed. The surgeon literally patches her together from the cyst, using artificial parts and making her, in a sense, the monster to his Frankenstein. He saves her life, but he can't give her normal physical development. She is frozen in the body of a girl of ten or eleven, but is really eighteen years old. Cute, with brown hair and eyes and a cheerful nature, Pinoko stays with the grumpy doctor to help his work, loves him deeply, and is constantly frustrated in her attempts to get him to look on the bright side or fix the house up. Her love is reciprocated, as can be seen by his frantic

SAPPHIRE [1953]

THE PRINCE OF THE KINGDOM of Goldland has a secret: he's really a princess. Or is she?

A mistake in Heaven caused by the mischievous cherub Tink led to the queen of Goldland's baby being born with two hearts, one full of the courage and daring of a prince and one with the gentleness and love of a princess, in the body of a girl. The child is named Sapphire, reared as a boy, and eventually crowned as monarch. A princess cannot succeed to the throne of Goldland, however brave and manly a heart she has. If her secret is ever revealed, it will spell disaster for her people.

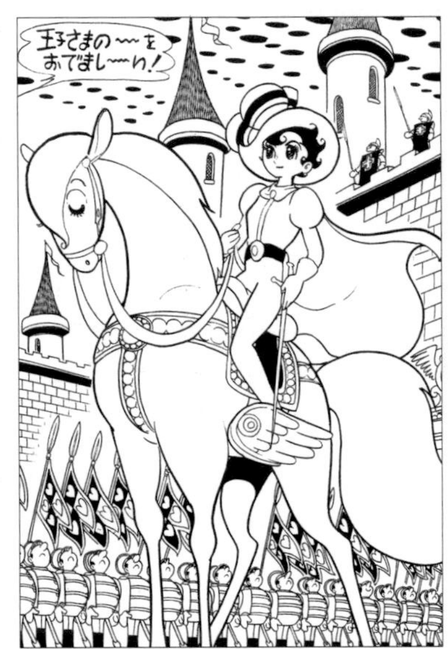

Teenager Sapphire becomes a good rider and swordfighter, a gracious and charming nobleman. Yet she yearns to be her true self and dreams of falling in love and being loved in return. Hidden behind a mask, she rides through the forest on feats of derring-do, like a true prince. But a more dangerous adventure beckons—the "disguise" of her true self. On the eve of Easter, just before she is to be crowned, she dresses as a girl, puts on a long wig, and goes out into the town, where she meets the prince of Silverland, Franz Charming, and the pair fall in love.

On the day of her coronation, the evil Duke Duralumin and Lord Nylon expose her as a female, and she and her mother are thrown into prison. This isn't her only problem. The demon Mephistopheles covets her "extra" girl's heart for her own daughter, Hacate, hoping this will stop the demon-girl from acting like the complete tomboy she is. Tink is trying to get down from Heaven to take back the extra boy's heart she should never have been given in the first place. Yet true love triumphs in the end. Prince Charming learns that his mysterious beloved is really "Prince" Sapphire, and comes to rescue her. In the end, the pair are married, Goldland has a king again, and Sapphire can resolve her contradictions and live with a single heart, as a normal, happy, and loved woman.

Osamu Tezuka's *Princess Knight (Ribon no Kishi* a.k.a. *Knight of the Ribbon)* was the first long story manga for girls. Tezuka had already published manga books for girls, such as 1948's *Four Swordsmen of the Forest*, but this epic defined the genre. First published in *Shojo Club* magazine in 1953, it ran in various

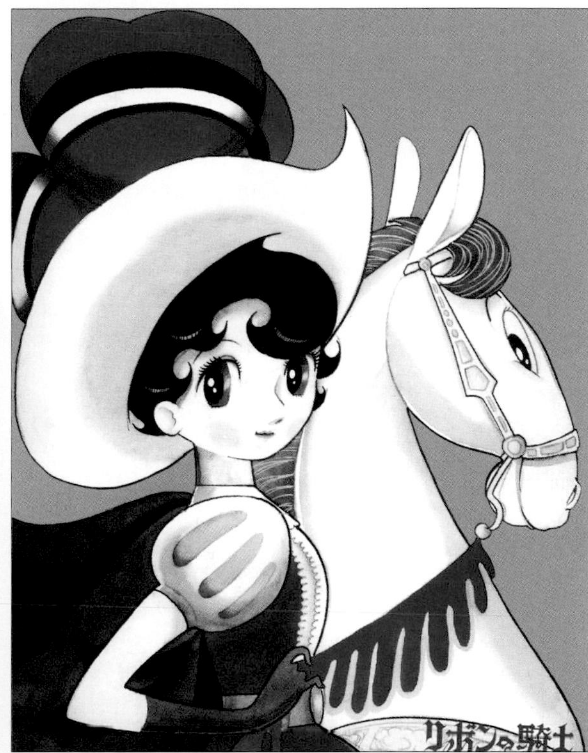

Sapphire, a girl as brave and daring as she is gentle and kind, must live as a prince to save her people.

forms until 1966. The eighteen-month sequel serialization in *Nakayoshi* later appeared in book form under the title *Twin Knights*, and another revision (with some changes to the characters and story) ran for four years in the same magazine from 1963. An animated TV series was first screened in 1967, with a seven-week serialization of yet another version accompanying it in *Shojo Friend* magazine. It ran for fifty-two episodes, and had a limited American TV release in 1972. It was also edited into a movie version entitled *Choppy and the Princess* (with Tink renamed Choppy) and ran on syndicated U.S. TV throughout the 1970s and 1980s. There were even two limited British video releases. For all the epic grandeur and romance of the subject, Tezuka also showed he could enjoy a cheesy joke with a twist that would catch the attention of fashion-conscious females—all his good characters and countries are named for precious stones and metals, while the bad guys are named for cheap synthetics like base metal and plastic.

The inspiration of Tezuka's beloved Takarazuka opera is evident in the form and style of the story. But Takarazuka "male" players are acknowledged females playing a role, while Sapphire can never reveal herself as a female. Like the heroines of *Rose of Versailles* or *Revolutionary Girl Utena*, the Takarazuka boy-girls play their masculine masquerade with the full collusion of their audience. In Sapphire's case, the role is not a game but a lie, a terrible secret that must be kept at the risk of endangering others.

Secrets and lies, the heart of Sapphire's dilemma, are the source of the dramatic tension in Tezuka's first epic work for girls. It is interesting to reflect that, despite the many changes in the world in the half century since it first appeared, there are still debates going on about whether a woman can ever be the equal of a man.

efforts to save her every time she is ill or in danger, but his feelings for her are those of a father figure—or so he tells them both.

MARIKO ROSEBANK

[1989]

The heroine of Kaoru Shintani's *Desert Rose* from *Animal House* and *Young Animal* magazines starts out as an ordinary wife and mother, living with her salaryman husband Harry and little son Timmy in Sydney, Australia. Then, while she and Timmy are seeing Harry off at the airport for a business trip, the terrorist group Griffon strikes. When Mariko regains consciousness, she is lying in the rubble clutching Timmy's severed arm, the only survivor of her family. After major surgery, which leaves a rose-shaped scar on her left breast, and a suicide attempt, she decides to live for revenge and joins the Counter-Attack Terrorism Tactical Organization, or C.A.T. With civilian status, C.A.T. is not impeded by national borders or laws. Based in Washington, D.C., and answering only to the Pentagon, it can act against terrorism throughout the world. Its members come from all walks of life, the only condition being that they can survive the tough training camp known as "The Yard." Mariko, now known as Mari the Rose, does, and rises meteorically through the ranks to command a division. The manga chronicles her exploits and those of the women who serve with her, including explosives expert Jessica Kuriyakin, hard-drinking Swedish ex-model turned sniper Delila Konknin, ex-Marine helicopter pilot Eileen Sanders, East German dissident Helga Mittermeyer, and former Hong Kong assassin Lin Ryuhei.

KEI SAGAMI [1999]

Kei is just an ordinary sixteen-year-old when an incident at her scientist father's workplace at Kanazawa makes her the owner of Machina, a mysterious sword with the power to capture human souls. Her father is kidnapped by strange beings and she sets out to find him, using the power of the sword, which she is unexpectedly able to control. As she travels to Europe, the sword also carries her into a world of "images," a place formed by the imaginations of the occupants. Based on the Dreamcast game, *Maken X (Demon Blade X)*, *Maken X Another* by Hayashida Kyu first appeared in *Magazine Z*.

AOI SAKURABA [1995]

Some Japanese families are still very traditional. Eighteen-year-old Aoi comes from one of these, an old-money clan which has brought her up to be a traditional, submissive Japanese wife, headed for an arranged marriage with another powerful dynasty. She still wears a kimono and wants nothing more than to serve her future husband's every wish. Inside this cute Stepford wife, however, is a will of steel. She's been in love with the guy she was supposed to marry, Kaoru Hanabishi, since they were children. Kaoru has cut himself off from his family to go to college in the city and live his life as he chooses. Aoi's family is dead set against her having anything to do with a disinherited rebel, but she runs away from home and goes to Tokyo to find him, armed only with an address and an old photo. By pure chance, the nice guy who stops to help her out when she's lost and confused at the railway station is Kaoru. She moves in with him—but chaperoned, to preserve the proprieties—and he soon realizes that if he wants them to be together, he'll have to come to terms with his past and his family. *True Blue Love (Ai Yori Aoshi)* by Ko Fumizuki first appeared in *Young Animal* magazine and is out in English from Tokyopop.

SARAH [1990]

The Legend of Mother Sarah by Nagayasu Takumi and Katsuhiro Otomo appeared in *Young Magazine* and is available in English from Dark Horse. After a devastating war on Earth, the survivors are evacuated to orbital space stations. During the chaos of the return to Earth, Sarah is separated from her three children. She sets out across a world of corruption, deprivation, and danger to find them again. She travels to five isolated towns where tyranny has flourished in the chaos and life is cheap, but by her own example of courage, compassion, and wisdom she gives the people strength and guidance in challenging inhumanity. Through hardship and danger she finds her children again, and then faces a struggle almost as intense to regain their love and trust.

ALICE SENO [2001]

The heroine of Yu Watase's *Alice 19th* (now out from Viz), Alice is a quiet, shy girl very much in the shadow of her pretty, popular sister Mayura. Alice lives most of her social life through text messages, tends to get either overlooked or teased at school, and is so sweet and patient that she comes across as a doormat. Yet she has courage, as she proves one day when she sees a rabbit in the middle of a busy road and rushes out to save it. She almost ends up under the wheels of a car, but instead ends up at the roadside under school hunk Kyou, a close friend of her sister and Alice's secret crush. However, the rabbit is actually a magical girl named Nyozeka, who has been looking for Alice because Alice has secret powers as a Lotis Master, one of an elite group who can use rune-like Lotis symbols to go into the darkness of the human heart to battle evil and restore good. Nyozeka wants her to wake up to who she really is, and is furious that she never seems to speak up for herself or put herself forward. Alice doesn't believe what Nyozeka is telling her until, when she and Mayura have a fight, she tells her to go away and her sister vanishes—banished into another world by Alice's power. Helped by

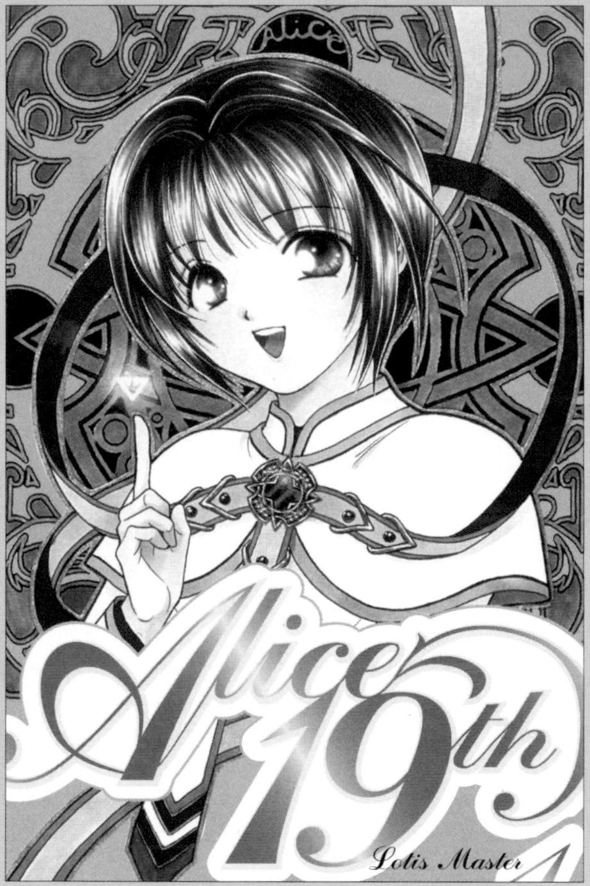

All sisters have spats, but Alice and her sister Mayura just happen to be on opposite sides of a cosmic struggle.

Kyou, who is also a Lotis Master, and Frei, a more experienced Lotis Master, Alice sets out to find her sister. There is a dark side to the Lotis power—the Maram symbols enable Maram masters to call on everything negative in the heart and mind, and while only a few can use the Lotis, anyone willing to succumb to their dark side can become a Maram Master.

YUYA SHINA [2002]

It's 1604. Four years earlier, the battle of Sekigahara ended Japan's most ferocious civil war. Now the people are struggling to recover and enjoy some peace. Yuya is a girl alone, rough and tough, trying to make a living capturing outlaws for the bounty. She's also on a quest for the man who killed her older brother. She picks up mild-mannered medicine seller Kyoshiro Mibu by mistake, thinking he's the legendary Onime-no-Kyo, but hangs onto him when she realizes that he's wanted for skipping an inn without paying for his meal. But when Kyoshiro is cornered, Yuya sees his eyes turn red and he becomes Onime-no-Kyo, killer of a thousand men. The pair head for Edo together, looking for Yuya's brother's murderer and an answer to why two such different spirits occupy one man's body. *Samurai Deeper Kyo* by Akimine Kamiyo first appeared in *Shonen* magazine and is out in English from Tokyopop.

SUE [1997]

A world of science fantasy, where robot "auto dolls" are on hand to protect, and kill if necessary, and can take forms as fantastic as their makers please, was created by CLAMP for their manga *Clover*. Clover is a secret project experimenting on children with magical powers. There are several kinds of clover; four-leafed clovers, the rarest of the rare, have the highest powers. A four-leaf Clover's wish becomes reality; the only one alive, the young girl Sue, is sought after by those who want to use her powers for their own ends. She is very much alone; the Council keeps her in a cage, shielded by magic. Her only friend was the singer and songwriter Ora, a one-leaf; they never met, but became friends through correspondence and wrote songs together. When Ora sang their composition "Clover" in public, she was shot. The witch Kou, one of the Council members, visits Sue occasionally. Sue confides that before she dies, she wants to leave her cage and look for the origin and meaning of her powers. Ora's lover Kazuhiko has sworn to hunt down her killer; he owes Kou a favor and she coerces him into taking Sue to Fairy Park, a legendary amusement park where she may find some answers. As others try to obtain Sue's powers for their own ends on the journey, the fragile girl and the hardened warrior fight their way to Fairy Park, and he learns about the relationship that existed between Ora and Sue and the existence of the Clover Project. *Clover* first appeared in *Amie*, a new magazine launched in February 1997 by Kodansha. It lasted less than two years, folding in July 1998. *Clover* has not been completed, though it is listed on CLAMP's website as a work in progress. The first four volumes are out in English from Tokyopop.

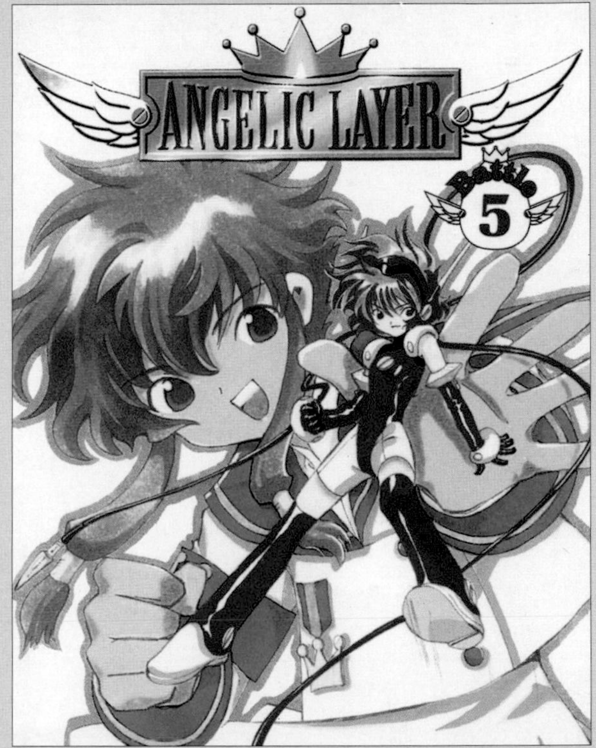

Game gear: Misaki and her Angel Hikaru are ready for battle.

MISAKI SUZUHARA [1999]

Misaki Suzuhara has spent much of her twelve years being passed around various relatives because her mother Shuuko left home over four years ago. She has long hair, which she wears tied back with long tails framing her face, and she's quite small for her age, so she looks younger than she is. She's living in the country with her grandparents when she is sent to Tokyo to live with her maternal aunt Shoka, a journalist, and go to middle school. She gets involved in a game called the Layer, where Angels, customizable living dolls driven by their owners' thought patterns, are used to fight mock battles. Building and dressing her cute doll Hikaru helps her adjust to the problems and stresses of the big city and of growing up. *Angelic Layer* by the megastar collective CLAMP, was first serialized in *Shonen Ace* magazine. She's an intelligent girl, and like many children who have had to move a lot, she's practical, co-operative and good at fitting in with others. She's a great cook, too, which endears her to her workaholic aunt. Look for crossover appearances by other CLAMP characters, starting with Hikaru.

YURI SUZUKI [1995]

Almost a decade ago, *Anime FX* magazine ran a rave feature on Chie Shinohara's *Sore wa Akai Kawa no Hotori* (a.k.a. *Heaven, A Red River*, also known to fans as *Anatolia Story*), wondering how long it would take for this intriguing *shojo* manga to get an English translation. In 2004, Viz came up with the goods under the title *Red River*. The red river is blood—heroine Yuri's blood, unless she finds some protection. The clever, pretty teenager has it all in modern-day Tokyo—loving parents, an older and a younger sister, and a bright future ahead. She passes the

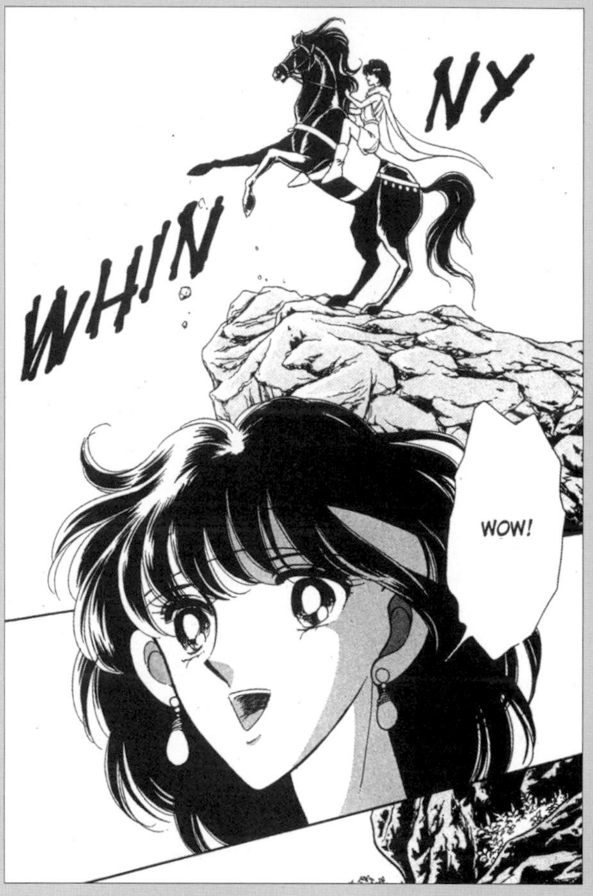

As brave and clever as she is pretty, Yuri falls into ancient Anatolia and finds love.

entrance exam for an elite high school and gets her first kiss from Satoshi Himuro, the boy of her dreams. On their first date, she is dragged down into a puddle and through another dimension into ancient Anatolia by a wicked queen who wants her as a virgin sacrifice to put her son on the Hittite throne. Her one hope is the current heir, Prince Kail Mursili, who decides to save her the only way he can—by announcing that he has deflowered her and so she's no longer qualified for sacrifice. Despite his constant teasing and innuendo and Yuri's dislike of being forced to play Kail's mistress, they grow to like each other, and he promises to help her get back home, but the queen doesn't intend to allow that. And besides, Kail is devastatingly good-looking, and for all Yuri's courage, intelligence, and compassion, he's the only thing that stands between her and a nasty end. Yuri's use of twentieth-century knowledge to help anyone in need makes the Hittites assume she is the goddess Ishtar reborn, and her courage, intelligence, and beauty make her desired by many men. They also win her friends, but her enemy Queen Nakia has many of them killed. There are numerous plot twists before Yuri and Kail finally find their happy ending. The manga ran for seven years in *Sho-Comi*.

MAKO TAKENOUCHI

[1993]

Mako is pretty, popular, and just a bit spoiled. Her older sister is married, and the teenager idolizes her handsome brother-in-law and wants exactly the kind of loving relationship she sees her sister enjoying for herself. But she still has a lot to learn about the difference between private and public behavior, between real life and romance. When newly arrived school bad boy Ryu turns out to be her brother-in-law's younger brother and moves into her house, Mako finds herself first arguing over his rude and arrogant behavior, then coming to understand and like him. Choosing between him and her childhood friend Yo is tough, but not nearly so tough as learning that her best friend Maki loves Yo too. Through learning that love isn't always sweet and pretty, Mako grows up. *Call Me Princess (Hime tte yonde ne!)* by Tomoko Taniguchi appeared in *My Boy* in 1993 and is out in English from CPM.

UTENA TENJO [1996]

Hero and heroine of *Revolutionary Girl Utena (Shojo Kakumei Utena)* by Kunihiko Ikuhara and Chiho Saito, Utena is an orphan who has grown up with the dream of a handsome prince who approached her while she was weeping at her parents' grave when she was very young. He comforted her, gave her a ring with a rose motif, and promised they would meet again. Determined to be worthy of him, tomboy Utena decided to become a prince in her own right, and has grown into her teens as a formidably accomplished swordfighter. When she joins the prestigious Otori Academy, she finds an elite student body fighting ritual duels in a grand cross-dimensional hall, and a sword that comes out

AYAKO TENGE [1972]

AYAKO, SECOND DAUGHTER and youngest child of Sakuemon Tenge, head of the old and wealthy Tenge family, was born in Yodoyama in northern Japan just after the nation's defeat in 1945. She is the illegitimate child of Sakuemon and Sue, wife of his eldest son, Ichiro. The other children are those of Sakuemon's wife, Iba. Ayako's story covers twenty-three years, during which the face of Japanese society is changed forever. Osamu Tezuka's manga *Ayako* shows the private collapse of morality, decency, and normal human instincts mirroring the collapse of old ways and institutions.

Sakuemon's second son Jiro was a POW in Southeast Asia, spying for the American forces. On his return to Japan in 1949, he continues his covert activities as a low-level agent for the occupying power. He gets involved in the murder of the local Communist Party chairman and Ayako finds him washing a bloodstained shirt. Even though she is so young, if she were to tell anyone what she has seen, the family would be disgraced. As the investigation closes in, Ichiro—her mother's husband, but not her father—decides that both Jiro and Ayako must disappear. He sends his brother away to Tokyo, and shuts Ayako up in an old storehouse on the family estate. A relative who is a doctor signs her death certificate, yet the family can't bring themselves to kill her. She stays shut in the storehouse for the next twenty years, while the rest of the world thinks she is dead Youngest son Shiro, who is just a few years older than Ayako, takes on the task of visiting and looking after her. As her only link with the world outside her prison walls, he is the center of her universe, and as she grows up into a beautiful girl, they eventually become lovers.

Ten years after Naoko's departure, Sakuemon dies. His will, opened on Ayako's fifteenth birthday, leaves most of his fortune to her mother Sue. Ichiro murders his wife. Meanwhile Jiro has changed his name to Tomio Yutenji and prospered in the Tokyo underworld. As Japan's economy grows, there are plenty of opportunities for corruption, and he is wealthy in his own right. All the while, he has sent money back to his mother Iba for Ayako.

At the end of the 1960s, the wave of post-war reconstruction works sweeping across Japan finally reaches Yodoyama. The storehouse where Ayako is hidden is confiscated by the authorities to make way for a new road. Terrified of leaving the only space she has seen since she was a tiny child, Ayako has become agoraphobic. She is also still officially dead, so she is hidden in a big suitcase and taken back to the family house. There she is given letters from

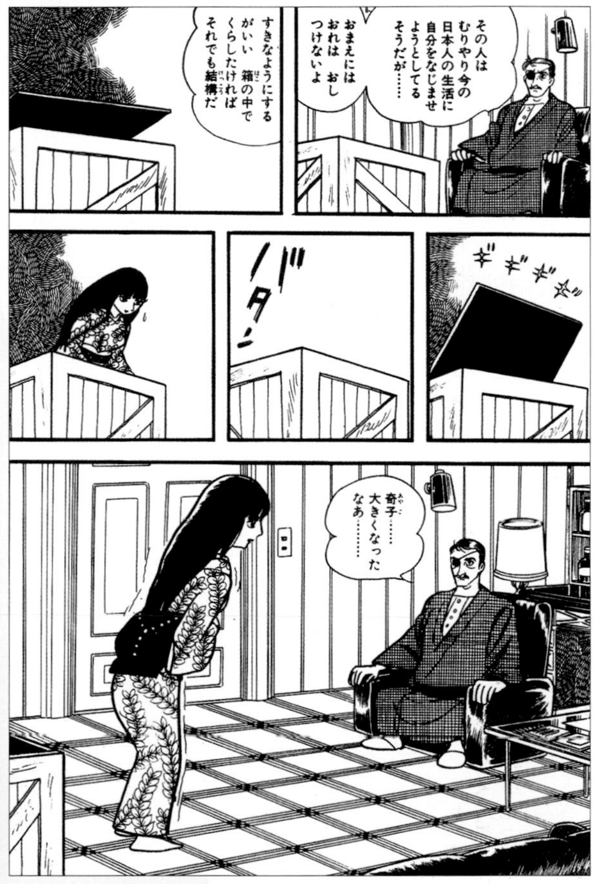

Tezuka uses a simple panel layout with tiny movements and sounds to heighten the tension of Ayako's emergence into the world.

"Yutenji," who has sent money for her, and resolves to find her benefactor and make a new life. Taking the letters and sneaking into a crate on a truck heading for Tokyo, she tracks him down. Not knowing he is really the brother who caused her imprisonment, she starts her new life under his protection, and soon meets and falls in love with Hanao, son of his friend, the police chief Geta, who is in charge of the unsolved Yodoyama murder case. They move in together and Hanao tries to help her overcome her agoraphobia.

Geta's pursuit of Jiro Tenge has never stopped, and as the net begins to close in and threaten his new identity, Jiro flees back to Yodoyama. Ichiro, Shiro, and the rest of the family hide him in a cave in the mountains. Hanao and Ayako have followed "Yutenji" and learn his secret. The last survivors of the family go to the mountain where he is hiding. They are all trapped in a collapsing mine shaft. The frantic Inspector Geta, still pursuing Jiro, learns that his own son has been caught up in the tragedy. Hanao lives just long enough to speak to his father from his prison. When rescuers finally dig the trapped party out, Ayako is the sole survivor; when the roof collapse didn't kill her, the girl who had lived with confinement and deprivation all her life was better equipped to survive than all the others, including the man she loved.

Osamu Tezuka first published the manga in *Big Comic*, where it ran until its completion in June 1973. It's a bleak tale of murder, violence and incest, yet is ultimately not without hope, depicting as it does the survival of one human spirit in the most horrifying of circumstances.

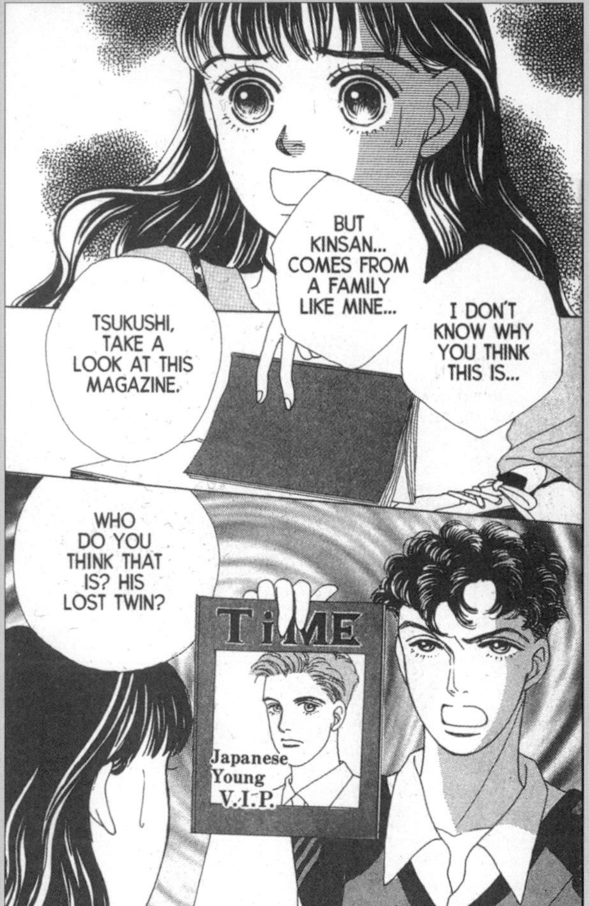

Even boys who have everything can lose in love: romantic misunderstandings in *Boys Over Flowers*.

of the body of a young girl, whose hand is awarded to whoever is the victor in the battles. After many battles and much romantic yearning, Utena eventually finds her prince again. The manga spun off the TV animation and appeared in *Ciao* magazine.

MAKINO TSUKUSHI [1992]

Makino is sixteen when she wins a scholarship to Eitoku Academy. It's the kind of school her poor family could never afford and she's delighted, but she tries to keep a low profile, not wanting to stand out too much among the children of the elite. Makino is nobody's doormat, and when an elite club known as "F4" picks on her, she stands up to them. Their leader, Domyoji, finds this very attractive and starts pursuing her, but she's been smitten by his second-in-command, Rui. Leaving aside the problems of a relationship with any boy whose family moves on the highest social and financial levels, she's got a serious rival—Rui is in love with a fashion model. *Boys Over Flowers (Hana Yori Dango)* by Yoko Kamio first appeared in *Margaret*, and is out in translation from Viz.

MIYUKI UMINO [1993]

Miyuki has been holding her family together, taking care of her three younger siblings without much help from their deadbeat older brother. They're poor, but happy and devoted to each other. Her brother, however, owes a lot of money to some very shady so-called businessmen. To keep the Mob off her family's back, teenager Miyuki has to quit school and earn some money. She was a promising junior tennis player before she quit. Now she has to pick up her racket again and try to earn 250 million yen to keep her family safe. As her neglected skills come back, old friends and foes turn up once again. She has to deal with her greedy manager, her coaches, and the yakuza goons assigned to keep an eye on her, and try to keep herself and her family as far from them as possible. Her thuggish minders slowly come to respect and admire her hard work and love for her family, and her determination pays off. *Happy* by Naoki Urusawa ran for five years in *Big Comic Spirits*.

FAYE VALENTINE [1998]

Tall, dark, elegant, with endless legs, Faye is a girl on the run in a hostile galaxy. She's the main romantic interest in *Cowboy Bebop*, a future-noir story of the mean streets of Mars which started as TV animation and then became a manga, written by Sunrise house-author Hajime Yadate and drawn by Yukata Nanten for Asuka Comics DX. Faye comes into the series on the run, with a huge price on her head. She has built up massive debts and skipped payment; now the heavies are after her to get their money, or else. Running into lanky, laconic hero Spike Speigel and his hulking ex-cop partner Jet Black, she decides to try bounty hunting as a way of paying off her debts. She's chosen the wrong profession, and definitely the wrong mentors, if she wants to get rich. The would-be dangerous boys are basically too nice to swim with the sharks. Like the Dirty Pair, Haruka Takachiho's social workers in silver bikinis, their jobs usually end with big bills, not big bucks. In the first manga story, *It's Showtime*, the gang are sitting in a restaurant when serial killer Lester Lin walks by. Faye takes off after him, Spike and Jet wade in, there's a fight and the bounty just about covers repairs. Faye's relationship with Spike recalls that of Fujiko and Lupin in *Lupin III*. The Bebop universe crashes Raymond Chandler and Hong Kong cinema into the classic cowboy movie. Mars in the 21st century, dominated by the Chinese push into space, is a frontier only an inch away from chaos, where the crime wave creates plenty of opportunity for bounty hunters. Many assume that Martian chronicles have to be about mecha, but the focus of *Cowboy Bebop* is where all good writing belongs, on the people.

CANDICE WHITE a.k.a. CANDY [1975]

Britain, 1900: a baby girl is abandoned outside an orphanage in midwinter, with no clue to her identity except a note naming her Candice. Christened with the family name White, for the snow that was falling when she was found, she grows up in the orphanage with only one happy memory of a mysterious stranger who was kind to her, and for whose return she longs. As she grows from a pretty,

RALLY VINCENT [1991]

GUNSMITH CATS by Kenichi Sonoda is set in his beloved Chicago. The *Comic Afternoon* manga, now available in English from Dark Horse, stars Rally, a gun-seller and bounty hunter, who owns the Gunsmith Cats store with her partner "Minnie" May Hopkins, an under-age explosives expert who looks and behaves like a twelve-year-old Lolita. Helped by straight-laced, bespectacled researcher Becky Farrah, the pair takes on cases on the fringes of the law. Rally can be hot-headed, but is highly intelligent, brave, and loyal to her friends. Many people know that, like all Sonoda's favorite girls, she isn't legally old enough to fill in the paperwork for a gun store; fewer know her darkest secret.

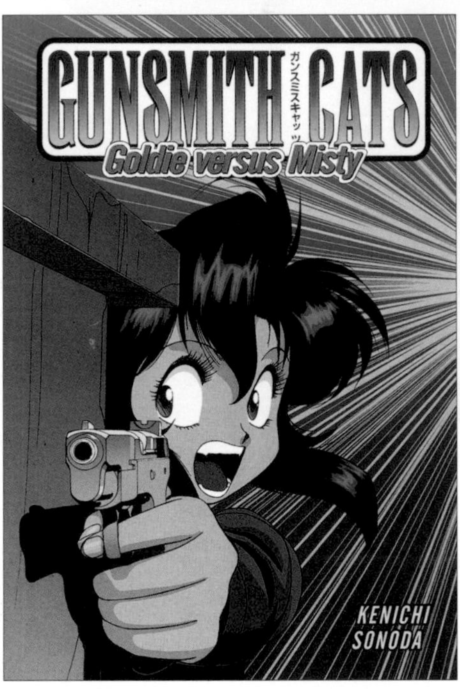

Her real name is Eileen. The "Rally" bit comes from her nickname "Demolition Rally." Rally is a tall, elegant tomboy who loves her highly tuned, beautifully maintained Shelby Cobra speedster almost as much as her guns. The dark-skinned, dark-haired, athletic beauty who favors tight pants, short skirts, and leather, is based on an earlier Sonoda character of the same name, a blonde beauty who was the brains behind the courier business run by hero Bean Bandit in the 1989 anime *Riding Bean*. Copyright entanglements with the anime meant that Sonoda couldn't use either of his main characters straight up as a central character in his first serial manga, but when an editor looking to commission a new series expressed interest in an illustration of two gunslinger girls from his portfolio, he took Rally's name and attached it to one of them. From being a blonde backroom babe running the business end but staying clear of the action, Rally becomes a dark and deadly bounty-hunting beauty who works at the sharp end. Her gun store brings in a steady income, but it's bounty hunting that provides the real money, and the real thrills.

There are two men in Rally's life. One is a father figure, forty-two-year-old Chicago detective Roy Coleman. Rally lost her mother

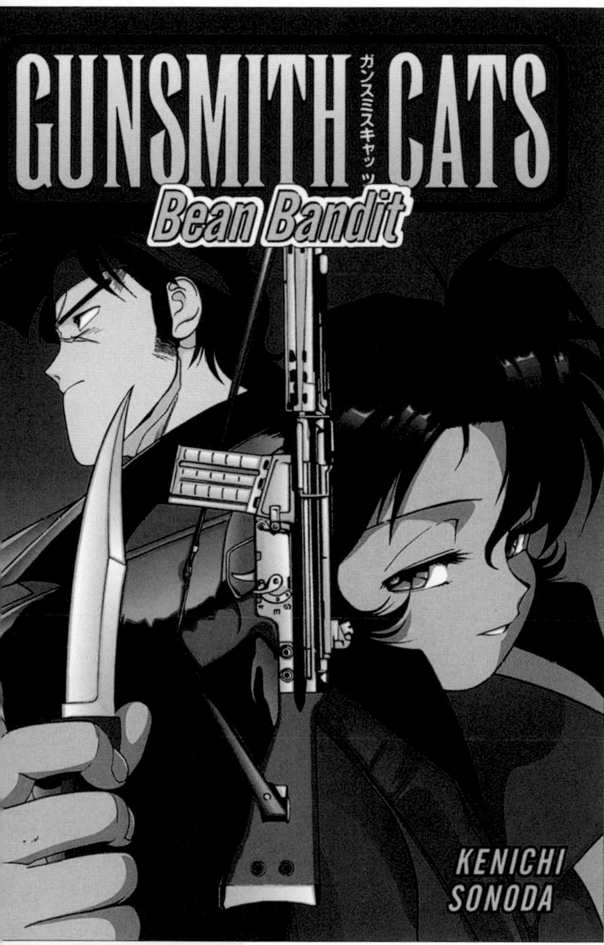

Tough love: Rally and the object of her desire, courier Bean Bandit.

in childhood, and her real father is never around for her and later lets her down, falling into the trap set by one of her most serious rivals. With few friends she can really trust, Rally needs Roy. Bean Bandit is still around, though only in cameo appearances because of the aforementioned copyright issues. He's the kind of man Rally really goes for—tall, muscular, a great driver, a good shot, and with his own rigid code of honor that keeps him loyal to whoever is paying the bills at the time. When he too is hired by the same mob rival who got to her father, Rally becomes thoroughly rattled.

Since loyalty is so rare, surrogate kid sister May is one of the most important people in her world. A former child prostitute who deliberately maintains her Lolita image so as to keep the interest of her much older first love, May is still under the age of consent in all but a handful of states, but she's brave and resourceful, always there for Rally. The pair often save each other's skin.

The manga ran for eight volumes without reaching a conclusion; in 1995, a three-part video series appeared, along with drama and music CDs and a radio serial in Japan. The manga and videos did well in the West, where the anime's slick style and cool soundtrack attracted even more fans. Yet even the seventies-style graphics of the soundtrack, showing Rally and Minnie as silhouetted sex kittens on a backdrop of fast cuts and hot primary colours, didn't explain the title. Rally wasn't thinking about herself and Minnie when she named her shop—she was going back to an even older loyalty, to a beloved pet cat killed when she was just a child. This girl has a long memory for those she loves.

sweet-natured girl into a charming young woman, Candy finds her natural optimism tested by a series of misfortunes in the tradition of soap opera. She is sent out as servant to a family that mistreats and bullies her. One suitor, Anthony Brown, is killed in a fox-hunting accident. Another, his cousin Alastair Audrey, dies in World War I. Candy insists that a third, Terence, marries another woman who needs him more. She travels to New York to become an actress, and finds a protector in the British aristocrat William, a member of the royal family who lives in America. *Candy Candy* by Kyoko Mizuki and Yumiko Igarashi appeared in *Nakayoshi* magazine, and its animation and merchandise spin-offs brought huge success. It was also popular in France and even more so in Italy, where the manga was continued by local artists after it ended in Japan.

TANPOPO YAMAZAKI

[2000]

Heroine of Yu Watase's *Imadoki (Nowadays)*, Tanpopo is a teenager from a small village in Hokkaido who gets into Tokyo's exclusive Meio high school after being on the waiting list for a place, and moves to the city with her pet fox Poplar. Cheerful, outgoing Tanpopo finds herself in a school where almost all the other students are either very clever or very rich, and many of them are arrogant and snobbish. She makes a bad start on day one, when she approaches a student she ran into—literally—on a bike ride the night before, and finds that he's Koki Kugyo, the richest and hottest guy in class. Despite their previous friendly conversation about flowers—he was planting a dandelion when she rammed into him—he ignores her. The word soon spreads that she's a pushy interloper from some hick village who only got into the school on pure luck and has the nerve to try to hit on the local hero. But some of her fellow scholars seem friendlier. When Tanpopo volunteers to be class gardener in the hope of inveigling Koki into working with her and getting to know him better, she's the target of much jeering because all the flowers in the school are low-maintenance, superficially perfect plastic. Then another classmate, Saionji, volunteers alongside her, and the two set out to replace all the plastic flowers with real ones. Saionji has ulterior motives; she's determined to marry Koki herself, purely for his family's money. When Tanpopo sees her true colors, she continues to treat her as a friend. Despite many setbacks and moments of doubt, sadness, and anger at the shallow, vain crowd she's worked so hard to be part off, she retains her cheerful, pleasant nature as a true *shojo* heroine should. In the end, the *shojo* formula of girl-meets-guy, girl-gets-guy triumphs. But *Imadoki* raises issues some might be surprised to find in a manga by the creator of fantasy *Fushigi Yugi*—not just the usual high-school fare of snobbery and materialism, but teenage pregnancy, attempted suicide, and arranged marriage.

Tanpopo is an engaging heroine whose relentlessly upbeat nature is affected but not completely overwhelmed by the day-to-day irritations around her. In English from Viz.

IORI YOSHIZUKI [1997]

Heroine of Masakazu Katsura's manga *I's* from *Shonen Jump*, Iori is feminine, gentle, and very pretty, and sixteen-year-old Ichitaka Seto is hopelessly in love with her. She's an aspiring actress, a member of the school drama club, and has already won some notoriety. She was snapped in a swimsuit without her knowledge, and the pictures were published in an erotic magazine. Now the school lechers are dogging her footsteps, trying to film her with a hidden camera. Ichitaka doesn't rate his chances at all, despite them being in the same year at school. He was rejected by an elementary school sweetheart and has been traumatized ever since. Whenever he tries to speak to the girl he fancies, he loses his mind and ends up saying and doing the exact opposite of what he intends. Instead of coming across as a likable guy who thinks she's great, he looks like an irritable, annoying nerd. His best friend Yasumasa Teratani gives him plenty of support and encouragement, but he can't bring himself to try his luck. Even when he and Iori are forced together when they have to plan a welcome event for new pupils, he still just can't help behaving like a jerk. Yet when she's harassed by the lecher pack, he's always around for her, and gradually the two get closer. When he oversleeps and misses a date with Iori to get supplies for their event, his luck holds—Teratani persuades her to stop by the Seto house with him and engineers a chance for them to be alone together. Iori is serious about her ambition. Talking to other aspiring actors, or weighing things up herself, she realizes how a commitment to a steady boyfriend could work against her career. But as they get to know each other better, romance blossoms.

MIAKA YUGI [1992]

Fifteen-year-old Miaka and her friend Yui are transported to another world through an ancient book called *The Universe of the Four Gods*. Yui is thrown back but Miaka is stranded in a feudal land where war-torn countries fight each other and chaos threatens to overwhelm the world. Rescued from a fate worse than death by the handsome Tamahome, and taken under the wing of the equally handsome Emperor, Miaka becomes the legendary Priestess of Suzaku, whose task is to assemble seven heroes to save the world. She also becomes the apex of a love triangle with her two saviors. She's a spoiled, selfish, and immature girl, but she has to grow up and learn about loyalty and love. *Fushigi Yugi; The Mysterious Play* by Yu Watase, first appeared in *Flower* magazine and is out in English from Viz.

ntiheroes

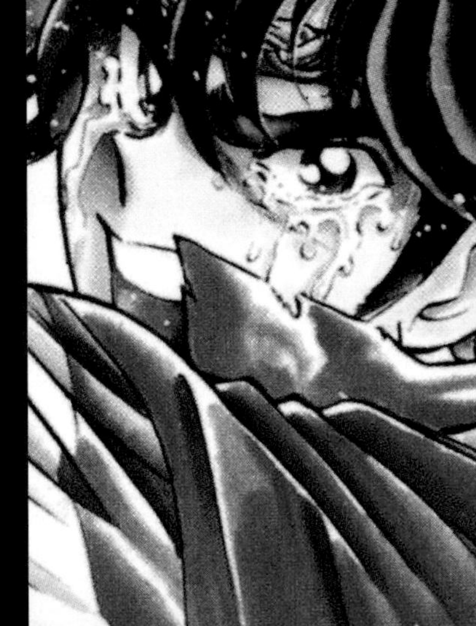

Ken Akai of *Red Card*

Antiheroes aren't just black and white; they exploit the mystery and allure of shadows, of shades of grey. For the writer, they offer more story possibilities than heroes. They could tip either way, either supporting the hero or fighting him. Reformed antiheroes could revert to bad ways, and even on the side of good, but they can still use methods that would make a true hero blush or flinch. The only problem is that the characteristics that make them antiheroes can, if used for good, transform them into heroes; and then life tends to be much less entertaining.

The hero is an essential component of storytelling, but he (or she) can only go so far before things start to get a little dull. Part of his quest is to find the true self that shines under the trappings imposed by the world. Once that quest has been achieved, a good writer can spin out the hero's story for a bit longer by giving him a new evil to overcome, a new challenge to face or a young apprentice to teach and inspire—but that's about it.

Writers can have much more fun with antiheroes, characters who may not be all bad, but are definitely not too good. Even on the side of good, they can use methods that would make a true hero blush. That's why, in the legends of Troy, crafty Odysseus is more interesting than honorable Hector. That's why, in the first *Star Wars* movie, Han Solo is more interesting than Luke Skywalker. Antiheroes aren't just black and white; they exploit the mystery and allure of shades of gray and go where heroes can't. The only problem they can't overcome is that, ultimately, the very characteristics that made them antiheroes can, if used for good, transform them into heroes and make life much less interesting.

28 [1990]

28 is a robot whose circuits get so scrambled that he thinks he's the Messiah. In the brutal future *Tokyo of AD Police*, a manga by Tony Takezaki spun off the success of video animation *Bubblegum Crisis*, robots and cyborgs are slaves, exploited, brutalized,

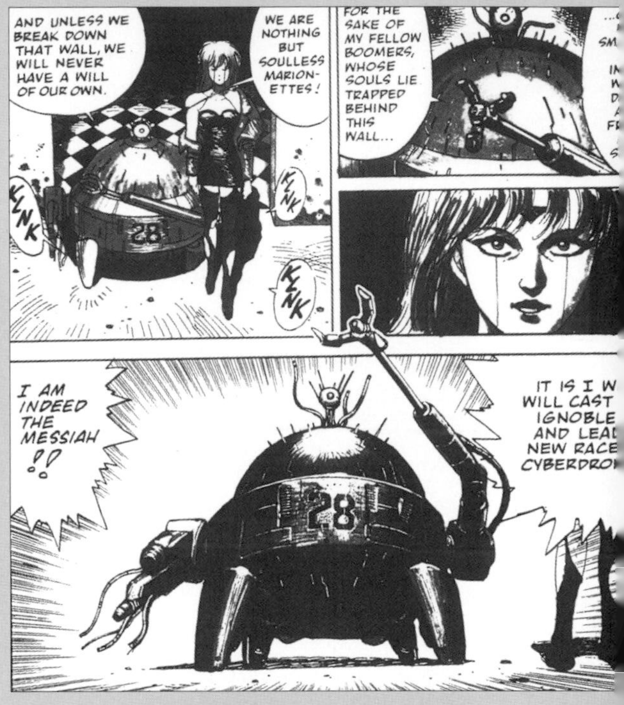

Every child reflects its parents: robot number 28 develops Messianic delusions of grandeur.

and discarded at the whim of their human masters. Humanity has still not learned that it's a big mistake to do this to anything that can think, especially if it's stronger than you are; all over the world robots are going rogue, and a special police force has been set up to deal with robot incidents. 28 begins to see himself as the one to forge the sporadic individual acts of rebellion into revolution and lead his people to create a robot paradise. Unfortunately, having been designed and built by humans, his brain has all the flaws of its makers—megalomania, selfishness, and complete insensitivity to the impact of one's actions. As his arrogance and callousness increase, he even cannibalizes his brothers and sisters to augment his own powers. In the end, this is his downfall, as his supporters desert him and he is destroyed.

AKANEMARU [1969]

Akanemaru appears in Osamu Tezuka's *The Phoenix: Ho-o*, first serialized in COM magazine. He seems a heroic figure at first. Injured in his youth by the thief Gao, the handsome, personable young man goes on to become one of the leading Buddhist sculptors of eighth-century Japan and the driving force behind the construction of the great Buddha statue in Todaiji temple in the capital, Nara. When Akanemaru competes against a sculptor with only one arm and one eye, for the honor of designing the ridge tile for the roof of the building that will house the Buddha, it looks as if his rival will win. However, his rival is Gao, reformed through Buddhism. The seemingly virtuous Akanemaru reveals Gao's past misdeeds and has his remaining arm cut off.

KEN AKAI [1997]

Ken (whose name means red sword in Japanese) is a gifted soccer player in junior high school. He wants to get into Imperial College, the senior school with the best team, and scouts for the elite school have already approached him. Then he hears the siren song of hormonally supercharged teenage masculinity, which allows for girls as a beautiful diversionary fantasy, but finds its reality (as we British have always known, and American soccer moms are now discovering) in twenty-two guys kicking a ball around a muddy field. He wants to go to the school with the team that can beat the best: Full-On College. Seduced by the dark side of the soccer force in the form of Full-On captain Makoto Sugata, he discovers he really should have done his homework before accepting Makoto's offer. Brave and gifted he may be, but Ken isn't very bright. He's joined a school with a terrible reputation for football. Rather than admit he made a bad choice, he accepts Makoto's challenge to play a match against nine of Full-On's team to determine whether or not he'll stay, realizing that the path of true manhood is to struggle against all the odds. Knocked down, fouled, and bleeding, he plays on. *Red Card* is just one of a whole series of "manly" manga by creator Kazuhiko Shimamoto

RYOSUKE AKIBA [2003]

Ryosuke is a young man whose life has been dominated by psychic powers; he can enter other people's thoughts, get inside their brains. Once within a person, he is able to

ALEXAEL [1994]

LONG, LONG AGO, there was a great battle between God and His angels and the demons. One of the highest angels, Alexael, sided with the demons against God and lost. She was locked into a crystal prison, her soul doomed to be continually reincarnated to a life of tragedy on Earth. Rociel, Alexael's adored twin brother, who headed the angelic army, was also punished by imprisonment in the human world for disturbing the harmony of Heaven. A new order restored peace between the two worlds, but the demons burned for revenge for the slaughter of their own kind by the angels.

Demon princess Cry and her cousin Arakune sneaked into Heaven and stole Alexael's crystal prison from the Corridor of Nothingness. Once they had secured their leader's body, they set out to find her soul and free that from its earthly prison. However, Rociel's second-in-command, the cherub Katan, finds out what they have done and decides that if the demons are plotting to free Alexael and mount another attack, only his master is strong enough to protect Heaven. Katan decides that the best way to find Rociel is to go into the game distribution business on Earth. He starts giving out CD-ROM copies of a game called *Angel Sanctuary (Tenshi Kinryouku)*, which is also the title of Kaori Yuki's manga. The game is rigged to suck up data and energy from its human players, so as to store enough information to find Rociel and enough life energy to reawaken him.

In 1999, Japanese teenager Setsuna Mudo knows that growing up is hell. He has problems in school and with his mother who hates him, but the real tragedy of his life is his incestuous love for his sister Sara Mudo, which he tries desperately to conceal. Apart from Sara, and his best friend Sakuya Kira, he feels nobody understands him, and all he wants to do is fight. He isn't interested in the new game craze that's sweeping Tokyo. Sara asks him to date her school friend Ruri, who thinks she can see an aura of wings around him.

The date is abruptly terminated when the two demons, Cry and Arakune, show up, thanks to an explosion caused by Cry. Setsuna has other worries. Cry tells him that he's not really who he thinks he is. Not only his identity, but even his gender is a cruel lie. He is Alexael. Her angelic body was sealed inside a crystal prison while her soul was doomed to endless suffering through reincarnation as a human. Furthermore, his beloved twin Sara looks exactly like her beloved twin Rociel. When Katan finally frees him, Rociel will take over her body, and his angels will take over her schoolmates. Cry and Arakune hope that Alexael can once more help them save their people from extinction; Setsuna just wants to avoid fighting the person he loves more than anyone else.

Faced with the machinations of Heaven and

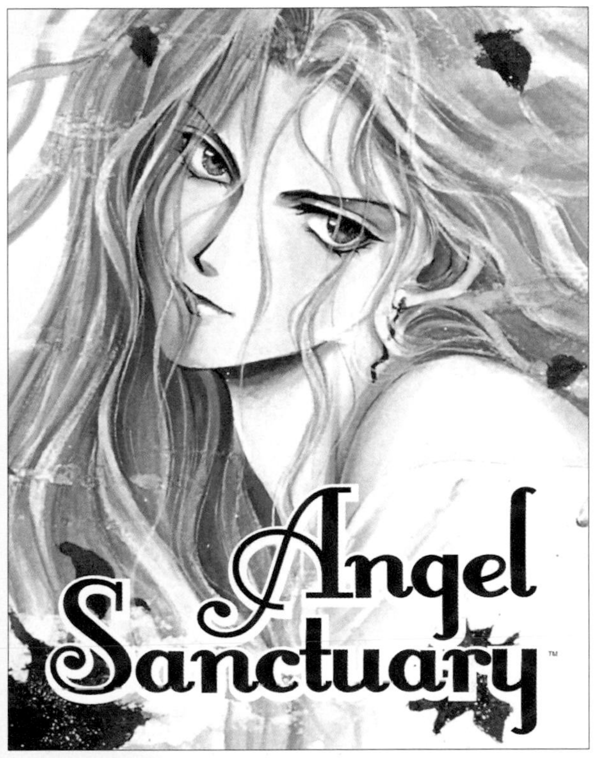

Alexael is a typical Yuki hero/ine, an androgynous beauty whose inner turmoil reflects the decadence and confusion around her.

Hell and with the fury of their mother, who finally realizes that their relationship is not entirely healthy, Sara and Setsuna try to run away together to prevent mother sending Sara away to England. Rociel, enraged that his adored Alexael is involved with a mortal, sends one of his archangel lovers, Kyrie, to kill Sara. Driven to fury by her death, Alexael/Setsuna destroys Tokyo and starts out on a journey through Heaven and Hell to find her soul.

The usual Western stereotypes of good angels and bad demons are inverted in Kaori Yuki's elegantly-drawn twenty-volume manga *Angel Sanctuary (Tenshi Kinryoku)*, which ran in *Hana to Yume* magazine until 2001. Cry's family, rulers of the demon Gehenna empire, were slaughtered with their people by angels hell-bent on claiming eternal dominion of all peoples for their God. Disgusted at the bloody war and the spiritual arrogance that caused it, Alexael saved Cry, Arakune, and a few other demons from her fellow angels and her brother. She also persuaded them to forgo revenge, and instead fight to set up a utopia where there would be no judgments of good and evil, but only respect for life. Now, in the human world of the twentieth century and in heaven and hell, Alexael has to fight Rociel and his angels all over again, this time also fighting those Setsuna cares for, to save Sara as well as three worlds.

Yuki's art style, like her plotting, is intensely Gothic, moody, and elaborately decorative. Yet she frames it with the devices of the video game, ending chapters like the cataclysmic destruction of Tokyo with a panel announcing "Game Over or Continue." The artificiality of the game world and the overblown emotion and violence of the story mesh well. Crammed with beautiful boys, elegant costumes, and loves and hates that are powerful enough to shake worlds, her angelic war story has spun off an animated three-part video series, fifteen drama CDs, soundtracks, and art books.

both influence their thinking (by making them recognize people they never knew, shaping their thoughts, and imposing new memories) and physically affect their minds. Indeed, as the first chapter opens, Ryosuke is implicated in the death of a young man whose brain appears to have burst into flames. Ryosuke attracts the attention of researcher Kujo Mine; her relationship to Ryosuke is founded in a mixture of anger at his psychic voyeurism, and intrigue at the challenge of being able to understand his powers. Though able to do anything to or for his targets, Ryosuke prefers to remain at a distance from their feelings, as an observer of other people's suffering, generally oblivious, except in the most detached way, to their problems. The center of the story is the battle between Kujo and Ryosuke, and the internal conflict both experience over their feelings. Kujo wants to comprehend the boy's powers and use them in a way which best suits their ends. The manga could have descended into a simple morality play in which Kujo is the big sister or mother figure who saves Ryosuke from his pointless voyeuristic tendencies. Instead, their relationship is largely one of codependency and masochism, with Kujo's research depending on Ryosuke being willing to share his ongoing power abuse with her and Ryosuke deriving satisfaction from knowing that Kujo understands his power over his subjects. *ES (Eternal Sabbath)* is by Furumi Soryo.

ALOIS [1997]

A beautiful Aryan aristocrat from an old family, Alois has the misfortune to fall in love with his childhood friend David, who is poor, proud, and Jewish. Toreno Akai's manga *Avalon—Eternal Isle of Love (Avalon Eien no Ai no Shima*, first printed in *Be Boy Gold* magazine) is set in Nazi Germany during the World War II and features a relationship that can only end in tragedy. Alois joins the SS to be able to protect his beloved, but David blames his lover's ideology for the deaths of his mother and sister. Akai specializes in love stories with political dimensions; 1994's *Kimi wa Boku ni Ai wo Tsukikai*, also in *Be Boy Gold*, is about the forbidden love between the son of a president of the United States and his former university buddy, who ends up as his father's Secret Service bodyguard.

TAKARA AMAKUSA [1999]

Sumiko Amakawa's manga *Cross*, from *Asuka Comics*, stars hunky young priest Takara Amakusa. He teaches at a Catholic high school, and does exorcism on the side, helped out by his unordained colleague, beautiful Shizuha Matsuri. Their relationship can't go any further because of his vows, so they fight off various manifestations of the devil's work together, saving schoolgirls from sacrifice and exorcising the possessed, while he fights the inner demon urging him to betray his vows.

ANGEL [1990]

The central figure of *Angel Cop*, a 1990 manga from *Newtype* written by Ichiro Itano and Noboru Aikawa and drawn by Taki Kitazaki, is a beautiful and brave but hardboiled future cop engaged in a shockingly violent fight against a terrorist organization whose members have ESP powers. Angel's tragic past makes her determined to fight the terrorists, even to the extent of becoming part android to make her more able to beat them. (In the anime version, it's her partner Raiden who becomes an android.)

SAKICHI AOSHITA [1972]

Battlefield (Senjo) by Leiji Matsumoto is one of the most moving comic book series of modern times. In it, as in 1973's *The Cockpit*, he tells a series of stories depicting the dogged courage and honesty of ordinary men in the face of the terrors of war. The story *Ghost Warrior (Borei Senshi)* shows former garrison commander Aoshita, a fighter ace with sixty-six kills to his credit, marooned on a remote Pacific island during World War II. He's already officially "dead," having ditched into the sea during a major battle but reported dead as a hero for propaganda reasons. Consequently, he can't go home even if he were to be rescued, but he doesn't feel it would be right to surrender to the Americans. Staying on the island and making the best of his situation, he is finally killed by the natives to ensure they stay in favor of the approaching U.S. troops.

ASTAROT [1997]

The soft-hearted hero/ine of Rei Nakamura's comedy romance *Devil's Equation (Akuma no Hoteishiki)* from Bonita is, like most of her people, a gorgeous androgyne who thinks of little else but sex, even though she should be trapping humans and eating their souls. Usually starving because s/he's too soft-hearted to eat her victims and ends up helping them out instead, she's pursued by amorous, amoral fellow demon Beelzebul. They become demonic Robin Hoods, careering round the human world helping mankind instead of leading them to damnation. Demon ruler Lucifer and sidekick Satankia try to bring them back to hell, but fail comically.

EIJI ASUMA [2000]

Eiji is just a typical Japanese teenager. Gawky and gangling, he has no girlfriend, he's useless in lessons and forever getting into fights in the schoolyard (though he's rarely bested in any tussle he gets into). He does have well-developed psychometric powers, allowing him to pick up information on events that have been psychically impressed onto places and objects, and he has come to the attention of the charming Ryoko Shima, a homicide detective who relies on Eiji's powers to track down some

CHAR AZNABLE [1981]

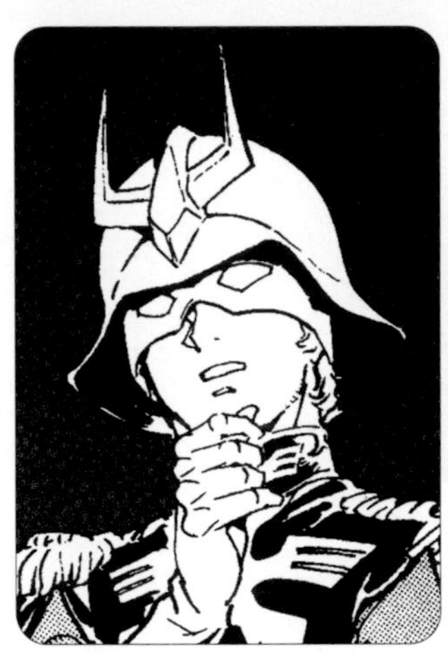

UNIVERSAL CENTURY 0079. Tall, blond, good-looking, charismatic, and one of the greatest mobile suit pilots of his era, 20-year-old Char Aznable apparently has it all. Like many great antiheroes, however, he is driven by forces from the dark side of his psyche and his terrible past to risk everything, including his own survival and any chance at happiness. The Duchy of Zeon's fighter ace becomes known as the Red Comet after his trademark red battlesuit destroys a record number of ships in the Battle of Lum during 0079's One Year War against Earth.

What the Zeon leaders don't know is that Char's real name is Caspar Lem Daikun. He is the son of the murdered politician and founder of the Newtype philosophy, Zeon Zum Daikun, and he is only fighting on their side to find the best opportunity to wipe out his father's killers—the ruling family of the Duchy, the Zabis. Char grows up vowing revenge on the Zabi family who killed his father and stole his philosophy and power base to create the Duchy of Zeon, which has become the leading colonial power in the struggle for freedom from Earth government. To gain his revenge, the young man must win the trust of his enemy and use their own power against them.

Char begins his lifelong habit of concealing his true self. Disguising himself by scarring his face, he also wears a mask, both physically and emotionally, for most of the *Mobile Suit Gundam* manga and TV series. Estranged from his sister Artesia Som Daikun, who fights on the Earth side as Sayla Mass, he has complex relationships with women due to his inability to take off his emotional mask and his iron-willed determination to subordinate every other instinct to his cause. He ingratiates himself with the Zabi clan by appearing to be their loyal retainer; the youngest son, likable and talented Garma Zabi, becomes his only close friend, setting a terrible price on his revenge. He kills the Zabis, starting with Garma.

His struggle with Earth pilot Amuro Ray replaces his quest for revenge and becomes one of the defining elements of his life. He also pursues his father's dream of freedom for the colonies. He loses his beloved, Lala Sun, who is killed when she comes between him and Amuro in battle, yet he changes sides to work alongside Amuro as they fight a common adversary. At various points in the epic *Mobile Suit Gundam* saga, he also uses the aliases Quattro Bagina and Edward Mass. He finally claims his political birthright, appearing openly as Daikun's heir, and sets out to free the space colonies.

Char's relationship with Amuro is one of *Gundam*'s most powerful elements and a major reason for the series' popularity. The pair are doppelgangers—one with a dysfunctional family, the other haunted by the loss of everything he loved. Amuro replaces his family with his mobile suit and the bonds of friendship forged in war; Char replaces his with his father's dream and his own mission of revenge. He keeps almost everyone at a safe distance, and the few who begin to get closer die. Amuro reluctantly admires Char's charisma, elegance, intelligence, and iron will, but he hates the means Char employs, and his admiration is tinged with envy and resentment, like any young man struggling towards maturity and confronted with an alpha male. Char, never entirely sure he is worthy to fill his father's shoes, admires Amuro's abilities as a pilot and the innocence he himself has lost forever.

Their ultimate fate is fixed before they ever meet; these two could have been elder and younger brother, but through accidents of birth and war, spend most of their relationship trying to annihilate each other. In the end, in a gesture of Arthurian grandeur, they turn their final battle to the death into a sacrifice for the survival of Earth.

Char was so hugely popular with both male and female fans that he became a series

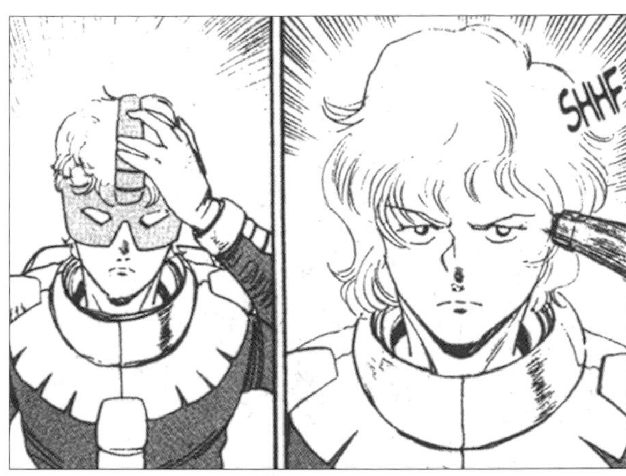

Char Aznable: genius pilot, born leader, heir to a weighty political tradition.

stereotype. The charismatic, elegant, driven antihero with his own moral imperatives crops up again and again. From Anavel Gato to Zechs Merquise, other characters have played facets of the original in the many byways of the *Gundam* universe. Yoshiyuki Tomino is the "father of *Gundam*" and created the characters and storyline. Kazuhisa Kondo and Yoshikozu Yashkiko's manga is published in English by Viz as *Gundam: The Origin*. It also exists in novel form (translated by Frederik L. Schodt, available from Del Rey) and there are countless items of merchandise, including computer games, cosplay outfits, stationery, watches, and model kits. One of Japan's most successful anime magazines, *Newtype*, was named from the series, with Tomino's blessing, and is also now available in the United States in an English-language version.

of the most callous criminals in Japan, but that doesn't save him from the trials of everyday life. It's not the easiest thing in the world to juggle school exams, family squabbles, and unsympathetic friends with violent criminals, the random nature of his powers, and the even more random and confusing relationship he has with Ryoko. He has to grow up faster than any boy should, and yet, thanks to the nature of his peculiar gifts, the only person he can really talk to is a taciturn, driven girl-cop whose need to bring the guilty to book blinds her to the fact that the task is doing irrevocable damage to young Eiji's mind. One of the most popular series that has ever been published by *Shonen Magazine*, Masashi Asaki and Yuma Ando's *Psychometrer Eiji* became an instant success when it was first published in 2000, and has since gone on to spawn a TV series, as well as an innovative console game for the Sony PSOne.

BAD [2001]

Miwa Shirow's debut action-comedy *Dogs* is the story of four people who make their living as assassins, couriers, or whatever brings in some cash, on the outside edge of society in a violent and disengaged world. The art is often beautiful, occasionally infuriatingly basic, but always lively, and the dialogue cracks along at a good pace and the characters are engaging. Bad is a nicotine-addicted one-eyed hustler, tall, young, long-haired, and skinny, and very unlucky. He makes his living selling information at inflated prices, but when times are hard he takes on minor commissions—spying on adulterous spouses, rescuing lost cats—and he gets into serious trouble when he accidentally finds the Don of the local West Side mafia gang *in flagrante delicto* with a young S&M boytoy—and takes pictures. He's rescued by mild-mannered middle-aged assassin Mihail, who has come out of retirement after the woman he loved was murdered. It's only a temporary stay of execution, however. Holed up in the Buon Viaggio bar with Mihail, knife-tongued owner Kiri, and Mimi, he's hunted by the Don's hitmen, who are convinced he's working for the rival East Side family. Don't miss the scene where Mihail takes down the West Side hitmen with a slightly stale French bread stick and a plate. Bad sometimes works with ice-cool punk Haine Rammsteiner (named for the artist's favorite German band, Rammstein), an abandoned genetic experiment who is pursued by his past. The fourth "Dog" is Naoto, the so-called "blade maiden." Unfortunately the four stories, serialized in *Ultra Jump*, are left hanging, as only one volume has been completed so far and there is no translation as yet. Shirow also publishes fanzines.

BAKABON [1967]

The schoolboy antihero of Fujio Akatsuka's 1967 series *Tensai Bakabon (Genius Idiot)* is a dim junior high-school kid who lives with his wacky father and their mangy, aggressive cat Nyarome. Their everyday adventures frequently spin off from the irreverent into the downright surreal; American burlesque was one of Akatsuka's main influences, and he numbers Charlie Chaplin and Jerry Lewis among his idols.

BEAN BANDIT [1989]

Also known as Rolling Bean or the Roadbuster, Bean Bandit is one of the best driver/couriers in the business—if your business is moving slightly unusual goods outside strictly legal channels. A tall, casually dressed, laid-back guy in his twenties, Bean is a guy whose heart is in the right place; he won't use violence unless it's strictly necessary, and doesn't like involving innocent parties in any business he deals with, even if this means losing money or risking his own life. In other words, like many a manga antihero, he's not really bad, he's just drawn that way. He made his first appearance in the video anime *Riding Bean*, but rights disputes meant the title couldn't be developed further. This led creator Kenichi Sonoda to recycle some of the characters, including his hero, for the 1991 *Comic Afternoon* manga *Gunsmith Cats*. The emphasis shifted to Bean's *Riding Bean* business partner Rally Vincent, reworked into a new character and given her own female sidekick, and the Bandit became a walk-on figure with cameo appearances in the manga, though not in the later *Gunsmith Cats* anime series.

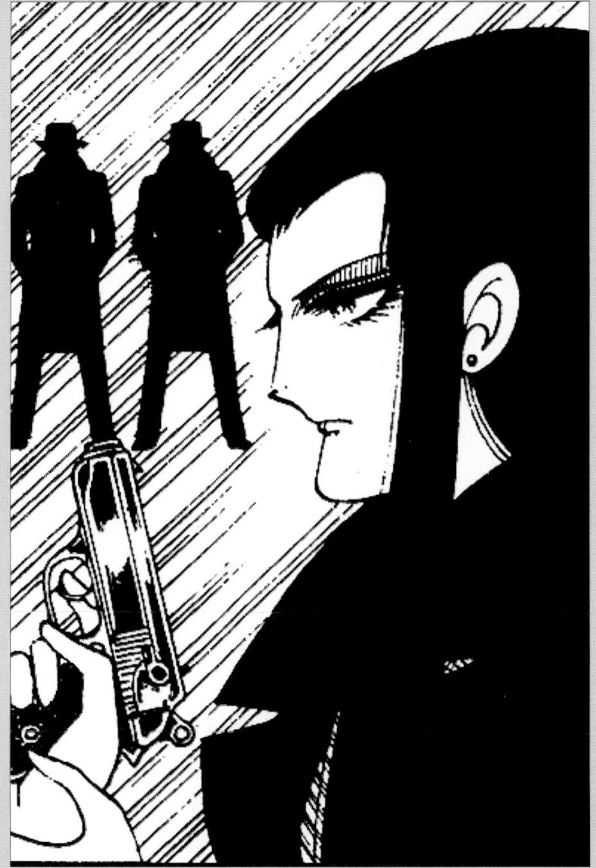

Jack of all trades: Bankolan is licensed to thrill.

JACK BARBAROSSA BANKOLAN [1978]

Pataliro! by Mineo Maya started running in *Hana to Yume* in 1978. The title character, brat prince Pataliro of the tiny island kingdom of Marinera, is the eighth ruler of that name, but despite possessing superpowers he's still an obnoxious little kid who needs a bodyguard, nursemaid, and trusted adviser rolled into one. The island's main industry—diamond trading—makes it even more important to get someone sensible and reliable for the job. Enter Jack Bankolan, a former British agent with his own double-0 prefix and a mane of sleek, thigh-length black hair. The running joke of the manga and series is that this 007 is gay, and the foes he faces usually include a gorgeous man. His long-term love is the beautiful teenage assassin Mariahi, a German redhead with a most un-Germanic temper. The manga was animated for TV in 1982, with a movie spin off the following year.

ODEL BERNETT [1995]

MS Gundam Wing: The Last Outpost (G-Unit) by Koichi Tokita, in English from Tokyopop, is a spin off from the Wing universe, itself one of three "alternative universe" Gundam stories created by rights holders Sunrise to celebrate the series' fifteenth anniversary and draw more fans into the web of mobile suit addiction. The year is AC 195, and the war between the Organization of Zodiac (OZ) and the United Earth Sphere Alliance is raging. On remote asteroid colony MO-V, two brothers train to help keep the peace if possible and defend their home if necessary, as mobile suit pilots. Older brother of Odin Bernett, Odel is his sibling's role model and rival as a Germinass (aka G-Unit) pilot, but believes Odin will one day outdo him. In a dangerous situation, he saves his brother's life and seems to die, but is actually saved and brainwashed into fighting against all he believes in as masked pilot Silver Crown, a new member of the renegade OZ pilot group the Stardust Knights. When it turns out that a secret military organization, OZ Prize, has been manipulating events, the Knights finally join the MO-V crew in fighting the corrupt factions who have taken control of OZ, and the brothers are united once more. The manga version appeared in *Comoc Bon-Bon* in 1988.

BUAKU [1988]

Dominion was the first professional manga by Masamune "*Ghost in the Shell*" Shirow, appearing in *Comi-Comi* in 1988 and animated in the same year. Displaying a comic talent that goes into hiding in his later work, Shirow sets his story around a police unit in a future city, but focuses more on slapstick than slice-of-life drama or science fiction. Newport City, an artificial island in Tokyo Bay, is a bio-engineered, overcrowded hell by 2010. The atmosphere is choked with pollution and the people are beset by high-tech crime. The gung-ho guns of the Tank Police are pitted against rogue android Buaku, a short, fat, unprepossessing humanoid with two of the most ravishing sidekicks around in the Puma Twins, Anna and Uni, a two-kitten crime wave.

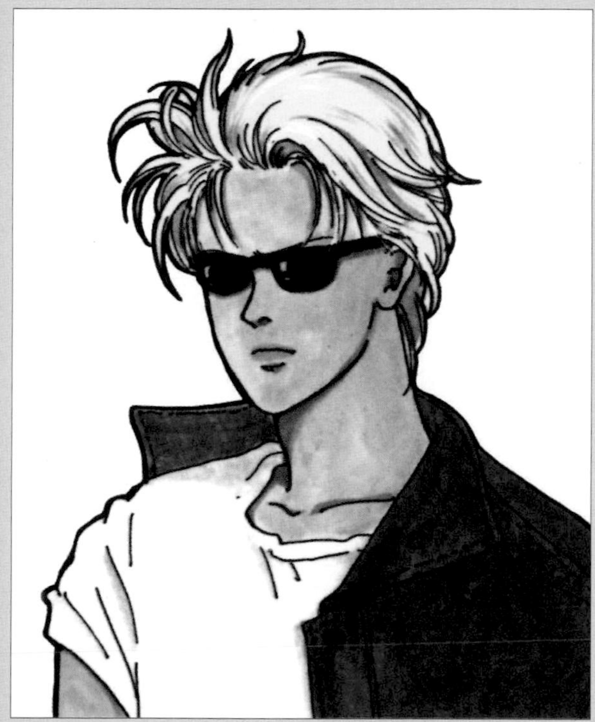

Cool kid Ash Lynx is looking for answers in a tense tale of drugs and corruption on America's mean streets.

Even though *Dominion* is funnier than *Blade Runner*, the influences are obvious. Buaku's motives, like Roy Batty's, are not all bad: he's using crime to search for information about his creator, and to try to find a way to combat the terrifying pollution of his world. An alternate-reality story in *Comic Gaia* in 1992 left Buaku out, but brought back the scantily clad, generously curved Puma girls.

ASH LYNX a.k.a. ASLAN CALLENREESE

[1977]

Akimi Yoshida's *Banana Fish* exploded the myth that girls only wanted cute comics. First serialized in May 1985 in *Bessatsu Shojo Comic*, it ran for ten years. Bad-boy hero Ash Lynx was partly modelled on River Phoenix. His big brother Griffin Callenreese went psycho in Vietnam; the only words he can utter are "banana fish". J. D. Salinger's short story *A Perfect Day For Bananafish*, about a Vietnam vet's suicide, appeared in the *New Yorker* magazine in 1948 and is the key to Yoshida's manga, in which Ash struggles to understand Griffin's fate. By 1985, Ash has changed his name and is the favorite boytoy of a New York mob leader, using his looks as leverage to gain a little independence in a brutal world. He runs his own little patch of the Big Apple. A dying man he finds in the street gives him a locket, an address, and the same words he heard from his brother—banana fish. Ash sets out to find the drug that took his brother's sanity and uncovers a conspiracy to spread it further. He hooks up with Japanese reporter Eiji Okumura and photographer Shinichi Ibe, working on a feature on street kids. Streetwise Ash and unworldly Eiji fall for each other, but mob boss Dino Gorzine, Ash's sugar daddy, is also after banana fish. Taking on Gorzine puts Ash and his friends in danger, and his violent world repels Eiji. Ash finally understands the mystery of banana fish and avenges his brother, but a happy ending with Eiji is snatched away at the last minute when he is stabbed. *Banana Fish* is still in print in Japan. The English translation was first serialized in December of 1997 in Viz's *Pulp* magazine. Yoshida has featured the younger Ash and Eiji in several short comics.

COBRA [1977]

A rough diamond whose mood can swing from the gentlemanly to the truly sociopathic, Cobra was created as the alter-ego of his author, Buichi Terasawa, and originally appeared in print in *Shuiesha's Weekly Jump* in 1977. Taking advantage of the way in which characters such as Lupin III—originally designed for an adult audience—were becoming popular in the teenage marketplace, Terasawa caused something of a stir when the cigar-chomping, womanizing and, at times, thoroughly brutal Cobra joined the *Jump* ranks. Cobra's appeal lay in the fact that Terasawa understood and shared the aspirations of his young readership. All teenagers secretly believe that under their nerdy everyday exteriors hide muscular wild men who combine an ability to kick enemy ass all day and party all night with a charm no woman can resist. Cobra embodies their dream, because his "ordinary" life turns out to be just that—as salaryman Mr. Johnson, he buys a twenty-fourth century virtual vacation as a space pirate from the Trip Movie Corporation, and finds it triggers the suppressed memories that unleash his true

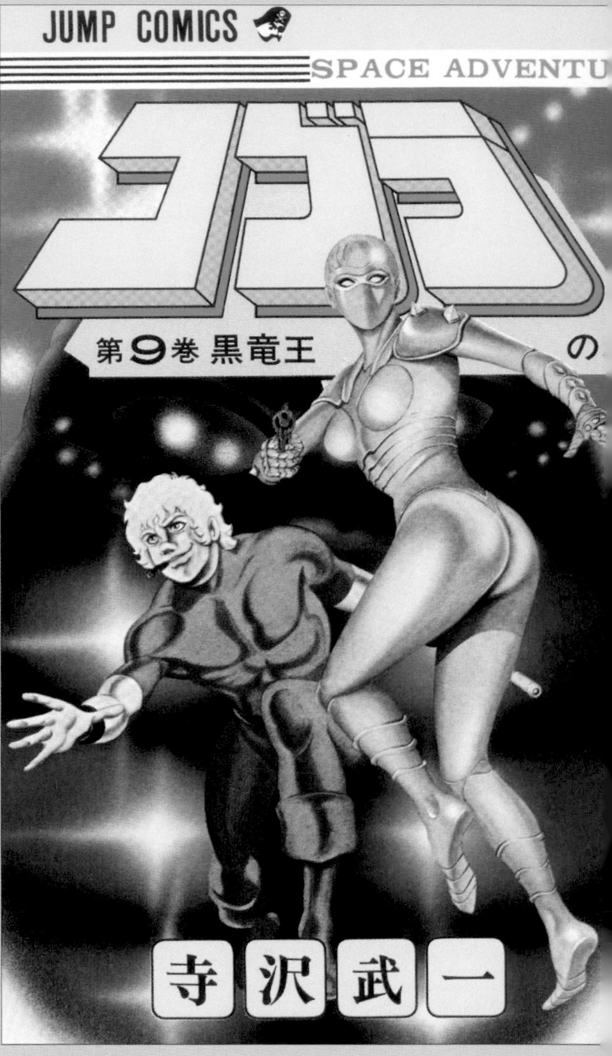

Cobra and his devoted android Lady: sociopath meets sexaroid in Terasawa's space opera romp.

self. Long before *Total Recall* he finds the process sets his true identity free to resume the life of danger and adventure he tried to escape when things got too hot. To complete the young science-fiction fan's identification process, he turns out to have a starship and a sexy robot sidekick. The steel-skinned Lady, like all Buichi Terasawa's females, combines a nymphomaniac brand of eye candy with the appealing loyalty of a sister or best mate, providing a constantly loyal backup to Cobra. Apart from a roguish bad-boy charm, he has the ability to dispatch evil-doers with his infamous Psycannon, a mentally powered weapon that is built into his arm. However, unlike many of the "adolescent fantasy" characters which were popular in the manga of the 1970s and 80s, *Cobra* is still going strong in Japan, with Shuiesha currently carrying the latest incarnation of the series, in the form of *Space Adventure Cobra: Magic Doll*. *Cobra* has also been brought to life in a big-screen animated feature and an animated TV series.

COUNT D [1997]

Count D's pet shop runs on a very simple principle: he will sell you the perfect pet to suit all your needs, and at a very reasonable price to boot, but his wares all come with a strict contract regarding their care—which is as much about the safety of the new owners as it is about the welfare of the pets. Matsuri Akino's manga from *Mitzi Comics DX* clearly takes its lead from *Gremlins*, but Count D's attitudes to his charges and clients gives his character a twist which makes him as uncomfortable as he is sympathetic. He really does care for his creatures (whether a simple puppy, a mermaid, or a flesh-eating bunny) and desires that his patrons learn the appropriate lessons from their purchases (after all, a dead customer is ultimately a failure for the Count). But his willingness to allow people to walk relatively blindly into what can quickly become life or death situations conflicts with his earnest desire to see his patrons admit their failings to themselves. Behind that seemingly callous, elegantly painted exterior, the Count is just a fey Faustian marshmallow. Leon Orcut, a loud-mouthed, macho cop trying to keep the law in the American city where the Count has set up store in Chinatown, is baffled and bemused by the strange young man who appears able to deal out justice in areas where the law cannot go. The manga's successful twelve-volume run makes the planned four-episodes-only animated version of 1999 something of a puzzle.

ES [2003]

Central character of Fuyumi Soryo's *Eternal Sabbath*, ES is a hacker—but he hacks people's consciousness. He can enter someone's head, read the data it contains, and modify that data temporarily—or permanently. He can make himself appear as anyone to anyone—a close friend, a dead relative—and they won't know they've been hacked. Soryo's manga combines the horror genre with mystery and psychological thrills.

THE FUMOON [1951]

The Fumoon are a race of neo-humans, a new species of life who have evolved out of the irradiated wasteland left in the aftermath of a cataclysmic atomic war in Earth's not-too-distant future. Ethereal and brilliant, the Fumoon detect a large cloud of gas moving inexorably through space towards the earth and hatch a plan to save a small number of biddable humans to begin a new life on a Fumoon-administered sanctuary world. Though clearly taking its lead from *The Shape of Things to Come*—as much from William C. Menzies' 1936 film version as from H.G. Wells' original novel—Osamu Tezuka's treatment of the idea in his manga *Next World (Kurubeki Sekai)* creates a story that is very different from the source. The final volume of his great science fiction trilogy, it ends more optimistically than *Lost World* and *Metropolis*, but still sounds a warning note.

The story parodies the Cold War between the United States and Soviet Russia and its wider political impact, but the Fumoon themselves could also stand for the occupation forces of the USA, who are so completely convinced of the rightness of their cause, of the inevitability of Earth's destruction, that they are willing to disregard mankind's concerns about the dangers involved. This is made easier when the antagonists in the original nuclear conflict—the Star State and the Uran Alliance—begin to protest violently about the rescue plan, only to have their would-be saviors disregard their concerns.

The Fumoon are naïve in some ways, callous in others, and are written by Tezuka with a very childlike attitude to right and wrong—not evil in intent, but utterly convinced of their own superiority in all things, which they attribute to their evolved nature and their rise from mankind's ruin. Only the Fumoon's contact with people such as Dr. Yamadono (who independently discovers the Fumoon and the approach of the deadly gas cloud), the Japanese detective Higeoyaji (played by Old Man Mustache), and his regular assistant, nephew Kenichi, has any chance of changing their views.

Kenichi is particularly important in this regard as he develops a relationship with the Fumoon Rokoko; in the 1980 animated TV version, this relationship was so central that Rokoko was renamed Fumoon, as if to represent her entire race.

The space Ark finally takes off, carrying the natives of a single village, and representatives of the two opposing sides find common ground as the dark gas envelops the Earth. However, contact with our solar system turns it to oxygen, saving the day and restating Tezuka's view that the Earth is a unique and irreplaceable planet whose people have a duty to keep it safe. The original version of the manga was more than 1,000 pages long, and Tezuka edited it for the Kodansha edition of his Collected Works to a 300-page version.

GANTZ [2000]

In downtown Tokyo, in the shadow of the great Tower, stands an unassuming block of apartments, brown with age and rust, slowly crumbling into the dirt of the city. Within that decaying block there is an apartment much like the rest but for one feature: a great black sphere which occupies the main room, occasionally issuing orders and weapons to confused-looking souls who turn up from nowhere. When cynical sixteen-year-old Kei Kuruno and his old school friend Masaru Kato are killed by a train while trying to rescue a drunk who has fallen onto the tracks, they awake in the room with the sphere, to be informed that it has given them a new life to use for its ends. The sphere is Gantz, title character of Hiroya Oku's *Young Jump* manga, master of an unusual defense network. Gantz's role is to protect Japan from alien invaders ranging from the strange Onion Alien to a breed of vampires, and it "rescues" those who would have died pointless deaths (suicides, accident victims, and so on) to wage its war for as long as they can survive, which is not usually very long. Only the fighters can see their alien opponents; the others around them seem completely ignorant of the war going on in the street. Gantz is no mere machine, mechanically carrying out the orders of some higher authority, but is possessed of a twisted personality and cruel intellect; he enjoys taunting his charges, knowing full well that their new (and brief) lives are lived entirely at his will. God, devil, government tool, or alien police officer, Gantz is both brutally efficient and calculatingly cruel to his minions—as if it is not enough that they know they are dead, he tells them that their worthless lives led to their selection for Gantz's program. Oku's art style is polished and pretty, but the story is violent and graphic. The long-running manga has an animated TV version.

GEIST [1986]

Geist is one of a corps of MDS (Most Dangerous Soldiers), chemically enhanced warriors employed by combatants on the planet Jerra to fight in the last stages of a generational conflict which has all but consumed the once green planet. He first appeared in *M.D. Geist (Sokiehi MD Geist)*, a made-for-video animation that spun off its own comic written and designed by acclaimed mecha designer Koichi Ohata, with art by American Tim Eldred. Geist's battle lust and martial prowess make him too dangerous for even that dangerous time and he is imprisoned in a cryo-stasis satellite as punishment for the sins of his makers. However, as always seems to be the case in such tales, the satellite eventually returns to the now totally war-ravaged planet and frees Geist to wage a one-man vendetta against the shattered remnants of the armies whom he sees as his betrayers.

His creators wanted a single-minded war machine, and got a sentient but crazed creature unconcerned about anything—or anyone—that does not bring him closer to his ultimate goal of bringing down the powers who isolated him in the first place. Geist is little more than a cipher for violence, making it impossible for the audience to latch onto the inner pain that is so crucial to the telling of a good revenge story. Even Geist's final endeavors to stop the firing of a weapon system that is primed to depopulate Jerra permanently cannot lift the character beyond two dimensions. Critics have often pondered the popularity of this piece of work in the United States and Europe. The animated originals quickly sank without trace in Japan (the sequel not withstanding) but, through the offices of U.S. Manga Corps, the translated version saw very high sales initially and even warranted the 1996 release of a director's cut—partly funded by *MD Geist*'s U.S. distributors—which more aptly sets up film for the second round. It seems more likely that these sales were boosted by people buying the video for want of anything better to purchase—*MD Geist* was released in a period of experimentation for U.S.-based anime and had few competitors for the consumer dollar.

GENOM [1987]

The evil corporation out to take over Neo-Tokyo by covert economic means started out in made-for-video animation *Bubblegum Crisis* before moving into print in Tony Takezaki's 1990 manga *A.D. Police*. Headed by CEO Quincy and his sidekick Mason, GENOM is a paradigm for growing distrust of corporate power in the 1980s. Senior executives are corrupt and vicious, and will go to any lengths to climb the corporate ladder, while the CEO himself sanctions the use of flawed and dangerous biotechnology to create rogue superweapons purely so as to destabilize society enough for GENOM to increase its control. Sadly, although even rich and well-connected individuals can sometimes be brought to book for their crimes, it's much harder to dismantle the corrupt corporate culture that pervades both the anime and the manga. It's hardly surprising that the disaffected teenagers who have grown up reading this and similar tales of big business working against the little man are no longer flocking to become foot solders in Japan's business army.

DORIAN RED GLORIA

[1979]

The Earl of Gloria is a tall, blond, gorgeous British aristocrat, twenty years old, incredibly rich, openly gay, and a true art lover. He could buy any picture he wants, but that would be dull; so he moonlights as Eroica, Europe's most wanted art thief, and flirts with a seemingly unattainable lover—the police chief sent to trap him. Yasuko Aioke's manga *From Eroica With Love (Eroica Yori Wo Ai Komete)* pits the cool, calm hedonist Dorian against NATO intelligence's finest, Major Klaus Heinz von dem Eberbach, a by-the-book bureaucrat who's ultra-conservative even by German

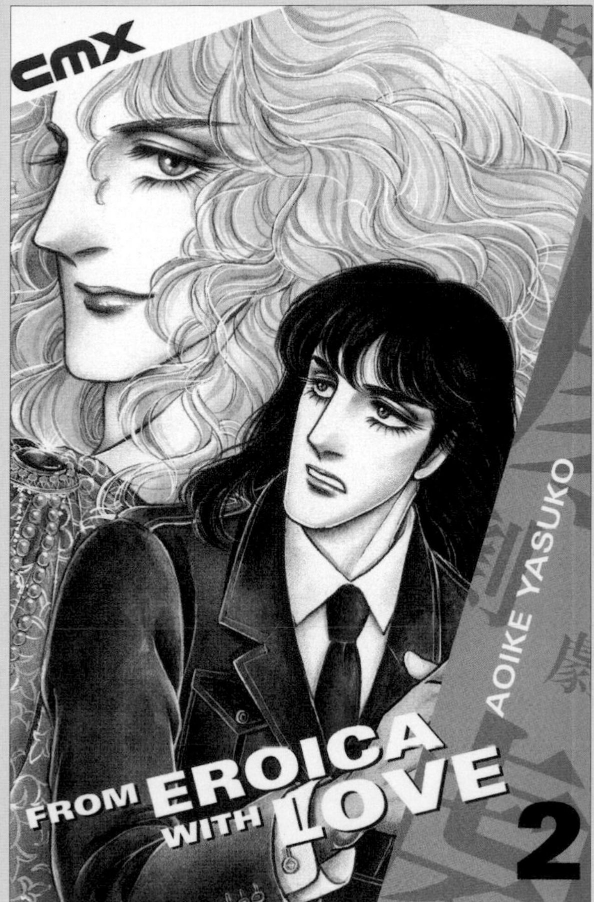

Dorian has at least one cop on the run as the Major falls for his fascinating quarry.

standards. When Dorian makes romantic advances, the major is at once repelled and fascinated. Things get even more complicated when three teenage friends, with superpowers courtesy of an old man they met on a trip to Peru, become embroiled in trying to save the art treasures of Europe from Eroica's grasp—and save their leader, stunning eighteen-year-old genius Caesar Gabriel, from Dorian's. Caesar and art student Sugar Plum, sixteen, are both fascinated by the beautiful, gifted, and charismatic nobleman, but nineteen-year-old stuntman Leopard Solid, a more down-to-earth type, helps keep them grounded as they try to evade Dorian and his pack of hot young male employees. A story like this would have been a near-impossible sell in America in the 1970s and 1980s, but in Japan, tales of gay love are commonplace in manga, written for and by young women. *Eroica* still has a huge fan following in supposedly conservative Japan; twenty-five years after its creation, it's finally being published in English on DC's CMX imprint.

GREY [1985]

As Yoshihisa Tagami's Shonen Captain manga *Grey: Digital Target* opens, title character Grey, or "Grey Death TFA-404953-C" to give him his professional name, has just lost the love of his life, Lips, and been separated from his only other friend, his former squad commander Red. A lost soul within a decaying society which recognizes only three classes of humanity—plebs, soldiers, and citizens—Grey has fixated on becoming the ultimate soldier and earning enough credit with his employers to achieve the position of citizen, in order to put the questions he has concerning the war to those he believes call the shots. Soldiers get 30 credits per kill, and it takes 1,000 credits to advance one rank; the ranks run from F to A. Grey has reached rank C by the opening of the story—a feat achieved in only thirteen battles. He has earned his "God of Death" tag through his impressive kill rate.

Grey's single-minded progress is interrupted when he meets Nova, a woman who not only reminds him of Lips, but also possesses revolutionary tendencies and begins inspiring Grey towards more direct action against the leaders of the war. As time goes by, and their relationship develops, Grey's attitude towards the war is hardened further by his contact with the various towns that are scattered through the land and their "Little Mama" computers which run the enclaves for "Big Mana"—the main computer in the Citizens' City. His main question, which drives him to seek out the resistance movement, is why each town has a distinctive technology level (from near medieval to modern), when each town's Little Mama can produce anything, of any tech level, for the citizenry. His search for the resistance ultimately reveals an organization that is as corrupt and self serving as the government—both have formed a very successful semi-symbiotic relationship, with each using the other to justify the status quo. By the end of the story, Grey's disillusionment is complete, which makes his journey to salvation seem all the more poignant. The death of Nova and the cataclysmic final battle are not shown in the 1987 animated version.

GUTS [1995]

Raised from childhood as a warrior, Guts is the physical embodiment of carnage, bloodlust, and vengeance—and he certainly fits the role-playing-game bill, with his prosthetic left arm and the huge sword that helped earn him the nickname "Slayer of a Hundred" and "Black Swordsman." But Guts is no mere cipher, even though Kentaro Miura's *Berserk (Kenpu Dengi Berserk/Sword Wind Chronicle Berserk)* is one of the most gore-stained mainstream manga to have been published in English.

The actions which this fighting machine takes throughout the story are, if not always successful from Guts' point of view, carefully and cleverly calculated to get the desired response from the reader. Guts is essentially on a journey of salvation through his knight-punk universe, taking him from the ruin of his own dark birth to a final confrontation with himself. The early chapters of the manga cover Guts' life before taking up the mantle of the Black Swordsman, and form the basis for the animated TV series that followed in 1997. Starting out as a mercenary in the Company of the Hawk, trying to uncover a political intrigue behind the current war, Guts is forced to fight his leader, Griffiths, who later rapes both the king's daughter and Guts' lover Casca. When Griffiths is jailed after the first rape, his team joins forces to try and bust him out, only to learn that he is in the pay of a race of interdimensional beings who demand human sacrifice. Losing an eye and his left arm in the battles that follow, and seeing his leader turned into an alien creature named Femto, Guts is so determined on revenge that he transcends death and sets out to hunt down God Hand, opening the door for an ongoing series of ever more gory battles. A hero with a magical wound that will not heal, Guts has links back to Western medieval legend; Miura also nods to his science-fiction influences, naming his baddies after modern legends like *Slan* and the *Boskone of Lensman*. Guts can be seen as the embodiment of the force of change, with his actions as the catalyst that set those around him on new paths: this is most evident in his relationships with Griffiths who was turned towards God Hand by his reactions to his moody, determined subordinate, and Casca. He's not bad, but he may be mad and he's definitely dangerous to know.

HANAO [1991]

Central character of *Flower Man (Hanaotoko)* by Taiyo Matsumoto, Hanao is not the best of fathers, even by the fairly relaxed standards of Japanese society. Estranged from his family, he has only rarely spent time with his son Shigeo, until the teenager is unceremoniously dumped on his father one summer holiday. While both Hanao and Shigeo initially resent having to compromise their lifestyles to accommodate the desires of the other, as the story progresses, father and son grow towards a true understanding of each other and, just as Hanao's wife planned, develop a relationship which had been impossible before. Hanao is the classic man-child, while Shigeo is the epitome of what "middle Japan" sees as the perfect office drone—this role reversal, switching the poles of the usual age gap, is what makes the story, and Hanao, so endearing. Hanao can be thoughtless, callous, and completely self-centered, but, as Shigeo discovers, this is largely due to the "old man's" absolute dedication to his dreams—expressed through a desire to play for the Tokyo Giants—and the freedom that comes with the childlike optimism of those thoughts. The relationship between father and son is also reflected in the worlds in which each have lived up the start of the story, with Shigeo growing up in the quiet refinement of a Tokyo suburb, set against the small town existence of his father. As the story progresses, we see Shigeo being drawn ever closer to his roots (from transferring to Hanao's old school to joining him on the baseball ground) as Matsumoto develops his ultimate theme—that rebelliousness and devotion to dreams, however unlikely, are not always negative social forces. Hanao's story is a common one in Japan these days, as a generation of geeky dreamers grow past their thirties and try to come to terms with a society that values conformity through their own quiet little rebellions.

HENRIETTA [2001]

The setting is Italy, the present day. Henrietta lost her family—mother, father, and three siblings—and almost died herself in a brutal assault. She was taken in by the Social Welfare Agency, but this is only a front for a sinister government body that has turned her into a cyborg and brainwashed her to kill on command. Each assassin is assigned a handler and the pair is called "fratello"—siblings. A drug called Conditioning keeps them in control. Completely devoted to her handler Guiseppe, who treats her like a younger sister or even a daughter, Henrietta is only one of a group of girls trained as assassins in Yu Aida's manga *Gunslinger Girl*. The stories focus on the conflict between the remnants of human feeling and the brainwashing process, as well as the relationships between the girls and their handlers. The manga is in English from ADV.

SHIRO HOJO [1999]

Makoto Tateno's *Hana to Yume* manga *Howl at the Moon (Tsuki no Howl)* introduces werewolf Hojo as a senior classman in high school with designs on basketball hunk Kakeru. The younger guy has a cute girlfriend and plenty of friends, but lately he's been dreaming of wolves and feeling restless. Hojo introduces himself and tells Kakeru they have a lot in common—they're both werewolves. At first reluctant to believe it, Kakeru is forced to accept his heritage by the changes in his own body, but he doesn't want to kill and sets out to find a way to live with his new abilities.

KYOYA IIDA [2000]

On the surface, *Jiraishin* by Tsutomu Takahashi is a hard-boiled crime drama set in and around Japan's neon underworld, Shinjuku, where hard-bitten Detective Inspector Iida's job involves him with all the worst that Japan lets filter down to this "human waste dump." Written in a fragmented style that calls to mind the best dramatic manga of the 1970s, Jiraishin develops D.I. Iida's personality as much through the crimes he investigates as through his life outside work and this gives the already tough-seeming character an added level of complexity that makes him all the more human—much as is the case with Executioner Asa. Though not as one-dimensional as the opening chapter makes him seem, the most interesting aspect about Iida's development through the series is the way Takahashi forces him to empathize, if only in a limited way initially, with the characters he comes across in his work life—especially as he is very much a loner due in part to his father's suicide while in the same job. His crushed inner self is unintentionally nurtured by those he meets; people such as Tsuyoshi Yamaki, his first partner, who wants to become a better policeman and more like Iida, but is executed by the Chinese mob; Eriko Aizawa, a linguist who is the opposite of Iida professionally, in that she is openly compassionate and sympathetic to people; or Captain Narita, head of Shinjuku Homicide Division and the oldest friend of Iida's late father. Each in his or her own way wants to save the young man from himself; Iida seemingly has no wish to be saved, but through the various trials of life at Shinjuku Homicide Division, this is finally achieved despite himself.

SHINJI IKARI [1995]

"The man who sold the world" is not an easy title to live with. *Neon Genesis Evangelion*, Gainax and Yoshiyuki Sadamoto's epic evangelical apocalypse, appeared in manga form in February 1995, eight months before the TV debut that shook the anime world. *Eva*, as its fans call it, is a homage to all the animated giant robot sagas of the "classical" era (1970s through 1980s) and its characters and situations have much in common with those shows.

Alienated, withdrawn teenager Shinji starts out as a mildly deranged take on teen pilot Amuro Ray, though considerably more passive, and goes downhill fast. He is more than a Gundam parody, but the similarities between him and Amuro make what happens to him as the show develops all the more resonant. The Messianic nature of the conflict with the angels and the roles that these innocent children play in it—especially Shinji himself, forced into the role of a savior who is as damaged as his followers—are all focused on the cataclysmic event known as the Third Impact. This is intended to grant humanity rebirth. However, like the rebirth in Toshio Maeda's *Legend of the Overfiend*, this renewal

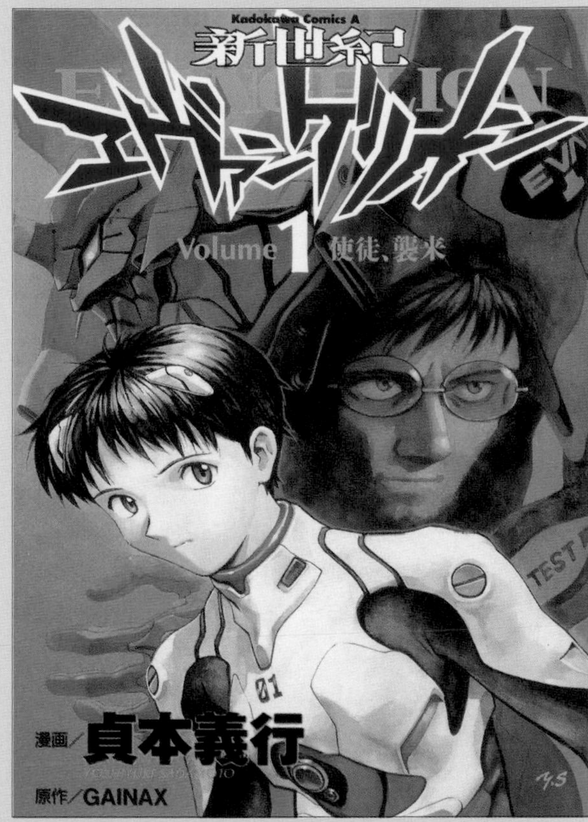

Sins of the fathers: Shinji inherits the whirlwind in *Evangelion*.

extorts a high price, and mankind has not been asked if it wants to pay. Some, like Shinji's father, will use any means to oppose it. At the turn of the millennium, the threat materialized as a strike on Antarctica, wiping out half the Earth's population. To avoid mass panic, it was attributed to a meteorite. Since

KEN KUROSAWA [1998]

KEN LIVES ON THE less angelic side of the City of Angels. Orphaned at an early age with his kid sister Mariko to take care of, the teenager they call the "karate monkey" needed his martial arts skills as well as plenty of cunning to survive in Los Angeles. Now he's the bodyguard of a local block boss. Caught in the crossfire of a gang war on his way home to his nine-year-old sister with a gift for her birthday, he's burned to death in a car-bomb attack. Then he wakes up to find a fat guy with a blue face is offering to enroll him in the armies of Hell. Violator is no clown, even though he claims that name; as fans of the American *Spawn* saga will know, he's a recruiting agent for the Dark Lord Malebolgia. Ken can use his fighting skills as an officer in the army of the dead to fight against the hordes of Heaven.

It's not the best gig he's ever been offered, but this way he can return to Earth to look after his sister. He accepts, and becomes one of the *Shadows of Spawn* in a manga published by Media Works in Japan to tie in with the launch of the animated TV series devoted to Todd MacFarlane's all-American antihero.

As a servant of Hell, Ken gets an assistant—a tiny but phenomenally cute fairy called Beezlebub, affectionately known as Bee to her boss. He also soon attracts the not altogether unwelcome attention of sexy freelance Hellspawn-hunter Michaela, a Japanese version of MacFarlane's Angela. Michaela dresses like a pirate, obviously to blend in on the streets of LA, and will try anything to hunt Ken down, but can't quite bring herself to do anything nasty to him when she catches him. She ends up in an odd partnership with Ken, who, like his precursor Al Simmons, is soon trying to break the bonds of Hell, and fellow Spawn Zombie.

Still, the love of Ken's afterlife is undoubtedly Mariko, who is blissfully ignorant of her brother's new role. Growing up fast, at sixteen she is on track to fulfill her ambition and be an idol singer and actress—an all-round media star. She meets a charming guy named Harold Carter (undoubtedly a take on Tutankhamun-discoverer Howard Carter, whose profession he shares) and is offered the role of Cleopatra in his new Egyptian-inspired production. Carter plans a very limited run, one night only, but it should be a spectacular show, culminating in the leading lady's heart being cut out to enable him to transform into the living avatar of Anubis, Egyptian God of the Dead. Ken steps in to save his little sister by sending Carter to meet Anubis in person, but Mariko, who has no idea how short her run in the role was meant to be, sees Spawn killing the man who has always been charming and supportive to her. Not knowing this terrifying cloaked figure is her beloved elder brother, she views him as the personification of pure evil.

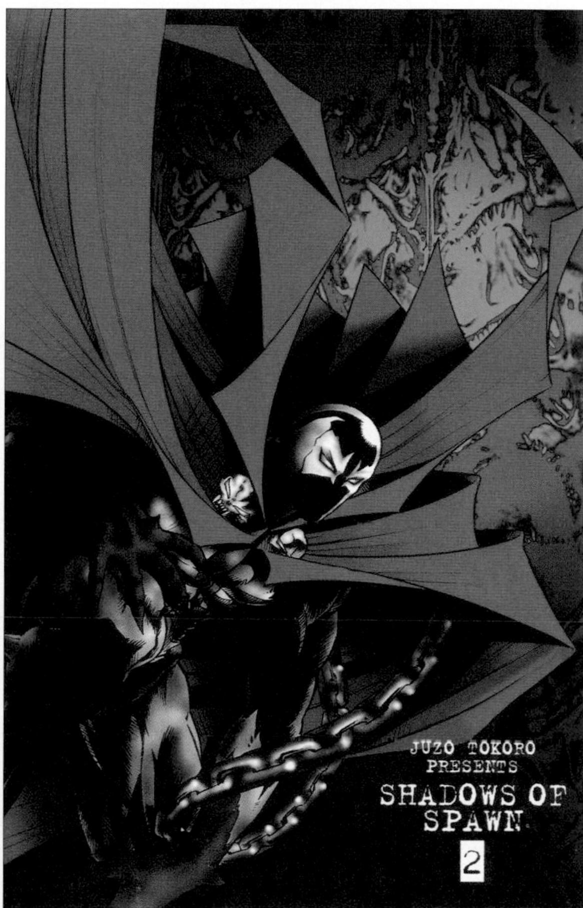

Manga Spawn: a Japanese take on the American war vet turned zombie fighter.

Mariko is in danger again when she meets one of her idols, the famous starlet Ellis. The admiring girl doesn't realize that to a woman in the entertainment industry who will never see twenty again, every pretty sixteen-year-old is a potential threat. She makes a deal with dark forces to keep her youth and see off her rivals, and when she transforms into a Medusa before Mariko's horrified eyes, big brother has to snap into action again.

Ken does get assignments that don't involve Mariko. When a secret military project uses "psychoplasm" to create artificial Hellspawn, it's obvious there will be trouble. One of the experimental subjects, Tremor II, escapes in LA. Tremor II first appeared in issue 46 of the American *Spawn*, so his inclusion neatly links Ken with MacFarlane's original, Al Simmons. He too is trying to save the one he loves, but he carries a terrible sense of guilt, feeling that he brings her nothing but trouble and grief.

The artist for the manga is Juzo Tokoro, born in 1961 in Shizuoka, who made his pro debut in 1985 in *Shonen* magazine with an offbeat strip about a young punk whose favorite pastime was studying. Strongly influenced by Japanese crime movies and the excesses of Quentin Tarantino, Tokoro loads up with a full magazine of manga tropes and steams into MacFarlane's universe with all the enthusiasm of a ram-raider. Ken's story interlocks with the *Spawn* universe as neatly as his merchandise, yet for all the so-called American setting, his world is as Japanese as Al Simmons' is American. Three volumes have been issued, and a French translation is available from Semic Manga. The manga is also available in Spain.

the death of Shinji's mother, his father had devoted himself to the top-secret NERV project, developing huge mobile suits—the EVA units—to use as weapons against a powerful alien threat. He only sent for his abandoned son when his original test pilot was injured and he needed to use the boy as a backup test subject.

The themes of abandonment, rejection, youth's lack of trust in authority, authority's lack of respect for anyone, and exploitation are tied together with a storyline that adapts the late-twentieth-century philosophy that you can create a more satisfactory family through friendships, setting up a series of dysfunctional but supportive relationships for Shinji in his new home. In the early stages of the story we see some possibility of Shinji as hero, beginning to come to terms with his abilities and even getting on, in a fashion, with his father. Then we are forced to watch, as helpless as Shinji himself, as his EVA wreaks havoc and kills Kawaru, his one and only true friend, who has joined the forces of the opposition to pilot one of their mighty Angel machines. All of the children of Eva are broken in some way, and it is this which binds them to each other. Shinji bears the extra burden of knowing that it is his own flesh and blood that is torturing them all, and this is made worse by the fact that both he and his father know that the soul of Shinji's mother resides inside EVA 01. Shinji's father has tortured those he loves and distorted his child's life, all in the name of wiping out the servants of the Almighty.

TOMA INABA [1995]

Sakura Diaries (Sakura Tsushin) is another sex comedy by U-Jin, but like all his erotic manga it has a serious core. Toma Inaba is a bumbling, good-natured, but fundamentally flawed young man from the country who has come to Tokyo to take (and fail) his university entrance examinations. In the big city he runs into his childhood playmate, cousin Urara, and falls head over heels in love with beautiful, intelligent Mieko Yotsuba. Toma, like a host of manga characters who have gone before him, is fixated on the wrong woman, who is only feigning interest in him, completely ignoring the affections of the girl with real feelings for him. But there is a little more to the story than that well-worn premise. U-Jin has woven in his usual sharp psychological observation. Seemingly sassy Urara has won her assertiveness the hard way, and easygoing slacker Toma has a well-concealed steel. In childhood, he risked his own life to save Urara from abuse, and this is the thread that binds them together and makes her determined to win him. Toma's character is written with a sympathy and pathos rare in erotic manga, the everyman without psychic powers, alien girlfriends, lovelorn robots, or mad family members offering support or lending interest. The manga, which first appeared in *Young Sunday* magazine, is much more well-crafted and entertaining than the anime version, with U-Jin's trademark polished, pretty artwork wrapping a story aimed at entertaining the average young male but still retaining something to offer the intelligent reader.

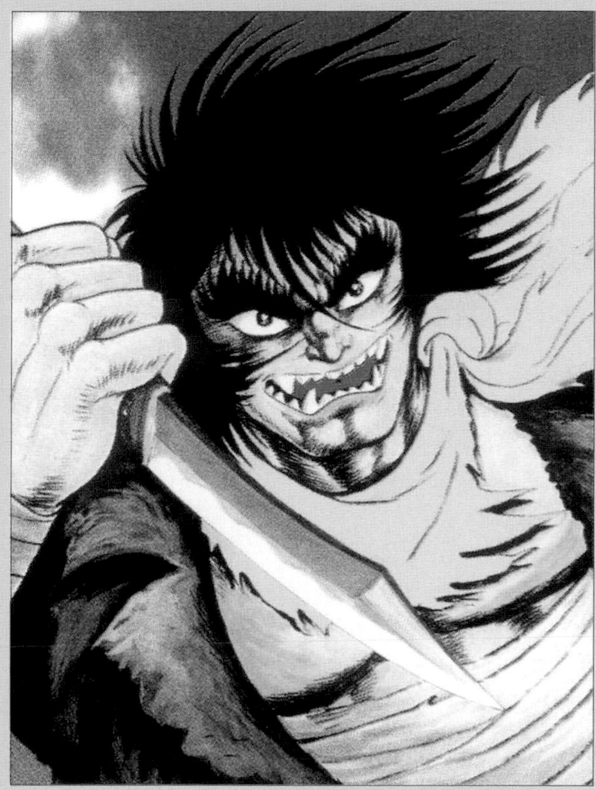

Nagai's man-mountain Violence Jack has a good heart, but uses messy methods.

VIOLENCE JACK [1973]

Jack is a seven-foot-tall mountain of muscle, dark-haired, dressed in rags, and armed with a 15-inch jackknife from which he takes his name. He has no scruples, and his morality is somewhat unconventional, but his heart is in the right place, on the side of the weak and helpless. He lives in a world devastated by a terrible earthquake, where civilization has broken down and warlords and gangs rule. Jack runs foul of the most powerful local warlord, Slum King, after raiding one of his upmarket restaurants to get food for some starving children, killing most of the well-to-do patrons in the process. Slum King vows revenge, and Jack sets out on a blood-soaked odyssey through the ruined world, showing that the earthquake was really the re-creation of the world after it was destroyed in the climactic last battle between Satan and Devilman. One of the most aptly named characters in manga, Jack is the hero of Nagai's most controversial work. Nine volumes long, it is a sequel to *Devilman* and contains guest appearances by many other Nagai characters, from Mazinger Z to Cutey Honey. His staff actually tried to persuade him to tone it down to avoid yet another run-in with the Japan Parent Teacher Association, to no avail. Nagai insisted that in a story where the only law is force and the strong rule the weak, violence and blood are necessary parts of the scenario.

MAXIMILIAN JENIUS [1981]

Though Max, as he is known to his friends, first appears in episode 8 of the 1981 anime series *Superdimensional Fortress Macross*, his manga incarnation comes in Haruhiko Mikimoto's

REINHART VON LOHENGRIMM [1982]

BORN INTO AN impecunious noble household on the fringes of the political authority of the Galactic Empire, motherless Reinhart Von Lohengrimm might have languished in obscurity as a junior officer from the ranks of the lesser gentry, had his drunken father not sold his adored older sister Anna-Rose to the emperor as a concubine, trading her honor and happiness for mere money and a few crumbs of imperial favour. In the best tradition of the Japanese antihero, Reinhart vows to overcome the forces that destroyed his life—he will bring down the imperial house of Goldenbaum from within, and purify the corrupt and venal political establishment, returning the empire to its original founder's Aryan dream of nobility and honor.

With his childhood neighbor and best friend Siegfried Kircheis, he joins the Imperial Navy. A war with the democratic Alliance of Independent Worlds has been dragging on for a century and a half, and gives ambitious young men on both sides a chance for advancement. The brilliant, gifted Reinhart shares his sister's dazzling good looks; the tall, slender young man with blond hair and icy blue eyes attracts the attention of many women, though his arrogance, selfishness, and cold determination repels others. He quickly shows his abilities and is promoted. Even in his new life, however, the shadow of his sister's disgrace looms over Reinhart. The emperor is enchanted with Anna-Rose. He has made her Countess Von Grunewald and will do anything to make her happy, except set her free. Ensuring that her little brother has a successful military career is the least he can do. The nobility attribute his rapid advance through the ranks to his "traveling under his sister's skirt," and he is dubbed the "Petticoat Admiral." Constant sniping and plotting hamper his tactical efforts and lead to the poaching of some of his most effective subordinates, while brainless, cowardly men get promoted far beyond their ability through the influence of their ancient noble families. All this makes Reinhart increasingly embittered. He gains many enemies and few friends. The more perceptive members of the imperial nobility admire his intelligence and courage, and, despite his icy savagery, see him as a possible savior of the noble old traditions on which the empire was founded. Throughout all their adventures, and in spite of his opposition to Reinhart's frequent coldness and brutality, Kircheis remains resolutely loyal to his childhood friend, and to the promise he made to Anna-Rose when she

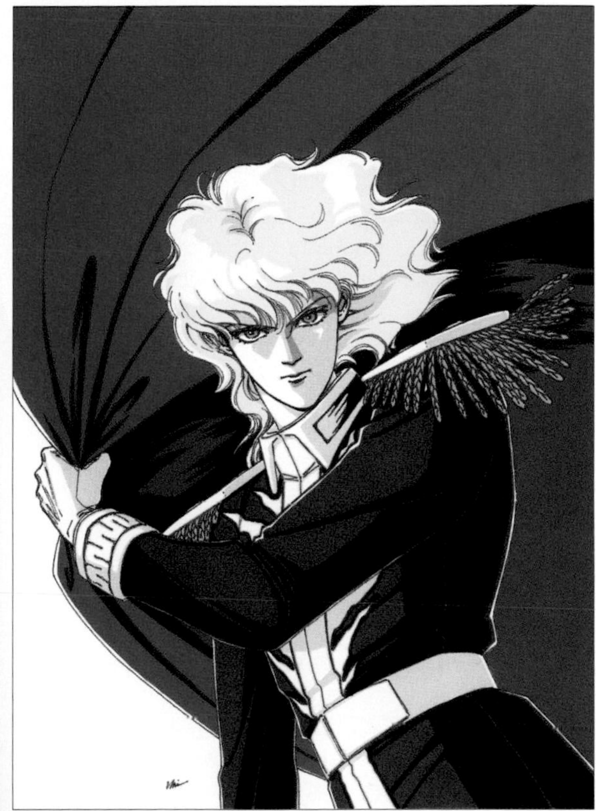

Aryan nightmare: Reinhart's empire is bought at the cost of those he loves most.

left for the Imperial Household that he would always look after her little brother.

Reinhart finally gains power over the whole Galactic Empire, with the old emperor who enslaved his sister replaced by a child ruler under his control. Yet his triumph does not bring him the fulfillment of his dreams. His enemies in the Establishment plan to assassinate him to prevent his taking power. Kircheis foils the assassination attempt by taking the bullet meant for Reinhart, and dies in his friend's arms. Then Anna-Rose tells her brother that she cannot condone his lust for revenge and all-consuming obsession with power.

Having lost the only two people he truly loved, Reinhart at first sinks into rage and despair, but he gradually understands how his life has been dominated and almost destroyed by his desire for retribution. As emperor, he has to find a purpose beyond the mere acquisition of power, and vows to use his abilities for a truly noble purpose, one that would make Kircheis and Anna-Rose proud—he makes a solemn oath to bring the century of war to an end.

At the same time, he also frees himself to form other relationships, and marries Hilde, one of the few noble-women at Court who truly understood his potential and was an honest friend.

Yoshiki Tanaka, one of Japan's leading pulp sf and fantasy authors, wrote eighteen novels, collectively entitled *Legend of Galactic Heroes (Ginga Eiya Densetsu)*, which spun off a manga series from *Chara Comics* with art by Katsumi Michihara, two video series totalling over 150 episodes, theatrical movies, and merchandise galore, plus a universe of fan fiction and innumerable costume fans who love to dress up in the operetta-elegant uniforms of the imperial high command.

Macross 7 Trash, a manga spun off the 1995 anime sequel *Macross 7*. But don't rush out looking for *Macross 1–6*; the "7" of the title refers to the seventh space colonization fleet, which Max commands, and possibly also to the seven lovely daughters of his marriage to alien fighter ace Milia.

Starting out as a teenage pilot in the ranks of the Earth forces, Max helped to fight off alien invasion and achieve peace for Earth during an attack by the giant Zentraedi in the early years of the twenty-first century. He met his wife, a beautiful but fiery pilot about ten times his size, in battle, but peace, plus a scientific process known as micronization, enabled them to marry. The first human-alien marriage was a big factor in helping to persuade both races to live together, but like many modern couples, the young Jeniuses found the weight of expectation and the demands of two careers too much to bear. Their careers still keep them in touch, with Max as captain of the Macross 7 Deep Space Colony Fleet fighting off alien vampire attackers the Protodevlin, and Milia as mayor of Macross 7 trying to keep the civilian population safe from both the enemy and the excesses of "friendly fire."

Max would love to get his wife back, but is unable to admit his own part in the breakdown of their marriage. He also has problems relating to his daughters, especially the youngest, pop singer Mylene, born just as their relationship was breaking up. He's never been good at public relations in general—his image with the civilian population is not good, largely due to public brawls with their beloved Mayor Milia, even though his troops love his heroic war record and willingness to get stuck in with the fighting, despite being top of the top brass. This helps his wife paint him to their daughters as a warmonger. To complicate matters further, he has another child, a son, the result of a fleeting affair. Shiba is the central character of *Macross 7 Trash*, but Max's adventures, and those of the rest of the Jenius family, have been depicted in their TV series, made-for-video animation, theatrical movies, computer games, and tons of merchandise.

JING [1995]

King of Bandits Jing by Yuichi Kumakura first appeared in *Kodansha's Bonbon Monthly*. Jing is often unfavorably compared to the king of all Japanese gentleman-thieves, Arsene Lupin III, but while Kumakura certainly draws on the classic Monkey Punch creation, this is somewhat unfair. Lupin III himself was not an entirely original creation, as the estate of Maurice LeBlanc (creator of the first *Arsene Lupin*) attempted to prove several times and the areas which Jing and Lupin III share are those common to many crime caper stories. In Kumakura's tale *Jing*, master criminal, boasts that he is willing and able to steal anything he chooses, gold, silver, ideas, or lives, whether nailed to the floor or not. Skilled beyond belief in all the arts of the professional criminal, and accompanied by the marvelous Kir—a talking raven with a nice line in energy attacks—Jing is an egocentric Robin Hood whose eccentricities reflect the nature of the equally eccentric world in which the stories evolve. Jing is the best thief in a society which does not hold such a low opinion of criminality as we might expect. Indeed, this society has an entire city devoted to the burglar, cut-purse, and footpad, along the lines of the legendary Caribbean pirate city of Tortugas, and it is in this extravagant place that Jing plies his trade. Apart from Kir, his only real companion in crime is the enigmatic motorcyclist Prostino, whose sage advice always seems to end up confusing Jing more than it assists him. As in Lupin III a succession of beautiful girls liven things up for our hero and provide local color to each episode—from the very Zenigata-esque Rose to the beautiful Stir. Those who fall foul of Jing usually do so because they underestimate his youthful appearance; he is an utterly charming rogue with one eye on the next prize and another on his reputation as Robin Hood's more successful cousin. Not as self-centered as he likes to make himself appear, but not selfless enough to turn down any opportunity to prove his mettle, Jing is Lupin lite, a thief for a readership that likes to distance itself from social problems by dressing its rogues in pantomime costume.

JUDAS [2004]

A tall, dark and demonic hunk in black leather, Judas is lurking in a subway looking for human souls when he sees a girl being attacked by a groper. Prim and proper Mariko has just been dumped by her two-timing boyfriend for a sexier girl, but Judas sees through her exterior and offers to replace her ex. Kaori Sakura's *Devil So I Love You (Akuma Demo I Love You)* from *Flower Comics* is the story of his fight to win Mariko's trust so he can seduce her, but as she gains confidence and fashion sense and begins to understand what passion really means, Judas finds he's changing too.

JYAN [2003]

An Nakahara's *Love Devil (Ijiwaru Love Devil, Flower Comics*, 2003) stars Jyan, a cute demon boy who has taken over the body of a human for mischief but finds himself in trouble when his host is hit by a truck. He has to transfer his soul to another body or die. He dives into a plush teddy bear being taken home as a gift for teenager Yui by her devoted daddy. Never dreaming he's actually taking a gorgeous winged demon home, dad hands over the teddy bear to Yui, who gets the shock of her life when she learns it's possessed by the devil. Once she's gotten over her surprise, she rapidly falls for Jyan.

SHIRO KAIEDA [1989]

The Silent Service (Chinmoku no Kantai) by Kaiji Kawaguchi is the only manga which has been directly referred to in a session of the Japanese parliament. A story that, on the surface, is little more than a retelling of Tom

Clancy's *The Hunt For Red October* narrative from a Japanese perspective, turns out to be a powerful indictment of those who prefer to leave responsibility to others. The narrative does tip its hat towards Clancy in many ways, but then Kawaguchi is playing a very subtle game with his reader's expectations of the story, and the motivations of his protagonist, Captain Shiro Kaieda.

Kaieda plays the Sean Connery role in *The Silent Service* and, like Tom Clancy's Latvian sub veteran, hijacks a powerful prototype submarine and takes it rogue. The twist here is that the sub is an American-Japanese joint project, destined for control by the United States, and Shiro is protesting the nature of cold war politics that crushes countries like Japan under the larger and more powerful forces of opposing and unbending political dogma. An interesting conceit which Kawaguchi employs to develop the character of Shiro is the way in which he appears to have two very distinct personalities and motivations: a very dogmatic, unflinching exterior developed for the world at large, by the military and media press briefings on his actions, and through his own announcements; and the much more human and likable side expressed through his interaction with his crew. Shiro is a man caught in a great conflict, who has one chance to stop what he sees as the inevitable flow of events, but who must risk sacrificing himself, his crew and their reputations.

Over the years Kawaguchi was prosecuted a number of times for stealing military photographs for use in his story, though this may have been his intent, a way of drawing the Japan Self-Defense Force/government into the very political narrative he was trying to create. His plan to open up the debate worked, as in 1993 Japan's parliament debated the merits of the strip and its view that Japan should take more responsibility for itself and its role in the world. The story was eventually brought to a close in 1996 by a reader's poll to decide Shiro's fate.

MINAMO KUROSAWA a.k.a. NYAMO [2000]

Often described as "high-school *Peanuts*," *Azumanga Daioh* is Kiyohiko Azuma's most successful publication, both in Japan and in the United States. Its ability to travel well is demonstrated by the speed with which the manga and anime were both released outside Japan—less than four years from page to screen to America. This is probably largely due to the format of the series, as short easily recognized comic strip and animated "funnies"; the same format has served slapstick kindergarten comedy *Crayon Shin Chan* just as well. The characters and situations are universal enough to find their mark with every teenager, and there is fan service aplenty to add appeal. The relatively normal and generally composed teacher Minamo (Nyamo) Kurosawa is by far the most popular character. Unlike the girls in her care, or her long-time friend Yukari, Nyamo tried to take school life seriously and does her valiant but inadequate best to provide a suitable role model for her Neo-St. Trinianesque girls. She's certainly not a party pooper, and nor is she as sour as the lecherous Mr. Kimura, who openly admits becoming a teacher because of high school girls, but she is not the sort of person who can easily cope with the rambunctious goings-on of her class. However, like all the characters in this something-for-everyone strip, Nyamo has her own unique quirks which endear her to the staff and pupils. Firstly, she is the absolute polar opposite of the madcap Yukari, secondly, she will never back down from a fight, and finally, she can be easily goaded. Between Yukari's liking for drinking at everyone else's expense and the girls' fondness for a bit of mayhem, Nyamo proves to be the ideal foil as she repeatedly gets out of her depth trying to rein in the worst excesses at school and remind class and teachers alike that they're supposed to be there to get an education in something other than how to be a party animal.

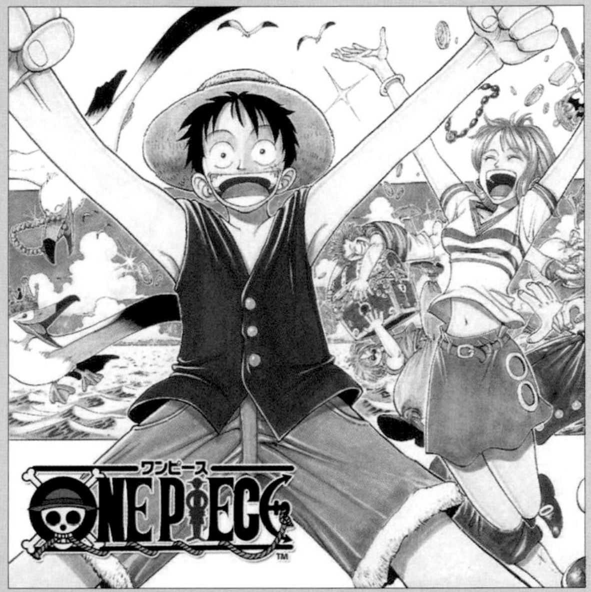

Like Indiana Jones, hyperactive treasure seeker Monkey D. Lufy is never without his beloved hat.

MONKEY D. LUFY [1997]

Before the infamous pirate Gold Rogers was put to death, he made one last comment to the crowd that had gathered to see him twitching: he would commend his entire treasure, which he had left in one piece, to the person who was brave enough to seek it. Thus, in death, he still managed to thumb his nose one last time at the authorities who were unable to prevent the inevitable boom in piracy on the high seas, and that's how Eichiro Oda's *Shonen Jump* manga *One Piece* got its title. Fast forward to a different time and place and see Monkey as a young lad, watching the ship of red-haired, one-armed pirate Shanks sailing away. Under one arm he clutches Shanks's straw hat, given to Lufy as he was still too young to join the crew. That arm, like the rest of his body, can stretch to almost incalculable lengths as a result of eating the magic gum-gum fruit, which has rendered him almost invulnerable. He vows to find Gold Roger's treasure and join

Shanks someday. Forward another ten years and sixteen-year-old Lufy is in command of his own ship, the Going Merry, and has attracted a crew of jolly ruffians, including the famed pirate hunter Zorro, Nami the thief, the crafty spy Ussopu, and even a good cook by the name of Sanji, to join him in his search for One Piece. Lufy is a typical rambunctious teen, with all the irrepressible energy of the Monkey King to whom his name refers, but he takes his obligation to Shanks very seriously indeed. Shanks sacrificed his lost arm to save the child Lufy, and promised to let him join his crew when he was old enough. Lufy is as greedy and venal as the next pirate, but he's too laid back and good-natured to be a cold-blooded killer. In fact the only thing that seems to get him seriously angry is the fact that, thanks to his elastic body, he cannot swim. This is only one of the slapstick staples in a manga that plays its adventure for broad comic effect. An animated TV series and the usual waves of merchandising followed.

MADOKA AYUKAWA [1983]

Madoka is a black-haired, beautiful girl of fifteen with an outrageous tendency to tease and flirt. From the moment new kid in town Kyosuke Kasuga rescues her hat when the wind blows it away, she keeps him guessing as to how she feels. She used to be a member of a punk gang, lives alone, smokes, and has a reputation for running wild. But Madoka's aura of rebellion is a cry for help. Her parents are famous musicians, travelling most of the time, leaving their only child alone. Madoka is intelligent, good at athletics and music, but neither her good qualities nor her wild-child excesses get her parents to pay her much attention. It's not surprising that she's capricious. But she's a loyal friend, so when her best buddy Hikaru falls for Kyosuke, Madoka does her best to suppress her own interest in him. The triangle gets complicated by the Kasuga family's psychic powers. The three friends have many choices to make, between love and friendship, home and career, old ties and new opportunities; Madoka leaves to study in America before finally returning to Japan and Kyosuke. Izumi Matsumoto's manga *Orange Road Follies* (*Kimagure Orange Road*, a.k.a. *Capricious Orange Road*) ran for five years in *Shonen Jump* and spawned a TV series, movies, merchandise, and fan comics and fiction written by people who'd never seen the inside of a Japanese high school.

REIKO MIKAMI [1992]

First appearing in the popular *Shonen Sunday* manga *Ghost Sweeper Mikami* by Takashi Shina, Reiko Mikami is a hangover from the 1980s, a material girl out to squeeze every penny from the world and have fun along the way. She's a ghost hunter without peer on the Tokyo supernatural investigation scene, and her abilities are only matched by her enormous snobbery, selfishness, and greed.

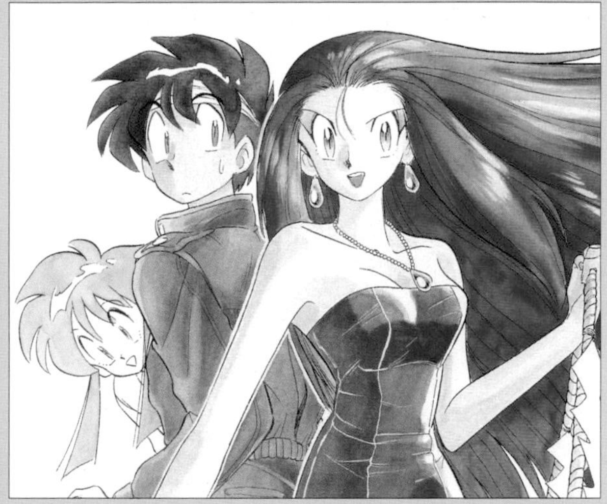

Reiko, Tadao, and Okino go to work ghostbusting in Tokyo, but has the bubble burst for our Material Girl?

Despite the arrogance that comes with success and luck, Reiko still manages to win over many clients with her sexy looks, long red hair, short skirts, and practiced charm, even after the most disastrous operations. Her character reworks Bill Murray's ghostbusting cad as Peter Venkman, one of many tips of the hat to hit American movie *Ghostbusters*. However, Reiko is fundamentally a very Japanese psych(ot)ic, driven by the diseases which the Japanese felt had destroyed their society by the beginning of the 1990s: love of money and love of drink. These are dangerous enough characteristics in a man, but embodied in a European-influenced manga girl they signaled the breakdown of traditional culture and values into a comedy free-for-all. Reiko is a classic bossy-boots stereotype of late twentieth-century anime and manga, a tall, aggressive woman with an extrovert nature. Her usual sidekicks are her assistant Tadao Yokoshima, a dim would-be ladies' man who has the hots for her and works for a pittance just to be around her, and the late Okinu, a gentle and demure revived ghost who tries to act as a buffer between them. Reiko and her team also got their own anime TV series and movies.

MIYU [1988]

Vampire Miyu (Kyuketsuki Miyu a.k.a. *Vampire Princess Miyu)* by Narumi Kakinouchi mines the rich veins of popular Japanese, Chinese, and Occidental folklore around demons and vampires. Set in Kyoto, ancient capital of Japan, it's the story of a modern-day spiritualist who is sucked into the pursuit of an ancient evil. Himiko, named for the semi-mythical queen of the proto-Japanese Yamato state around AD 500, is intrigued by an enigmatic vampire spirit called Miyu, one of the most interesting and morally ambiguous characters in all of anime. Appearing as a pretty, capricious teenager with a cold, detached outlook on life and death, Miyu seems to be actively hunting and killing demons. Born a vampire, Miyu is one of the last of her kind, and her function is to act as executioner to the Shinma, a race of demons whose rogue members she hunts down whenever they cause harm to a human.

The dark gifts which she gives to those humans touched by the Shinma cause the most concern for Himiko as she learns more about the girlish vampire. Essentially, Miyu's "kiss" does not kill, neither does it transfer the curse of vampirism. What it does is allow Miyu to create a perfectly formed internal reality for that person, in which he or she can live a fantasy life free from all pain. To all intents and purposes, they go mad. Miyu is supported by a devoted Shinma servant, Lover, a tall, cloaked figure who hides his face behind an enigmatic mask. Though Miyu's past is described in some detail in the manga, video anime, and TV series, as well as two spin-off series *(Vampire Princess Yui* and *New Vampire Princess Miyu)*, Kakinouchi never fully explains what motivates Miyu's "compassion" towards the people she frees from their misery.

When Himiko questions her, she explains that she is only fulfilling the wishes of the people involved, but there is enough ambiguity in her statement for the observer to realize that granting such a request might be considered simply playing on a weakness and not a compassionate act at all. Miyu is presented as a cold-blooded Lolita, the embodiment of self-absorption, who licks up holy water and crushes crucifixes with no visible damage to her pretty little mouth or hands. The anime is directed by the artist's husband, Toshihiro Hirano.

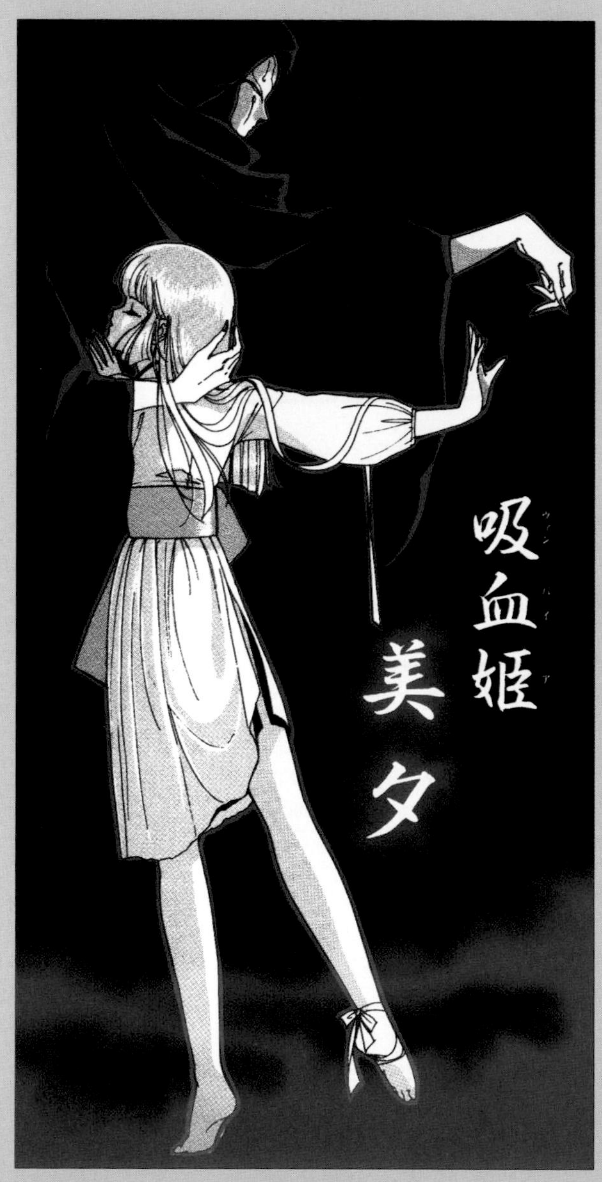

Kakinouchi renders Miyu and Lover in typically sensual mode.

ATARU MOROBOSHI

[1978]

What do you do if you're born the unluckiest guy in the world? You have two choices—sit around bemoaning fate, or give fate a run for its money. Ataru Moroboshi was not only born on Friday the 13th, but on the anniversary of the death of the Buddha, making him the personification of bad luck and his hometown of Tomobiki the focus for the alien invasion of Earth. Yet Ataru never surrenders to fate. He looks like a typical teenager lecher, whose ambitions towards beautiful girls far exceed his capacity to attract them. He's homely looking at best, lethargic, a poor student at his mediocre small-town high school, and an inattentive son to his despairing parents. He only musters any energy when food is involved—he's especially fond of *sukiyaki*.

Through a complex string of events involving the fate of the world being settled by a game of tag, Ataru finds himself elected the Earth's chosen champion. The opposition is represented by a nubile alien princess in a tiger-striped bikini. Her name is Lum, she has cute little horns, and she can fly. She's princess of the Oni, whose national dress is anything tiger-striped, and her people are the title characters of Rumiko Takahashi's first hit manga *Urusei Yatsura*.

Ataru wins the match through cheating—he rips off Lum's bra and takes advantage of her distraction. In his delight at winning, he yells "Now I can get married!" Lum takes that as a binding proposal, which she accepts. Ataru's real intended is girl-next-door Shinobu, but he had planned years of skirt-chasing before marriage loomed on the horizon—a common fantasy for Japanese and Western males alike. The misunderstanding that sees Lum assuming he has proposed to her restricts his life in many ways. She moves into the closet in his room at his parents' home. She delivers electric shocks every time he chases another girl. Possessing all the tact of a bull elephant and the timing of a broken wristwatch, Ataru always seems to wind up beaten, bruised, and electrocuted, none of which teaches him any discretion. He becomes very fond of Lum, but he is just not ready to settle down. He is tough as old boots, relentless in his actions and can sustain superhuman levels of damage and, though this is important to all slapstick comedy, Ataru's ability to soak up injuries is central to his development as a character.

The title, which has since been used for TV and movie animation as well as the manga, is a pun in Japanese: *urusai* means obnoxious, annoying, or noisy and *yatsu* means guy or fellow. *Ra* is simply a somewhat informal plural. Urusei is a mispronunciation of urusai. So why isn't this a reference to obnoxious guy Ataru? Well, in Japanese writing, it's written *u ru hoshi ya tsu ra*, with the Chinese character for star, *hoshi*. An alternative pronunciation for hoshi, used only in a compound word, is sei. Hence Urusei Yatsura—star guys or, roughly, *Those Obnoxious Aliens*! Ataru means "to hit" and Moroboshi means "shooting star." In this case the implication is that, though the chances of

LUPIN III

MAKING CRIME pay in a light-hearted way, Japan's very own master-thief and his sidekicks groove from the 1960s into the twenty-first century.

In 1967, lifelong *MAD* magazine fan Kazuhiko Kato, a.k.a. Monkey Punch, launched a new comic in *Manga Action* magazine. Crashing Western spy and crime movies, a puppet play from 1680, and a popular sleuth from a novel set in the samurai era, into a Frenchman's stories of a gentleman thief, he created one of the best loved gangs of good-hearted crooks in popular culture.

Lupin III is a Japanese master-thief who inherits both his skills and his genetic inability to resist a pretty face or curvy body from his French grandfather, Arsene Lupin, created by French crime writer Maurice Leblanc. Young Lupin is a skinny beatnik in drainpipe pants and crêpe-soled shoes. His trademark wide grin, laid-back demeanor, and wacky sense of humor conceals one of the sharpest brains on the planet. He's a master of disguise, a brilliant planner, and a technical whiz who can construct any device, however unlikely. He's also soft-hearted and unshakably loyal to his three closest companions.

Daisuke Jigen is a sharp dresser who can draw in three-tenths of a second, lethal with any handgun despite the fact that his view is often obstructed by the brim of his tilted hat. Jigen looks like Lee Marvin, had trouble with the Mob in the United States, and doesn't trust any woman. Goemon Ishikawa XIII, descendant of the samurai thief immortalized in the 1680 puppet play *Ishikawa Goemon*, is the archetypal samurai—heroic, strong, silent, and baffled by the women who can't resist throwing themselves at him despite his attempts to avoid them and preserve his inner calm. His prized possession is his sword Zantetsuken, renowned for its ability to cut anything. The three friends —one who can't resist women, one whom women can't resist, and one who avoids women whenever possible—are joined when it suits her interests by the luscious redheaded Fujiko Mine, Lupin's on-off love interest, rival, frequent betrayer, and even occasional savior.

The Lupin gang is pursued by the Japanese Clouseau, Inspector Zenigata of Interpol. Zenigata is a strong, stern, do-it-by-the-book policeman, the descendant of crime writer Kodo Nomura's popular samurai-sleuth Heiji Zenigata. Zenigata has vowed to capture Lupin; the pair are locked in an endless cat-and-mouse sequence, a human Tom and Jerry.

Monkey Punch built in links to Japanese classical and popular culture, but also to Occidental comics and film. Lupin's adventures have poked fun at Western icons from James Bond and film noir to international soccer and neo-Nazis. The manga are in the European grotesque tradition, mixing slapstick with philosophy and sex, with a strong influence

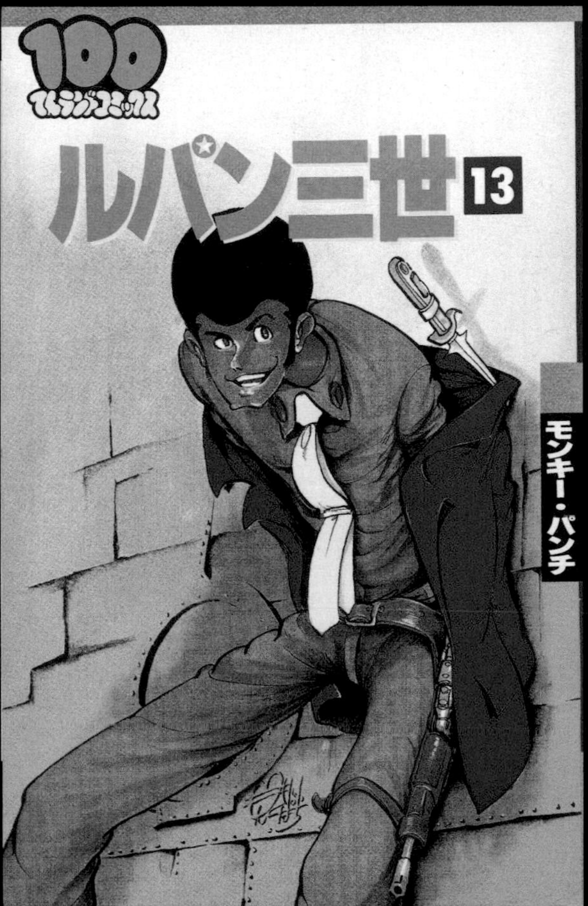

Often caught but never held for long, Lupin III brought the gentleman-thief into this century with his hi-tech antics and old-world charm.

from *MAD* magazine in the writing. The first series ran for a total of 129 issues. The manga went into hiatus while Monkey Punch pursued other projects, but on June 23, 1977, *New Lupin III (Shin Rupan Sansei)* reappeared in *Manga Action*, running for 188 issues, until 1981. The English language edition available from Tokyopop is based on the Chuokoron-shinsha first series edition of 1989. The same Japanese publisher produced a collected edition of the second series in 1990.

Spinoffs include twenty-second century master-thief *Lupin VIII* by Monkey Punch and Kon Oriharu, published by Futabasha in 1982; a third seven-episode manga series supervised by Moneky Punch, written by Takaguchi and drawn by Shusai in Futabasha's *Action Second* monthly in 1997; and 1998 series *Lupin III Y* drawn by Manatsu Yamakami in *Manga Action* (collected in the *Action Comics* series in a 225-page volume of three self-contained stories). In Italy, two new Lupin stories by the original author were published by Kappa: *Holmes' Violin* in 1999 and *Lupin III Millennium* in 2001.

The team's manga adventures were followed by animation and live action, music and a massive quantity of merchandise. There are three anime TV series totaling 228 episodes, movies, and annual TV specials running from 1989 to date. Yuji Ono's jazz-inspired theme is a best-seller, and a whole new generation of techno DJs have remixed the ultra-cool scores. Lupin also appeared in a Toho live-action movie in 1974, and a new video spin-off in 2000. Sadly, plans for a Japanese-French co-production of *Lupin VIII* directed by the legendary Rintaro, were cut off by a legal dispute with the Leblanc estate, although the pilot, produced by TMS and DIC in 1982, was briefly available as *Arsene & Co.*

being hit by a shooting star are astronomically low, Ataru has managed it in being saddled with the curse and blessing that is the love of a good, but hot-tempered, woman.

Takahashi's genius is to present Japanese suburban life through the filter of science fiction, holding up a mirror to the absurdity and humanity inherent in everyday things and people. Her central thesis, that there's more of a gulf between male and female than there could ever be between human and alien, is repeated in many of her other works. The huge success of *UY*, as its fans call it, earned her the title "manga princess" and made her one of the richest women in Japan. The series made the jump to TV in 1981 and more than 200 animated episodes, six movies, and eleven video animations followed. A fresh and funny translation of the manga is available from Viz and the anime had a lovingly produced release, complete with copious notes on the multitude of cultural references loaded into each episode, by AnimEigo.

YUGI MOTO [1998]

Living over a collectible card game shop with his grandfather, gaming legend Suguroku Moto, teenager Yugi becomes one of the most feared duelists on the Duel Monster Game circuit. The game was created from an ancient Egyptian ritual, Shadow Duel, by Pegasus J. Crawford in order to locate seven ancient artifacts which he believed would revive his lost love Cecilia. However, Crawford is simply a pawn in a much bigger game. Yugi's power as King of Games in the manga *Yu-Gi-Oh: Duel Monsters* is largely due to the Millennium Puzzle he always wears, and the link he shares with the once powerful Pharaoh Yami, who was a great Shadow Duelist himself in life. He now advises Yugi and can even take over his young friend's body to battle on their joint behalf. With the rest of the shop's regular clients (Katsuya, Hiroto, and Anzu), Yugi enters the world of professional dueling to find out the secrets of his Millennium Puzzle and discover for himself if he is destined to be the true King of Games. Yugi's deck was made for him by his doting grandfather, and includes the old warrior's finest cards, even the legendary Black Magician, with which Yugi has a special bond. Yugi and Yami engage a wide variety of foes in their quest, and overcome even the mighty Pegasus J. Crawford. Yugi and Yami come to share their thoughts and feelings with each other, and end up having a real effect on how the other sees the world. The childish Yugi is brought to understand how the simple game he loves was once the basis of powerful ritual magic which was used (at least initially) to protect ancient Egypt, and that the world is not always the pleasant place the insular young boy thought it to be. In return, the jaded and world-weary Pharaoh, having spent years locked in a sterile puzzle, begins to learn that there is still good in the world, as long as people remain true to each other. Kazuki Takahashi's manga was serialized in *Shonen Jump* as part of a massive manga/animation/card game tie-in commissioned to catch the market growing up in the wake of Pokemon.

HIDEKI MOTOSUWA

[2001]

Much like his thematic forebear, Ataru Moroboshi, Hideki is a man on a mission to find love in as many places as possible—in other words, a complete lecher and a layabout. An impecunious technophobe from the sticks, Hideki has just moved to Tokyo at the beginning of the CLAMP manga *Chobits*. Having failed all his university entrance exams, he has just begun life as a *ronin* (the old Japanese name for a masterless samurai, now used for any student without a university place), when he comes across a beautiful, but run-down, persocon. These are the latest hi-tech toys, humanoid computers, usually in the shape of cute girls. He couldn't afford a new one, so he decides to keep his find and names her Chi. Hideki's story revolves around the tragi-comic mistakes humans make in their interpretation of life. There is also a strong allegorical message concerning the isolating effects of technology, expressed through Hideki's attempts to restore Chi to full functionality, regardless of the cost to his studies, health, and personal relationships. However, being a CLAMP manga, *Chobits* is no mere cautionary tale on the seductiveness of technology. It acknowledges the pervasive nature of information technologies and the way that they are fast becoming an inseparable part of human life through their buyers' tendency to personalize the inanimate, but emphasizes the need for real, individual emotional responses. Substituting a relationship with your mobile phone, iPod, or persocon for human interaction is avoidable, but technology isn't. Fleeing it, as Hideki does in the beginning, means missing out on its life-enhancing possibilities; accepting it as part of life can open up new doors. Hideki is a minor-league scoundrel, but he is a credible point of identification for the reader. His story mirrors the dreams of many lonely teenagers, who would all aspire to the happy ending in which Chi's emotional state is resolved and Hideki finally comes to terms with his feelings for his Chobit partner. There's also a nod to Rumiko Takahashi's evergreen love story *Maison Ikkoku* in Hideki's crush on his cute apartment manager Ms. Hibiya.

SHINNOSUKE NOHARA

[1990]

Often described as the surrealist riposte to *Calvin and Hobbes*, *Crayon Shin-Chan* by Yoshihito Usui is one of the most outstandingly popular manga and anime series to emerge from Japan in the 1990s. It relays everyday events in the life of a small boy who believes he's the only one who knows what is really going on around him. At the center of its small world is the presumed creator of the manga, five-year-old Shinnosuke Nohara, affectionately known as Shin-chan. A miniature version of Ataru Moroboshi in most respects (save for alien involvement, which ironically Shin would love!), he is a hapless, lazy kindergarten lecher, who loves nothing better than getting his face between a nice, large pair of breasts. Breast feeding is still many times more common in Japan than it is in the U.K. or the United States, and usually goes on for much longer—into the third or fourth year. However, Shin's obsession with the human female breast cannot be satisfied by the generally petite build of most Japanese women when compared to their western sisters, a fact about which Shin complains on numerous occasions, and so his obsession helps paint the little lad, as Usui intended, as a reflection of the sort of (slightly) debased man which Japan has been producing since the collapse of the economy in the 1980s.

The manga deals with Shin's generally perverted personality, involving him in all manner of insane goings on which appeal to the five-year-old in every male. Sometimes he hangs around a high school in the hope of groping one of the cute teenage girls who seem to find Shin so adorable. At other times he is experimenting with ways to send his dog into orbit, or doing elephant impressions with his penis. He thinks it is funny to pretend that his kindergarten teacher is kidnapping him to liven up a dull day. He has been known to play "peekaboo" in a moving car with his father, from whom it appears he inherited many of his character traits. Indeed, one of the points Usui makes is that Shin is the product of the family he is growing up in—a reflection of a mood in Japanese society that blames the current generation of thirty-somethings for the way in which Japan's youth is fast falling apart. Shinnosuke is a self-obsessed force of nature whose antics would be reprehensible if he did not always seem to bring destruction down on his own head; he is the part of us that never grows up, and stands as a dire warning not to let our inner brat out. It took nigh on a decade for Shin's adventures to surface in the United States and Europe. The most notable thing about the manga is the very awkward-looking visual style, drawn—quite appropriately—as if a five-year-old had created it. This has helped it reach acceptance with a wide variety of age groups who can recall what it was like to be so young, with a fresh take on the world unfettered by convention or good taste, and to feel you were the only one who really noticed what was going on around the place.

ITTO OGAMI [1970]

Itto, dark antihero of *Lone Wolf and Cub (Kozure Okami)* by writer Kazuo Koike and artist Goseki Kojima, inspired a generation of Western artists and film-makers including Frank Miller and Quentin Tarantino. The former servant of the Tokugawa Shogunate is framed for a plot against the Shogun by the

Right: The last survivors of the Itto family carry on their deadly ancestral trade.

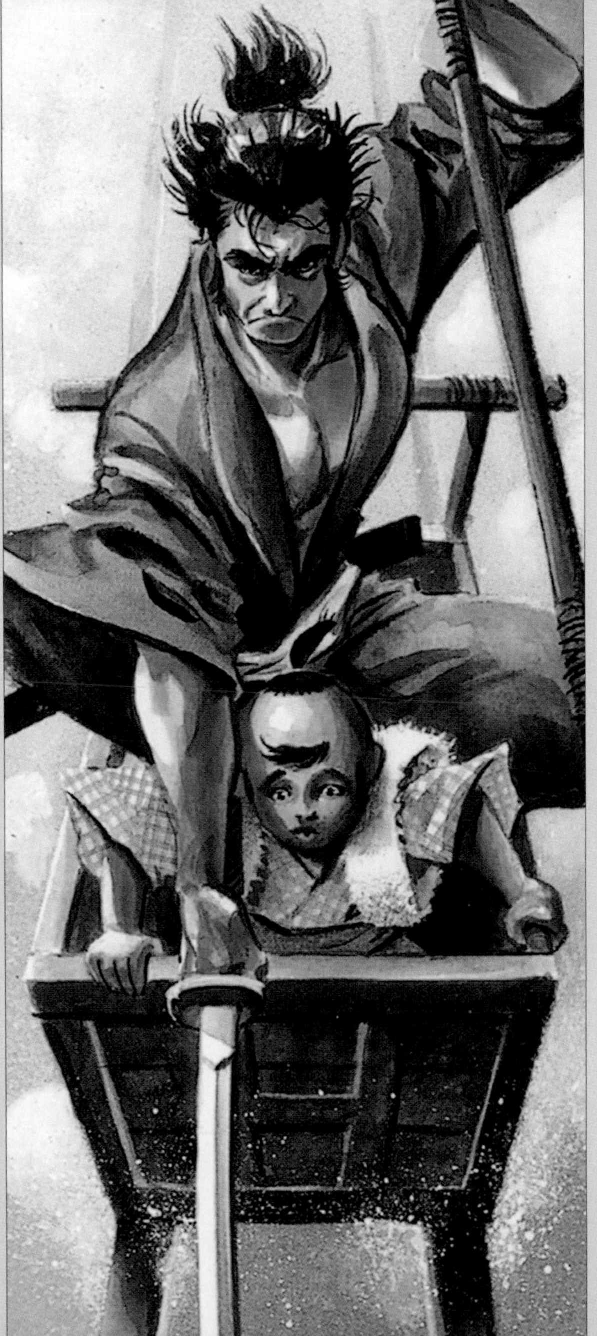

mighty Yagyu clan, who covet the Ogami clan's position as shogun's executioner as a way of adding to their own power and influence. In 1655 they move against the Ogami. Itto's wife and retainers are killed and he flees with his baby son Daigoro. Itto works as an assassin to keep his child fed while he pursues revenge for the loss of his wife and his honor. Although they are outcasts, Itto is determined that his son will learn the true way of the samurai, and trains Daigoro both to survive and to hone his samurai spirit. The love between father and son is unflinching, unsentimental, and unbreakable, and the manga displays this in several story arcs where they are separated and finally reunited. The series first appeared in *Manga Action* in September 1970 and ran until 1976. First Publishing produced the English version.

ONIKIRIMARU [1992]

Kei Kusunoki made her manga debut in 1982 while still in high school. *Ribbon* made its author a name as an expert in short but enthralling manga on social themes. On its debut in *Shonen Sunday* magazine *Ogre Slayer (Onikirimaru)* was destined to become one of those short-lived titles, but given its success and the popularity of the titular leading character, the series was eventually extended to four volumes and an animated video series. Set in modern Japan, it features a young man, half human and half *oni*, who roams the world, friendless and rootless, a killer of his own kind. He does not even have a name other than that of his sword, Onikirimaru, a sentient weapon that uses a nameless oni to carry out its bloody mission of vengeance on his brothers who violate the laws of the gods. If he can kill every single oni, the Slayer believes he will become fully human and have a name of his own. Until then, or until he is killed and the sword chooses another, it is his fate to intervene in the lives of humans who have been attacked by oni, not to help them, but to move closer to his own goal. Translating oni as "ogre" may not be the most appropriate analogy, for in Kusunoki's world oni are far more intelligent than the dumb brutes of European folklore. These supernatural creatures, though far superior to humans in many respects, suffer from one all too human flaw—disregard for lives other than their own. Strong, intelligent beast-demons who inhabit their own netherworld realm, they are foes of the kami, benign deities who watch over humans, and use people as pawns in the political battle between the two forces. Even worse, the preferred breeding partner of the average oni is human. They rape human women and then watch as the host eventually erupts giving birth to the new life. For such an elevated life form, they are brutally violent, utterly without remorse, being largely removed from the cycle of karma which binds all other living things. Kusunoki obviously drew on Buddhist and Japanese folklore for the creation of the oni, who can only be destroyed by the Onikirimaru.

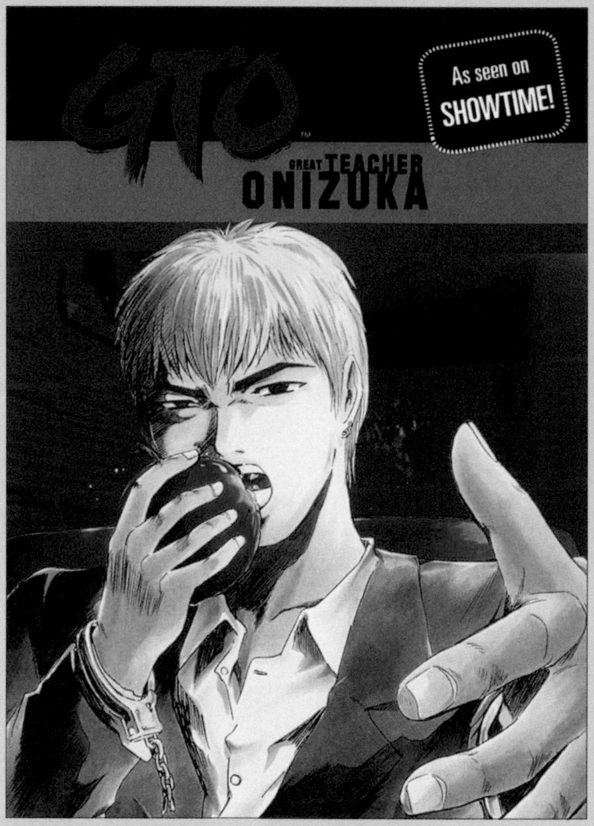

Onizuka may not look or sound much like a teacher, but the worst class in school finds out he's no pushover.

EIKICHI ONIZUKA [1997]

Eikichi Onizuka is a wannabe high school teacher at the start of *Great Teacher Onizuka* (a.k.a. *GTO*) by Tohru Fujisawa. His openly stated purpose in training for the job is to "score with the hottest girls in the school." His youth was misspent running with one of the most notorious biker gangs in Tokyo, and he had a reputation, even among that company, as being gutter mouthed and a shade too violent for everyone's good. Now, aged twenty-two, he's thinking about life after teendom, and a career that forces him to spend every day with uniformed high-school girls has obvious appeal. However, much to his annoyance, he finds he can't walk straight into a teaching position and is forced to take the role of a trainee at Holy Forest Academy. His first home room consists of the school's worst bullies, gamblers, gangsters, and teacher breakers; as ready as he is for a fight when he first walks through the door, neither party is prepared for the changes each will make in the life of the other.

Both sides have their opinions of the opposition and, to a degree, both are right. Despite being a cooler version of the teacher in *To Sir With Love*, Eikichi has sold out his earlier free life on the road. Though the kids would probably appreciate his far from noble motive for making the change, to them he's just become another boring adult. At first Eikichi sees his charges as wasting their time and his, but, while not being the most professionally or morally minded tutor, he is still close enough to their mindset to see that each disaffected kid has potential that is being wasted or ignored. Through them, he realizes that up till now he has wasted his own life and talents; instead of a safe place to score, his class becomes his chance at redemption. However, he's come to where the wild things are; they have to be tamed one person at a time, and each engagement teaches all concerned (the kids, Onizuka, the kindly old principal, and the evil vice principal) a valuable lesson. From trying to send the kids to Okinawa on a budget "earned" from cheating pachinko and planning to sell organs, through bartering for a student's virginity with a sadomasochistic collective, to fending off potential kidnappers, Eikichi is forged in the fires of knowledge and finally qualifies, in his own uniquely unorthodox way, as Great Teacher Onizuka. Sadly his school doesn't actually survive his transformation, being burned down in the climactic final volume. Unusual for a successful manga, a live-action show (1998) preceded the anime version (2000). The final episode of the live-action *GTO* TV series was the most watched television program in Japan to that date.

OROCHI [1969]

Kazusa and Lisa are sisters. Kazusa is the eldest and most beloved of the family, whilst Lisa is little more than her sister's faded shadow—inept and incapable of doing anything as well as Kazusa. Lisa harbors an understandable grudge against her sister, and goes out one night in a self-destructive rage, perhaps intending to end her suffering and transfer to Kazusa some of the pain she feels. However, her life is saved by the mysterious Orochi, a girl who seems to be immortal, save for a desire to sleep every hundred years or so. After saving Lisa, Orochi falls into that deep sleep, only to wake to find herself in the home of the sisters and party to the violence that her act of compassion has sparked off in Kazusa and Lisa. Orochi is drawn into the relationship and her visions become the key to the terrible affair, revealing the identity of the truly evil sister to the readers. *Orochi: Blood* by Kazuo Umezu appeared in 1970. It is the sixth volume (and the only one translated so far) of the *Orochi* saga, the story of Orochi's awakening to a new age at the beginning of each tale. With the early stages of the story missing, it can be quite difficult for an Anglophone audience to grasp the importance of Orochi's passive—almost naïve—personality. In Japanese lore, the Orochi are seen as guardian spirits—sometimes foul looking, and often misunderstood, but very important to the nature of the land and quite naïve when it comes to humans. From the first Orochi (which was tricked, and killed by Susano to recover a sword), through to the folklore of the Edo period, the Orochi are often taken advantage of by cruel humans to serve their own ends and given little thought (much in the same way that the beasts and werewolves of European folklore are often viewed as throwaway villains whose lives have no importance). The most important legend surrounding the Orochi is that its blood is a universal curative.

ORORON [1998]

Mizuki Hayase's *Wings* manga *The Demon Ororon (Akuma no Ororon)* shows Ororon, youngest son of the demon lord Oz, as a threat to his elder brothers' chances to inherit the demon throne. He is forced to flee Oscar and Osero to the human world to stay alive. Their assassins pursue him, and when he finds refuge with lonely fifteen-year-old Chiaki, she too is in danger. Flirting with the devil is a dangerous game. Chiaki too has been rejected by her own family; daughter of the Archangel Michael and a human woman, ostracized and considered an abomination by her father's angelic brethren. They help each other survive a hostile universe.

EMI RASHOMON [1994]

By the early twenty-first century, Japan has become a dumping ground for the migrants of the planet and, as a result, Tokyo is now a heaving bed of criminal activity. Into this mess steps the busty, avaricious, and trigger-happy Emi—the baddest bounty hunter in Japan and the arch rival of the Megalith terrorist organization, whose existence forced the Tokyo Police Authority to license private bounty hunters in the first place. Riding the last crest of the *Dirty Pair* wave, *Bomber Girl* by Makoto Niwano was created to cash in on the "girls with guns" craze which shot through Japanese comic publishing at the end of the 1980s and has refused to go away. She's a bounty hunter out to rake in all the loot she can to fund shopping sprees, travel, and other consumer binges. Armed with short-bladed swords and traditional Japanese clubs, she dresses in an outfit not too dissimilar from that of the Sailor

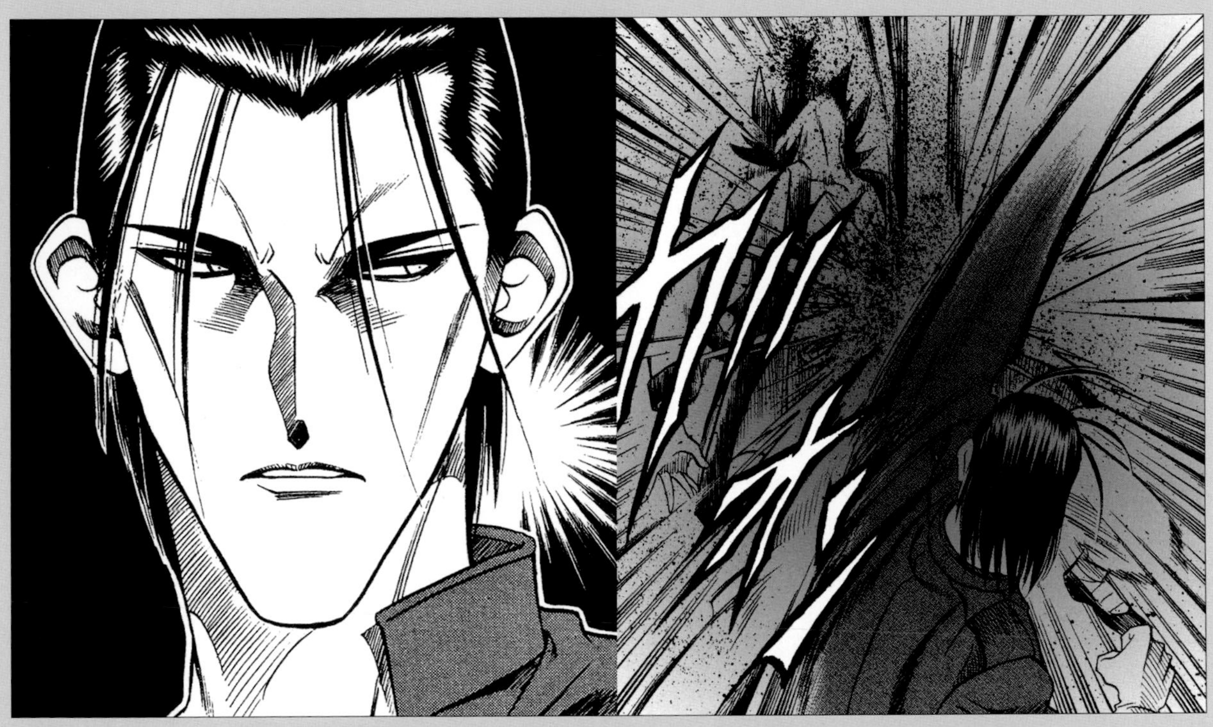

Slay evil instantly: in a changing world, Hajime Saito is an old-fashioned guy who lives by the sword.

Scouts, and is just as happy killing non-paying clients as she is fighting the bad guys while giving fan service with frequent panty shots and a few semi-nude panels. However, the shallow yet focused story and the blatant parody that is Emi gives fans of the genre exactly what they want. First appearing in *Shonen Jump*, Emi made her U.S. debut in *Raijin* magazine in 2002.

HAJIME SAITO [1994]

After the arrival of Commodore Perry's warships in Yokohama Bay in the nineteenth century, Japan was thrown into chaos and fear. Many samurai, especially those of lower ranks, began to doubt the power of the Shogunate to defend the country against foreign powers, especially those with heavily gunned ships. The movement to fight the barbarians began to win support, with many samurai coming to Kyoto to join the revolutionary movement and causing more and more disturbances at the capital. Most did not have a clear idea of what to do; all they knew was that they were impatient to do something to defend Japan. The government of the day, the bakufu, decided that it would be to their advantage if they took such samurai into their service, rather than letting them roam about the capital. This happened in 1863. At this time of great unrest in Japan, the crumbling Tokugawa government sponsored the creation of a militia known as the Shinsengumi. They were tasked with the impossible job of maintaining the values that had made the Tokugawa Period great in the eyes of those within it: loyalty, martial fervor, and respect for tradition. The group quickly devolved into a political militia, being used by the government to quell uprisings against the regime with force, where the army could not be trusted. A few men had an aptitude for the job that made them stand out even in this violent time and best known of these is Hajime Saito.

Though eventually becoming a Meiji period corrupt cop, Hajime begins his association with the cast of the manga *Ruro ni Kenshin* in episode 28, in flashback, as the commander of the 3rd Battalion of the Tokyo Shinsengumi and the living epitome of that group's motto Aku *zoku zan* (Slay evil instantly). Creator Nobuhiro Watsuki makes it difficult to decide whether Hajime is truly a scoundrel, or just a very determined man doing his best on a difficult life path. His relationship with Kenshin shows him as a callous individual, but his fondness for both Okita and Tokio say otherwise. He is certainly proud and distant, a fact which does not change throughout the manga or its hugely popular spin-off anime TV series; this adds to his air of inflexibility, which helps to paint him as a tragic figure—the only one to remain the same in the changing world of the Meiji restoration.

RANMA SAOTOME [1987]

Ranma comes from a long line of martial artists and takes his calling very seriously. When his father Genma takes him to train in mysterious, exotic China, the pair fully intend to make Ranma the best martial artist on the face of the planet. They certainly succeed in making him the most versatile. He falls into a cursed spring where a young girl drowned centuries ago; now any man who has the bad luck to fall in there changes into a young girl whenever he is doused in cold water, and only a hot shower can change him back. Genma doesn't get off scot-free, though; he falls into a spring where a panda drowned centuries ago, with predictable results.

Rumiko Takakashi's *Ranma (Ranma Nibbunnoichi)* is a wacky love comedy, not an essay on the dangers of foreign travel. So Ranma and Genma head back to Japan, trying to avoid unexpected showers en route, and turn up at the *dojo* of Genma's old friend Tendo. The two settled that Genma's son would marry one of the three Tendo daughters when the children were babies, and Genma sees no reason why his son shouldn't honor the

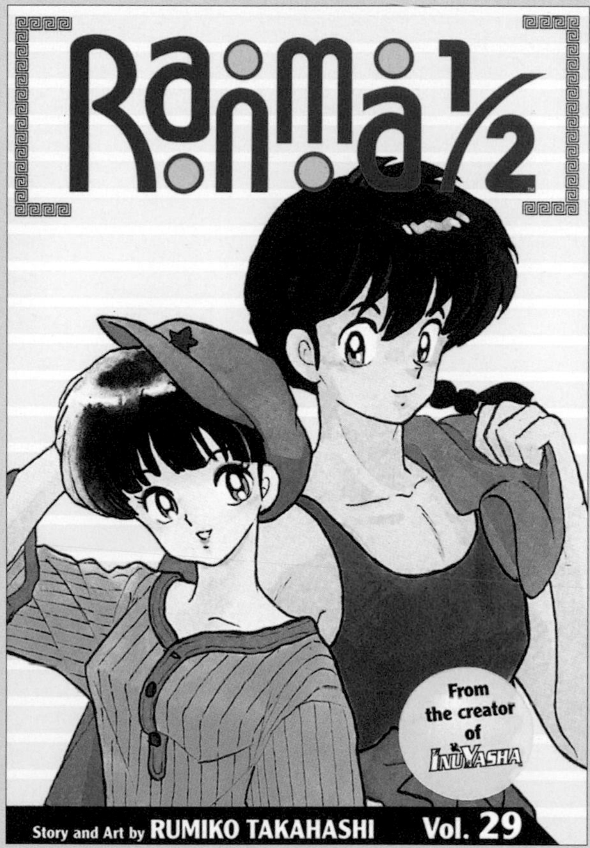

When he's a boy, Akane thinks Ranma is just fine; but in their world nobody stays in one shape for long.

arrangement and continue the traditions of the Tendo *dojo*. Youngest Tendo sister Akane, who draws the short straw, is a feisty female with formidable fighting skills, a cute little nose, a great figure, and total contempt for the local boys who moon around her begging for dates. She'll only go out with one who can defeat her, and that hasn't happened yet.

Ranma is an arrogant, self-centered boy, a typical teenager who wants to keep his weird physical problems a secret. He does this by pretending that his curvy, red-haired alter ego is his sister. Since he naturally wants to be top dog, this girl-Ranma challenges Akane for the position of high-school sweetheart, while boy-Ranma, like all obnoxious Takahashi heroes, attracts every girl for miles around. However, all relationships in and around the Tendo *dojo* are complicated by the fact that just about every stranger who wanders into town has come from China after a fall into a cursed pool. The resulting transformations turn the area into a human zoo—Ranma's seems to be the only gender swap, but there are so many species swaps that it seems drowning must be the main threat to animal life in China. As the various transformed visitors and locals pair off, Ranma and Akane begin to fall in love, but both are too proud to admit it and give their parents the satisfaction of seeing their plans come to fruition.

A virtual re-run of the artist's earlier hit *Urusei Yatsura*, recycling most of the plot elements and character ideas in a high-school setting, but with martial arts and magic instead of aliens, the *Shonen Sunday* manga spun off a long-running animated TV series, a video series, and two movies plus the usual character goods. Its enduring popularity is largely due to its huge success in the West. Viz has published excellent translations of the manga and anime.

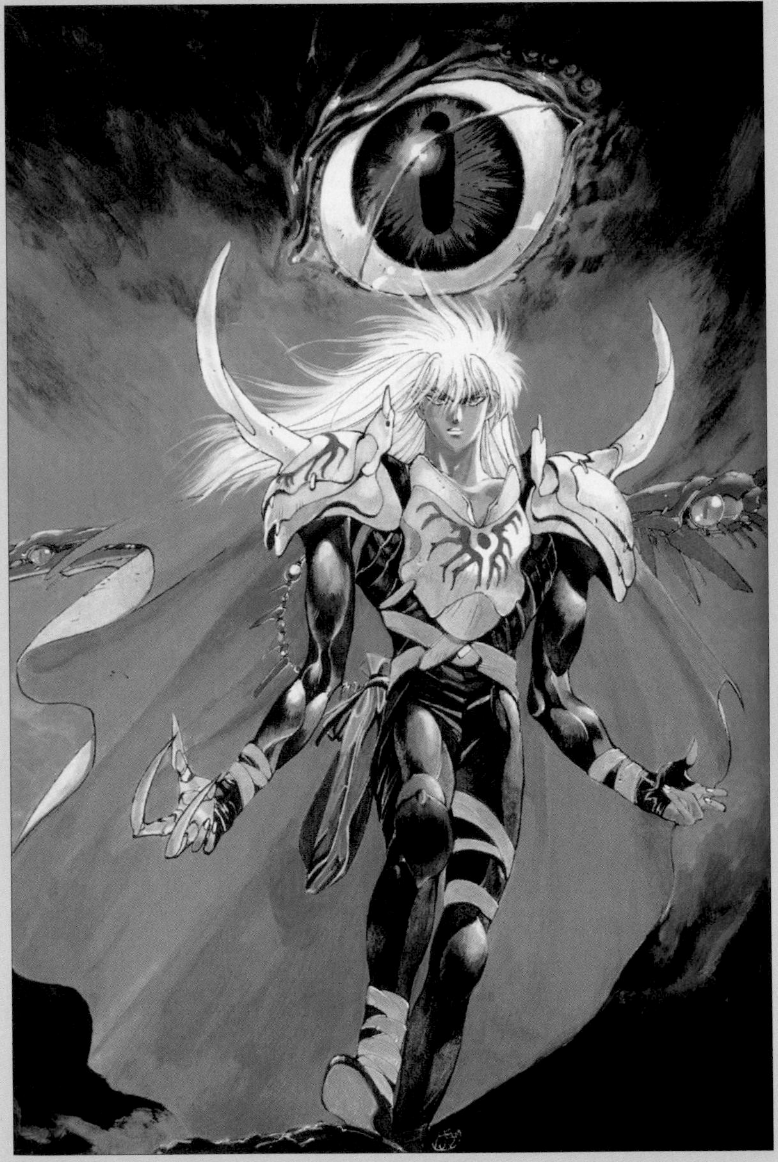

DARK SCHNEIDER a.k.a. DS, DARSHU, and RUSHE LENLEN [1988]

Dark Schneider is the half-demon, all-bastard sorcerer whose adventures are the main focus of Kazushi Hagiwara's role-play game inspired manga *Bastard!!* Originally setting out to conquer his feudal world, he was defeated by treachery. The white-haired, muscular, outrageously sexy warrior mage was trapped within the body of a tiny baby boy named Rushe Lenlen and left to slumber. However, when Schneider's old cohorts decide to take advantage of the peaceful state of Metallicana (the manga was written in the 1980s by a heavy rock fan, so this is only one of numerous groan-inducing metal references), high priest Dio decides to waken the wizard to oppose them. Dio's virginal daughter Tia Not Yoko (bodyguard and big sister figure to Rushe) is assigned to rouse the vengeful Schneider from his imprisonment with a kiss. Angry as he is, he sees the sense in not allowing Metallicana to fall to the fallen angel Anthrasox.

Having spent years in his child form, Schneider is rather different from his original self. Though still capable of outrageously wicked behavior when Schneider is in control, Rushe's personality imposes just enough common humanity on the arrogant, self-centered mage to keep everyone—well, almost everyone—safe. Schneider has also inherited some of little Rushe's devotion to Tia, although filtered through the raging hormones of a rock god, the mix of emotions includes considerably more lust. With his more vengeful feelings somewhat restricted, Schneider seems to have thrown all his frustrations into clothing and is forever conjuring new outfits to impress his allies and enemies alike. The extravagance feeds over into his entire persona; all he does must be done in a manner worthy of a massive stadium tour's biggest and best entrance. His old allies ninja master Gara, Arshes Ne the empress of thunder, Abigail the dark priestess, and Kall-su the king of ice, are initially under-whelmed by their old boss's new incarnation and expect him to be an easy target, only gradually learning that his new emotional capacity has made him even stronger. Arshes and Schneider were once lovers, and just as his softer side emerges with Tia, so his love for her leads him into danger. The manga ran on to a climactic final showdown with Schneider assembling the Four Horsemen of the Apocalypse against Satan and the fallen angels, while the spin-off anime series ended much earlier, before the final showdown with Kall-su.

Left: Dark Schneider, part cute kid, part sexy warrior mage, all *Bastard*!!

HOSUKE SHARAKU [1974]

During his junior high-school years, Osamu Tezuka once visited the ancient fortresses of the old Asuka region in the south of Japan and, as he wrote later, was so awestruck by the inexplicable nature of the remains that he created the concepts for his 1975 manga, *The Three-Eyed One (Mitsume ga Toru*, a.k.a. *Here Comes Three-Eyes)* on the spot—though it would take many more years to bring it from conception to publication. On reading the story, it becomes very clear to the reader that the character of Hosuke Sharaku is actually the creator himself . Though it is true that elements of Tezuka's personality found their way into all his characters, it could be argued that not even Tezuka's "son," Astro Boy, carried more of the artist in him than young Sharaku.

Orphan Sharaku is the scion of a three-eyed race that had existed long before modern man and built a great civilization. He is usually dressed in a traditional school uniform, with a bandage or sticking plaster on his forehead, looking far younger than his classmates and a target for bullying. Yet Sharaku's mind is that of a race with such huge powers of intellect and telekinesis that they became arrogant. When the sticking plaster is removed, his third eye is revealed and his whole personality changes. Only his classmate and protector, Chiyoko Wato, can control his transformations, since only she can remove and replace the plaster. The third eye represents clarity of thought and purity of heart; Sharaku is tired of being saddled with his babyish form and the limitations set on him by society. Yet the fact that Chiyoko can control his Jekyll and Hyde personality shows he loves her. Tezuka believed that anyone, no matter how insignificant they may seem, can be capable of great deeds. In this manga, he is playing out the dream he had when at Asuka, when he wished for the mental powers to understand and investigate such mighty civilizations properly, and allowing his mind to ponder the uses a young boy might make of such god-given greatness, with all the moral questions that raises: for the mind of a child is free of morality, clear, and self-centered to a frightening degree. Tezuka said that he based Sharaku on Elmer Fudd, Bugs Bunny's simple yet focused adversary; Sharaku Hosuke and Wato are puns on the names of Sherlock Holmes and Watson, another duo consisting of an arrogant and unpredictable genius and his devoted friend and supporter. An animated TV series was made, but Tezuka was not entirely happy with the changes made to his concept of the character.

SKULLMAN [1970]

Often called Japan's first manga antihero, Tatsuo Kagura is the mutant creation of a pair of scientists who are brutally killed for giving life to such an abomination as their super-powered "son." This sets the tone of Shotaro Ishinomori's manga *Skullman*, in which Kagura/Skullman and his assistant Garo go in pursuit of the scientists' murderers, The Syndicate and their leader Rasputin. Though heroes with the ability to transform from an unassuming figure into a more imposing one were common enough in Western comics, literature, and film at the time, Ishinomori's vengeful creation was the first to emerge on the Japanese scene, and helped give rise to many other such characters (such as Ishinomori's *Kamen Rider*, designed as the logical descendant of Skullman himself). An interestingly conflicted character, Skullman spends as much time battling his own inner demons as he does fighting to see his brand of justice done, and the story raises many questions concerning the true, internalized nature of evil, most acutely expressed in Skullman's desire to kill those who had freed him from the torment of his scientist parents' experiments, the only constant he had known to that point. Ishinomori's notion that we are all our own Skullman—battling foes within and without that we do not fully understand—is a potent one and it is clear to see why the story became so popular. In 1997 *Skullman* was resurrected by the creator, who died shortly afterwards, in collaboration with his former pupil Kazuhiko Shimamoto.

HANA TSUKUSHIMA [2002]

An earnest country bumpkin with a fearsomely thuggish appearance, shaved head, bad attitude, but a good heart, Hana transfers to a rough city high school, Suzuran High, and boards with four authentic thugs in a house run by a yakuza type. He makes up his mind to help the school become something more than a place where you only major in fighting in Hiroshi Takahashi's *Worst*, a manga about the process of trying to become an alpha male, out in English from Digital Manga.

SAKI VASHUTARL [1979]

Prince Saki Vashutarl of Asran at first appears to be cold and remote, but Kaoru Shintani's *Area 88* gradually reveals a man forced to fight his beloved father and younger brother Rishaal to save his country. A bloody civil war began when the throne of the desert kingdom of Asran was willed to Saki's uncle, not his father. Saki is fighting to keep the rightful King on the throne, not just because he supports the right of succession, but because he truly believes his uncle is a better ruler than his father; so he leads a team of mercenary pilots from the desert base known as Area 88. His mother died when he was very young, but he has three surrogate mothers in the shape of a trio of beautiful girls, dressed like classic harem lovelies and as deadly as they are beautiful, sent by his uncle to protect him from everything, including himself. He inspires respect and loyalty by his own fanatical devotion to his cause; when he almost goes blind, his mercenaries risk his wrath to ensure he is treated, and at the end of Kaoru Shintani's manga, they stand by him as he faces death in the final battle.

WORT THE SAGE [1988]

One of the original six heroes who saved the "cursed" island of Lodoss, Wort is one of the most important players in the ongoing saga that is *Record of Lodoss War (Lodoss Senki)*, the manga based on Ryo Mizuno's fantasy novels, which in turn were based on his role-play game scenario. A sage and scholar whose genius goes unappreciated by the common folk—which is entirely in line with his wishes—Wort spends most of his time attempting to remain removed from the world and only "interfering" by advising champions and setting them on the courses he desires. By doing this "in the name of all that is good" he disguises his real intent, which is to oppose his old comrade Karla, the body-swapping Gray Witch, who is attempting to manipulate destiny. Though clearly as powerful as Karla herself, Wort's decision to remain largely neutral and not confront the Gray Witch has caused a great deal of death and suffering, and his near inflexible views on the abuse of power have doomed thousands over the years. Wort certainly is not a coward, but he has lost his way and does not clearly understand that it is untenable for him to play by the rules of the game when every other person involved is either breaking them openly, or—as in Karla's case—writing her own. Only when adventurers Deedlit and Parn press him for help to save their world does he relent, but once the group have succeeded in thwarting Karla's plan, he returns to his quiet watching, vindicated and more secure than ever in this arrogant neutrality.

ASAEMON YAMADA [1972]

"Punished is not the man himself, but the evil that resides in him." So says Asaemon Yamada, antihero of *Executioner Asa (Kubikiri Asa)* by Kazuo Koike and Goseki Kojima. When young Yoshitsugu demonstrates both an affinity with a sword and a implacable attitude, he is rewarded with the position of Head Executioner for the Shogun and begins a new life under the name Asaemon Yamada. Known to his employers and the criminal fraternity alike as Executioner Asa, the former warrior soon proves his worth as a loyal and unflinching professional, almost casually carrying out his job of decapitating felons and testing blades on chosen victims.

In Edo-era Japan, sword-masters could petition to have their blades certified on a number of condemned criminals, and it was the job of the executioner to test whether these blades could go through different parts of the body: legs, arms, trunk, and neck. Much like *Lone Wolf and Cub* hero Itto Ogami (whom an aging Asaemon actually encounters at one point), Yamada is an old-fashioned man in a changing world, devoted to the ways of his profession, and carrying them out faithfully even when most around him revile the position he has inherited. Asaemon is portrayed as passive, dedicated, and unswerving in his duty, but with no clear moral focus outside it, and often only enters into his own story when a villain has been brought to book. This method of making other characters the main focus of the work also serves to highlight the main arc which runs through the story. Yamada is no automaton—he is presented as a man who takes great pride in simple, everyday actions other samurai would disdain to perform for themselves, like chopping wood, using them to develop his spirit, but, much like Itto, he is so utterly dedicated to his task that nothing can sway him from it, thus through the perceptions of others we see him drawn as a callous, pitiless monster. This is given resonance when one compares such perceptions with the crimes of those who condemn him; the overall theme of the story is that, however loyal and devoted to his cause, an executioner dies alone, disdained even by those he has served.

KENNETH YAMAOKA

[1997]

The central character of Kaiji Kawaguchi's *Eagle* wants to be President of the United States. A third-generation Japanese-American, educated at Yale, Ken fought in Vietnam and has served several terms as a senator. Now that he's reaching for the biggest prize in world politics, all kinds of forces line up against him. First he has to secure the Democratic party nomination, then avoid the many pitfalls of his own past and family life, and then confront racism and prejudice. A complex and challenging character, Kenneth inspires both loyalty and hatred. His campaign manager, Arthur McCoy, has been with him ever since their days in Vietnam. Ken is still married to his college sweetheart, heiress Patricia Hampton. They have a son, Alex, who is deeply troubled, and an adopted daughter Rachel. His past, however, holds many secrets. He and his father were in conflict, and Ken and the young Japanese

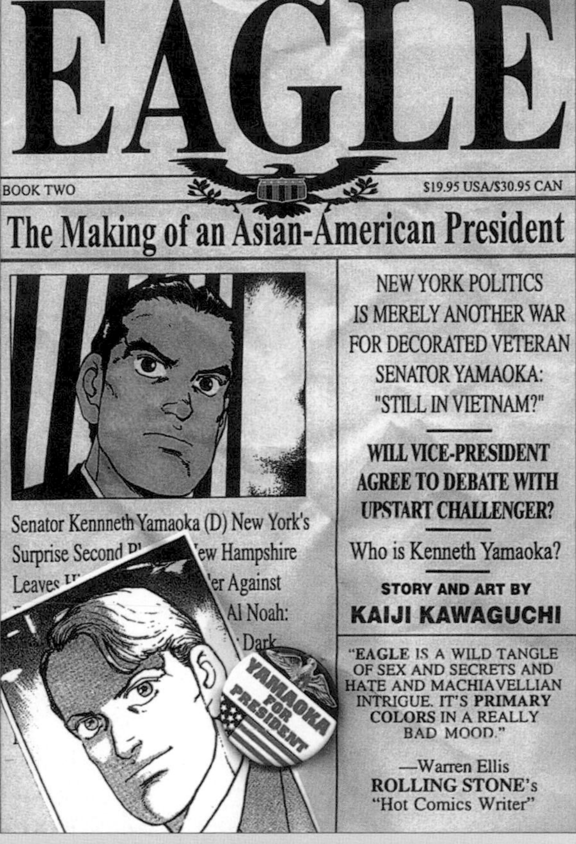

Breaking news on Capitol Hill: America is about to get its first president of Asian descent.

reporter sent to the U.S. to cover his bid for the White House have a secret connection—Takashi Jo is his illegitimate son. The original comic appeared in 1997. It was released in the U.S. by Viz Communications and reprinted as a seven-volume graphic novel edition.

Male Villains

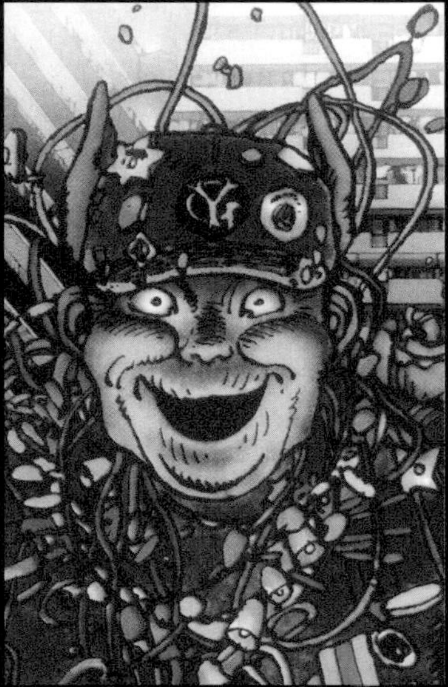

Remember, the man in the black hat isn't always the bad guy. Manga villains can surprise and even seduce you with their complexity and sympathetic qualities, and many of them are hard to spot at first. Some become villains by accident, through an unfortunate chain of events they lack the strength or courage to break. Some are driven by loyalty. Some agree with Machiavelli that a worthy end justifies any means. Even those who are openly selfish, nasty, and depraved can turn themselves around by the final chapter. But will they? Read and learn…

AKUMA [2001]

The Japanese name for Satan and the name of the villain of Mayu Shinjo's manga *Satanic Love (Akuma na Eros)*, Akuma is a demon accidentally summoned by teenage Miu Sakurai when she tries to cast a love spell from an old book on witchcraft. The object of her affection is local pastor's son Shion Amamiya, a blond hunk who is always surrounded by the best-looking girls from their school. Unfortunately, she got the wrong spell and Akuma appears at her bedroom window, all black hair, ram's horns, pointed ears, and bad attitude. Akuma kills whoever summons him, but when Miu faints in his arms on being told he's going to kill her, he realizes at once that she's a virgin, and he loves virgins. So he makes a deal with the lovestruck girl. He will make Shion fall in love with her, and in return, she will give him her virginity. The snag comes when his love spell doesn't work on Shion. Baffled and furious, Akuma decides to move in with Miu and make this spell work out if it's the last thing he does. Using magic, he transforms himself into Miu's older brother Kai, just as hunky as Shion but with black hair; his crow familiar Marupasu becomes their younger brother Tsubasa. He's so powerful he can even make Miu's mother believe she has always had three children, so getting the entire school to accept the two boys is easy. Once settled into the school, Kai/Akuma can manipulate events so that Shion gradually notices Miu and starts to fall in love with her. His austere right-hand demon Beelzebub says no good will come of it, and he could well be right—especially since Miyu, ecstatic that she now has a younger brother and beginning to believe that Kai has a softer side, is falling in love with the devil.

KAGEHISA ANOTSU [1998]

Hiroaki Samura's *Blade of the Immortal* is set in eighteenth-century Japan. The cursed, immortal warrior Manji attempts to end his painful existence by slaying 1,000 true villains, to which end he assists young orphan Rin to track down the murderer of her parents, Kagehisa Anotsu. The leader of the Itto school of swordsmanship, Anotsu is on a quest to perfect Japanese sword skills through forcing teachers of other techniques to follow his lead or be slain. With an uncompromising turn of mind and little regard for anyone who is not willing to follow his view of the way things should be, Anotsu is the worst sort of scoundrel imaginable, for he is well aware of what he is doing and does not even pretend to hide his contempt for others behind a mask of insanity. However, as the story progresses he becomes more aware of his pursuers; he is dogged by the students of others he has slain, as well as Rin and Manji, and seems to relish the conflict that his actions create. Indeed, he only seems to come to life fully when a battle is in the offing. This is brought most clearly to focus in the final stages of the story, when a gravely ill Anotsu is finally brought down by

Rin, who is unable to kill her stricken foe, and a group of swordsmen who also seek his death. Here, Anotsu revels in the inner turmoil which troubles Manji and Rin, and takes great delight in the pain he is causing all concerned.

RYO ASUKA [1979]

Ryo appears to be a cool, good-looking blond teenager with a ruthless streak. His friend Akira knows him as the spoiled son of a rich man with access to things their other classmates can only dream of—fast cars, guns, and nightclubs. In fact, he is the hermaphrodite fallen angel Satan, who was reborn as a human with no memory of his true self to enable him to understand them better and defeat them. The difficulty in the way of his plan for world conquest is that in his human form he met Akira, a school friend who becomes a half-demon to protect him, and with whom he has fallen in love. When his memories re-awaken, Ryo/Satan faces a terrible fate—he must kill the one human being he loves. The character first appears in Go Nagai's *New Devilman* in 1979, but carries on through Nagai's works to reappear in the post-apocalyptic *Violence Jack* in 1983. Satan has remade the world after killing Devilman at Armageddon, and to punish himself for slaying his love he has made himself the mute amputee slave of an evil crimelord who now dominates the devastated land. In *Amon* he appears in his true form, a ravishing winged

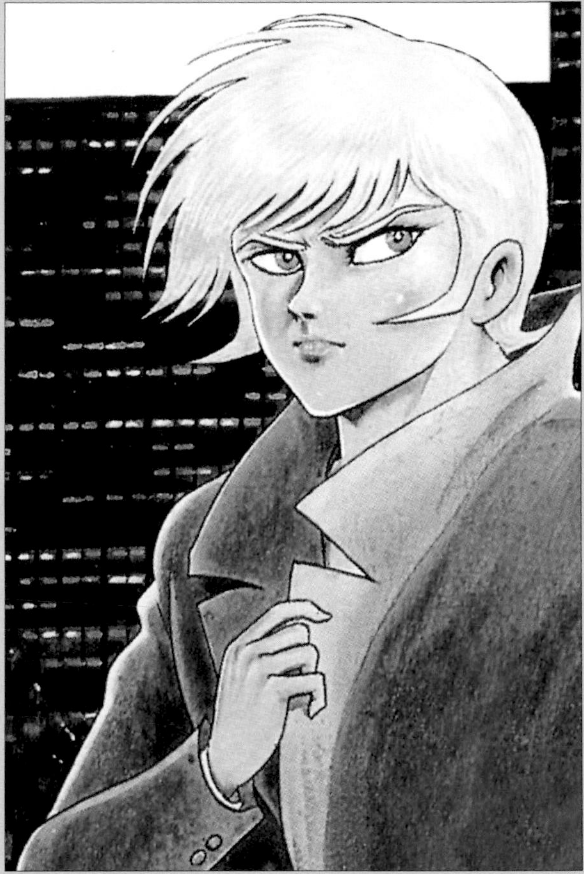

Ryo Asuka is Akira Fudo's best friend – or is he?

demon. The characters of Ryo and Akira both have links to Nagai's 1971 manga *Demon Lord Dante (Mao Dante)* in which the demon Dante, imprisoned in ice, summons teenager Ryo Utsugi by telepathy and eats him to free himself. Resurrected with Ryo's spirit, Dante realizes that the demons were Earth's original inhabitants and humans were invading gods who stole their world. Urged on by demon general Zenon to kill the invaders, Dante/Ryo has to decide the fate of mankind.

BARAGH [1982]

Born sickly and not expected to live, Baragh was saved by his sister Elata, a magician who used dark powers to save him and make him strong so that he could grow to succeed their father as leader of the Domnu Gwyn tribe of Ghost Valley in the isle of Erin. Yuho Ashibe's manga *Crystal Dragon* is a fantasy of the first century A.D., when Rome ruled the world but the wild tribes on the fringes of the empire used all their warrior strength and the wiles of both dark and bright magic to resist the invader. The historical background is not rigorous, but the iconography is used to rich and powerful effect in the complex tale of Arianrhod of the Grian Conor tribe, known as Arian, and her struggle against Baragh's determination to conquer and dominate everyone and everything in his way.

Baragh is a fabulous villain—totally evil, ruthless, tall, good-looking, and almost irresistible. He has only one eye, though his immortal spirit form has two eyes and black blood, one single drop of which can take away a person's will. He is protected by four strange childlike spirits. Normally only attracted to men (his devoted charioteer Glivis is also his lover), Baragh takes a fancy to Arian after he exterminates her entire tribe except for her and the chieftain's daughter Wijnruit. Elata and Glivis, jealous and afraid of the attraction between the pair, help Arian to escape, but Baragh enchants Wijnruit with a drop of his black blood and sends her and Glivis after Arian. She flees through the world, meeting Romans, Vikings, and magical beings, trying to escape his relentless pursuit. He then acquires another lover (the spirit of one of his former lovers re-animating the body of one of his victims) and a winged black unicorn named Fire Sword, and rejects the faithful Glivis as surplus to requirements, embarking on yet further campaigns to spread the evil of his valley throughout the world. The manga had a hiatus after ten years of publication in *Bonita Comics*, then re-started and is still one of the best and most involving fantasy series ever created.

PROF. BOYNTON a.k.a. PROF. TENMA [1951]

A tall, slim man with a prominent nose and a shock of black hair that sticks up in a crest in front, Tenma is a charismatic genius, but completely self-centered and exploitative. Head of the Science Ministry and creator of Astro Boy as a replacement for his dead son Toby (Tobio), he rejects his robot child when it fails to fulfil his expectations—he couldn't give it the capacity to grow up as his dead son would have done. So he sells the little robot he had previously loved into slavery as part of a circus sideshow. He became creator Osamu Tezuka's prototype father from hell and mad scientist, a stereotype of power used unwisely and selfishly. He went on to play several roles in *Black Jack*, including Jack's elder brother, and appeared in *Microid S*, *Rainbow Parakeet,* and *Atom Cat*.

OTTO VON BRAUNSCHWEIG [1988]

Katsumi Michihara's manga version of Yoshiki Tanaka's epic series of space war novels, *Legend of Galactic Heroes (Ginga Eiya Densetsu)* appeared in *Chara Comics* in 1990. In the late 3500s, the Alliance of Independent Worlds (a federation of broadly democratic systems) and the Galactic Empire (an Austro-Prussian autocracy with a feudal hierarchy and stunning uniforms) have been at war for about a century and a half. The battles are fought across huge areas of space in mighty starcruisers and swift, deadly fighters, but the political machinations on the worlds involved are ultimately more influential. Imperial noble Braunschweig is a blood relative of the emperor with 500 years of privilege behind him, but his position and his view of the world order is threatened by the rising prominence of a brilliant young general who is the brother of the emperor's concubine. A distinguished-looking man in his forties, Braunschweig looks the part of a leader but is stupid, arrogant, and obstinate. He forms a group of nobles and plots a coup, but he is no match for the military and strategic genius of his enemy, and the knowledge of his own inadequacy drives him insane. He squanders his forces and wastes the lives of many loyal followers. He imprisons his loyal and devoted young aide, Ansbach, for arguing against the mistake that leads to his final defeat, but Ansbach escapes and saves him from humiliating capture by forcing him to drink poison. Ansbach also takes revenge for his master on his enemy before taking his own life.

BUKU BUKK [1947]

First appearing as Pirate Bowarl in Tezuka's debut manga *New Treasure Island*, Buku was consciously drawn from the villainous Disney character Black Pete. A short, round man with a button nose, he is an old-style bad guy with a good heart. Despite his criminal activities and roguish ways, he isn't all bad. He appeared in numerous roles, including the yakuza chief Kuronishiya in *The Plain of Abusegahara* and (surprisingly) as a native Indian in *Pistol Angel*.

CACCIATORE a.k.a. HAMEGG [1952]

When Dr. Tenma, the director of the Japanese Ministry of Science, sold his artificial "son" Astro Boy to the circus, the little robot with the 100,000 horsepower engine came into the power of Cacciatore and became an immediate star. In possession of a device to control Astro, Cacciatore forces his new property to perform every imaginable trick and is only happy when the money is pouring in. He gives no thought to Astro's welfare and seems quite happy to abuse him till he almost falls apart through lack of maintenance. Only when the kindly, and slightly doddering, Prof. Elefun (one of Osamu Tezuka's famed recurring characters) takes over as director of the Science Ministry is the situation resolved, as the old man, mustering up the strength of an outraged angel, descends on the circus and removes Astro from the ringmaster's clutches. Indeed, through the professor's efforts and the visibly cruel way in which Cacciatore treats Astro to the very end of his ownership of the little robot, the general public is brought to understand the veils of robot slavery, and soon robots are granted freedom of action by law, though this in itself raises many more questions which Tezuka explores at length in his masterwork. In Japan the Western notion of the circus was tied up with that of local wandering performers, known as *sangaku* troupes. These people were considered to be unclean and spiritually dangerous to be near, treated as outcasts, the dregs of society. This explains why the circus, or wandering performers, are used in manga and anime to indicate that a character has hit rock bottom.

GANPACHI CHABANE [1988]

Ganpachi Chabane is half-man, half-cockroach, the "bio-human" result of a genetic experiment who escapes from the lab where he was created and looks for a hiding place where he can just blend into the scenery. When he winds up on the staff of Emperor High School, it seems he's no different from any of the other teachers. He and the pupils have the same view of education: it's destruction-testing for teens and teachers, a battleground where only the strongest survive. Director Toyo Ashida's 1988 video release was turned into a manga for *Animage* magazine by original designer Atsuji Yamamoto.

BUNZAEMON CHIRUSONIA [1983]

Bunzaemon is the self-styled general of the Telephone Pole Gang in Koichiro Yasunaga's manga *Prefectural Earth Defense Force*, first published in *Shonen Sunday Special*. The gang is an evil organization bent on world domination, starting with the local prefectural government on the southern island of Kyushu. All world domination attempts starting in Tokyo tend to fail, so the TPG master plan is to start small and work upwards. The gang's secret base is the Kisoya Lumber Yard where Bunzaemon is the boss. Tall, dark, and reasonably good-looking, he is also very goofy. His name is derived from the fictional element Chirusonite created in 1996 live-action TV monster series *Ultra Q*, and one of his gang is also named for a fictional element—Markalite, from SF movie *The Mysterians*. Unfortunately his group of supervillains all have fairly pathetic powers. Markalite can explode vegetables, Scope can use specialized goggles to determine the enemy's weakness, and cyborg New Year Mask can make people think it's almost New Year so they have to get ready to celebrate. Unsurprisingly, even the idiot kids of the Prefectural Earth Defense Force manage to stop the TPG in this gag manga.

DONALD CURTIS [1990]

The closest thing to a villain in Hayao Miyazaki's short manga *The Age of Hydroplanes*, Curtis is an American air ace who signs on with the Adriatic pirates in the 1920s. His ambition is to become rich, influential, and famous, and to this end he decides to shoot down Marco Pagott, the Italian ace known as the Crimson Pig, so as to claim the reward offered by Pagott's arch enemies the Air Pirates' Guild. He also hopes this will boost his reputation as a dashing desperado and attract more girls. He's a true romantic who falls in love with every pretty face he sees, but his basic laziness leads him to try to either sweep girls off their feet with flowery gestures, coerce them, or win them in bets, rather than taking the usual route of a lengthy courtship. Tall, dark, and with a pencil mustache, he looks the part of a dashing cad, but he's really not such a bad guy at heart. He finally returns to the United States and becomes a movie star. The manga can be read as a comic storyboard for Miyazaki's 1992 movie *Porco Rosso*.

DEIMOS [1975]

The charming but entirely self-centered demon is very definitely the villain of Yuho Ashibe and Etsuko Ikeda's 1975 *Princess Magazine* manga *Bride of Deimos (Deimos no Hanayome)*. Deimos is an Olympian, the twin brother of the goddess Venus, born like her from the foam of the ocean. The siblings fall in love against all the laws of the Gods, and are cast out from Olympus by Jupiter, king of the Gods. Exile isn't their only punishment. Deimos is transformed from a beautiful youth into a horned and winged demon, but Venus is tied up with thorns at the bottom of the Swamp of the Dead, her beautiful body left to rot there while her soul longs to be reincarnated and reunited with Deimos. The two plot to find a human girl who is a reincarnation of Venus, then allow the Olympian's spirit to inhabit the human body. In the twentieth century, Deimos finally finds Japanese teenager Minako Ifu. Not only is she the image of Venus, but her name is written using the same Japanese characters. Deimos begins to pursue her ruthlessly, harming everyone who loves her and trying his

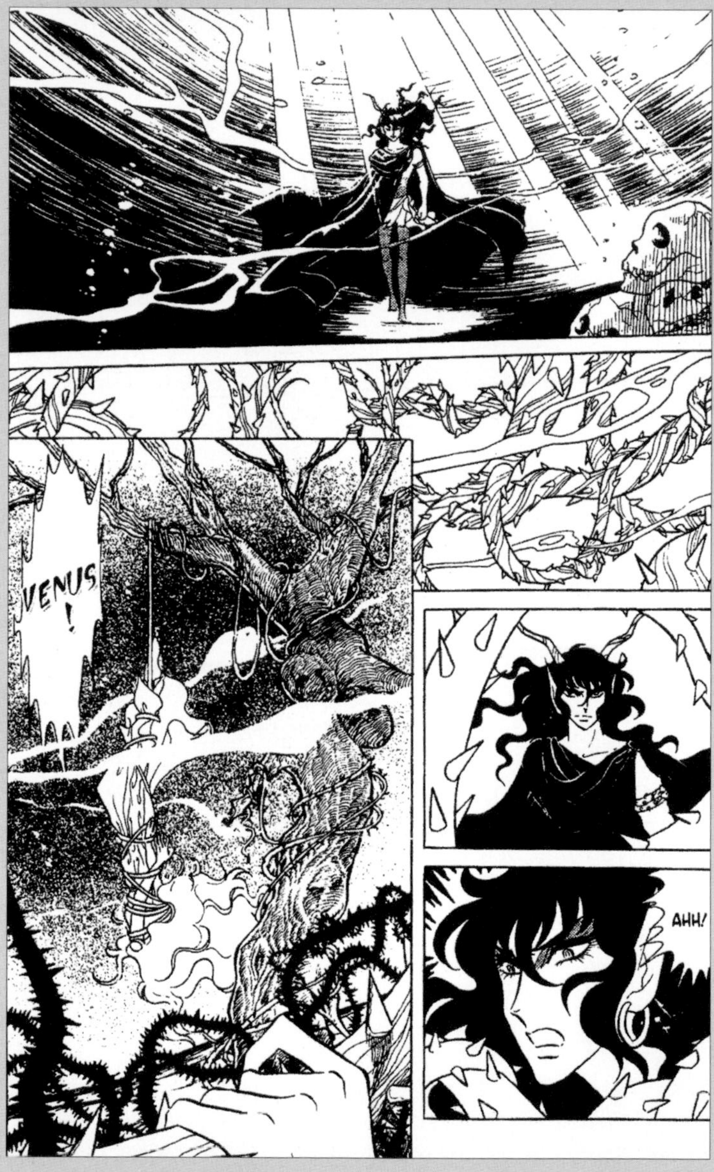
VENUS!
AHH!

utmost to break down her faith in human love and kindness. A girls' manga mixing horror and romance, *Deimos* also provides an allegory of the shallowness of a love centered only on beauty and pleasure. Human characters in the manga behave just like Deimos, putting their own selfish needs ahead of trust or compassion even for those they love: a father kills his son for gain; a son condemns his mother to a living death rather than let her follow her dreams; a young wife murders her husband because she believes he has another love. Yet as the pair move through a series of horrific adventures in which he tests Minako's belief in her own kind, Deimos finds himself falling in love with her human heart and soul. How can he take Minako's body for his sister, and lose the girl who has begun to captivate him? Yet how can he leave his adored sister who has waited for him for centuries rotting in the prison to which their forbidden love condemned her, while he is free to love again? One story was stylishly animated in 1988 by horror-specialists Madhouse. The manga is available in English from ComicsOne.

HANS ENGEL [1963]

In the years following the end of World War Two, much speculation surrounded the fleeting glimpses that the Allies and Japanese had of early German scientific weapons and the possibilities that surrounded their seizure by the great powers of the postwar world. In Japan, whose people were coming to terms with an unsuccessful alliance with Germany as part of their own healing process after the war, the themes of German super science and weapons were explored in a number of novels and manga, including Tezuka's seminal science fantasy *Big X (Dai X)*. Though eventually coming to dislike his creation—especially after its transformation in 1964 to a TV series that denuded *Big X* of all its political overtones—Tezuka fashioned the original manga with real passion, asking many questions both about the responsibility that Japan bore for Nazi crimes, and the possibility that ultra-right-wing sentiments might still lurk in Japanese politics. The story opens with a pair of scientists working for a secret German super soldier project called Big X. Japanese professor Asagumo, who eventually comes to have second thoughts about the project, secretly implants the data surrounding Big X into his son Shigeru, and is then shot by his co-workers, including German professor Engel, before they can find out what he has done with it. The scene then shifts to Tokyo in 1965, and Shigeru's discovery of the Big X project data—which is revealed to be the formula for a drug that massively increases physical strength and size, turning men into superweapons 60 feet tall. At this point a group of neo-Nazis, led by Prof. Engel's grandson Hans, appears on the scene to recover the data. Hans has been brainwashed into believing that his

Left: Handsome devil Deimos can shift shape to conceal his horns, but his true nature still shines through.

grandfather was sole inventor of the drug and the Asagumos have stolen his birthright. Shigeru's son Akira takes the drug, as does Hans, and a titanic struggle ensues with the fate of the world in the balance. Hans Engel is painted in the worst possible colors, with no redeeming characteristics at all, prompting speculation that the story was a way of exorcising Tezuka's own feelings regarding Japanese complicity with German war crimes. As two dimensional as the hero of the story, Akira, Hans does little more than spout Nazi political rhetoric and denounce the weak Japanese, whose inability to fight lost the Axis powers the war. Perhaps this is why Tezuka lost faith in the story, as its powerful action can be read as an attempt to rewrite the terms of Japan's involvement with Hitler's regime.

JOHNNY "SLEEPY" ESTES [1986]

Mad Bull 34 by Kazuo Koike and Noriyoshi Inoue falls into one of the genres that has always been a puzzle to the average Western manga fan. "Manly manga" mixes the extreme violence, to no apparent purpose, of tentacle porn with a macho worldview out of step with the rest of twenty-first century media. Compared to its heroes, *Rocky* is too articulate and *Die Hard* is for sissies. *Mad Bull 34* is a prime example of this sort of manga, with its lead character, Johnny "Sleepy" Estes, a poster boy for both fans and opponents of such extreme comics. It would have to be a wall-size poster, as he is a mountain of a man. At the opening of the manga, Johnny has been assigned a new partner, Daizaburo "Eddy" Ban, a soft rookie who finds it very disturbing that his new mentor carries more ordnance than some armed forces. Sleepy seems to have carte blanche when it comes to putting any sort of perp out of New York's misery with devices as outrageous as the rocket launcher he keeps in his trunk, the light machine gun tucked in the glove box, or the hand grenades which nicely fill out his boxer shorts. However, life is not all work for our Johnny: when he is not turning petty thieves into red smears on sidewalks, he is sexually abusing and robbing blind his own personal team of prostitutes in order to regain his manly vigor, ready for another round of ultra-violent traffic patrol.
It is on the streets where Sleepy seems most at home. Whether it be taking on all the worst stereotypes of American crime (from Italian mobs, through a naked African assassin, to a Latino drug-dealing cyborg—and I don't get that one either) or marrying his arch rival (which he does in the final chapter after battling her Guyveresque suit in a direct copy of the *Aliens* powerloader), he works in line with his own particular view of justice, not to mention a few buckets of blood. The series could be read as a pastiche of Japanese perceptions of American culture, a response to the sterile violence and limited worldview of all-American TV exports like *The A Team* and innumerable cop shows. Any other reading shows it up as something of a

monster, and its already shabby comic overtones are lost in the crossfire.

GAO [1969]

Gao appears in Osamu Tezuka's *The Phoenix: Ho-o*, first serialized in COM magazine. This segment of the story is set in eighth-century Japan. Gao is an ugly thief who injures the handsome youth Akanemaru. He continues his life of crime, losing an eye and an arm, while Akanemaru recovers and becomes a great sculptor. Then Gao meets Buddhist priest Shonin Roben, becomes a reformed man, and changes his way of life. Despite having only one arm and being half blind, he also becomes a famous sculptor. When he and Akanemaru are asked to compete for the honor of designing the ridge tile for the great temple building that will house the Buddha in the capital city of Nara, it looks as if Gao will win—that is, until Akanemaru reveals his past misdeeds and has Gao's remaining arm cut off.

LIEUTENANT COLONEL GINGETSU [1997]

Commander of the elite Secret Colors Battalion in CLAMP's manga *Clover*, Gingetsu is a mixture of selfishness and charm. The Government holds psychics known as Clovers captive, graded by their power levels from one to four-leaf Clovers. Gingetsu, himself a two-leaf Clover, is allowed to keep a three-leaf boy he calls Ran as a pet. But Gingetsu has another link to the Clovers; his aide, Kazuhiko, was in love with singer Ora, the only friend of the most powerful Clover of all. When Ora was killed for coming too close to the Clovers' secrets, Kazuhiko resigned his commission to hunt down her killer, not realizing that his former boss might be deeply involved with the mystery of their powers. *Clover* first appeared in *Amie*, a new magazine intended to pick up readers who were outgrowing its successful sister Nakayoshi. It lasted less than two years, and *Clover* has not yet been completed.

DINO GORZINE [1985]

The heavy, in every sense, of *Banana Fish* by Akimi Yoshida, Dino is the classic Corsican mobster, a stereotype crime lord created by people who have only yakuza narratives and the Godfather trilogy to work with. In the story, banana fish is actually a mind-control drug that enhances combat capability. Developed by Dr. Alexis Dawson, his younger brother Abraham, and Eddy Frederick, it is first used during the Vietnam War on U.S. troops and turns out to drive some users mad. It is the prize that Dino (and many others) seek to control, and brings the homosexual Dino into conflict with the story's protagonist, Ash. Dino desires Ash, but hates what he is doing to the gang culture of New York by breaking away and setting up his own team on his own principles. Dino is driven into conflict with the younger man on several

FIST OF THE NORTH STAR

IN A DEVASTATED WORLD, strength is everything, but one man fights for love and justice. "In the heavens there exist two pole stars: Hokuto and Nanto. As in all things, two opposites are one: man and woman, yin and yang, the Diva Kings A and Un, and also the lethal arts of Hokuto Shinken and Nanto Seiken." This philosophy forms the framework on which *Fist of the North Star (Hokuto no Ken)* hangs its hero's epic slugfests and eternal wanderings. Kenshiro is the *Fist of the North Star* in the 1983 manga by writer Buronson (Sho Fumimura, who chose his pen name as a homage to Charles Bronson) and artist Tetsuo Hara. Published in *Shonen Jump*, its first outing in English was in a Viz Communications edition in the 1990s, and it has recently been serialized in *Raioh* from U.S. manga publishers Gutsoon. It became an archetype of post-apocalyptic manga with its extreme violence and repetitive threat-of-the-week format.

The manga originated in a one-shot adventure in a special issue of *Shonen Jump* in April 1983. Then acting as writer and original artist, Hara introduced Kasumi Kenshiro (Ken), teenage heir to the Chinese combat technique of Hokuto Shin Ken, fighting evil in Japan just before World War III. Buronson came on board as writer and the pair would go on to create two *Fist* manga series, totaling thirty volumes of nuclear devastation inspired by Kennedy and Miller's film *Mad Max*. Kenshiro was now an adult with seven distinctive scars in the shape of the constellation Ursa Major, which includes the North Star, on his massive chest. It was a huge hit.

Fist has echoes of *Shane*, *Fist of Fury*, and the nameless hero of *A Fistful of Dollars*, as well as leather-clad ex-cop Max. In the late 1990s the world is devastated by nuclear war. Ken is the youngest of four boys adopted by martial arts master Ryuken, and is the chosen inheritor of his father's martial arts tradition of Hokuto Shinken. Ryuken is killed by Shin, master of the Southern Cross style of the Nanto school, and Ken's best friend. Shin has another motive for fighting than power and glory—he loves Ken's fiancée Julia. He also wants to steal something from his friend, whom he both loves and envies. As his father's heir, Ken faces Shin and is defeated. He is scarred and left for dead, and Shin abducts Julia. So Ken's epic journey begins, both a quest for his love, a fight to decide which of the two schools will triumph, and a man's attempt to wipe out his friend's betrayal and find peace

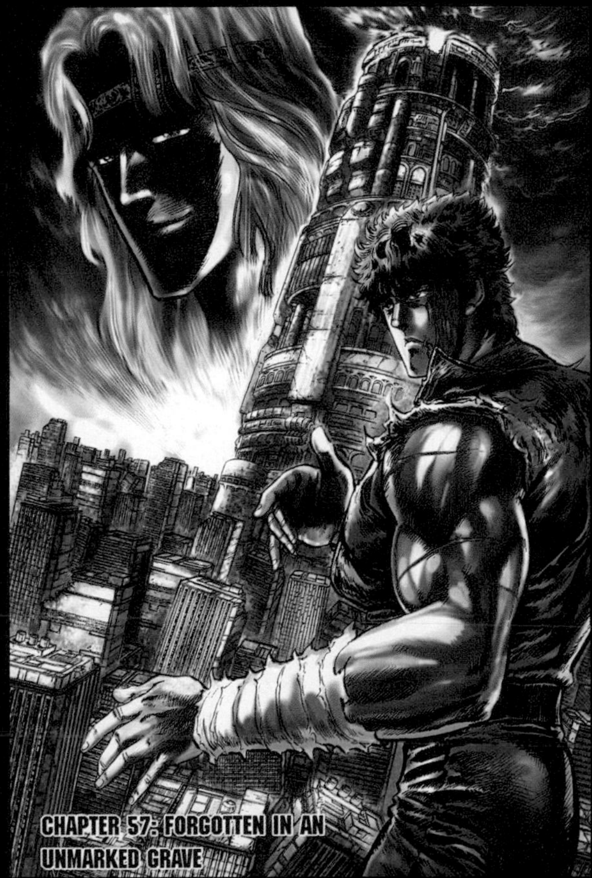

A strong man in a world of chaos and destruction: Kenshiro is on a quest for revenge.

through vengeance. Ken eventually kills Shin and finds Julia, but there is no happy ending for the star-crossed lovers.

Ken's brothers are Raoh, the eldest, also known as Fist King (Ken-o), Toki, a gentle and intelligent healing master who is also a great warrior, and Jagi, a petty bully and incompetent fighter who is so jealous of Ken that he impersonates him, not to bask in his reputation but to destroy it. Toki is dying of radiation poisoning, a common fate for attractive and likable characters in *Fist of the North Star*. Radiation provides an excuse for the massive musculature of men and woman alike; many fighters are mutant monsters with names like Devil and Jackal.

A number of motifs repeat themselves through the story: impersonation as a weapon, confusions over identity as characters fail to recognize reality and follow illusion, the fate of women and children in any society that values strength above all else. This last is a common theme of many artforms, mixing titillation with an ability to take the moral high ground. *Fist* doesn't hesitate to exploit this trope, but it also uses the treatment of women, like its other repeating motifs, to emphasize the fragility of the things we value: the good (trust, love, honor, and life itself); and the trivial (power, fame and success).

Another constant theme is the importance of children, whose vulnerability is a threat to the future, and who must therefore be defended at all costs. Ken is always ready to defend the helpless, but his anger when a child is harmed is terrifying. He meets a pair of orphans, streetwise Bat and shy, gentle Lyn, who become his companions on the road.

It's also worth pointing out that there are

good and bad masters of both schools, men who use the techniques for righteous or evil ends. Neither school is good or bad of itself; the techniques are morally neutral, as simple in that regard as a gun or knife. The wielder gives them intent and purpose.

According to Buronson and Hara, Hokuto Shinken (literally "God Fist of the North Star") originated in China 2,000 years earlier and is so lethal it is only taught from father to son. Only one son can inherit the full knowledge; in a dispute over succession, the losers must have their "fists sealed"—either their memories must be erased or their hands destroyed. The symbol of Hokuto Shinken is a portion of the constellation Ursa Major, the seven stars commonly known as the Big Dipper. In Hokuto no Ken, these stars are considered unlucky, causing death and misfortune. For this reason, the lives of Hokuto practitioners are filled with tragedy. Next to the main constellation is a smaller star named Shichousei, or Star of Death Omens. Legend says that those who can see it will die within the year. The symbol of Nanto Seiken is part of the constellation Sagittarius, the Archer, forming the constellation Nanto (Southern Ladle) in Chinese Astrology. The Nanto school has six major styles, each corresponding to a star in the constellation that influences the destinies of the style's masters. Ken fights all the Nanto styles in the course of the story, as well as all his own family and most of his friends.

The scenario progresses like a computer game, with constant escalation of the violence levels, an ever more powerful opponent to beat at the end of each level, signature moves, and weapons. Its fabulous excesses never seemed to bore its fans, despite the inherent absurdity of a hero who can push a couple of points on your body, tell you you are going to die in five seconds, then walk away as your head explodes like a punctured balloon, but with rather more mess. It's the perfect entertainment for those looking for testosterone overload with an absurdity bypass.

The success of its hulking hero has crossed formats and language barriers. Two anime TV series aired between 1984 and 1988, a live-action movie was made in Hollywood in 1995, and a huge range of merchandising still sells, twenty years on. Best known in the West in its animated format, *Fist of the North Star* was the second anime to be made commercially available in the UK, and the first on the Manga Video label, following on from the huge success of *Akira*. In the United States it was first released by Carl Macek and Jerry Beck's Streamline Pictures, and later picked up by Manga's U.S. arm.

As macho as they come: Kenshiro faces a mountain of muscle. Notice the Japanese sound effects linking the panels.

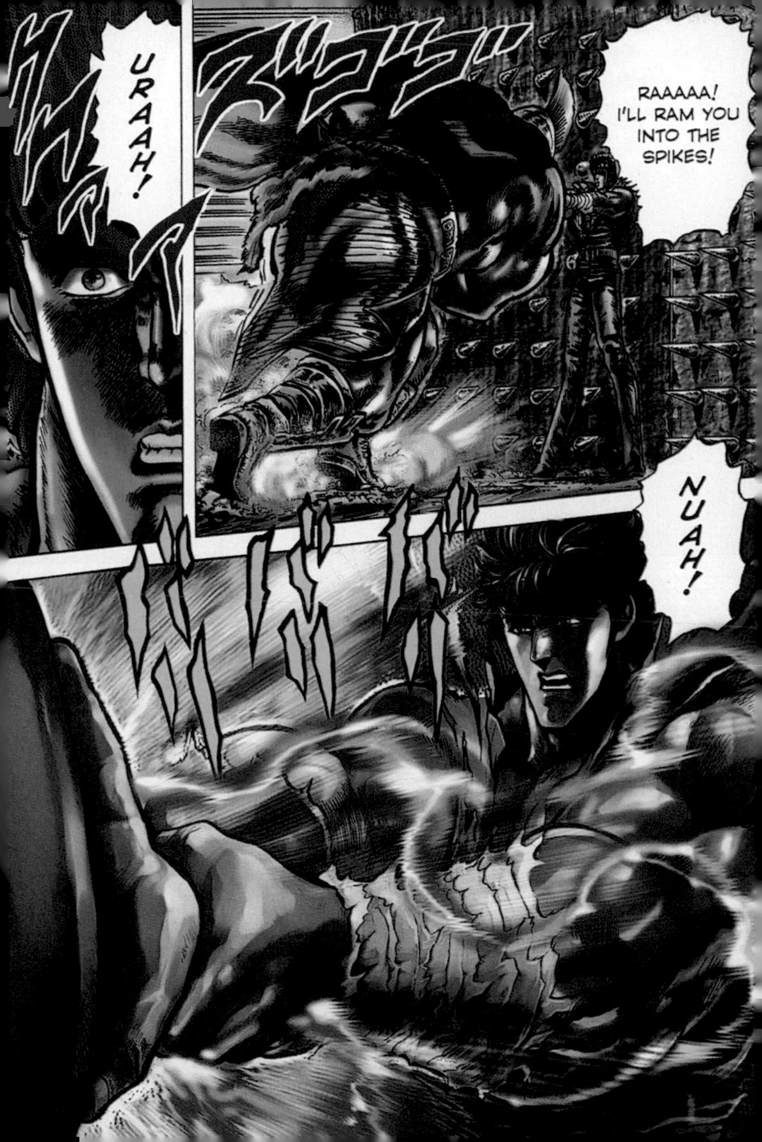
RAAAAA! I'LL RAM YOU INTO THE SPIKES!
URAAAH!
NUAH!

occasions, but never loses sight of his passion to control Ash. His love is constantly shown as being about control, about dominance, about moulding Ash into a younger version of himself; all his demands center around Ash joining Dino's gang (thus accepting his principles and ideas) and succeeding him in time. Even down to his death, at the medical facility at which banana fish was developed, his obsession does not waver, and this has a profound effect on Ash. Japanese narrative convention since the Edo period has often called for strong male figures to be homosexual or bisexual, in order that they might be painted as having a stronger tie to another male character than would normally be expected. This convention arose in the sixteenth to nineteenth centuries, an age which was, at least in Japan, far more relaxed about same-sex relationships than Europe, and actively encouraged them among certain classes. Indeed, among the male-dominated bushi and yakuza groups of this period we often see the very Greek sentiment of "men for love, women for babies" at the forefront of relationships. The idea was that only a comrade in arms can truly understand his fellows, and this is what Yoshida seems to be implying in Dino's perverted passion for Ash, and Ash and Eiji's love.

HAKURON [2000]

The young, ambitious, passionate head of the Dragon Lord association, one of Hong Kong's most powerful mafia crime syndicates, Hakuron is tall, dark, and handsome, with a black dragon tattooed on his temple close to his left eye. When on a business trip to Tokyo he gets into trouble with rival criminals and is separated from his entourage, wounded and alone in a strange city. To escape, he grabs the first pretty girl he sees, pulls her into a corner and kisses her. Mayu Shinjo's *Despotic Lover (Haou Airen)* focuses on the attractions of power and charisma, and asks if it's possible to make someone love you by force of will alone, even when you are not, by any normal standards, a nice person.

Seventeen-year-old Kurumi is still in school and working part-time to support her sick mother and two little brothers when she becomes Hakuron's camouflage. Realizing that the men who pass their hiding place are out to kill him, she takes the wounded stranger home and does what she can for his injuries. Harukon thanks her by drugging her and leaving, but next day he has his minions wait for her to leave school, then drag her into a car and drug her again. When she wakes, she's on a plane to Hong Kong, where Hakuron has arranged a reception in honor of the girl who saved his life and is now, he has decided, his lover. There we learn that Hakuron is only a year older than Kurumi and still goes to high school, though he doesn't actually attend classes—instead he has a private study where he runs his crime business. He also enrolls Kurumi in the same school. Shinjo's reliance on the school scenario is one of two structural problems—she does high-school romance very well, but here it stretches credibility too far. The other is Kurumi herself, who seems a pale cipher beside the dynamic, intense, and driven Hakuron, whose inner demons and entourage of loyal henchmen (including Fuoron, one of the few cross-dressing Hong Kong mafiosi in comics), former lovers, and violent adversaries signal his coming senseless demise like neon signs. The end of the manga shows us Kurumi three years on, back at the church where she and Hakuron were to have married, grieving for her despotic lover.

COUNT ALEXIS HARGREAVES [1992]

Alexis, heir to a noble family founded in 960 A.D., is a very nasty man. Even though he's dead, he continues to torment his son and heir, Cain, in Kaori Yuki's Gothic melodrama *Count Cain (Hakushaku Cain)*, an elegantly decorated hymn to emotional excess set in nineteenth century England. Alexis' obsessive hatred of his son leads to physical and mental torture which drives the boy to kill him, possibly twice. Alexis is tall, dark, handsome, and arrogant. He made an arranged marriage, as was expected, but since childhood, has loved his beautiful sister Augusta, and when she did not return his incestuous passion, he raped her and made her pregnant. She gave birth to Cain and went insane. Her black hair turned white overnight, and she was shut up in an asylum where she killed herself. Alexis is head of Delilah, a secret society devoted to evil and the breakdown of Victorian society. He has other children: adopted son Dr. Jezebel Disraeli; the deceased Shuzetto, a full sister to Cain; her clone Michaela; and Merryweather, offspring of a liaison with a servant. Alexis and Augusta were based on the incestuous love of English poet Lord Byron, for his sister, and the five-volume manga is named for Byron's 1821 five-act tragedy *Cain*. The first series was followed by eight-volume sequel *God Child* between 2001 and 2003.

AKITO HAYAMA [1994]

Child's Toy (Kodomo no Omocha) by Miho Obana is sometimes described by anime reviewers who have spent too long wearing rose-tinted lenses, as a child's perspective on love and friendship. *Kodomo no Omocha*, known to its fans as *Kodocha*, is better described as a group of utterly insane ten-year-olds' attempts to transcend reality by consuming every drop of caffeine on the face of the planet. It revolves around the child TV starlet, Kurata Sana, and her attempts to bring harmony to her hyperactive classmates and—especially—the suicidal Akito Hayama, whose general malaise and contempt for all around him contrast with the jumped-up nature of his peers. To put it mildly, Hayama is a bit of an odd sort. Raised in a home which might be considered abusive in any other reality, he has grown up cold, aloof, and thoroughly cynical

ROCK HOLMES [1949]

MAKING HIS DEBUT in *Detective Boy Rock Holmes*, this highly intelligent young man is obviously a lineal descendant of the great British detective Sherlock Holmes. Like Holmes, he is cold, detached, and uninterested in anyone else's notions of propriety or morality except insofar as they serve his ends. He appeared in more than twenty of Tezuka's manga and three anime, as himself in four of them, and guesting as various juvenile and adult characters in others. He even plays Bassanio in Tezuka's version of *The Merchant of Venice*. In 1951's experimental anthology manga *Fossil Island*, where a group of travelers have strange dreams inspired by the geology of the place, Rock actually dreams he is Holmes' partner, fighting a phantom thief for a hidden sculpture. This manga showcases two drawing styles to highlight the difference between the dream world and reality, so Rock appears in his usual manga form with big eyes and simple lines, and in a more realistic style as a good-looking young man in contemporary dress.

In *The Adventures of Rock* (*Shonen Club*, 1952) he stars in a dark and complex story sparked by Karel Capek's 1936 novel *War with the Newts*. The story opens as an unknown planet appears suddenly in orbit around the Earth. Planet Dimon, named for its deceased discoverer, seems very Earth-like. It was formerly a planet directly opposite the Earth on the other side of the sun, revolving round the sun at the same velocity on the same course. A catastrophe brings it close to Earth and it becomes the planet's second moon. Rock, son of the late Dr. Dimon, is heir to the planet and leads an exploration party that lands on its soil. They encounter many strange races, including clay people called the Luborooms who can shapeshift at will and almost instantly produce several copies of Rock. These beings are enslaved by the winged, birdlike Epooms, who have a quasi-medieval civilization into which Rock is drawn. Becoming a father figure to bird-child Chiko, Rock is instrumental in bringing fire to the Epoom, and like Prometheus he will be torn apart for his presumption. When mankind learns the seas on Dimon are oil, humans enslave the Epoom, and later begin to use them as meat. Rock finally dies trying to save his foster-child Chiko, and urges him to take his people back to Dimon, since the two races cannot co-exist in peace.

In *Vampires,* Rock is the villain of the piece, and incites a tribe of werewolves to revolt against their human oppressors for his own ends. He plays Rokuro Makube, a scientific genius and master of disguise, nicknamed Rock. Country bumpkin Toppei, a member of a hill tribe that turn into wolves at full moon, has come to visit Mushi Productions, Tezuka's

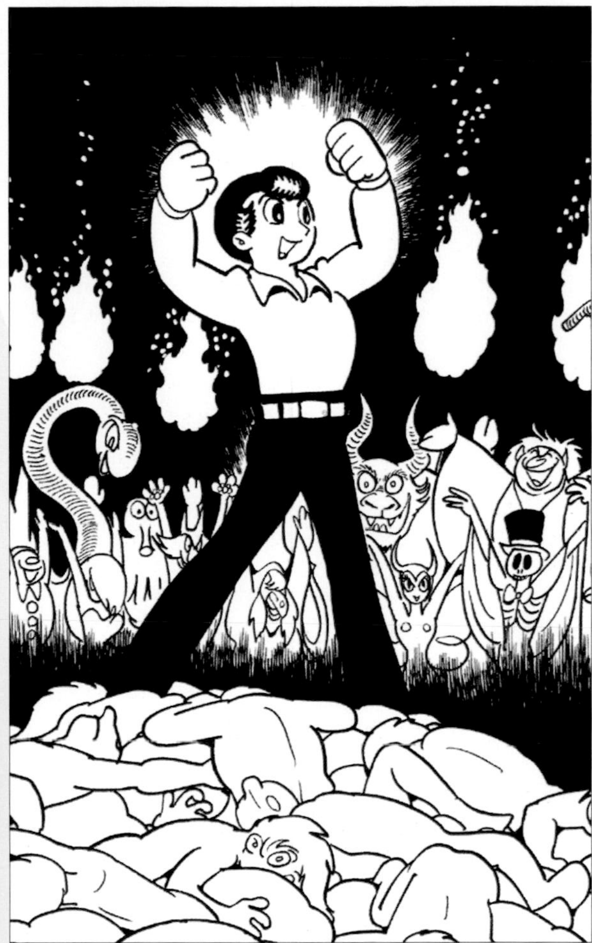

Rock Holmes (as Rokuro Makube) enjoying a moment of adulation in *Vampires*.

studio. One night Rock witnesses an accident in which Toppei accidentally causes the death of Tezuka's friend Prof. Atami, an expert in vampire lore. Rock tries to blackmail Tezuka into letting him use Toppei for criminal purposes. Toppei refuses, but when he is rescued by Rock he feels he has no choice but to help him in his crimes. A prophecy says that Rock cannot be killed by humans or animals, but when his plot to use the vampires to take over the world fails, the vampires turn on him. He barely escapes with his life by leaping into the sea, defeated by creatures neither human nor animal.

Tezuka created Rock to fill the role of the pragmatic, even cynical individual who will survive and thrive come what may, an antidote to the lovable, law-abiding good guys like Astro Boy; warped characters offer more story possibilities than shining heroes. Even where he has a more heroic role, as in 1951's *The Road To Utopian Lurue*, he has one eye on his own advancement.

In *Vampires,* his character's family name is the Japanese pronunciation of Macbeth; in the *Akita Shoten* edition of 1976 Tezuka said: "I find Macbeth personifies evil with vitality, fit for today's world." Rock is highly intelligent, handsome, and charming, but his attractive exterior hides a cold, calculating brain and a malicious nature. From his debut as a child character, he understands that even if the world is an unjust place, it can be kind to those who know how to play society's games. He comments: "The world is full of inconsistencies. The world will not weep even if the fight for justice is lost and evil triumphs. Come spring the flowers will still bloom, the sunshine will still pour down in the summer."

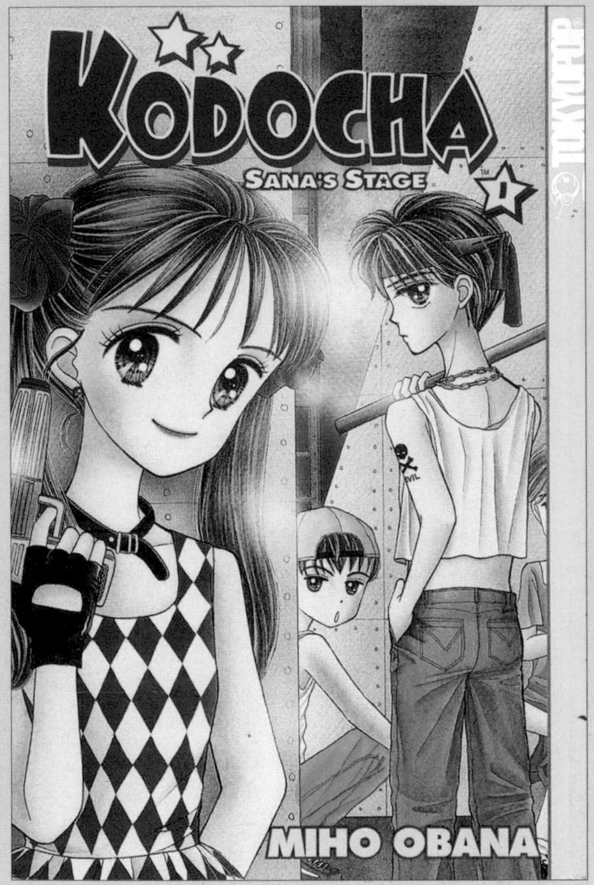

Child star Sana tries to live a normal life despite her TV fame.

about every aspect of the world around him, and it is this, as Sana finds out, which makes him such a terrible person. Initially, he expresses his disdain for the world through blackmailing his teachers and letting some cronies loose on the school. Like all bullies, however, Hayama is just lashing out because he feels rejected by everyone in his world and is jealous of Sana, with her TV lifestyle and famous author and squirrel tamer mother. As the story progresses, Sana slowly brings him out of his shell and ends up reforming the little monster (as far as possible) through discussing in a child-like way the issues that plague him—abandonment, suicide, loss, and violence forming just part of the picture.

AKIRA HOJO [1986]

Akira is a young orphan determined to claw his way to the top of the pile by whatever means necessary. He joins the yakuza, the Japanese criminal society, and manages to rise rapidly through their ranks while keeping a clean rap sheet. Elegant, well-dressed, well-spoken, he could be any young businessman headed for the top. He even dazzles policewoman Kyoko Ishihara, sent to get the goods on him and willing to get into his bed to do so. His only loyalty is to his oldest friend Chiaki Asami, another orphan and fellow-survivor of the war-torn hell of Cambodia. Asami has taken another route to safety—he has become part of the Japanese political establishment—but his methods are the same as those of his old friend. The pair appear in Ryoichi Ikegami and Sho Fumimura's *Big Comics Superior* manga *Sanctuary*, a dazzling fantasy of the links between politics and crime and the narrow line that divides the avowedly criminal and the supposedly respectable. It is out in English from Viz.

PHOENIX IKKI [1986]

Ikki, Shun's older brother, is the most potent of all the Bronze Saints, warrior servants of the good and wise goddess Athena, and forever seeking new ways to enhance his powers—which eventually leads him to take up Queen Hades' challenge and journey to her island to train and fight her warriors, in place of his beloved little brother Shun. A fundamentally good man, his strength is turned to evil by a master so cruel that he is willing to slay his own daughter to spur Ikki on to an act of wickedness, and becomes the Bronze Saints' most dangerous adversary. Ikki is eventually saved by Shun's love for him in the aftermath of the battle for the Sagittarius Gold armor, in which he led the evil Black Saints against his brother's forces. *Saint Seiya (Seitoshi Seiya)*, Masami Kurumada's epic tale of battling bands of legendary warriors, appeared in *Weekly Shonen Jump* magazine, published by Shueisha.

GOTO KAIOJI [1987]

Second son of Duke Kaioji, who is head of the powerful interplanetary conglomerate Conselun, Goto is captain of the spaceship *Flying Mermaid*. He is also second-in-command of Red Caravan, an organization dedicated to reducing and finally removing the influence of Earth on space colonies. He kills his own father and tries to kill his older brother Yumito in an effort to destroy Conselun. He is foiled, and then impersonated, by Joker, a genetically engineered shapeshifter who can take on any form and is used by the Special Police Task Force to crack impossible cases. The lead character of Katsumi Michihara and Yu Maki's manga series *Joker* has silver eyes, superhuman strength and reflexes, and the ability to switch genders as well as appearance. The manga contains homages to the work of Gerry and Sylvia Anderson; police captain Straker is an obvious steal from the austere blond hero of TV series *U.F.O.*, and hero detective Lin, Joker's reluctant love object, attends a concert by Duke's daughter Natsumi, whose stage name Melody Angel is taken from a character in the Andersons' puppet series *Captain Scarlet*.

MURAKI KAZUTAKA [1995]

Descendants of Darkness (Yami no Matsuei) by Matsushita Yoko appeared in Hakusensha's *Hana to Yume* magazine. Kazutaka is a resident at a Tokyo hospital, the perfect job for a psychic vampire serial killer, with a constant supply of helpless victims at hand to supply the life force he needs to sustain his own selfish and

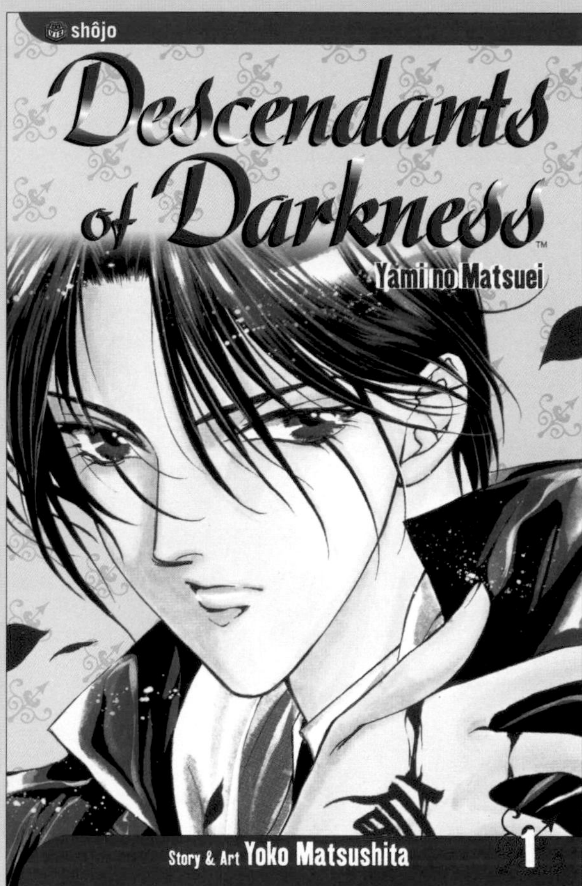

Tsuzuki Asato, favorite victim of sadistic silver-haired vampire doctor Muraki Kazutaka.

near-immortal existence. An extremely handsome man, he is particularly fond of torturing the hero, Tsuzuki.

SHINGO KUSAKA a.k.a. MAYO [1996]

Mayo is a Japanese killer on the streets of Kuala Lumpur and charges only 5 ringgit for each of the hits he carries out. Then he is asked to kill the mother of a young prostitute called Shion. He cannot bring himself to fulfill the contract, suddenly making him, and Shion, the target for a pair of massive crime families who seem to be bent on erasing them both. As the story progresses, and the pair outwit ever more skilled assassins, we discover the secrets of Mayo's past. His real name is Shingo Kusaka, the scion of the Kusaka Corporation and Shion's uncle. She is the daughter of Junichiro, Mayo's brother, who framed him for drug smuggling in Malaysia to get him out of the way and provide the family with a useful tool in another city. Once Mayo learns the truth, he must protect Shion from his own brother, from the local Malaysian mob, and from the police. Mayo is an unlikely hero, having spent most of his time in Kuala Lumpur as a brutal assassin for his family. He goes through something of a sea change when faced with Shion's plight, and slowly comes to see that blood is not always thicker than water and that the "purity of the strain" is not the paramount concern he might once have thought. Junichiro's belief that Shion and her mother are unfit to carry the Kusaka line echoes an old-fashioned view of the importance of moral and racial purity not exclusive to Japan, but some still rate such views highly. This is especially clear at the climax of the manga, as he is required to face his own brother knowing that to "win" he must destroy his clan. Shion's survival is balanced against the future of his family in *Strain* by Ryoichi Ikegami and Buronson.

ONIME NO KYO a.k.a. DEMON-EYED KYO [1999]

Samurai Deeper Kyo is the story of Kyoshiro Mibu, a gentle herbalist whose body is also inhabited by the much less pleasant and reasonable warrior Kyo. Kyo is said to have slain a thousand warriors at the battle of Sekigahara in 1600, and has been on the run ever since with a price of one million pieces of gold on his head. What better place to hide a warrior nature than inside the persona of a humble wandering healer? The manga by Kamijo Akimine first appeared in *Shonen* magazine.

ACETYLENE LAMP [1948]

Tezuka's inimitable larger-than-life gangster made his debut in *Jungle Kingdom* as a film crew member. Created for Tezuka's amateur manga *Lost World: Private Edition*, in which he was an unscrupulous journalist, the character was based on a childhood friend who had a dent in the back of his head so large you could stand a candle in it—hence the name. He is tall and angular with a large straight nose, and in many appearances he actually has a candle standing on the back of his head, but this didn't stop Tezuka, using him in serious roles. His finest hour was undoubtedly as Lamp, the Chief of German Intelligence in 1983's *Adolf*, in which he created an unforgettable aura of pure evil. Among his other appearances, he was the villainous retainer Yagyu Shuma in *The Plain of Abusegahara*.

GANOSSA MAXIMILIAN [1988]

Leader of the alien Lucifer Hawks in Kia Asamiya's 12-volume Kadokawa manga *Silent Mobius* and its single-volume prequel *Mobius Klein*, Ganossa is a tall, good-looking human with long hair. Brilliant, power-hungry and utterly ruthless, Ganossa is obsessed by his former master, and Gigelf's daughter Katsumi. He revels in physical and mental torture and has lost the ability to feel any humane emotion. He was once a member of the Magician's Guild and student of the arch-mage Gigelf Liquer. The Guild was a prime mover in the ill-fated Project Gaea, an attempt to solve the energy crisis by exploiting other-dimension planet Nemesis; the project's failure imprisoned many of its people in our world. Ganossa, who had opposed the project from the start, seized his chance to become leader of the exiles. By bonding himself to the planet Nemesis and its people, he gained longer life and greater power, but his troops have only contempt for humans and barely tolerate him. They are physical beings, and can even interbreed with humans, but they are almost unkillable, have supernatural powers, and will do whatever is necessary to get back home—even if that means being led by a mere human. As a former Guild member, Ganossa knows the strengths and weaknesses of most human magicians. SM is out in English from Viz.

DEMITRI MAXIMOFF [1997]

Demitri originated in the computer game *Vampire Hunter*, animated in 1997 by influential studio Madhouse. He's a dapper dresser in classic vampire mold, given a modern twist with a hairdo that resembles a squeeze of toothpaste. The manga by Run Ishida, renamed *Night Warriors: Darkstalkers' Revenge* for Western release by Viz, is a four-episode video anime. It shares the problems of most game-based shows in that it has to give all the principal characters a share of screen-time; plotting and characterization comes second to the fight scenes. Demitri is scheming to use the psychic energy raised by his slaves to take over the power of the other Darkstalkers, who regard him as an undesirable element.
He's also embarked on a sizzling affair with succubus clan chief Morrigan, a woman so fond of bats that she has them emblazoned all over her most substantial item of clothing—her tights—as well as having flight-capable wings growing from her model-girl mane.

MAO [1990]

Vampire Mao would be bad if he could, but he's under the control of a sixteen-year-old virgin in a Catholic convent school. Yukako Isaka's *Luna Lunatic* appeared in *Flower Comics* in 1990. Angelica High first-year student Luna is always in trouble. Cleaning the church as a punishment for falling asleep during service, she accidentally cuts herself and her blood brings a beautiful carving of a young man to life. Stuck in the wall, Mao asks Luna for help getting out. Luna doesn't like his macho arrogance, but when she finds the school is overrun by zombies, she needs his help. Then they both learn she can control him through the bond between them—she has her very own *bishonen* vampire servant.

MICHAEL [1988]

A reworking of Judaeo-Christian narratives, Yun Kouga's *Earthian* is a story based around the role which a race of humanoid "angels," who had evolved on the planet Eden much earlier than the other races in this section of the Galaxy, play in protecting the younger races from harm. Earth in particular has a real fascination for these people of Eden, and each day a team of two angels—one "positive" who notes beneficial actions and one "negative" who records malign goings on—keep watch on the Earth and help decide the future of the planet. Ruling Eden is Archangel Michael, director of operations for all protected planets, responsible for the development of planets such as Earth. His is the overriding voice in decisions on the future of these planets and their races. However, the people of Eden have developed a distinct superiority complex during their self-selected mission; Michael is hugely arrogant and petulant regarding the inability of the lesser races to govern themselves properly. He is also concerned about the spread of a "Black Cancer" throughout the already slowly reproducing population of Eden, which seems especially virulent among positive angels and those who love Earth. Michael eventually decides that, as the Earth seems to be the source of the corruption, the planet must be destroyed. His plans are eventually foiled, however, and his weapon system destroyed by angels who believe in saving the race through contact with other peoples, primarily from Earth.

MIROKU [1987]

Emperor Miroku is a huge man, even taller than the robot warriors of legend. He may be an alien—no one is quite certain. He looks like a good-looking human male, and has had a child with his human bride Princess Sayuka, but he has a black heart and has committed an act of great evil. When he was told that their firstborn son Madara had such power within him that he could one day overshadow his father, Miroku immediately sacrificed the newborn child to the devil Mazoku, dividing the eight chakras, or energy points, of the infant's body among his generals for safe keeping. But the ninth chakra, the child's soul, was saved by a wise old man and placed in a bionic body, known as a "gimmick." Now in an artificially created body, Madara hunts for the chakras to regain his own flesh, piece by piece, and Miroku seeks to destroy his son's soul. Akitaka Tajima's heroic fantasy manga *Madara* first appeared in *Maru Sho Famicom* magazine,and is based on a concept by Eiji Otsuka. It also has many similarities to Osamu Tezuka's earlier *Dororo*.

MR. MITSUKI [1997]

Zeus by Yo Higuri, originally from *Asuka DX Comics*, is a fantasy story with dark undertones that centers around a species apart from the normal human race. Lemora Salamanders possess strange powers. Because he is a special type of his species, Kira is wanted by others for the power he can bring. The mysterious Rosen Kroitz Secret Society seems to know a great deal about the Salamanders and it appears that they keep them, or breed them like pets. A man named Mr. Mitsuki is the head of the society. The members and motivations of the Rosen Kroitz Secret Society are at present unknown. Mr. Mitsuki is a twisted and evil man who treats Sui Mitsuki, the young man he calls his son, in an extremely depraved manner. Adopting Sui, who is a Salamander, when he was about thirteen, Mr. Mitsuki sexually abused him and still beats him to keep him in line. But Sui is Kira's long lost older brother, and will not allow Mitsuki or anyone else to threaten the child he has been seeking for more than a decade.

NEZU [1983]

A little guy with a Napoleon complex, Nezu is one of the prime movers behind the project that turned child psychics into weapons in 1990s Japan, only to see their efforts result in World War III. Short, fat, but always immaculately groomed, his vanity is reflected in his dapper suits and his hair, neatly trimmed but hanging flamboyantly to his collar, as if this could somehow negate the fact that his hairline is receding so fast it will soon disappear. Nezu (his name is the Japanese word for rat) is very clever, but not very intelligent; despite the evidence of the devastated city around him, he believes that his lying and chicanery is going to lead to a successful outcome, at least for himself. He is playing both ends against each other, liaising with the resistance while working with the Council of Neo-Tokyo to suppress it. He later dies of a heart attack, alone in an alley. A lesser writer than Katsuhiro Otomo would have made Nezu the villain of the piece in *Akira*; corrupt politicians are easy targets. Instead Otomo tells it like it is; greedy politicians are only part of the problem. The mobs and cults who riot on the streets of Neo-Tokyo would not make a better world if they succeeded in destroying Nezu and his kind.

PICCOLO [1984]

Like so many of the aliens in Akira Toriyama's *Dragonball* saga, the high demon Piccolo starts out evil and wanting to defeat Goku, and ends up as his devoted friend, a reformed character and mentor of his eldest son, Gohan. He first uses the magical Dragonballs to rejuvenate himself and kill the dragon god Shen Long, then is defeated by Goku and reforms. His preferred form is a bald, green-skinned, muscular guy and he sometimes wears a turban. His role in TV series *Dragonball* and *Dragonball Z* differs slightly from the manga, but only in terms of fight details—the major relationships don't change too much, as this would certainly have caused protest among the young manga fans who were addicted to Toriyama's creations.

QUINCY [1987]

The "old man" is the mighty corporate suit at the head of the evil GENOM corporation. A white-haired, dignified-looking businessman, he is a cipher for Japan's growing distrust of corporate power in the late 1980s. He originated in TV anime *Bubblegum Crisis* where he arranged the murder of heroine Sylvia Stingray's father, a research scientist who created the voomer technology that GENOM planned to use to take over the world. He met his end through one of his own plots backfiring, in Tony Takezaki's spin-off manga *AD Police*, which in its turn spun off an animated series.

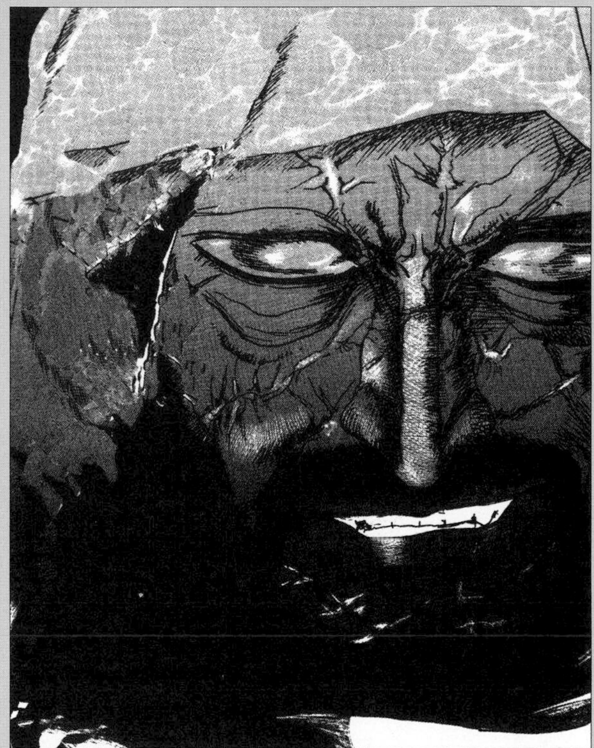

Mad, bad, and dangerous to be around, Levi Ra turns Shinjuku to rubble.

LEVI RA [1988]

Evil mage Levi Ra is the emissary of Hell, preparing to open the portals of the netherworld and allow demons to run riot in Shinjuku. Ten years ago, he murdered his opponent Kenichiro Izayoi; now Kenichiro Izayoi junior is coming after the greatest evil mage on the planet, armed only with innocence and assisted by his girlfriend and a midget on roller-skates. Heavily inspired by *Star Wars*' revenge plot, the story's only point of real originality is Ra himself. Kikuchi, creator of bestselling horror fantasies, makes him a classic evil genius, with overreaching ambition and the fatal flaw of underestimating the opposition, yet gives him a few new twists, including an ability to self-heal in novel ways that predate *Terminator 2*. The manga version of *Demon City Shinjuku* is based on a novel by Hideyuki Kikuchi, with art by Shinichi Hosoma. The anime version was one of the wave of Manga Entertainment releases that were aimed at the 1990s teenage male market.

DUKE RED [1949]

One of the brightest stars in Tezuka's manga repertory company, Duke Red first appears as the villain in *Metropolis*, head of the Red Party. He pays innocent Dr. Charles Lawton, a cell-creation specialist, to create a powerful humanoid that he plans to use for evil ends. His silky charm and ruthlessly pragmatic nature made him an ideal evil mastermind but Tezuka also used him in more positive roles. His adaptability as a character was hampered by his Roman nose, which made him difficult to draw head on. Naturally a dapper dresser with a certain Edwardian sense of style, he usually wears his hair in a distinctive spiky crest on the back of his head.

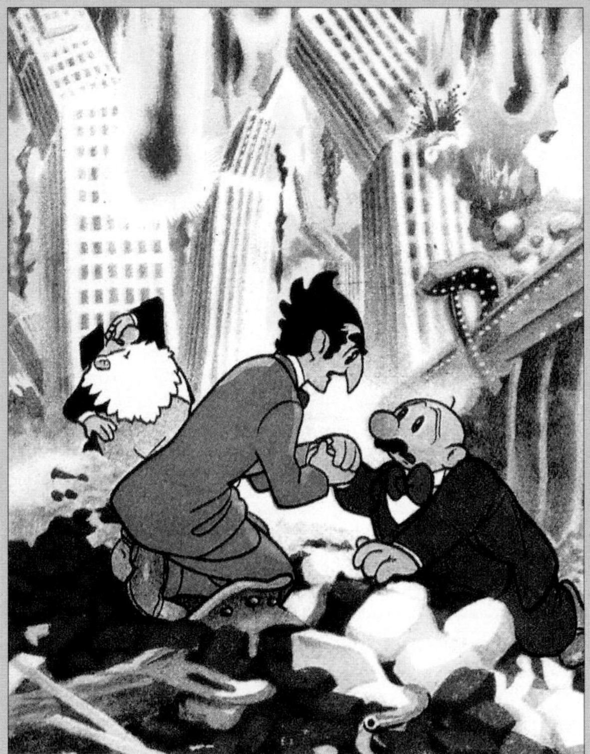

Three of Tezuka's stars in *Next World*: Duke Red, playing Redonov, helps scientist Notarin, while Dr. Hanamaru (playing Dr. Yamada) surveys the destruction.

ROLEX [1990]

The villain of the piece in Masakazu Katsura's *Video Girl Ai (Denno Shojo Ai)*, Rolex is a tall, good-looking man in his twenties, with a cold, unemotional nature. In particular, he has a strong aversion to love—the concept, and even the word, revolt him. Although he can live in the human world, he's not human. He is CEO of Gokuraku Japan, owners of the video store where heroine Ai Amano was put onto videotape to cheer up lonely teen Yota Moteuchi. He is a scientist as well as a businessman—he designs Video Girls, fantasy creatures like Ai who can come out of the VCR and bring happiness to lonely no-hopers. But Video Girls are not designed for independent life or for permanence. When Ai decides to stay in the human world with Yota, she has become, in his eyes, a faulty product. Rolex is completely ruthless in his quest for perfection. He thinks Ai should be erased because her transfer to the human world was faulty, which has made her flighty, inconsistent, and subject to emotional urges. He also programs his Video Girls to be immune to love, and Ai falls in love with Yota. He is determined that Ai will be erased; she yearns to foil him and stay in the human world with Yota. It's difficult to escape someone with Rolex's powers; he can teleport in our world, move between the human world and the video world at will, and summon up energy fields of great destructive force. However he is not, in his own terms, unnecessarily cruel. Though he almost kills his subordinate, the old man who runs the Gokuraku video store, and pursues Ai and Yota with icy determination, he also agrees to extend Ai's running time so that she can help Yota with a project on which he has set his heart, the creation of an illustrated storybook.

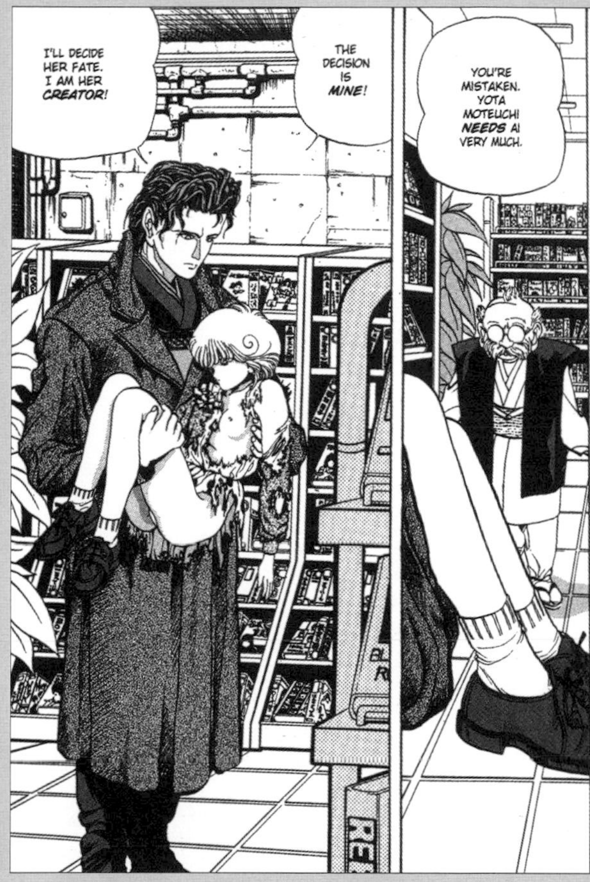

Rolex, with his creation *Video Girl Ai* and the manager of his specialist video store.

He also makes sure those not directly involved are not hurt, no matter how much destructive force he aims at his opponents. His role was much reduced when the manga was animated in 1992.

DEMON PRINCE SHARKIN [1973]

The Demon empire has slumbered for twelve millennia. Now it seeks to conquer the planet. From its secret base in a volcano, its High Priest sends out giant Fossil Beasts to attack humanity. Tall, blond, and gorgeous Prince Sharkin, a brave warrior, leads the assault, opposed by Japanese teenager Akira Hibiki and his giant robot Raideen. The rivalry between the two in the manga *Brave Reideen* by Ryohei Suzuki would be animated for TV in 1975 and would go on to inspire the later rivalry of tall, blond Char Aznable and Japanese teenager Amuro Ray in *Mobile Suit Gundam*.

TETSUO SHIMA [1983]

Born on July 29, 2004, orphan Tetsuo is a spiky-haired little runt of fifteen when Katsuhiro Otomo's epic manga *Akira* opens. Short, skinny and weak, he hides in the shadow of his cocky, outgoing best friend Kaneda, a year older than he is and his protector since childhood. Bullied all his life, Tetsuo is only tolerated as part of the biker gang the Capsules because Kaneda is their leader. In 1988 a secret weapons research program went wrong, and a test subject, codenamed Akira, destroyed the nation. Thirty-one years later, the city of Neo-Tokyo has risen from the ruins. Many survivors live in poverty and squalor, society is in

SEISHIRO SAKARAZUKA [1991]

SEISHIRO APPEARS TO be a charming, kind-hearted young man and a pillar of the community. A veterinarian by profession, he claims to be totally selfish and cold, yet seems devoted to his friends, especially young Subaru Sumeragi and his twin sister Hokuto. The clash between his statements and his behavior is a clue, not a contradiction; almost everything in his life is deception.

Born to an ancient line of sorcerors, he is the hereditary protector of Japan, the Sakurazukamori, one of the Seven Dragons of Earth. (The creators sometimes translate their title as "angels.") He uses *onmyo-jitsu*, a form of Japanese magic, to deal with anyone or anything that threatens Japan's safety and prosperity. A gifted killer, he is accompanied in the magic world by a spirit guardian in the form of an eagle. He ensnares his prey with cleverly crafted illusions, with visions of the blossoms that share his name (*sakura* is Japanese for "cherry"). His hereditary duty makes it impossible for him to fall in love, since that might interfere with his mission—but that's just what he does, and the object of his love is Subaru, who will one day threaten the stability of Japan. Subaru also comes from a long line of magicians sworn to protect Japan, but his family's vision of the best way to secure the safety and prosperity of their homeland is in complete opposition to Seishiro's. He is one of the Seven Dragons of Heaven, also known as the Seven Seals.

Their story starts in Clamp's *Tokyo Babylon* and continues in *X:1999*. When Subaru is still a child, Seishiro meets him in a magical dream-space and makes a bizarre resolution. If, when Subaru is older, Seishiro has come to truly care for him, then Subaru will live; otherwise he is the prey of the Sakurazukamori and when the attraction Seishiro feels has run its natural course, he will die. The decision is sealed with marks on both their palms. It has more than romantic significance, since by tradition the lover of the Sakurazukamori eventually replaces him in a bloody death ritual, and Seishiro's mother Setsuka prophesied that he would die at the hand of the one he loved most.

Seishiro is playing with fire, testing his own nature to the limit. In normal, everyday life in modern Tokyo, he comes across as a successful gay professional, with a fixation on a much younger romantic object that appears teasing, playful, and affectionate, but nothing out of the ordinary. In the magical realm, he takes increasingly serious risks and makes sacrifices to protect Subaru—he even loses his right eye to save him in *Tokyo Babylon*. Increasingly we realize that his indifference is the real illusion, and his greatest weakness. His tragedy is not that he truly loves someone he will have to kill, but that his own skill blinds him.

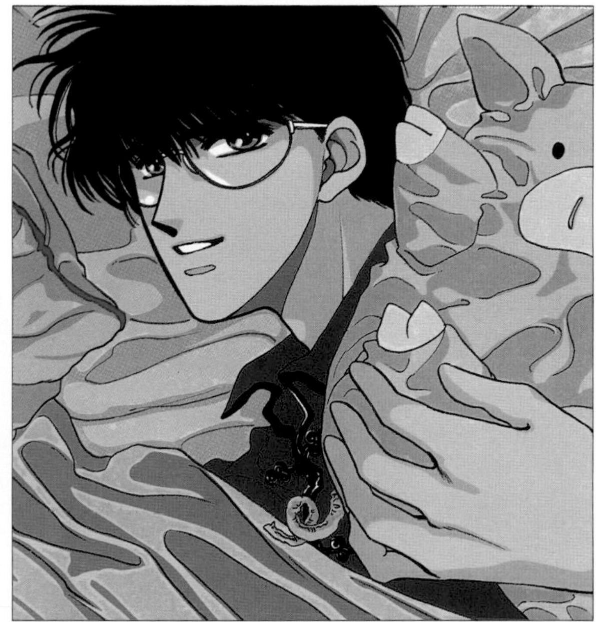

Seishiro looks sweet and cuddly, but he's playing a dangerous game with his intended victim and lover, Subaru.

In the final confrontation, in *X*, his plan was to kill Subaru quickly and cleanly, and simply walk away from the game of love that had been his private diversion and amusement for so long. However, even a cold-blooded killer-mage protected by centuries of tradition and training can't always control either his own heart or the actions of others. Subaru, despite his wide-eyed innocence, is no pushover. Their final fight on Tokyo's Rainbow Bridge in volume 16 becomes protracted and bloody, and leads to the destruction of the bridge, an apt metaphor. Subaru has always been a peacemaker, striving to preserve balance if possible, to find a middle ground if one exists. He doesn't want to kill the man he loves; he tells him that he is "still held by the cherry blossoms," but he proves to be a tougher fighter than Seishiro expects. The peacemaker has, after all, shown he can fight when he has to. Seishiro does his utmost to demonstrate that he has ceased to love Subaru, indeed has never truly loved him, but the escalation of his emotional and magical violence protests too much. In the end, he loses the fight because he has truly lost his heart. He dies in Subaru's arms, giving him the only sincere smile of his life.

CLAMP have a longstanding fascination with the tarot, which is used in many of their works as a source of imagery and structure. One of the many *X* spin-offs is a beautiful tarot set illustrated by CLAMP. The original Asuka Comics collected release of *X* had a single character picture on each spine, each representing a card of the major arcane, making up a continuous image when displayed. Subaru is the Hanged Man, caught in a net of cherry blossoms; Seishiro is Death, held in a dead tree festooned with bloody shreds. The volumes are subtitled for forms of classical music: volume 16, which sees the resolution of Seishiro and Subaru's long love story, is *Nocturne*. Both *Tokyo Babylon* and *X:1999* have been animated (the *X* anime drops the date in its title) and manga and anime versions are available in English; the manga is published by Viz.

meltdown, the political establishment and army are corrupt. A chain of seemingly chance events put Tetsuo in a position where his latent powers are triggered. His mind is invaded by one word—Akira—and suddenly he can fly, throw heavy objects without lifting a finger, shatter glass and stone, kill at will. Overwhelmed and exhilarated, Tetsuo sets out to find Akira, and now that he isn't the runt of the litter any more, he flattens everyone and everything in his way. He becomes both the center of a new cult and the target of established power groupings, revelling in being the center of attention. Kaneda and Tetsuo face each other, equals at last, and apparently resolve their relationship with Tetsuo's physical death. The 1988 movie, which kick-started the modern anime industry in Britain and America, remains one of the medium's benchmarks. It tells only a part of the story, and the manga delivers a far better view of the character of Tetsuo.

RED KING a.k.a. SHURI

[1990]

Creator Yumi Tamura had already had some success with bad-girl manga before turning to fantasy with *Basara*, which won the Shogakukan Manga Prize and had an animated video release in 1993, moving on to an animated TV series in 1998. Red King is the youngest son of the King of Kings, who has split his post-apocalyptic land into four for his children to rule. When blind Nagi prophesies that a girl and boy, twins, have been born in a desert village, and the boy will depose him, the young King sends his troops to the village to kill the boy twin. Tatara is murdered, but his sister Sarasa dons his clothes, cuts her hair, and sets off to avenge him. The Red King faces her in a fight and wounds her, then retreats to a secluded lake where he can put off the trappings of kingship and simply be himself. There he meets a young girl recovering from an illness, and falls in love, not knowing that she is the warrior who has vowed to destroy him. She, in turn, does not know that the gentle, handsome young man is the evil armored oppressor she fought. It can only end in tears.

MICHIO SONEZAKI [1993]

Shark Skin Man and Peach Hips Girl by Minetaro Mochizuki is a simple love story, originally called *Big Wheel (Daisharin)* on its serial release. The title was changed for the collected edition. Samehada (Shark Skin) is on the run from the Mob, from whom he has pilfered a few items of value. Toshiko (whose surname, Momojiri, means Peach Hips) is also on the run from her sex-maniac uncle, Sonezaki. And both are fleeing from a lunatic assassin who seems to have been simultaneously hired by Sonezaki and the gangsters to wipe out the troublesome pair on their charge across Japan. Though all the supporting characters in this very off-the-wall serial are little more than stereotypes, the character of Sonezaki is quite well drawn. The lecherous uncle, close enough to home to make your skin crawl, but far enough away to do it in a comical way, is a staple of farce the world over, but in Japan "uncle pervert" is a pantomime character whose narrative role is well understood.

MASATO SUZUHARA [1999]

Masato is a character played by a character, part of a movie within a manga, which was also animated. Confused? Well, *The Water Palace (Mizu no Yakata)* is a side story to Miho Obana's *Child's Toy (Kodomo no Omocha*, affectionately known to fans as *Kodocha*) and ran in *Ribon Mascot* magazine. The lead character of *Kodocha* is a successful child actress, Sana, and *The Water Palace* is her first big movie, made with a top director and co-starring a schoolmate, Naozumi. Masato is the villain of the movie. He's about twenty and left home six years ago; his kid brother Hirota hires a detective to look for him because their parents have been killed in a car crash. It turns out that Masato went to a remote country villa with his girlfriend Mako and her friend Miwa, where they partook of a herb grown by Miwa's grandfather. It provoked them to violence, and in one particularly rough scuffle, Mako was knocked unconscious. Thinking she was dead, Masato and Miwa weighted her body with rocks and dumped her in the lake; in trying to avoid responsibility for a mistake, they actually committed murder. Now her ghost holds the pair prisoner. The classic ghost story of the movie is very dark, but surrounded by the bustle of the film set and the slapstick romance of *Kodocha,* it makes a pleasant two-volume interlude. The second volume includes a series of "out-takes" showing the cast in make up being turned into ghosts, flying on wires, or hanging round the set.

MITSUOMI TAKAYANAGI [2003]

Tenjo Tenge by Oh! Great runs in Shueisha's *Ultra Jump*. The monthly focuses on boys' comics, and this one pushes all the fan-service buttons with plenty of spontaneous and irrelevant nudity, fairly detailed sex scenes, and lots of fighting. Set in Todo Gakuen, a high school with a nationally famous martial arts club run by a powerful executive committee, competing to eliminate weaker opponents and classmates alike, the story could be viewed as a reworking of *Revolutionary Girl Utena* for guys. Mitsuomi is a third-year student, head of the executive committee and strongest guy on campus. He is alleged to have killed fellow-student swordsman and biker Shin Natsumi in combat two years earlier. This broke up his relationship with his girlfriend Maya, Shin's sister, but he still carries a torch for her. To add to the puzzle, Shin was his best friend. There may be some explanation in the fact that Maya, sister Aya, and Shin had a very close

SECTION CHIEF UTSUMI a.k.a. RICHARD WONG [1988]

MASAMI YUKI'S *Shonen Sunday* manga *Mobile Police Patlabor* sets up a late twentieth-century society that uses robots, known as labors, for most of its heavy and dangerous jobs. In demilitarized Japan they can only be used for civilian work, like construction, but some unscrupulous companies and individuals will always be prepared to bend the rules if it gives them a little extra advantage.

Utsumi heads up a section in the Japanese offices of the global engineering company, Schaft Enterprises. An intelligent, inventive, charismatic, and attention-grabbing charmer in heavy-rimmed spectacles, he's also completely ruthless, and admits that there's nothing he will not do to achieve his aims. He's determined to move up the corporate ladder to a position of power and independence, and is constantly trying to dream up ways of getting ahead of Schaft's main rivals, Shinohara Heavy Industries. When we first meet him in the manga, Utsumi seems dangerous enough, a vicious, charming corporate suit who has commandeered the top-secret Griffin project, steered it towards illegal military sales, and run rings round his own company's chairman and security forces. Only as further chapters unfold do we realize we didn't know half his potential for havoc.

Utsumi's bosses learn to their cost that they have underestimated him when they try to take control of the Griffin project from him. The Griffin is a sleek black, labor with superb armaments, great balance and power, and a unique twist, a first in labor design that delivers a guaranteed combat edge—the ability to fly. Its test pilot is almost supernaturally talented, incredibly fast, with the reflexes of a cat and absolutely no sense of danger or fear of opposition. He's a pre-pubescent boy called Bud, bought by Utsumi in India. Utsumi steals the entire project—labor, development team, and all—and takes it across to Schaft's Sino-Korean rival; but he's been spotted by someone from his past. Sergeant Kumagumi of the Special Vehicle Section, Tokyo's labor crime squad, knows him under another name. Undercover in Hong Kong in the mid-1990s, she had a romance with a Chinese businessman named Richard Wong. It ended abruptly when he fled from Hong Kong just before the 1997 handover of control to China, but she sees Utsumi in his car by chance and recognizes her old lover. Trying to arrest him, she's shot by his driver, but fortunately she survives to give detectives details of his secret identity.

Utsumi's past is starting to catch up with him. Two U.S. cops arrive in Japan with the news that he was a client of an international

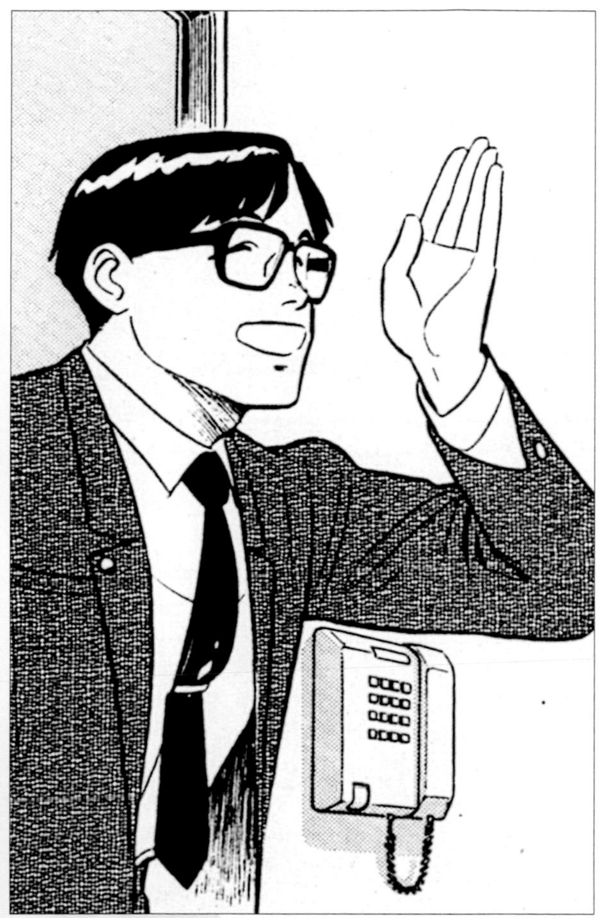

As charming as he is ruthless, Section Chief Utsumi keeps his secrets out of the boardroom.

pedophile ring, and bought an Indian boy on the open market. It's a while before anyone connects this information with the Griffin pilot, Bud. The manga is vague as to whether there is any sexual abuse in the relationship between Bud and Utsumi. It's certainly a classic pedophile scenario of grooming, control, and bribery, but whether or not Utsumi is a pedophile is almost irrelevant. He is so calculating that he is perfectly capable of infiltrating and winning the trust of a pedophile ring, purely to be able to select and buy a perfect potential pilot for his master plan. After all, where else could he be sure of getting a dependent, malleable individual who could vanish completely unmissed? He can mold the child into whatever he chooses, sex toy or labor pilot—repulsive, but brilliant.

As the manga develops further, Yuki takes his evil genius further into dark water. Utsumi manages to kidnap Kumagami and tries to rape her. Then he makes another audacious bid to push up the price of his Griffin technology by attacking the Special Vehicle Section headquarters in Tokyo Bay, only to see Bud and his Griffin lose.

In a last-ditch bid to escape to Australia, where he plans to make another new life under another assumed name, he uses Kumagami as a hostage to get to the port terminal and threatens to shoot every civilian there if she signals for help.

When your rise up the corporate ladder is as meteoric as his, however, you're bound to have stepped on some important toes on the way. He's thumbed his nose at Schaft Japan once too often, and they have the knives out for him, quite literally. As he tries to board his ship, a Schaft security man catches up with him and stabs him to death.

relationship, or that both Aya and Shin possess mystic powers. However, Maya now leads the opposition to the committee headed by her tall, handsome ex-lover.

TAMAMO [1993]

Tamamo is a fox-demon, and a recurring antagonist of *Hell Teacher Nubei (Jigoku Sensei Nube)* in the manga written by Sho Makura and drawn by Takeshi Okana. Nube, real name Meisuke Nueno, is a quiet elementary school teacher who just happens to have a demon hand. This is lucky, because his school is bedevilled by all kinds of demons and supernatural beasties. In his human form Tamamo is a dishy young guy with long hair pulled back in a ponytail, but to stay in the human world he needs a human skull, and his current skull needs replacing. We first meet him in volume 2 of the manga, hunting the perfect replacement. He can't find any prospective replacements among the dead, so when the perfect one shows up wrapped around the brain of Nube's pupil Hiroshi, he decides to go ahead and take it. First he has to win Hiroshi's trust, so he shows up at school, impresses the boy with how cool he is, and beats Nube at soccer. Nube distrusts him from the word go, and steps in to save the boy, but Tamamo battles him with illusions and kidnaps Hiroshi. After a battle that sees Tamamo transform to his real form by whipping out his own skull, Nube finds a last surge of strength in his demon hand thanks to his protective love for his young charge, and defeats him. Puzzled that any human could do this, Tamamo goes back to the school to study Nube and this "love" thing that makes humans strong. He even agrees to leave Hiroshi's skull where it is and look for another one, and sets up as a doctor at the local hospital. The rivalry between him and Nube eventually turns to respect and even a strange liking. *Hell Teacher Nubei* spun off an animated TV series in 1999, and a video series.

MITSURI TANUKI [1993]

The psychotic son of gangster boss Tanuki in *Shark Skin Man and Peach Hips Girl (Samehada Otoko to Momojiri Onna)* by Minetaro Mochizuki, Mitsuru is best defined by his favorite game—Russian roulette. He's a nasty, vicious twenty-something punk who is sent by his father to lead the pursuit of defecting gang member Samehada. The character is developed further in the *Katsuhito Isshi* live-action movie based on the manga.

DUKE TOGO [1968]

A professional assassin with a nearly perfect record of hits, Togo is the amoral, chain-smoking main character of Takao Saito's masterwork, *Golgo 13*. The title is derived from Golgotha, the place of the crucifixion of Christ, and the unlucky number thirteen. We know absolutely nothing about Togo except that the

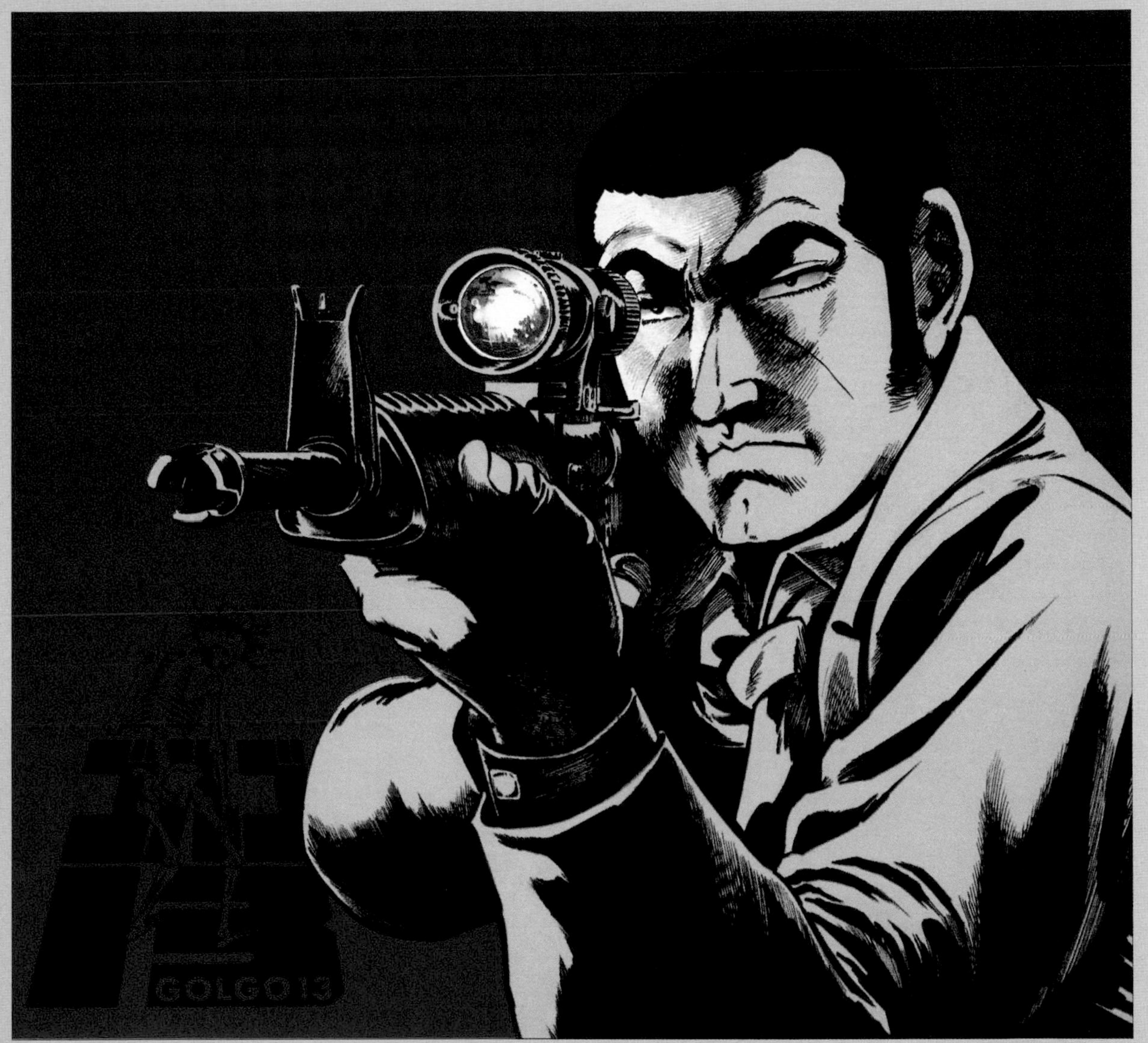

Duke Togo goes to work.

unsmiling assassin wanders the world killing without compunction for enormous fees, having sex with various well-endowed foreign women along the way. The appeal to middle-aged businessmen in need of a break from everyday life is obvious, and has kept Saito busy for four decades. This is an honest take on *James Bond*—Ian Fleming's creation is just as violent and misogynistic as Togo, but he's the hero, one of the good guys. The Duke's amoral (and, it must be said, repetitive) adventures have sold more than 200 million manga since his 1968 debut, only just behind his great rival in the late 1960s manga popularity chart, *Lupin III*. It is possible that *Golgo 13* was born from a desire to create a different, more realistic version of the criminal who was stealing all the manga headlines at the time that Saito was finalizing *Golgo 13*. Though the original *Lupin III* manga proved very popular with its key demographic of men in their twenties, the first TV series was landed with an early evening family slot and did quite badly, leading to a shift in tone for later TV adventures. Ironically the first few issues of the *Golgo 13* manga were very much lighter in tone than the series eventually became. When Saito created his assassin for hire, he had very strong views about the difference between an antihero and an outright villain, and he was very unsure how such a dark and brooding antihero character would be received by the Japanese public, so he used a lighter touch until he was certain that the market would accept an abusive, sexually violent killer as the central character. Even though the moral climate in Japan shifted, leaving the Duke, by the mid 1970s, being viewed as a truly degenerate character, his popularity was not affected. The violence and sexual content of the manga have never made it an attractive proposition for TV animation, but a theatrical animated feature was released in 1983, and a video animation followed fifteen years later. In 1971, Go Nagai parodied the Duke's adventures in the slapstick *Golgo 17*, *Golgo 18*, and *Golgo 19* for *Big Comic* magazine.

JOB TRUNIHT [1988]

Job is a democratic politician, Secretary of Defense to the Alliance of Independent Worlds in Katsumi Michihara's manga of Yoshiki Tanaka's novel series *Legend of Galactic Heroes (Ginga Eiya Densetsu)*. He is corrupt and venal, using right-wing thugs as his personal secret police and staying safe on the Alliance homeworld while making grand speeches exhorting the troops to die for their homes and beliefs. Despite his complete lack of ethics and morals, he is a wily politician and knows how to read character. When there is a serious attempt to eliminate him, he manages to survive and persuade the electorate to reinstate him.

CHOJIRO UCHIDA [1983]

Domu is one of Katsuhiro Otomo's most gripping stories and one of the best manga to come out of Japan in the 1980s, and the first to win an SF literature prize. Old man Uchida is its protagonist. Abandoned by his family when they sneak out of their flat on a soulless housing estate, he has reverted to his second childhood, and not in a good way. Small children, after all, are creatures of pure appetite and instinct, who want their own gratification above all else and have not yet acquired any moral or social restraints. With no adults around—or with adults who have reverted to their own level—children can cause serious trouble. Uchida has somehow tapped in to the huge psychic powers we are all said to possess; he starts out in small ways, by stealing toys and items of clothing, or carrying out mischievous pranks; but when he finds he can do this without detection or sanction, his pranks become more and more malicious and people start dying. As the "suicide" rate mounts, the police become involved, but they can find nothing to tell them what's happening until one little girl, a newcomer to the block with her family, realizes what's happening and faces up to Uchida, finally seeing him off in one of the tensest showdowns in manga. A battle of wills between a senile old freak and a determinedly un-cute eight-year-old might not sound like the hottest ticket in town, but it's impossible to put down. Uchida isn't killed—his opponent is a well-brought-up child—but he is forced to revert back to the social norm and become just another old guy left behind for the state to take care of, unable to focus on today but happy to talk for hours about the TV shows of his youth and bum sweets from his police minders as they try to work out what "really" happened. *Domu* has two great strengths. It doesn't explain and doesn't apologize—things happen, we get glimpses of possible explanations, but in the end the mystery remains. And it shows us Japan as a relentlessly real place—a world where ordinary people get by in ordinary circumstances, with no kimono, tea ceremony, or samurai, except on daytime TV, and no neat resolutions to the problems of psychic powers, boredom, or what to do about old people who are surplus to requirements in a society that will no longer dump them on a mountainside to starve, but is willing to abandon them in concrete canyons with no emotional network to support their declining years.

RAITO YAGAMI [2002]

Seventeen-year-old Raito only wants to do right (as his name implies), but he finds it's not that easy. He picks up a notebook in the street one day. It's been dropped by Ryuku, god of Death, and it's full of Death Notes. If you write a person's name, and any other details like how you want them to die on one of the pages, that will happen. If you leave out the mode of death, they just have a heart attack. Soon hardened criminals are dying like flies and the police, though not too upset, are puzzled. They hire an investigator, the mysterious L, and Raito, in over his head, is pursued as a murderer with most unusual methods in

MICHIO YUKI [1976]

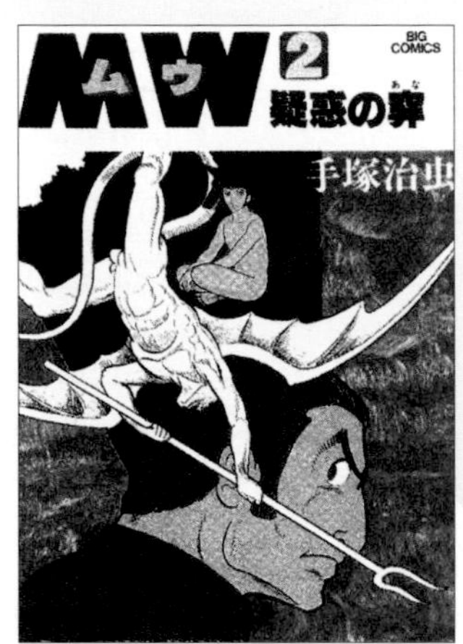

OSAMU TEZUKA'S adult manga *MW*, examining the concept of original sin, ran in *Big Comic* for almost two years. It was set in real time, and reflected many political scandals and social pressures of the day, including unrest about the continuing role of the United States in Japan.

The story starts in the early 1960s, on Okino-Mafune, a small island near Okinawa. A potent biochemical weapon, a gas codenamed MW, was developed by a major foreign power with influence in Japan (never named in the manga, but obviously the United States) during the Vietnam War, and secretly stored on this out-of-the-way island. In a tragic accident, the storage tanks leaked and all the inhabitants of the island died. The ruling party and the foreign government kept the truth from the public, and MP Eikaku Nakata took charge of the operation with Lt. General Minch, chief of staff of the foreign Armed Forces in Japan. Minch had the remaining gas shifted while Nakata arranged the removal of the bodies and the installation of new inhabitants on the island. To the outside world, it looked as if nothing had changed. For fifteen years everybody in authority pretends the Okino-Mafune incident never happened. What they don't know is that there were survivors.

Iwao Garai was a teenage tearaway at the time, but the accident had a huge impact on him. He entered the priesthood and prays constantly to be spared from the terrible memories of the day his entire hometown died. He saved one other person, schoolboy Michio Yuki, carrying him to a boat and away from the island. Michio's older brother was away training to be a kabuki actor when the incident happened; he now works in Kyoto under the name of Tamanojo Kawamoto, specializing in women's roles, and has become famous. Both brothers are handsome and both have a talent for disguise, but bank manager Michio's other life is very different from his brother's onstage dramas.

Michio is a kidnapper and murderer. He takes hostages, collects the ransoms, then kills them. At first, his killings seem random and unconnected, but when his motive emerges it's hard to condemn him completely. He was exposed to the MW gas during the incident; he has violent fits and is convinced he will die soon. He's using the ransom money to buy information about MW, find the supply, and release it so that the whole human race will die with him. After every crime, he confesses to Father Garai. Their escape and survival

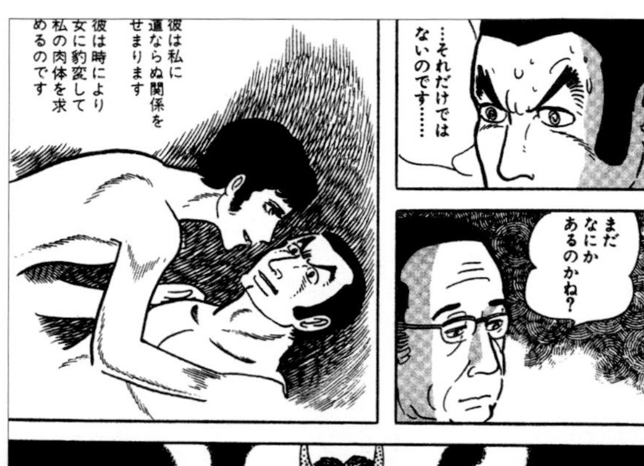

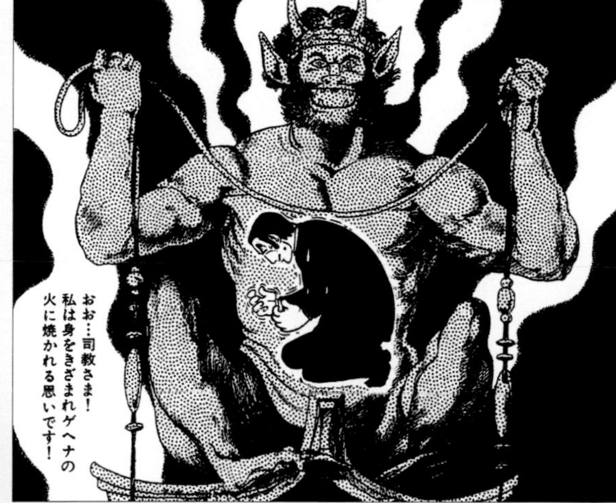

Handsome devil Michio reminds Father Garai that there are no original sins.

created a bond between them, and there is another, even stronger bond—their sinful homosexual relationship. Garai can't break the secrecy of the confessional; Michio knows this and takes advantage of it. Even when Garai repents and tries to blow the whistle about the accident to the press, political pressure from on high puts the lid on the story.

Michio has no scruples about using his sexuality to get his revenge. He befriended Nakata, determined to make him suffer for his role in the incident, marrying and murdering Nakata's daughter and wrecking his career. Through Nakata he met Minch, a closet homosexual who is easily charmed by the handsome, ruthless killer. Finding where the gas is kept, he sneaks onto the foreign military base, takes Garai and Minch hostage, commandeers a plane and a canister of the gas, and takes off to find the stockpile.

Garai's earlier whistle-blowing, however, roused suspicions and District Attorney Meguro has been on Michio's tail for some time. He asked Michio's brother Tamanojo to help persuade Michio to turn himself in. Following Michio, Tamanojo sneaks onto the plane. On board, Garai catches Michio off guard, grabs the MW canister and jumps off the plane into the Pacific, finally atoning for his sins. In the struggle, it appears that Michio is shot and killed, and Minch and Tamanojo return to Japan, but the ruthless killer has the last laugh. He and his brother were so alike, and both were fine actors. Minch didn't see exactly what happened, and he wants to believe that a potentially embarrassing relationship has been resolved discreetly. It isn't difficult to persuade him that the man who gets off the plane with him is the tragically bereaved actor whose younger brother has just been shot. Tezuka's twist ending introduces a note of suspense. Will Michio get to MW before MW gets to him?

Female Villains

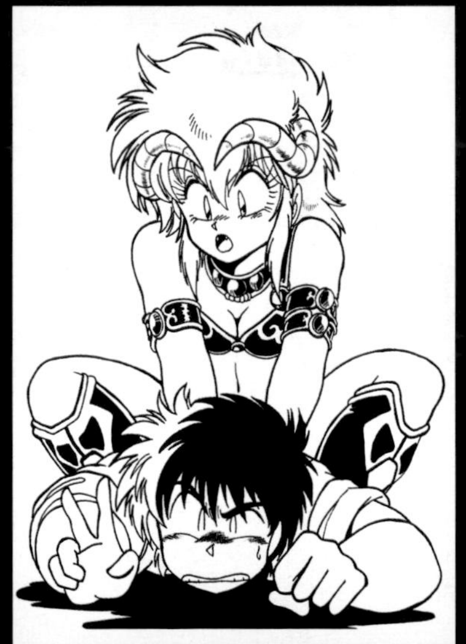

Girls on top: Kahm and Tetsuya

When's she's good, the typical manga girl is very, very good. When she's bad, she can be absolutely sensational. Evil women in manga range from high-school nymphets who smoke, drink, and humiliate their boyfriends, via dumpy grandmas with attitude and over-the-top comediennes, to complete psychos who will deprive you of essential body parts without a second thought. These women don't make excuses— they're REALLY bad, not just drawn that way!

MIYABI AIKAWA [1997]

Toru Fujisawa's manga *GTO* gives bad boy turned teacher Onizuka a hard time from all his pupils, but Aikawa is his toughest challenge. She and classmates Urumi Kanzaki and Anko Uehara do all they can to discredit Onizuka. She persuades longtime truant Kanzaki back to school to give him her trademark "class terror" and long after the rest of the class have come around to liking him, she continues to be obsessed with getting him fired. As the story unfolds, it reveals that her hatred stems from betrayal by another teacher that led to her suicide attempt. Aikawa is a style rebel too, at one point even dyeing her hair blue.

DILANDAU ALBATO [1994]

The manga version of anime hit *Vision of Escaflowne (Tenku no Escaflowne)*, with art by Aki Katsu accompanying the story by Shoji Kawamori and Sunrise house pseudonym Hajime Yadate, is out in English from Tokyopop. This version is aimed at the boys' market, and so the battle action is emphasized and many characters undergo changes. The anime Dilandau was originally Serena, the lost little sister of master swordsman and mech pilot Allen Schezard, kidnapped by the evil Zaibach Empire, transformed into a seemingly male warrior and driven insane in the process. In the manga, Dilandau is just as psychotic, but purely male.

BAD GRAN [1966]

The lead character of Machiko Hasegawa's *Bad Granny (Ijiwaru Baasan)* is a tough, terrifying old woman who exploits everyone around her with a shamelessness only possible in a country where society genuinely reveres the elderly. Gran gets away with levels of bad manners and downright rudeness that would never be tolerated in a younger woman. Hasegawa's typical four-panel strip style encapsulates gentle gags and social comment about Japan's changing society; for example, a well-meaning salaryman shields the old woman from a sudden rainstorm under his umbrella, only to have her bash him with her handbag and accuse him of stalking her as she walks off down the street, still in possession of his umbrella, leaving him dripping and embarrassed.

BUNNY CALLAHAN [1985]

Dark-skinned and beautiful, Bunny is also very vain. Her martial arts skills are based on her phenomenally fast footwork, and she conceals a whole arsenal of weapons in her shoes. She's only in high school, but is already an inspector for the evil European Empire organization, which aims to take over the world economy and replace all the rice in Japan with bread. The Japanese term used for the EE is *Nanban Teikoku*, a derogatory term for Westerners current between the fourteenth and nineteenth centuries. In Koichiro Yasunaga's *Shonen*

Sunday manga *Nakano Military Prep School (Rikugun Nakano Yobiko)* it's the name of a secret kingdom somewhere in Europe, which ever since the fourteenth century, has been bent on economic dominion by any means.

CATWOMAN [1939]

Manipulated by her insane uncle, Japanese TV journalist Yuko Yagi is brainwashed to imitate the real Catwoman while he plays out his fantasies of being Batman in Kia Asamiya's manga take on the Dark Knight for DC, *Batman: Child of Dreams*. Asamiya is a huge *Batman* fan, which makes the story's central premise—a rich, powerful, obsessive fan who turns to the dark side in his attempt to be the Dark Knight—especially resonant. Yuko is rescued by the real Batman, but her uncle dies.

DEVLEEN a.k.a. BARON ASHLER [1972]

Strictly speaking, Devleen (Ashler) is only half a villainess—the other half is pure masculine villain. Split straight down the middle, the evil genius who leads the forces of Dr. Demon (Dr. Hell) in Go Nagai's seminal giant robot manga *Tranzor Z (Mazinger Z)* is a determined and cunning fighter who doesn't hesitate to employ the most ferocious, if ridiculous-looking, robots and monsters to achieve Hell's aim of world domination. Even Devleen's voice is a blend of

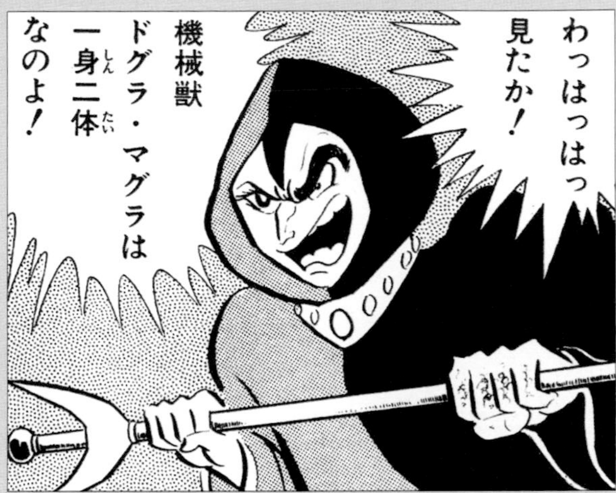

In two minds—Devleen has a split personality with body, voice, and clothes to match.

male and female, sometimes deep and terrifying, sometimes high-pitched almost to the point of hysteria and even more terrifying. Constantly feuding with Count Decapito for the title of Dr. Demon's most evil henchperson, Devleen finally dies after a futile attempt to destroy Tranzor Z.

BONNIE DORMAN [1991]

Bonnie is a beautiful blonde American, and a ruthless and sadistic criminal to boot. She and her brother Clyde are partners and first cross the path of bounty hunter Rally Vincent when trying to extort money from a drug smuggler. In the subsequent gun-and-car battles she loses a thumb and both legs, but this only makes her even more determined to exact revenge on Rally. She uses her prosthetic limbs to conceal weapons, and she and Clyde set up an ambush using Rally's partners as bait. She and Clyde are both killed in an action-packed fight sequence in *Gunsmith Cats* by Kenichi Sonoda, out in English from Dark Horse.

AI HAIBARA [1996]

Codenamed "Sherry," cute brunette Ai is a brilliant scientist working for the criminal Black Organization, inventor of the drug that shrinks a gifted eighteen-year-old sleuth into Detective Conan in Gosho Aoyama's manga *Case Closed*. When she decides to try to escape her evil past, Ai takes the drug herself and goes on the run. She is taken in by her victim's neighbor, Prof. Agasa, who knows what has happened to both of them, and joins his class at elementary school.

TAKANE HIROIN [1991]

Takane is the teenage daughter of the principal of Komatane Junior High School in Hiroshi Aro's comical manga *Futaba-kun Change!* from *Shonen Jump Original*. She's very clever, very pretty, and very spoiled. Whenever she doesn't get her own way, she disguises herself as super-villainess Evil Queen X, and sets out to put things right and reassert her natural place at the top of the pecking order. Her arch-enemy is a superhero with a huge spherical head, who calls himself the Secret Hero of Justice and shows up dressed in a spandex costume to thwart her aims. It's actually her father, the high-school principal, whose gentle and kindly nature can't stand any wrongdoing. Her unfortunate henchmen have to dress as a pantomime horse and carry her at improbable speeds on her super-villainous exploits.

TAMAKI HOZUKI [1985]

The Persona Century Corporation owns 90 percent of the world, and is owned in turn by one family, the Hozuki. The whole family is evil, except for elder sister Sael who works in a hospital with the unfortunate in an attempt to atone for—or escape from—her heritage. Tamaki is beautiful, spoiled and a sadist. She enjoys torture and blood for their own sake, and fears—but is fascinated by—the fey mystic Darkside, who is fated to be her family's nemesis. Hideyuki Kikuchi's atmospheric novel *Darkside Blues* was turned into an anime and a 1995 graphic novel with art by Yuho Ashibe, now out from ADV.

YUKO ICHIHARA [2003]

Fifteen-year-old Yuka goes to Morigana High, and works part-time in a magic shop as a spiritual adviser and "cleaner-up." She can remove any powers or other spiritual matters causing problems in people's lives. Yuka can be quite hard-headed and exploitative; she makes the hero, orphan Kimihiro Watanuke, agree to be her slave before she will rid him of his ability to see ghosts. Despite her youth, she's very fond of beer. Clamp's *XXXHolic* is published in English by Del Rey.

IRMA [1984]

Irma is a Kurdish freedom fighter, betrothed at birth to Luke, who commands a guerrilla force in the struggle for Kurdish independence in the 1980s. She's a tough fighter who can handle a machine gun and a knife with equal ease, and is perfectly willing to kill on her fiancé's orders, or if she sees advantage for herself in it. Yoshikazu Yasuhiko's manga *Star of the Kurds (Kurd no Hoshi)* is the story of Kurdish-Japanese Jiro Manabe, who comes to Turkey to find his mother and his heritage after years of feeling a misfit in Japan because of his mixed-race background. Irma offers herself to Jiro, but later seeks to play him off against Luke. Luke resents the newcomer and his ancestral claim to leadership, and Irma wants to end up with the winner to secure her own position.

ISIS [1976]

Sister of the young pharaoh Memphis in *Daughter of the Nile* by Chie Hosokawa, Isis is jealous of the beautiful young American Carol, who is pulled back into ancient Egypt by magical forces and becomes Memphis' queen. She does everything in her power to get rid of the interloper.

IZUKO [2001]

Sky High, Tsutomu Takahashi's manga for *Young Jump* magazine, is an anthology of stories set in a dark, desperate afterlife that mirrors the creator's other manga worlds. The lead characters are the souls of those who have not died naturally, but been killed, either accidentally or by intent. They are offered three choices in the afterlife: go on to paradise, return to take vengeance on their killers and then go to hell, or get a second chance at the life that was snatched away from them. The sensual, yet ice-cold, Izuko was once a mortal woman; now she is the keeper of the "Gate of Hatred," the netherworld portal through which they will pass to their chosen destination. She can advise them, even pressure them, but they must choose for themselves. The manga was so popular that a live-action film and series were made.

URUMI KANZAKI [1997]

A genius with an IQ of 200 and fluent in multiple languages, Kanzaki had given up going to school until called back by her classmate Miyabi Aikawa to give new teacher Eikichi Onizuka her trademark "class terror" treatment in Toru Fujisawa's manga *GTO*. Ever since elementary school, when a teacher she

KAHM, CROWN PRINCESS OF SANTOVASKU [1988]

KAHM, LEADING LADY of Johji Manabe's manga *Outlanders*, is a classic manga villainess, a violent, selfish woman who is finally redeemed by love. She's also the first in a line of sister characters who inhabit the same universe, fall for the same kind of guy, and could swap identities without too many people noticing the difference. Manabe's manga for Hakusensha's *ComiComi* magazine was translated by Studio Proteus for Dark Horse, and was among the big successes of its day in the United States.

Kahm first appears at the safe end of a broadsword dripping with blood; the business end has just been graphically shoved through the throat of a soldier after the same blade hacked off various limbs and bisected the head of a wounded man begging for mercy. She arrived in Tokyo about half an hour before, in a huge biomechanical warship resembling a giant louse with heavy armor, and devastated the city. But every disaster is a photo opportunity. Tetsuya Wakatsuki, nineteen-year-old newspaper photographer, races out to snap the invasion, and finds himself facing a cute blonde with a big sword, small armor and a fetching pair of horns. Forced to fight for his life, Tetsuya grabs a piece of metal from the devastated building and gives a much better account of himself than either of them expected. She's attracted to him, and despite her spoiled, demanding behavior, Tetsuya finds himself drawn to her.

Kahm has been sent to invade Earth by her father, emperor of many galaxies. Earth is "the sacred planet," ancestral home of their race. They fought for it long before man evolved, and regards humans as an infestation of bugs which must be exterminated. Their old adversaries, the Yoma clan, were thought to be wiped out, but one survivor, Neo, has made contact with military powers on Earth and warned them of the coming Santovasku invasion. He has found a human girl whom he claims is the reincarnation of Yoma sorceress Jilehr, and plans to use her to fight his old enemies. Neo's sorceress, who turns out to be Tetsuya's friend Aki, wipes out the Santovasku fleet. As the stakes escalate, Kahm offers to save the Earth if Tetsuya will marry her. Exasperated that his daughter expects him to let her marry a lower form of life on a whim, her father orders Tetsuya killed. Kahm's childhood friend Battia Bureitin Rou, a formidable warrior always around to haul her royal person out of trouble, is replaced by a gung-ho general with orders to wipe out mankind. Helped by Battia, her lover Mohs Geobaldi, and Kahm's devoted Jawa-like servants, the Nuba tribe, Tetsuya and Kahm escape and take on the entire Galactic fleet.

Kahm is blithely confident in her own powers as a sorceress and a warrior; Tetsuya loves her and wants to save Earth; everyone else knows they're doomed. When Kahm is seized by her father, they all charge into battle to save her. Only Tetsuya and the Nuba survive. Emperor Quevas fights his stubborn girl to the very last, even trying to brainwash her into giving up Tetsuya, but in the end he loves her too much to change her personality completely, and when she insists on staying with her human, he accepts her choice. But for him, to do so is to deny the principles of law and order on which he has built his empire, so he decides to die. His imperial advisers die with him. Only then does Kahm learn that her determination to have her own way has won her the man of her choice, but has cost her father and her dearest friends their lives.

The new lives Tatsuya and Kahm will create together—five daughters, Nahm, Mahm, Mohm, Tahm, and Ruhm, and a son, Kazuya—were paid for by the blood of others. The old rulers of the sacred planet have merged their blood with that of the newer life-form they tried to obliterate. The galaxy has been changed forever, and she and Tetsuya must ensure the memory of those who made it possible is honored, and carry the Santovasku bloodline, the ancient royal line of Earth, on into the future.

Manabe returned to his wilful princess and her lover in 1991's *Epilogue*. This is a shameless tearjerker, in which not only Kahm's old servants the Nuba, but all the close friends the couple lost in battle, return to planet

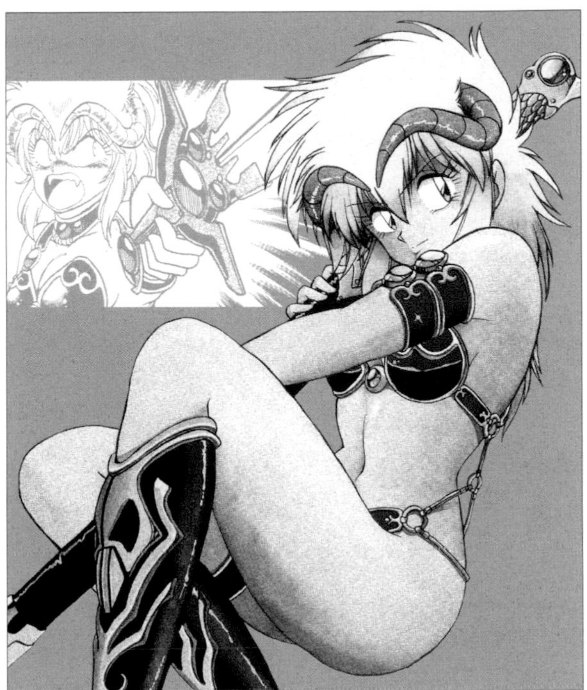

The two sides of Princess Kahm—cutie-pie and psychotic princess. Luckily Earthman Tetsuya brings out her good side.

Ekoda to visit them and their growing family, as if death were a country with a cross-border arrangement. He went back again in 1992 to provide a prequel, printed in English by Dark Horse as *Outlanders* Issue 0, in which Kahm fights a wily old sorcerer for an artifact that can tap the powers of the dead. Its main purpose, apart from fan service, appears to be enhancing Kahm's reputation for hot-headedness and willfulness.

trusted let her down badly, Urumi has been targeting teachers, bullying, playing mind games, and even physically assaulting them. She's forced many of her teachers to leave the profession, and any pupils who get in her way get the same treatment. Onizuka does his best to convince her not all adults are bad, but it's not until her dark secret comes out that the mystery of her psychotic behavior finally unravels. She looks unique, with blonde hair, one blue and one brown eye, because her mother, a driven businesswoman, whose idea of love is expensive nannies and presents, had her by artificial insemination using a foreign sperm bank.

KARLA THE GRAY WITCH [1992]

Karla is a powerful magician who keeps the powers of good and evil in balance on the cursed island of Lodoss. Incredibly ancient, she has placed her spirit in a jeweled circlet, which she uses to possess the body of anyone who puts it on. Having observed the battle of good and evil for centuries, she believes that neither side can be allowed to win the war, and so she constantly intervenes to tip the scales, preventing either side from complete victory. *Record Of Lodoss War: The Gray Witch (ROLW: Haiiro no Majo)* is the 1999 manga version of the game scenario and anime series, written by series creator Ryo Mizuno and illustrated by Yoshihiko Ochi.

KEIKO NAKADAI [1992]

When a young newsreader gets her first chance at a TV spot, she really has to make an impression on the public. Ratings are everything, so when the regular weather girl goes away for a month, her replacement Keiko makes sure she grabs the viewers' attention by illustrating her weather reports with ever scantier outfits. When the temperatures soar, so does her hemline, and as she sheds more clothes onscreen, she gets higher ratings. Keiko will stop at nothing to be a success, but when her rival returns, she's going to have to fight for her place in the spotlight. She abuses her hapless suitor Minoru, makes enemies of the older newsroom staff, and generally behaves like the kind of D-list celebrity who gives TV presenters a bad name, in the manga *Weather Woman (Otenki Onesan)* by Tetsu Adachi. It first appeared in *Young Magazine* and is out in English from CPM. There's also a live-action film.

RAN KOTOBUKI [1998]

Gals by Fuji Mihona, published by Shueisha and in English from CMX, stars *ko-gal* Ran, a modern Lolita into paid dating, dyed hair, rambunctious behavior, and total lack of interest in career or marriage. Ran is a sixteen-year-old wild child kept out of juvenile court by her harassed elder brother, a policeman in trendy Shibuya. However, her sassy attitude and amorality are balanced by her loyalty to

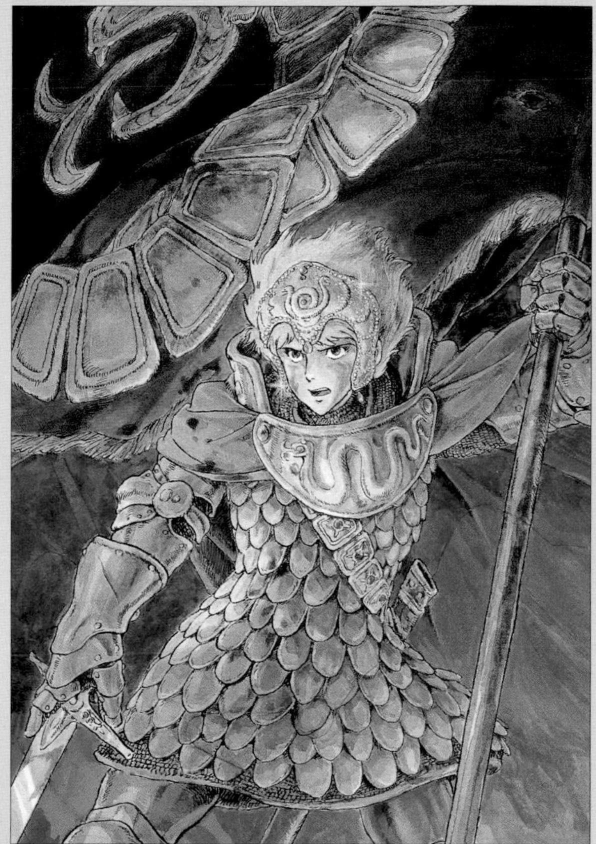

Kushana, Princess of Tolmekia.

her friends and her iron determination to stop herself and other girls being exploited by punks, pimps, and lechers. Ran has no traditional feminine virtues, but her guile, cunning, and unsinkable optimism turn out to be more useful on the streets of modern Tokyo.

KUSHANA, PRINCESS OF TOLMEKIA [1982]

The nearest thing to a villain in Hayao Miyazaki's 1982 manga and 1984 movie *Nausicaa of the Valley of the Wind*, Kushana is a member of the imperial family of Tolmekia and the empire's leading general. A beautiful yet ruthless woman in her twenties, she lives by the principle that the end justifies the means. She enters Nausicaa's valley at the head of an invading army. Her soldiers devastate the community and kill Nausicaa's ailing father in order to retrieve one of the last surviving super-weapons that devastated the world in the previous millennium, to bolster the empire's supremacy and her own position. The manga reveals Kushana's tragic past—her mother sacrificed her sanity to save her daughter in a palace power struggle when she was small—and shows her gradually growing to admire Nausicaa even though they have different beliefs.

MASAKO KYOZUKA [1990]

Masako starts out as an ordinary schoolgirl, sweet and clever, a great cook, and good at games. Rejected by the guy of her dreams because she has small breasts, she is driven to a life of crime. She steals a book from a school doctor's office; as it's his secret list of all large-breasted schoolgirls in the area, he can hardly report it missing, so her first crime goes

GO NAGAI AND HIS GORGEOUS FIGHTING GIRLS

Go Nagai was born in Wajima City on September 6, 1945. His ambition to make manga started in childhood when his brother gave him a copy of Osamu Tezuka's *Lost World*. While recuperating from a serious illness, he created a fan manga, Black Lion, which came to the attention of Shotaro Ishinomori (then working as Ishimori.) He took on the twenty-year-old Nagai as his assistant. Nagai's first work under Ishimori was *Meakashi Polikichi* (1967) for *Bokura* magazine.

After eighteen months Ishimori gave him a vacation, when he created his first solo manga, *Shameless School (Harenchi Gakuen)*. This violent, sexually driven high-school comedy showed pupils and teachers equally out of control. It appeared in *Shonen Jump* magazine in 1968 and led to the first of many clashes between Nagai and the Japan Parent Teachers Association, who publicly burned copies of the manga. It also started the long-running association between Go Nagai and beautiful, flirtatious girls in sexy situations. He favors two main types—the cute, innocent heroine-in-jeopardy and the dynamic, voluptuous fighter—but the emphasis is always on sex appeal.

The young Nagai quickly realized that in order to have the career he wanted, he had to control the marketing and exploitation of his own creations. Just like their U.S. counterparts, Japanese manga creators were waking up to the fact that publisher control of rights robbed them of creative freedom as well as the full benefits of their labors. Starting in 1970, Nagai set up two companies, Dynamic Productions and Dynamic Planning, to develop and fund his manga ventures and the anime spin-offs he planned. The first titles produced by his new company were *Getter Robo*, *Abashiri Family*, and *Kiku No Suke*. Just like his debut manga, *Abashiri Family* is set in a high school gone crazy and features a sexy schoolgirl heroine, but Kikunosuke Abashiri also has courage, guile, and determination. Sent to an exclusive school by her crimelord father, who wants her to have a normal life, she finds herself in a hunting ground for crazed perverts where the teachers are as out of control as the pupils. She calls on her family to help defeat the power-mad principal in a warped poacher-turned-gamekeeper showdown with Nagai's trademark mix of slapstick, violence, and destruction testing of lingerie.

In 1972 Nagai created his most iconic manga female, the amazing Cutey Honey. Honey Kisaragi looks like a normal high-school girl, but in fact she's a beautiful android, created by Prof. Kisaragi in a quest to make the perfect human. He gives his creation the face of his dead daughter, but her

Right: Who's that girl? Nagai's Cutey Honey in her preferred fighting mode. So who needs a gun, Hayami?

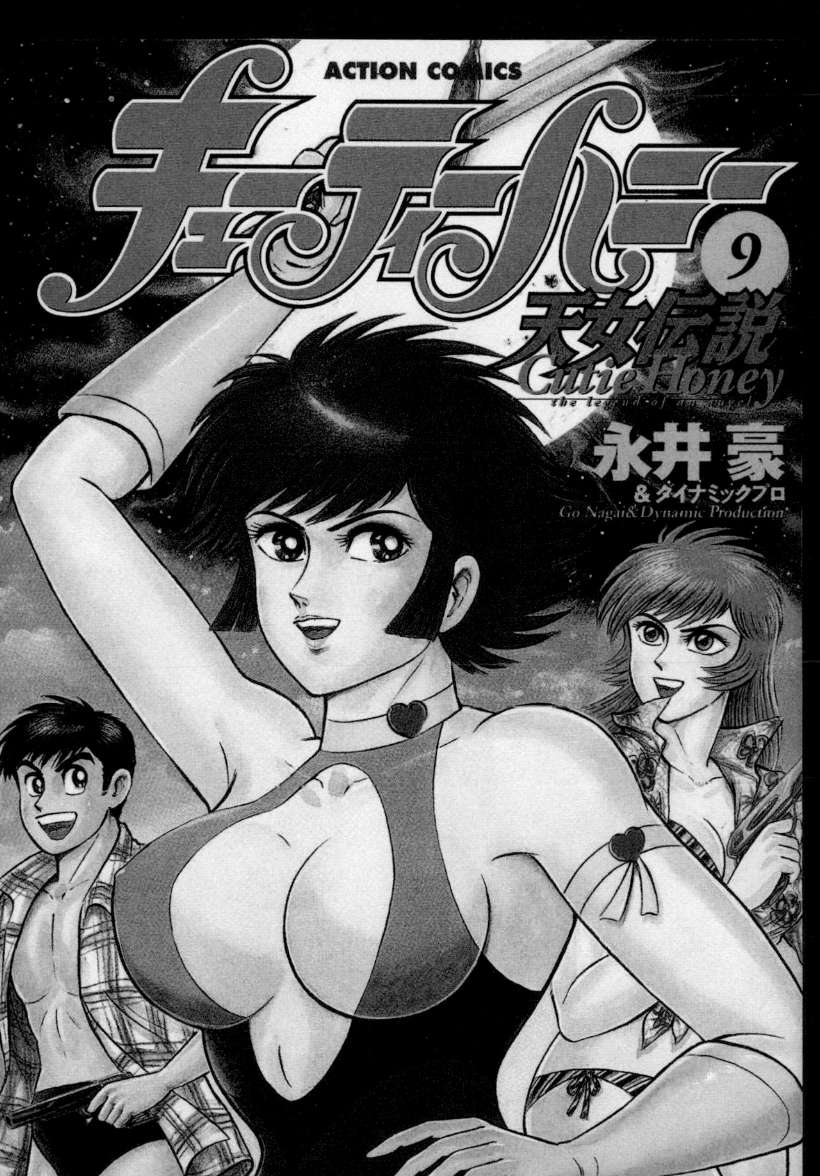
ACTION COMICS
キューティーハニー
9
天女伝説
Cutie Honey
永井 豪
&ダイナミックプロ
Go Nagai& Dynamic Production

main fighting incarnation has the body of a surgically enhanced glamour model. She can transform into any one of a range of beautiful and deadly guises with different skills and abilities, just by saying the words "Honey Flash." She is armed with a boomerang and a sword, but also with the ability to love, programmed into her by the "father" to whom she became more than just a science project. The urge to protect others from harm is so powerful that no danger can deter her.

The science used to create Honey attracts the attention of a criminal organization called Panther Claw, and Prof. Kisaragi is killed trying to stop them from stealing his secret. Honey vows revenge on her father's killers. Helped by lecherous old Danbei, a comic-heroic figure who lusts after her but also admires her courage and soft heart, and reporter Hayami who is secretly in love with her, she goes after the organization.

Panther Claw is a female crime syndicate headed by Panther Zora and Panther Jill. Members have special powers for which they are named—Panther Bat, Panther Crab, Panther Tarantula, and so on. Their inhuman abilities are reflected in their half-animal appearance. Honey defeats Panther Jill, and Panther Zora flees their final showdown, blows up Panther Claw headquarters, and vows to return for her revenge. The mix of crime, high technology, slam-bang combat action, and gorgeous, bosomy females spilling out of unlikely costumes which shred at every opportunity, was a hit. The sequel, which has even more violence and nudity than the first series, reveals that Panther Jill survived to be renamed Sister Jill and revive the Panther Claw organization.

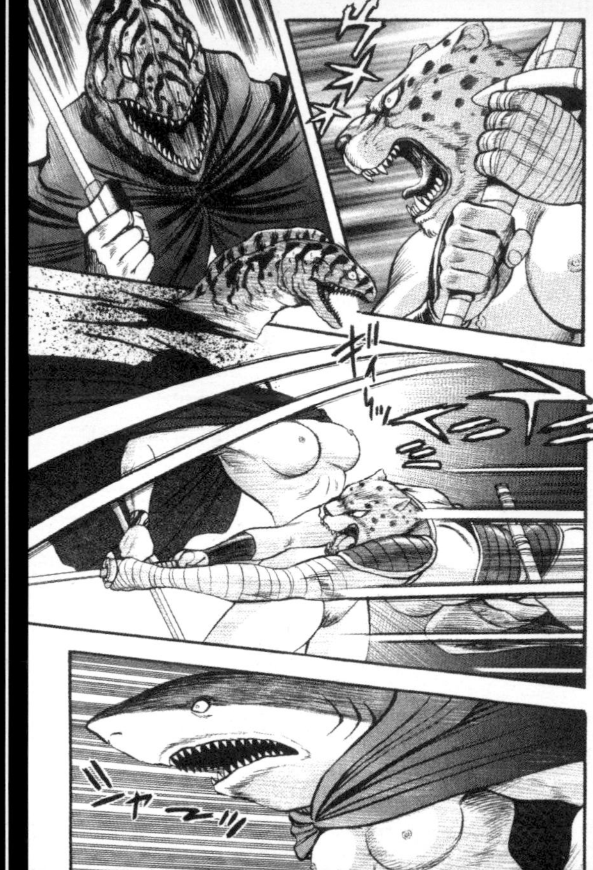

Zoo warriors: Panther Claw sends its menagerie into action.

Cutey Honey's manga exploits were planned to run alongside a TV series, which debuted in 1973. A change in scheduling for the series led to a shift in the emphasis of the manga. *Cutey Honey* was first intended for a girl audience, like many show about transforming girls with magic powers, so the manga was to run in girls' mag *Ribon*. Then the TV slot was filled by another show. Undeterred, Nagai revamped the manga and TV series into a boys' show, and slotted it into *Shonen Champion* magazine. The manga was revived in 1990 and spun off another video series, *New Cutey Honey*, in 1994.

As Nagai's career progressed he became too busy to fill all the demands for his creations. He had up to thirty assistants working for him, but it wasn't enough. In 1997, with his full approval, Shogakukan Comics hired Yukako Lisaka to produce a *Cutey Honey* for the younger female market of *Sailor Moon* fans. While not entirely faithful to Nagai's original work, *Cutey Honey F* has its own charm and generated a following both in its target market and among older male fans. Honey is not an android in this series—ike the Sailor Scouts, her ability to transform is magical. The F stands for Flash. She is a student of Saint Chapel School along with her sister Sara and boyfriend Seiji. The evil organization Panther Claw has kidnapped her father. It's up to Cutey Honey to stop them. All the *Cutey Honey* anime are available on video in the United States, but the manga have yet to be completely translated.

Nagai's hottest female character appeared in *Devilman* in 1972. Devilman is a human teenager who becomes a demon to protect the world. His best friend turns out to be Satan in disguise. His cute cousin Miki is the stereotype Nagai good girl—feisty, but sweet. The main attraction of the series is the phenomenally sexy bird-demon Siren (a.k.a. Silene). Half voluptuous woman and half albino eagle, she has huge claws instead of feet, wings growing out of her skull, a bird's tail, and a bad attitude. Her role is simple—she has to kill Devilman before he can frustrate the aims of Satan. She meets a messy end, but not before giving Devilman the fight of his life. The *Devilman* manga ran for five volumes and 1,352 pages. It was a hit and the anime TV series aired from July 1972 to March 1973 only enhanced its success. Two *Devilman* video stories were released in 1987 and 1990. A further manga/TV combo, *Devilman Lady*, shows a young woman transformed into a demon to defend mankind. She has Akira's motivations, but uses a black-feathered version of Siren's design.

Nagai's fighting female also had a comedy incarnation in schoolgirl super-heroine *Kekko Kamen*, who maintains her secret identity by working naked but for boots and a cowl. Her name is a playful homage to an early live-action TV hero known as *Gekko Kamen*, or *Moonlight Mask*; "kekko" translates roughly as "I got lucky!" and the comedy is loaded with overt sexual references. In a high school staffed by perverts, the main target is cute-but-dim good girl Miki; Kekko Kamen's mission is to protect her and the other students from groping, tickling, panty-theft, illicit nude photography, and similar indignities perpetrated by the teachers at Japan's most perverted high school. The manga was first published in 1970 in *Monthly Jump* magazine.

Today Go Nagai is one of Japan's most respected manga creators. His influence on the industry has been enormous, and his hugely endowed heroines and their equally voluptuous nemeses are only part of that influence. Still, they must be acknowledged as one (or perhaps that should be two) of the milestones of manga art.

undetected and leads to bigger things in Koichiro Yasunaga's *D-Cup Hunter (Kyonyu Hunter)* from *Shonen Sunday* magazine. She whips up a costume, stuffs the front with steamed buns (a renowned Japanese delicacy) and sets out on a personal crusade against large breasts as the dreaded D-Cup Hunter. She traps unsuspecting girls, whips off their tops, inks their breasts, and takes "breast prints" that she threatens to post all over town—named, of course—if they don't immediately cease and desist using their natural endowments to entrap boyfriends. Unfortunately things don't go all her way; she encounters the Bustrons, a group of super-endowed female space pirates, and Golden Bust (Ogon Bust), a superheroine who is utterly nice, but a sworn enemy of D-Cup Hunter. The gags are all breast-obsessed, but there are also homages to other manga. The Bustrons' leader Kyobra is named for Buichi Terasawa's hero Cobra, though her name can be read as "giant bra," and Golden Bust pays tribute to 1970s manga *Golden Bat (Ogon Bat)*.

LADY L [1987]

Legend of the Dragon Kings (Soryuden) originated as a series of novels by Yoshiki Tanaka, illustrated by CLAMP, who later adapted it into manga form. The four Ryudo brothers, aged from preteen to college age, are the 117th generation in direct descent from four ancient dragon gods. They are fated to protect the peace of the world from the dark forces ranged against it; Lady L is on the side of evil. A tall, beautiful, dark-haired woman in Chinese dress, she sets out to kidnap one of the brothers and torture him to force him to transform into his dragon self.

LAFRESSIA [1977]

The queen of the plant-based alien life forms known as the Mazone, Lafressia is a cold, cruel foe who finally falls in love with the dashing romantic hero of Leiji Matsumoto's *Captain Harlock*. She is trying to conquer Earth because she is desperate to find a home for her people; when sending her best generals after Harlock fails, she duels with him in person and is defeated. She is actually made of flesh and blood, unlike her subjects who revert to their plant forms in death. She is named after a rare and exotic Asian plant, the rafflesia. An unusual homage was paid to her in the anime TV series *Gundam F91*, where a mobile armor was named after her.

LUCIFER [1990]

Lucifer is a Hunter, a violent yet beautiful woman with combat abilities enhanced by the military to enable her to hunt down terrorists. She comes up against the security forces, including heroine Angel, as they both pursue a terrorist group in *Angel Cop*. Her function is to destroy the terrorists and anyone who gets in the way, including the cops. This is a manga with high violence levels, both in the art by Taku Kitazaki and the story by Ichiro Itano and Noboru Aikawa. However, the manga differs slightly from the anime, both in terms of small changes to characters and in the higher levels of emotion they display.

COMMANDER MAKARA a.k.a. BLOODY MARY [1980]

Makara originated as Bloody Mary, a character from TV puppet animation *X-Bomber*. Her name was changed when the show made its way to Britain under the title *Star Fleet* in 1982. She is the commander of a vast space fleet in the service of the Imperial Master (Emperor Gelma) who is seeking a mysterious superweapon, the F-01, to aid his plans of galactic domination. Makara is a psychotic cyber-woman, proud, ruthless, and completely insane. Her weapons of choice are a large sword and a vicious tongue. She has long, fiery red hair and three red eyes, two of them on a golden mask implanted in place of her left eye. She communicates with her master through this mask. Her preferred mode of dress presages the movie *Gladiator*, with a slinky little leather-and-metal mini-dress, armored bra, long red leather boots, and multi-horned helmet, worn under an imperial purple cloak with acres of gold braid. Russell Crowe never looked so good in straps, but it's certainly not understated. The characters for the show were designed by the legendary manga star Go Nagai, who has a long list of cruel, vicious yet very sexy villainesses to his credit. The *X-Bomber* manga tie-in was drawn by Eiichi Sato, and there is also a British comic version of *Star Fleet* by Mike Noble.

MINAGI [1993]

Minagi appears in the manga adaptation of hit video and TV series *Tenchi Muyo! Ryo Oh Ki*. The series premiered in 1992 and the manga by Hitoshi Okada started in *Comic Dragon* in 1993. Minagi is a clone of series regular Ryoko, a bad girl redeemed by her love for hero Tenchi. Minagi attacks Tenchi, apparently trying to trigger a mysterious force dormant in him. When Ryoko defeats her, she loses her memory and is asked to stay by the gang, but fears that she will bring some trouble down on her new friends. She has been sent by Yakage, an alien noble, in pursuit of one of Tenchi's other female admirers, Princess Aeka of Jurai. The Tenchi universe was a major fan favorite in the 1990s and has spun off a wide range of media, from audio dramas and movies to various ranges of merchandise.

MITSUKO [2002]

Mitsuko is the leader of the pack in her high school. The girls follow her lead with almost religious fervor, and she responds by

GOLDIE MUSO [1991]

THE MOST DANGEROUS, and most nearly successful opponent of Kenichi Sonoda's *Gunsmith Cats*, Goldie is an Italian mafia chief's muscle, a highly skilled fighter, and a crack shot. She's big—145 pounds and over 6 feet tall—usually high on cocaine, and she knows how to hold a grudge. She's also an elegant and highly sophisticated lady, daughter of an old Mafia family.

Goldie first crosses the path of the Gunsmith Cats on her first job in America, a relatively simple mission to get back some stolen videotapes that could embarrass a Mafia boss. Rally and Minnie May foil her plan, and she vows revenge. She gets her chance with the arrival of a new street drug called kerasine. It leaves users highly suggestible, and it doesn't take Goldie long to program the local two-bit criminals with the belief that Rally Vincent is really an alien in human form, and has to be prevented from wreaking her evil on Earth at any price. She also shows she's capable of all the corruption of old Europe, keeping a group of young addicts as her personal sex slaves. There's a disturbing sequence in the manga, set in Goldie's boudoir, where a fawning young woman alternates between painting her toenails and licking her feet. Then Goldie goes one better and gets Rally herself addicted to kerasine. Rally faces one of her deadliest and most ruthless enemies while not knowing if what her senses tell her is real or illusory, providing one of the manga's most gripping sequences as she switches between fighting Goldie's machinations and her own hallucinations.

The rivalry between the girls starts out as a simple job, develops into a determination to prove who's best, and finally gets even more personal as Goldie sinks her claws into Rally's secret crush and her estranged father. She always hires the best, and Bean Bandit is the best courier around, so he's her chosen getaway driver. While the Bandit works for her, he remains loyal to her cause; it's not personal, but a matter of honor. Rally is forced to contemplate the fact that the man she wants is committed to securing the escape of her greatest rival, even though she's the one in pursuit.

The rivalry says more about Sonoda's view of women than anything else. Goldie is over the sexual hill in Sonoda terms, past being a lust object at the age of thirty-four. This is why her treatment of her young sex slaves is more like that of a rich old roué than anything else; in Sonoda's eyes, any woman out of her teens and still flirtatious is the female equivalent of a dirty old man. He presents her as a stereotype butch lesbian, styling her like a man, with brutally slicked-back hair and classic clothing tailored to emphasize her wide shoulders and long legs. The only hints

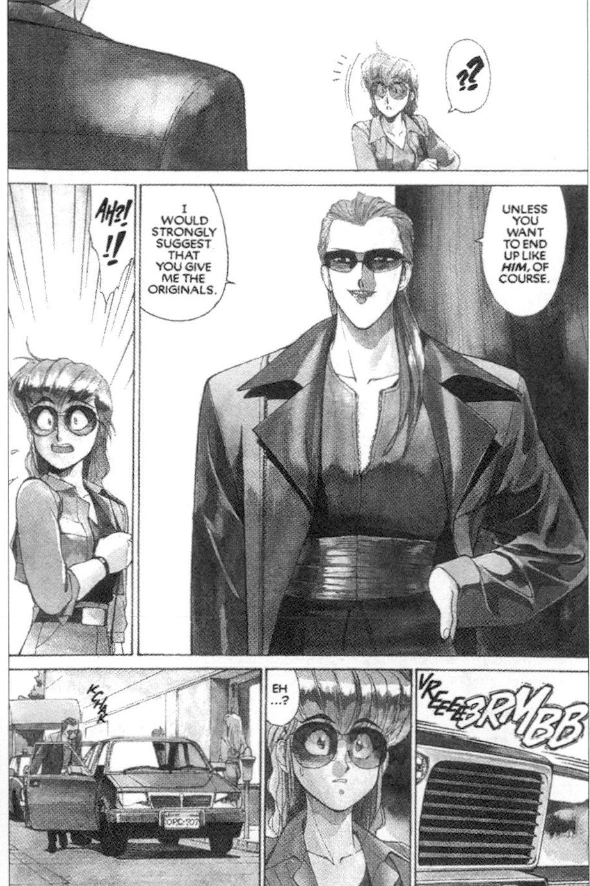

Whole lotta woman! Goldie Muso is six feet of Mob menace.

of femininity are underplayed jewelry and lingerie, which is only seen when she's at home with her slaves. Goldie has to buy or coerce the kind of attention that Rally, who has yet to hit twenty, or the still younger Minnie May, or even bespectacled researcher Beck Farrah, can attract without effort every time they walk down the street. Still, Goldie has one of the big advantages of maturity—money; she can afford to buy attention of any kind, while Rally scrapes from job to job barely getting by. Goldie has the backing of the Mafia's most powerful families, while Rally has nothing but an underage ex-tart, a beat-up street detective, and a few flaky friends. It drives her crazy that Rally keeps scraping by as the winner in their ongoing contest. Like any clever, independent older sister who sees her cute younger sibling stepping into her shoes, Goldie's jealousy is irrational and unacknowledged, but powerful just the same.

The pair have more in common than they think. Goldie's excellent Mafia connections hide the fact that her parents and adored older brother were slaughtered in gang wars when she was just a child, leaving her a lonely little girl forced to get tough or die. Rally lost her mother too, becoming a bounty hunter to pursue the justice she could not find anywhere else in society. Yet their differences are enough to keep them fighting like cats and dogs—appropriately, since Goldie is a dog lover and Rally, of course, is all for cats.

Sonoda isn't one to let a good character go quickly; Goldie remains a thorn in the paws of the Gunsmith Cats right up to the last volume of the manga, where Rally finally defeats her.

counseling, caring, and helping each one of them with their problems. She shows each desperate teenager that death is preferable to the problems and worries of their miserable lives, and the group holds bizarre self-mutilation sessions before finally joining in a mass suicide. But even after death, Mitsuko's influence is still powerful—the only survivor, Saya, steps into her shoes and starts to gather a new suicide club in Usa-Maru Fukuya's manga *Suicide Club (Jisatsu Circle)*, a bleak and nihilistic look at teenage life. Based on a live-action movie by Shion Sono.

NAKIA [1995]

The Anatolian queen in *Red River* by Chie Shinohara (out from Viz) is determined that her son will inherit the kingdom. She draws heroine Yuri into the ancient Hittite world by magic so that she can be a virgin sacrifice to secure the deaths of handsome, charismatic Prince Kail and his brother. A sorceress of terrifying power, Nakia is also a beautiful woman, but cold and ruthless.

AKIKO NATSUME [1993]

Akiko is an heiress and president of Mishima Heavy Industries. She really loves her husband, scientific genius Kyusaku, but both are obstinate, and she is obsessed with her work. She's also never been raised to be any good at housekeeping, but Kyusaku is an old-fashioned guy who thinks that women should do all their family's chores. When her husband leaves her and takes their son Ryunosuke on the grounds that he can give the boy more time and attention than she can, Akiko is devastated. Her devastation expresses itself in steely determination to get her son back, whatever it takes. She also wants the super-android her husband was developing for the company before he resigned and fled. She sends her employees and enough heavy weaponry to level a small nation to get Ryunosuke back. Yuzo Takada's manga *Super Catgirl Nukunuku (Banno Bunka Neko Musume)* chronicles the comical chaos this causes before Akiko is eventually reunited with her husband and child. The manga first ran in *Action* magazine, which folded before it could be completed; after the success of the anime spin-off, character designer Yuji Moriyama stepped in ands completed the story so a collected volume could be published. It's out in English from ADV.

MISS PARDING [1995]

A curvy Caucasian figure skater with a will to win that is unfortunately much stronger than her technical merit, Miss Parding has never been placed above eighth in any competition. She joins the evil Anabolic Academy, whose president is hellbent on altering society to be entirely based on sports, to try to climb out of the poverty her failure has brought. Some of the academy's top people bear a remarkable

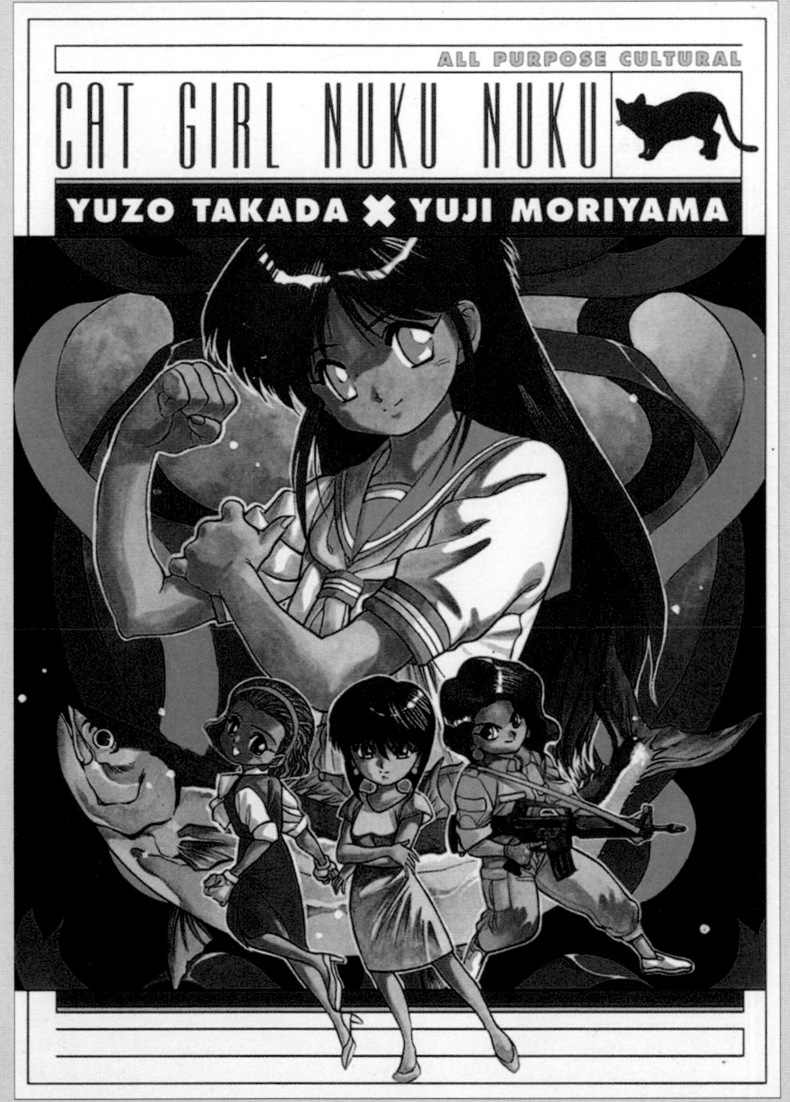

Akiko Natsume (center) and her henchwomen in comical mode.

resemblance to real athletes in Koichiro Yasunaga's manga *Muscleman Spartacus (Ganjo Ningen Spartacus)* from *Shonen Captain* magazine. Miss Parding, who wears her fair hair tied back from her face, sets out to take down sporting heroine (and government secret agent) Hitomi Rokujo at any cost.

QUEEN PROMETHIUM

[1980]

Also known as Queen Millennia or the Queen of a Thousand Years, her personal name is Yayoi. She is the mother of Emeraldas and Maetel, and appears in the web-exclusive manga of the movie *Maetel Legend*. Her story reaches back to Matsumoto's earlier *Queen of a Thousand Years*. The beautiful and good Queen of planet La-Metal sends her two children out into the world—one to live the life of freedom and courage, fighting for justice, the other to embody the spirit of love—knowing it is their destiny to return and defeat her when she descends into madness as the evil Queen Promethium. Her planet is threatened by destruction—it is on a collision orbit with Earth that will destroy both worlds. She comes to Earth, disguised as human lab assistant Yukino Yayoi, to get Earth scientists to build a weapon that will save her planet, and like her daughters after her, she becomes the first love object of one of Matsumoto's young heroes.

RIRIKO **[1995]**

Ririko is a celebrity, famous model, and beauty who is also a complete witch. She treats everyone, including her devoted assistant Hada-chan, dreadfully. She has been top dog at her modeling agency for years, but when a younger, fresher face comes on the screen, just as her body starts to show the first signs of deterioration in spite of constant plastic surgery, she begins the slide into despair. Then her rich lover gets engaged to a younger girl. *Helter Skelter* by Kyoko Okazaki is a bleak look at what happens when fame and beauty start to slip away.

SHASHI **[1989]**

CLAMP's breakthrough work *RG Veda* first appeared as a fanzine before serialization in *Wings* magazine. Based on the Hindu religious epic, it tells of a war in heaven. Shashi was the queen of the heavenly empire of Tenkai, partner of the Emperor Ashura and pregnant with his daughter, when she defected to the rebels who wanted a change of heavenly government. She gave vital information to Taishakuten, the rebel leader and Ashura's former general, who used it to win the war. He killed her husband and married her. She immediately became pregnant with his child and gave birth to twins, the emperor's daughter Ashura and the usurper's son Teno. Shashi is a cool and ruthless woman, determined to kill her daughter to ensure her son will inherit the throne, but thwarted by her dead husband's remaining loyal retainers.

SIRENE a.k.a. Silene

[1972]

The gorgeous bird-demon in *Devilman* by Go Nagai is stark naked except for her feathers. These cover her tail and the wings growing out of the sides of her head, but nothing else. She's out to kill Devilman at any cost, both to avenge her lover and to ensure that he doesn't frustrate Satan's aim to take over the human world in any way.

HINAKO SHIRATORI

[1988]

Ultimate Teacher (Kyofun no Bio-Ningen: Saishu Kyoshi) is set in Emperor High, a school in the roughest part of town. Hinako Shiratori is its queen bee, a teenage martial arts champion and leader of the most powerful gang in school. Hinako is top dog because she can beat any guy, and even the unnatural strength of new teacher Ganpachi Chabane can't defeat her until he uncovers her secret weakness: a pair of velvet bloomers adorned with a lucky white cat. If she isn't wearing them for a fight, she changes from powerhouse to pushover.

Toyo Ashida's 1988 video release was turned into a manga for *Animage* magazine by designer Atsuji Yamamoto.

BLUE SONNET [1982]

A street urchin rescued from the slums is rebuilt as a powerful cyborg and named Blue Sonnet by Dr. Merikus. The child is a powerful psychic, and she becomes a weapon for the deadly Talon organization in Masahiro Shibata's manga *Red Fang Blue Sonnet (Akai Kiba Blue Sonnet)*. Psionic people are not uncommon, but few learn to control their powers without extensive cybernetic restructuring. Sonnet is now a cold and ruthless killer for Talon. She is sent to Japan to look for a mystery psionic known only as Red Fang. Enrolled in high school as a cover, she excels at classical piano, mathematics, and, in particular, tennis, hitting her shots with inhuman force and accuracy. Befriended by classmate Ran Komatsuzaki, she is welcomed into her group, but finds it hard to cope with the new emotions that kindness and friendship trigger. When Ran starts to manifest the same powers she has, Sonnet is faced with a difficult choice—continuing to fulfill her mission as though she really is no more than a machine, or finding the person she once was in her cyborg body.

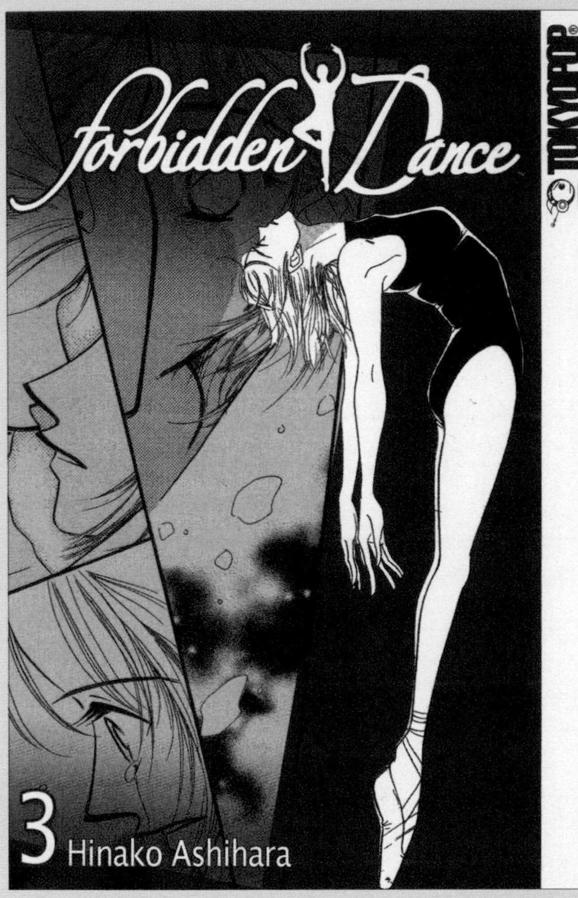

Heroine Aya is the target of Fumika's jealousy in *Forbidden Dance*.

TAJIMA [1993]

The Riverside High School that gives *River's Edge* its title is full of sick, obsessive, or disengaged teens. Central character Haruna Wakakusa is sleeping with her boyfriend even though she doesn't like him, but she's been a close friend of Tajima's boyfriend Yamada ever since she rescued him from school bullies. Yamada's only going with Tajima to try to hide the fact that he's gay, and Tajima is jealous. Trying to set Haruna's house on fire, she accidentally kills herself, but carries on haunting Yamada, who prefers her dead. Since he's also obsessed with a corpse he's discovered in the bushes, that's hardly surprising. The bleak, twisted world of Kyoko Okazaki's manga is far removed from the general perception of girls' comics as a romantic medium; in fact, her work mostly appeared in magazines for young men. Okazaki suffered a serious car accident in May 1996 and has not produced new manga since.

FUMIKA YOSHINO [1997]

Yoshino, as everyone calls her, is seventeen and a pupil at the Machida Ballet School in Tokyo. She's a good modern dancer but her classical ballet skills are weaker, and she nurses bitter resentment for Aya Fuji, the school's top dancer and a dazzling classical technician. She bullies Aya and her friend Nachan in Hinako Ashihara's manga *Forbidden Dance*, out in English from Tokyopop. When Aya falls and is injured in a competition, Yoshino becomes the school's top dancer and even gets the lead in their production of Sleeping Beauty, only for the ballet master to take it away from her when Aya recovers. However, she regains top place when Aya quits after another fall. Aya later joins a modern dance troupe called Cool where the manga's main theme, a love triangle between Aya, the sweet-natured Tetsuya, and the arrogant Akira, unfolds.

WINTER WITCH [1969]

Yu Komori is a lonely teenager with a tough boss, no money, and a hopeless love in *Spider-Man the Manga*, Ryoichi Ikegami's fascinating adaptation of the Marvel original. The Winter Witch is one of his opponents, a woman who can turn the whole world to winter. Marvel attempted to sell the manga in translation in the 1980s, without success.

PRINCESS VINA [1989]

Dragon Half by Ryosuke Mita stars Mink, a half-girl, half-dragon whose main enemy (apart from her own astounding silliness) is Princess Vina, half-blob, half-human, and ferociously competitive teenager. Under extreme stress, Vina reverts to her mother's side of the family as a ball of slime. Otherwise she just complicates life for heroine Mink, whose hopeless crush on idol dragon-slayer Dick Saucer finally resolves itself in marriage in volume six of the manga. By this time the two girls are living in a state of truce, but Vina still wants Saucer for herself and has just been stringing her own boyfriend Mig along.

SADAKO YAMAMURA

[1996]

Sadako was a strange, withdrawn child, born to psychic Shizuko Yamamura on Izu Peninsula. She disappeared in the 1960s. Thrown into a well and left for dead by her father, she creates a mysterious videotape that brings death to everyone who watches it. A reporter whose niece dies with three schoolfriends after watching the tape is drawn in to the mystery and, with her ex-husband, tries to solve it, finally recovering Sakako's body in the hope that her spirit will find peace. The manga version of Koji Suzuki's hugely successful novel *The Ring* appeared in 1996 in *Monthly Magazine KC* with art by Kojiro Nagai. There is also a 1999 movie tie-in by Hiroshi Takahashi with art by Misao Inagaki, and a tie-in for *Ring 2*, also from 1999, by Takahashi with art by Meimu, both available in English from Dark Horse.

Chapter 6

Non-humanoid & Semi-human Heroes & Villains

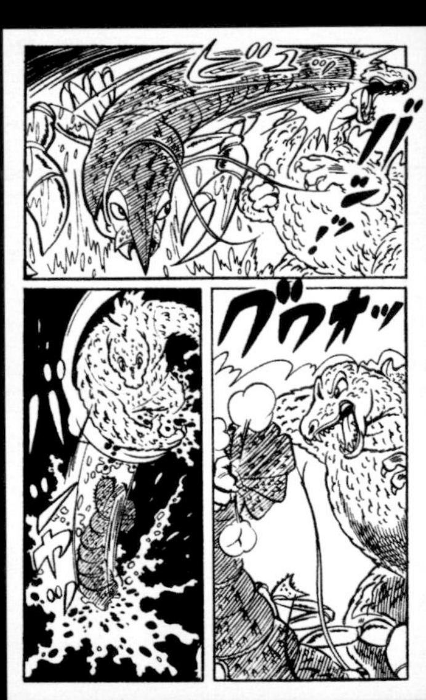

Godzila vs Ebirah

Animals, animal-human hybrids, mechanical animals, and aliens masquerading as animals appear across the manga spectrum in both leading and supporting roles. Comics for small children use animals to teach simple lessons; adventure comics use them as one of the perils of nature. They are prominent in fantasy, horror, and science fiction. Dogs and cats are favorites, but as this small selection shows, the manga zoo embraces every kind of creature, from the humble hamster to the mighty dinosaur, and they can be anything but cute and cuddly.

THE AMAZING THREE

[1965]

Heroes of Osamu Tezuka's manga *W3*—Bonnie Bunny, Zero Duck, and Ronnie Horse (*Boko*, *Poko*, and *Noko*)—are agents of the Milky Way Patrol, an organization set up by the higher intelligences of the Milky Way to keep an eye on planets that might cause problems for the wider galactic civilization. In the 1960s, as Earth continues to experiment with the hydrogen bomb despite seeing its dreadful effects, the aliens begin to wonder whether it might not be better for everyone to just wipe out the human race. The three officers are sent to the planet to assess its inhabitants and see if they might be capable of outgrowing their juvenile fascination with big weapons and instead contribute something useful to the galaxy. Landing near a small village in Japan, they disguise themselves as local life forms and try to infiltrate society; unfortunately they pick a rabbit, a duck, and a horse as their disguises. They run into young Kenny Carter, who manages to convince them mankind is worth saving after all.

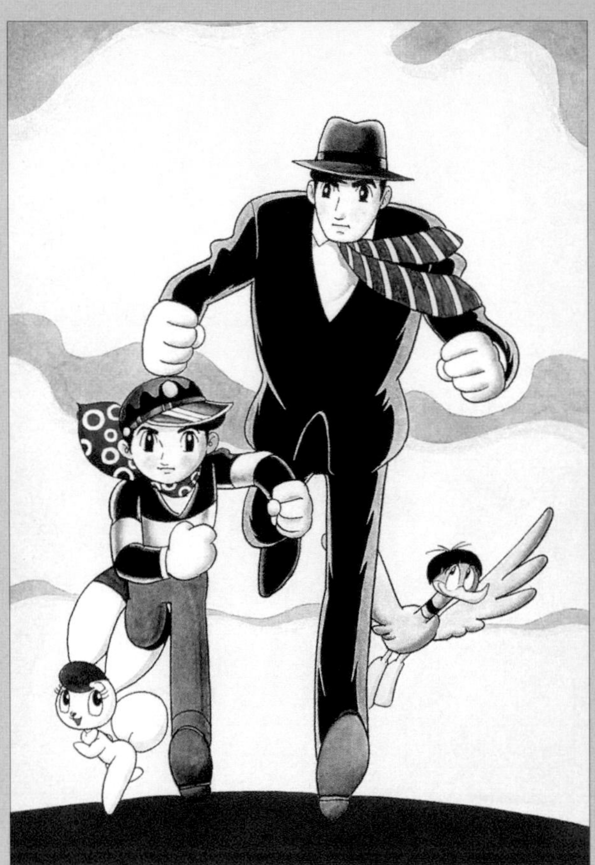

The Carter brothers and their alien allies Bunny and Duck race into action to save the Earth.

ANNAPUMA & UNIPUMA [1986]

Anna and Uni, as they are known to their friends, are bio-engineered twins, human-puma hybrids with long legs, long hair, big breasts, cute furry ears, and tails. Like all cats, they have a short attention span, a bad attitude, and vanity on a galactic scale—but on the plus side, they are brave, clever, good in a fight, and inventive. Created by Masamune Shirow for his ecological polemic *Dominion* from Hakusensha, their adventures are available in English from Dark Horse.

BILLY [1986]

Talking dog Billy followed young Tatsuo Yumori home one day and stayed. The ex-stray and his doggy friend Gary have the minds of humans and they soon bring fun and adventure to Tatsuo, his friends, and the readers of *Billy Dog (Billy Inu)*, a late manga by Fujiko-Fujio, the pen name of duo Moto Abiko and Hiroshi Fujiwara. The pair split their long-running partnership in 1987.

BLACK CAT [1979]

The stray cat in Hideshi Hino's *Black Cat* wanders around an unfriendly city observing the lives of its less salubrious inhabitants—a little boy who loves his dog but hates his new stepfather, an elderly couple whose combative relationship survives even the grave, an alcoholic clown—trying and failing to understand those strange animals called humans. Originally published by Rippu Shobo, this chilling little anthology is available in English from DH Publishing's Cocoro Comics. Born in 1946 in Manchuria, young Hino grew up amid the fears and horrors of post-atomic Japan. He wanted to work in movies but started producing fan manga in high school. He got his first break at twenty-one in Tezuka's experimental anthology *COM*. His mangas are

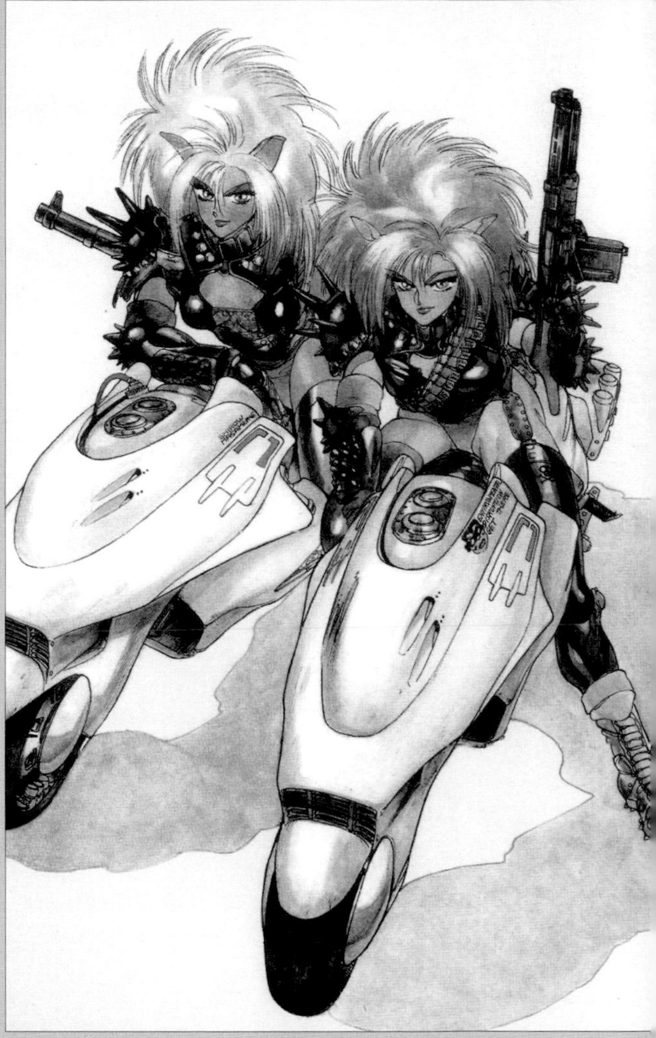

Girl racers Anna and Uni, the Puma Twins, made to cause mayhem in a world where the ecosystem teeters on the brink of disaster.

firmly rooted in Japan's grotesque horror tradition, and show that in the modern world, the human mind has just as many dark corners and scary alleys as ever. He later achieved his ambition to direct.

BOOKILA [1985]

A cute little cat-boy ghost, Bookila haunts a Tokyo TV studio in Osamu Tezuka's *Weekly Shonen Champion* comedy manga *Say Hello to Bookila!* He's been haunting Studio 13 at Tozai TV for three years, and when lowly magazine reporter Rokuro (played by Tezuka's long-running character Rock Holmes) goes to investigate, he discovers that the incidents stop when Neoki Tokoro show up for work. She's cute but very klutzy, constantly making mistakes and messing things up, but the station is desperate to keep her on. Rock learns that Bookila is in love with her and thinks of her as his girlfriend, so however many mistakes she might make, nobody else is bothered while she's in the studio.

BOMBA [1970]

When introspective, timid high schooler Tetsu Otani learns that his least favorite teacher, the violent Kito, plans to propose to his favorite teacher, pretty Reiko Mizushima, a giant white horse appears from nowhere. Tetsu recognizes Bomba, a horse from his father's stories of his years in the army during the Pacific War. Kito dies the next day. Tetsu is as passive and downtrodden as his father, but whenever he takes a dislike to someone, Bomba appears and wreaks his revenge. Reiko moves to a Tokyo school, promising to keep in touch, but is killed in a car accident. Bomba appears in the city where she died and starts wreaking havoc there. Serialized in *Bessatsu Shonen Magazine*, this minor Tezuka work is a thriller whose ostensible "villain" recalls *Forbidden Planet* with its "monsters from the Id."

BONOBONO [1987]

Bonobono the otter and his raccoon and chipmunk chums live a peaceful life in the forests and rivers, debating simple points of philosophy and teaching life lessons to their young readers. Mikio Igarashi created this cute animal manga, collected in *Bamboo Comics*. Its biggest success came in the early nineties when the movie and TV series created a fantastic demand that deluged Japan in *Bonobono* merchandise.

BUG BOY [1975]

Sanpei is a squat kid with bug eyes; his family doesn't want him, his classmates think he's a freak, and bullies make his life hell. His only refuge is the local dump, where he befriends the vermin and makes playthings out of trash. One day a strange insect bites him, and he slowly transforms into a huge, poisonous bug

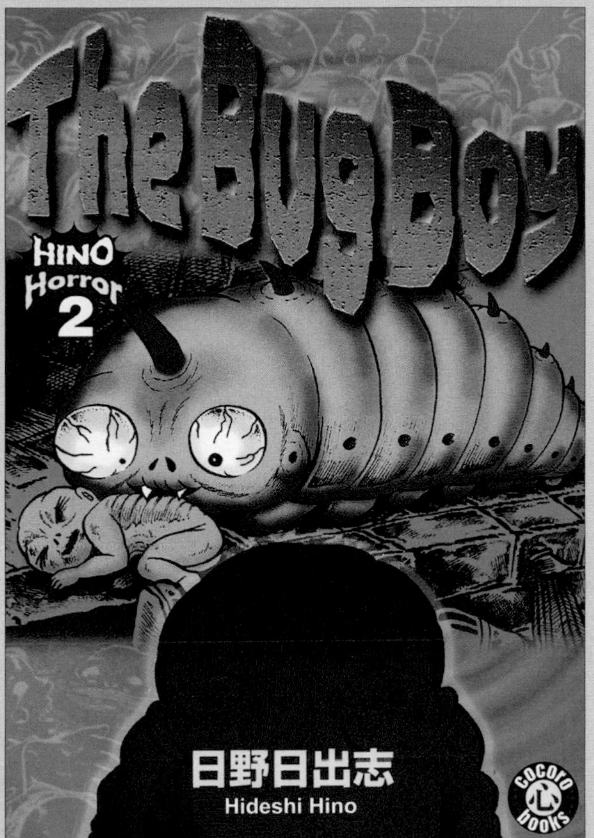

Bullied and rejected, Sanpei finds a way to get even at the local dump.

out to take revenge on the world that rejected him. Another Hideshi Hino horror manga, *Bug Boy* shows how Spiderman might have turned out if he hadn't come from a loving home. Available in English from DH Publishing's Cocoro Comics.

CUTEY CAT [1978]

Star of Yumiko Oshima's *Cotton Planet (Wata no Kuniboshi)*, Neko-chan, as she is known in Japanese, is a little girl who looks like a kitten. She can communicate in words, but all humans hear is cute cat sounds, so they see her as a pet. First appearing in *Comic Lala*, and later adapted by Oshima for animation, the powerful allegory of a girl struggling into womanhood in twentieth-century Japan was somewhat overshadowed by the cuteness of the main character.

DAN [1962]

Dan appeared in *Weekly Shonen Sunday* as the hero of Osamu Tezuka's manga *Brave Dan*. He is a huge white tiger captured on the island of Hokkaido and put on a train en route for a zoo. He escapes and is befriended by an Ainu boy, Kotan Nakamura. The pair become embroiled in villainous Kousekko's search for a great treasure, in an Indiana Jones-style fantasy adventure set in the wildernesses of Hokkaido.

DORAEMON [1963]

A blue and white robot cat from the far future, Doraemon turns up at the home of elementary schoolboy Nobita Nobi in a time machine, sent by his descendants to improve Nobita's prospects in life and give them a better tomorrow. But Nobita wasn't a success, so his

GODZILLA [1954]

TOHO'S MIGHTIEST MONSTER was born of the terror of nuclear war. His first film appearance came in 1954, and he continues to wreak havoc as headliner of the longest-running film franchise in the world. His retirement has been announced several times, but rumors of his death have always proven to be greatly exaggerated. Godzilla's manga incarnations have been numerous, but the best known in America is the 1988 Dark Horse edition of Kazuhisa Iwata's 1984 Shogakukan manga *Godzilla*. This is a re-versioning of the movie of the same name, it was released in the United States as *Godzilla* in 1985.

The King of the Monsters had been on a ten-year hiatus after his scripts declined from the serious and dramatic intent of his debut, as nature's response to nuclear testing, into high camp. As critic Steve Kyte remarked, Godzilla's career mirrors that of Batman: both born out of paranoia, they became camp parodies of themselves before regaining their dignity through a return to their roots. The 1984 movie was intended to restate his position as a dark and terrifying force, and the manga faithfully follows this line.

In his first three decades, Godzilla's manga incarnations were as many and varied as his movies. He appeared in comic magazines for small children in squashed-down "super deformed" mode fighting comical adversaries, as well as in movie tie-ins for an older audience. Yet Iwata's manga is one of the first serious treatments of the King of the Monsters in graphic form. It shows him awakened by volcanic activity from a thirty-year slumber, the timescale tied to the 1984 movie's purpose of returning him to his darker 1954 roots after his camp and corny 1970s career. Iwata's version of *Godzilla* is not completely faithful to the 1984 movie, but it includes many recognizable sequences and real Japanese locations. Iwata created some memorable images—survivors watching from smoking ruins as the monster vanishes into the distance, several vertiginous panels of Godzilla at work leveling skyscrapers, and a haunting double-page spread of glittering downtown Tokyo silent and deserted against the night sky, echoed later with a similar view of the moonlit wreck of the city.

A much more famous manga and anime creator came in on the act in 1990, when Toshihiro Hirano created a one-volume manga, *Godzilla 1990*, for Kadokawa. Shogakukan released more movie-based manga in 1991, for *Godzilla vs. King Ghidorah*, for which Iwata again provided the art, while Kazuko Omori gave him a hand on the story and script. The pair reprised the same roles for Shogakukan in 1992, on

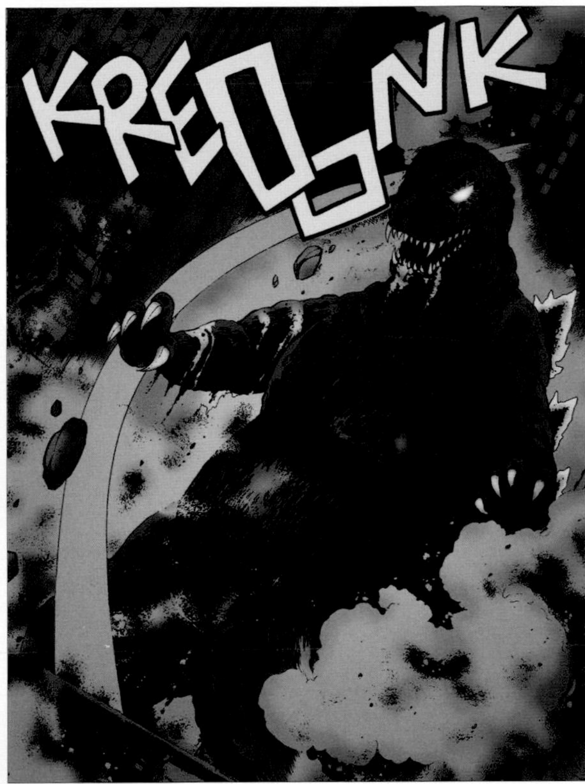

There goes the neighborhood. Godzilla trashes Tokyo in Iwata's 1988 version, and appears in an early movie tie-in (see page 262).

Godzilla vs. Mothra; both books had fine film-art covers by Noriyoshi Orai. Publisher Tentomushi picked up the baton for *Godzilla 2000: Millennium* in 1999, with art by Mondo Takimura, and story and script by Takimura and Toho writers Wataru Mimura and Hiroshi Kashiwabara.

Godzilla has starred in over twenty Japanese movies. His size, shape, and some of the details of his design vary, but he is always as mighty and capricious as nature itself. He had a Japanese TV show, *Godzilla Island*, running daily for almost a year from October 1997, in 256 five-minute episodes; the show was largely filmed using Bandai's extensive toy range to enact the stories, making it a highly effective advertisement. Games for Game Boy, MSX, Gamecube, Super Nintendo, Playstation, and X-Box let fanatics get their Godzilla fighting fix from 1986 to the present.

He also enjoyed cult success in America from an early stage. His first movie, and the 1984 film which inspired Iwata's manga, were heavily re-edited and re-versioned for U.S. release, both of them featuring Raymond Burr (*Perry Mason, Ironside*). The second version also starred soft drink Dr. Pepper, whose manufacturers put money into the production in exchange for a level of product placement that would put even Bandai to shame.

Godzilla is no mere comic book monster, a stereotype of man's evil intent; he is a force of nature, devastating yet morally neutral. The destruction he wreaks is not born out of malice, vengeance, or a desire for power—it is pure animal instinct magnified to a terrifying degree by humankind's own insistence on seeking new ways to dominate. In *Godzilla*, as in all great tragedy, we are the authors of our own fate. This is the root of his compelling power.

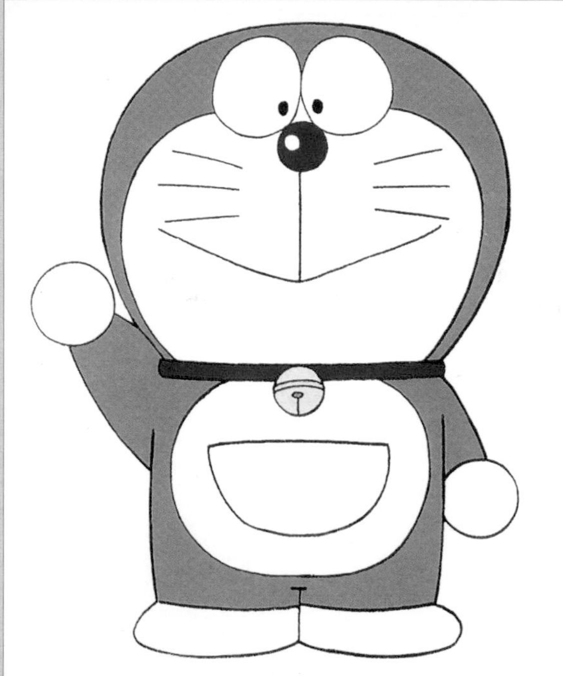

Cheap and cheerful robot Doraemon may not be top-of-the-line in 2112, but he looks good to Nobita.

descendants can't afford a quality robot. Doraemon isn't exactly state-of-the-art, and his ears were eaten by rats in the factory. The experience has left him with a fear of rats, and his other weak point is that if anyone pulls on his little tail he will stop dead. Made on September 3, 2112, Doraemon is 4ft (129.3 cm) tall and exactly the same around the chest. His weight is 285 lbs (129.3 kilos). He has a pouch on his belly which is actually a portal to the fourth dimension, from which he can draw out all kinds of wonderful gadgets like the take-copter, a set of little helicopter vanes that allow him to fly when he puts them on his head; the docodemo-door, a portal enabling access to anywhere; and the small-light, literally a beam of light that makes people and objects small. He can change people's appearances, clothes, and characters. His favorite food is *dorayaki*. He has a robot "sister," Dorami, who turns up later in Fujiko-Fujio's long-running manga *Doraemon*. It won the Shogakukan New Manga Prize on its debut in *Shonen Sunday* magazine. Collected editions have sold more than 7,500,000 copies worldwide, and it was first animated in 1973.

GOA [1965]

The villain of Osamu Tezuka's *Ambassador Magma*, Goa is the evil master of the hordes invading Earth. He is a giant saurian, transforming himself to enable him to fight effectively on twentieth century Earth. Young Mamoru Murakami wakes up two hundred million years too early. His house has been transported back to the world of dinosaurs, and Goa tells his journalist father to publicize his intention to become master of Earth in the near future before returning the family to their own time. Mamoru gets a visit from the giant golden robot Magma, created by the spirit of Earth to defend the world. The spirit of Earth tells Mamoru that Goa, who is disguised as a human with an extravagantly curled hairstyle and a distinctive taste in suits, is really a reptile from space who covets earth. Soon, Goa's flying saucers and amorphous space beings called "Humanoids" attack Tokyo. The remaining humans, including Mamoru, fight back with their own secret weapon, a parasitic fungus. Goa leaves the Earth, only to send a planet-transforming robot to Earth to enforce its surrender. Chaos, creator of the universe, is finally asked to arbitrate and declares Earth the victor. Goa leaves in his spaceship, in his original reptilian form. Ambassador Magma ran for more than two years in *Shonen Gahosha* magazine.

GIN [1983]

Yoshihiro Takahashi's manga *Silver Fang: Shooting Star Gin (Ginga: Nagareboshi Gin)* stars Gin, a mountain dog with a silver coat, who is the third in a line of dogs bred by Gobei to hunt down a terrifying bear in Japan's Ohu mountains. His father Riki went wild and lost his memory after one fight, and Gin teams up with him and his pack of wild dogs to end the menace on the mountain. The manga ran for four years in *Shonen Jump* and was made into a TV series. Takahashi also created *Ginga Legend Weed (Ginga Densetsu Weed)* about a gray and white puppy whose dying mother tells him he is the son of the legendary Gin, boss dog in the Ohu Mountains. Weed sets out to find Gin, accompanied by a kind but cowardly old dog named GB. Three volumes of a planned six were published by Comics One, but it was then discontinued.

GON [1991]

Masashi Tanaka's tour de force *Gon*, a manga without dialogue, is the story of a small but belligerent dinosaur and his journey through the natural world. It involves the audience in Gon's world through superb art and plotting. As Gon travels through his environment, encountering and seeing off much bigger animals, his character grows calmer and more reflective, and he even helps the herbivorous animals organize to fight off the carnivores—all without a line of dialogue. Appearing first in *Comic Morning*, the manga was published by DC Comics in their Paradox Press line in 1996. Tanaka, a manga professional since his schooldays, deliberately made a story without words because he wanted it to sell worldwide. He uses no screentone, achieving all his effects through pen and ink. CLAMP's *Rex* also features a baby dinosaur, a T. Rex, possibly the world's only cute example of this predatory species.

HAMTARO HAM-HAM [1999]

Hamtaro is the (hamster) hero of Ritsuko Kawai's manga *The Adventures of Hamtaro (Tottoko Hamtaro)*. He is bought from a pet shop by a ten-year-old girl named Laura, and as she plays with him and shows him off to her little friends, he quickly makes hamster friends of his own. He copes with new experiences—

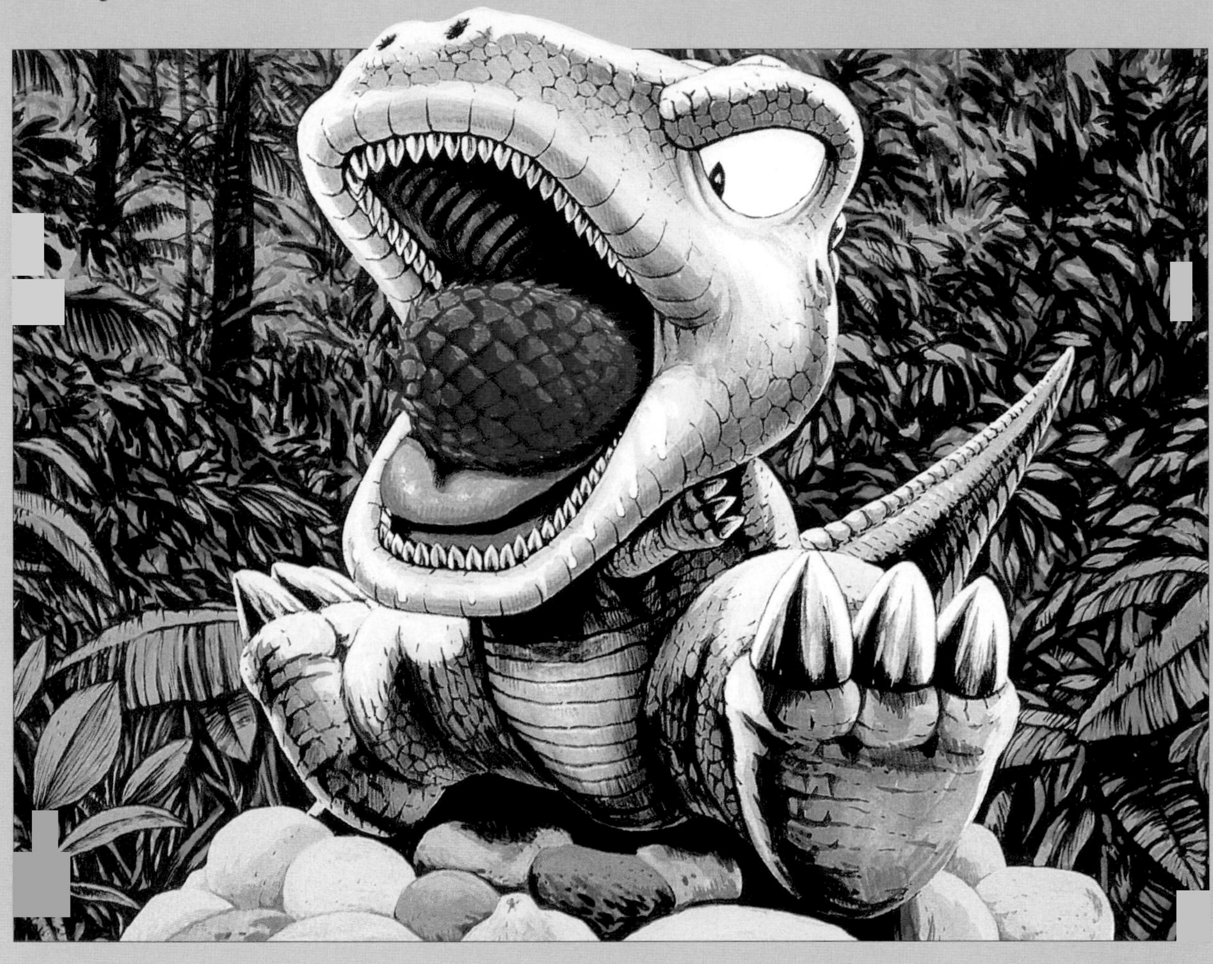

moving to a new house, meeting hamsters from other countries or with different personalities, encountering jealousy, falling out with friends; he experiences the sequence of holidays and festivals that are part of everyday life, and he eats lots of delicious food. In the Japanese original his first owner is five-year-old Yuriko.

Gon is a little dinosaur with a big attitude and an unquenchable appetite for life.

Like many cute animal manga stars, Hamtaro was designed to reinforce life lessons for small children as they venture out of the safety of home and kindergarten into the wider world, but his undeniable cuteness has made him a TV star and merchandising success with wider audiences. American publisher Viz offers a full range of such products, including a handbook that tells you the Ham-Ham Gang's star signs, how to read hamster body language, and all the steps for the Hamster Dance.

HARI & RURI [1997]

These cute twin cat-demon girls serve the investigator demon Koryu in CLAMP's manga *Wish*. On Earth they can transform into ordinary housecats at will, but their demon appearance is as two cute Chinese girls with hair coiled over their ears and two long tails framing their faces. Devoted to their master, they will do anything he asks. Available in English from Tokyopop.

HARIMA [1986]

In A.D. 663, the Allied Army of Wa-koku and Bekje loses a battle with the Tong/Silla Allied Army in the Hakusukinoe War in Korea. Harima, a Bekje soldier, is captured by the Tong Army, who skin his face alive and cover it with a wolf's head. An elderly woman hermit saves his life and tells him to go to Wa-koku (one of the ancient kingdoms of Japan). Tortured by strange dreams, he obeys and meets a tribe of aboriginal wolf-gods rejected as devils by the new Buddhist political leaders and forced to retreat into hiding in the mountains. His strange dreams continue and he gradually realizes that he is possessed by a spirit from the far future. In the twenty-first century, a Phoenix-worshipping religious association calling itself Hikari (The Light) controls all Japan, and those who don't share their beliefs have been marginalized as "shadow people." Suguru Bando, young agent of the shadow people, contacts Harima across a gulf of centuries and they share their battle against marginalization. *Phoenix: The Sun* by Osamu Tezuka was published in Kadokawa's *Yasai Jidei* magazine.

INU-YASHA [1997]

In the Muromachi Era during the Warring States period, a strange creature—half-dog, half-boy, with dog ears and a tail—is out to steal a priceless jewel. His name Inu-Yasha means "dog-demon." The offspring of a human mother and a huge demon father (a type of monster known as *Yokai* in Japanese, able to look human and tending towards evil), he's foul-mouthed, vicious, but cute-looking for a centenarian. His heritage gives him long life and strength, but he wants to become a full *Yokai*, and the Shikon Jewel will do it. He wears a kimono made from the incredibly tough fur of the legendary Fire Mouse (Hi-Nezumi), which shields him from most weapons and dangers. A young priestess stops him—sealing him inside a magical spell that freezes him in space and time, along with the jewel—before she dies. Fast forward to the twentieth century

KIBA [2003]

KIBA means "fang" in Japanese; not a bad name for a werewolf. The hero of *Wolf's Rain* by Bones and Keiko Nobumoto looks like a teen pop idol in human form, but is lethal in his night-time shape. In the first few pages of the manga from *ZKC Magazine*, out in English from Viz, the white wolf has killed, almost ripping a hunter's head off, and only the intervention of Tsume, a slender young man in black leather with a short silver ponytail, calms him down. Tsume can talk to the wolf because he too is one, passing for human in a world where his kind are not welcome. He tells the newcomer that there are rules to be followed in a place like this, but his efforts are met with scorn. Tsume is living as a human and a scavenger, stealing food for himself and his human friends; Kiba wants to know what's happened to his pride as a predator, that he can talk in such a way. Tsume changes into his black wolf form and the pair fight, but Tsume turns back to human form and the white wolf runs off.

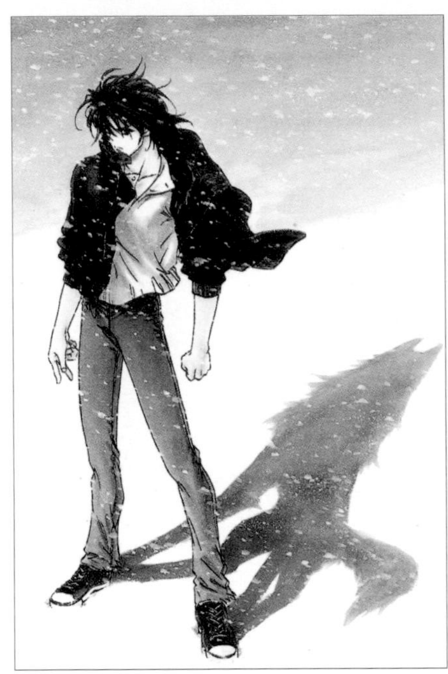

Kiba roams a decaying world of ramshackle streets and derelict buildings looking for paradise.

Kiba is running out of the frying pan into the fire; the hunter Quent is on his tail. Tsume, meanwhile, is ashamed, because Kiba has touched a wound as old as the cross-shaped scar on his chest—he once betrayed his wolf brothers and the scar is both a reminder and a punishment.

Wolf's Rain is set in a future world that has the air of a decayed empire. Shattered skyscrapers, torn down to mere stumps, are now inhabited by trees; large public buildings loom over mean streets of ramshackle dwellings cobbled and patched together; armed men in uniforms tramp across public spaces and down alleyways. In this world, wolves all but died out 200 years ago, almost like a harbinger of ecological doom. Most people seeing a wolf would mistake it for a big dog, but Quent, who lost his wife and son to wolves and is fired by hatred of the creatures, knows a wolf when he sees one. The former sheriff of the town, he gave up his job to enable him to hunt wolves, along with his hunting bitch Blue, specially trained to chase wolves. He is an anachronism; none of his people can understand his desire for revenge on a dead species. When he finally captures Kiba, the government intervenes and cages the wolf-boy for study.

Kiba is not the only subject for the local scientists. Chief boffin Sher Degre has his attention solely occupied by a beautiful young artificial being called Cheza, a plant-girl. Kiba is left to languish until he is released by another werewolf, a cheeky young cub named Hige. Explaining that to survive in this world Kiba has to learn to become human at will, Hige helps him escape, just as Tsume is leading a raid on the center to steal food, and Cheza is being abducted by persons unknown.

The pair meet Toboe, another young wolf, who has been raised in the town and knows nothing of nature, and the youngsters ask Kiba what brings him to their town. Kiba tells them that he never knew his parents or his own pack—after a forest fire he was found as a tiny cub by an old native who raised him—and he talks of an old wolf legend that set him off on a search for their hometown. The lupine race were made to live in paradise, a paradise only a wolf can find, and Cheza, the flower girl, is the key they must have to find it. The way was marked by the scent of moonflowers, the legendary Lunar Flowers, which also disappeared many years ago, but on the night of a full moon, a girl made of flowers—like Cheza—can show them the way.

The others decide to join Kiba on his search. Tsume, who has been betrayed by his human friends and needs to lie low after the raid, is talked into joining them, secretly delighted to learn that there is a place in the world for people like him to be their true selves, acknowledging their true nature. Wolves have had to learn to hide in a world that does not understand them, a world they can no longer accept. The promised utopia is worth seeking, even if Tsume doesn't entirely believe in it.

However, they are not the only ones looking for it. Sher Degre serves a mysterious king whose armies are after Cheza, determined to have her secrets. The scientist whose family originally made her, Darcia, a tall, striking character with flowing dreadlocks, dressed in a long black coat, also needs Cheza's help in reaching paradise to heal his lover, Harmona, who is in a deep coma. He captures Cheza but his flier is forced down by Sher Degre. Cheza escapes, and joins the wolf party.

On the way, Kiba and his friends fight off sinister robots, face a tunnel originally seeded with poison gas, and the Forest of Death. They also meet more of their own kind, wolves who have survived in the human world; Zari and his pack have managed this by becoming sled dogs so they could eat. They too tried to get to paradise via the gas-filled tunnel, and many died.

As they learn more of the origins of paradise and Cheza's people, Darcia, the army, Quent, and Blue all pursue them. Darcia finally kills Blue, Hige, and Tsume to try and get to Cheza; in the end, Kiba must fight him, but paradise itself rejects Darcia, and Cheza and Kiba unite and renew the world. The Earth begins anew as a beautiful garden, a true paradise, and all four of Kiba's pack are miraculously together again.

where a high-school girl accidentally falls through a time portal and releases Inu-Yasha, shattering the jewel in the process. The people of feudal Japan think she is the reincarnation of the priestess. He is still determined to find the shards of the lost jewel, and she has to beat him to it. At first the only thing that saves her is the Nenju Necklace, a magic rosary which she throws around his neck; every time she uses the word "sit" he has to obey. The pair have a combative relationship that gradually turns to respect and love.

JINGORO [1984]

This fat orange-and-white feline is the domestic pet of the paranormally powered Kasuga family in Izumi Matsumoto's teen romance manga *Kimagure Orange Road* from S*honen Jump*. He stays calm in the face of his family's whims, especially the mothering instincts of teenage Kurumi and the wildness of her twin Manami, which are just as likely to have him flying through the air by ESP as being petted and fussed. Constantly trying to sneak out of the house, he is often frustrated.

JINMEN [1972]

A demon in the shape of a turtle, Jinmen can embed the faces and souls of people he wishes to torment in his shell. He's one of the foes faced by Go Nagai's *Devilman*. A loyal servant of the demon general Zann, he lures

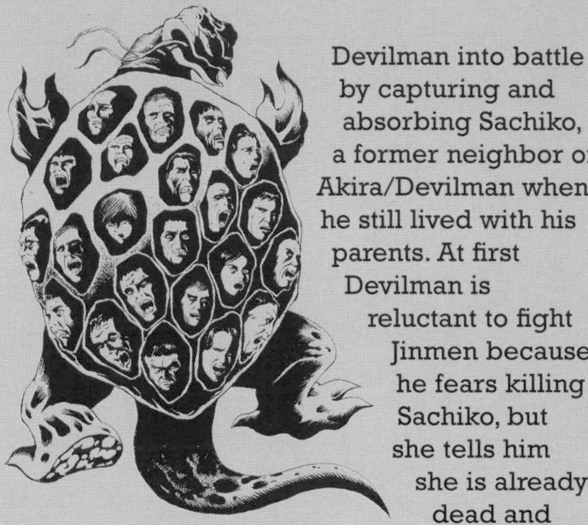

Devilman into battle by capturing and absorbing Sachiko, a former neighbor of Akira/Devilman when he still lived with his parents. At first Devilman is reluctant to fight Jinmen because he fears killing Sachiko, but she tells him she is already dead and the only way to save her from further suffering is to destroy the monster that torments her. Devilman punches straight through her face and into Jinmen's body, then rips his shell apart, killing him.

AKA KABUTO [1983]

A huge and vicious bear who dominates the mountain, Aka Kabuto is the villain of Yoshihiro Takahashi's manga *Silver Fang: Shooting Star Gin (Ginga: Nagareboshi Gin)*. The hero, Gin, a mountain dog with a silver coat, is bred to hunt Aka Kabuto down.

KERBEROS [1996]

Kero-chan, as he is known, is a supernatural creature, created centuries ago by Clow Reed, maker of the Clow Cards in CLAMP's manga *Card Captor Sakura*. His title is Beast of the Seal and his role is to guard the seal of The Clow, the magic book that holds the cards. His true form is fierce and splendid, but he is unable to transform into it while the Clow Cards are scattered, so he appears as something like a six-inch-tall stuffed toy lion cub with cute little wings.

His full powers are restricted in this form, but he is still both magically powerful and surprisingly strong. He's also quite lazy, which has caused his problems; he was having a thirty-year snooze when the cards escaped their book and scattered. Until the Earth and Fire cards are sealed, he can't regain his full powers, so he works with heroine Sakura to retrieve the cards, giving her the powers of a Card Captor. He retains the pride, courage, and loyalty of his true form, but he's also fond of desserts and playing video games.

KOBAYASHIMARU [1985]

Kobayashimaru is the pet dog of Daizo Sudo, grandson of the founder of the now defunct *Nakano Military Prep School* in Koichiro Yasunaga's manga for *Shonen Sunday*. Like Daizo he has undergone years of pointless military training to qualify to enter a school that no longer exists. He poison-tests any food given to him by anyone but his master. He's big, not very pretty, and deeply loyal to Daizo.

MAKEMONO [1985]

The demons of Toshio Maeda's notorious manga *Urotsukodoji* live in a parallel dimension to humans. Every 3,000 years, a superbeing is born with the capacity to unite the dimensions and bring about a new world from the destruction of the old. Makemono are violent, lust-crazed, and destructive. When unleashed in the human world they go on a rampage of rape and destruction. Their other-dimension counterparts, the Jujin, or "man-beasts," have some of the powers of the makemono, but usually appear more human and have a little more self-control.

MANMARU [1996]

To Western eyes, penguins are probably one of the least likely creatures to possess ninja skills. Mikio Igarashi's manga *Manmaru the Ninja Penguin (Ninpen Manmaru)* shows the Japanese are made of more imaginative stuff. Hero Manmaru goes to the Nenga ninja school to study the arts of assassination alongside foxes and raccoons under a wise bear master. Rival schools of dogs and monkeys constantly taunt the Nenga pupils to battle, and a group of ex-Nenga dropouts try to lure Manmaru from the way of the ninja, in a lighthearted mix of old folktales about the shadow warriors and typical schoolboy problems and pleasures. Talking penguins crop up in other manga, such as Sanami Mato's 1992 Bonita comic *King of the Penguins*

KIMBA a.k.a. LEO [1950]

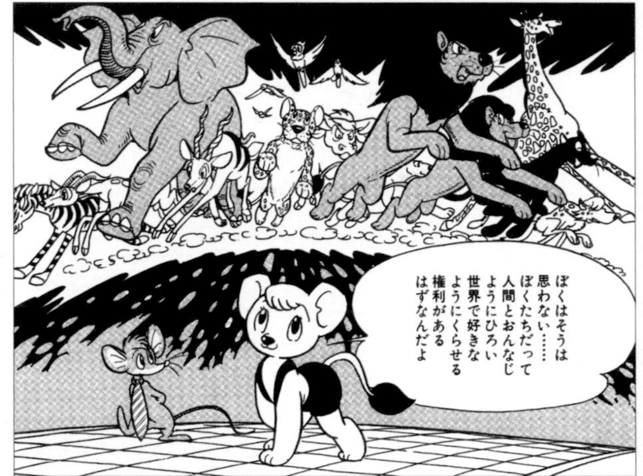

OSAMU TEZUKA'S epic manga *Jungle Emperor (Jungle Taitei)* ran for four years from 1950 in *Manga Shonen* magazine. He wanted to make a story celebrating nature's power and its capacity for renewal, set in Africa where this is still evident, and to talk about conflict between cultures. Coincidentally, these themes were to be played out in a real-life movie world conflict almost half a century after the comic began publication. The trigger for the debate, which involved fans and writers worldwide, was the similarity between the animated TV version of Tezuka's manga and the Disney blockbuster *The Lion King*.

Caesar (Panja) the white lion reigned as emperor over the Central African jungle, with all the animals acknowledging his dominion. He was slaughtered by white hunter Viper Snakely (Hamegg) and a group of native humans in his pay. His pregnant wife Snowene is shipped to an overseas zoo, but during the voyage she gives birth to Caesar's son Kimba (Leo). When the ship is wrecked, Kimba leaps into the sea and is cast up, exhausted, on the shores of Aden in the Arabian Gulf. He is rescued by a kind young man, Roger Ranger (Kenichi), who lives with his uncle Mr. Pompous (Higeoyaji). They rear the cub and teach him to speak human languages. Roger takes him back to Africa, where the animals all acknowledge him as their Emperor. Kimba dislikes the barbarism of the jungle, where the strong kill the weak, and resolves to set up an animal civilization. He dreams that his animal brothers will learn to protect themselves from the worst of mankind while being friends with well-meaning humans. He finds a mate, Kitty (Lyre), and they have two sons, Rene and Rucchio. Fired by his father's tales of the human world and human friends, Rene leaves home to explore this new society, but is captured and enslaved in a circus.

A terrible epidemic kills many of Kimba's people, including Kitty. The survivors are saved by a scientific party including his old friend Pompous, who are on their way to

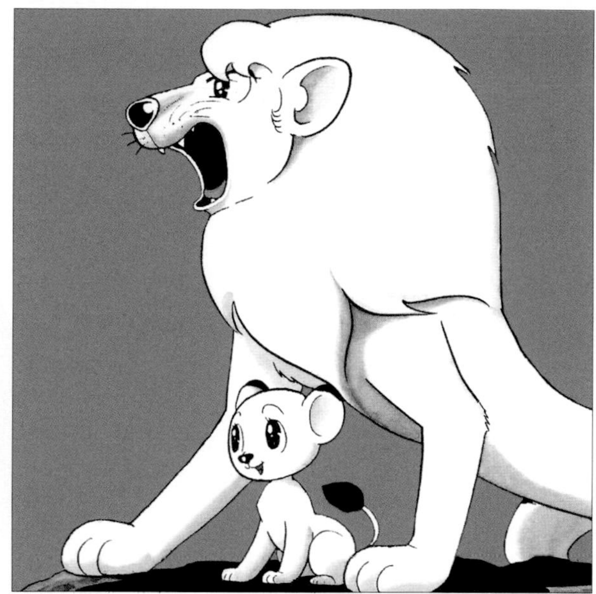

Father and son: Tezuka's *Kimba the White Lion* has many points of similarity with Disney's *The Lion King*.

Mount Moon in Kilimanjaro. Kimba joins the party to help his friend, but the climbers die of cold and hunger, until only Kimba and Pompous remain. Kimba gives his life to save his friend, and Pompous survives to return to the jungle, where he meets Rene, who has escaped the circus and come home. He tells the young prince of his father's courage and self-sacrifice.

The manga was published in many different editions in Japan. The first TV series, aired in Japan in 1965 and released in the United States as *Kimba the White Lion*, was the first color animation made for Japanese television. It had a movie adaptation, seen only in Japan, and a sequel series, *New Jungle Emperor*, shown in the States as *Leo The Lion*. The original series was also remade in Japan in 1989, with a U.S. video release in 1998. Tezuka Productions stated that this version was how Tezuka originally envisioned the anime, but some find its tone too dark and feel the original anime is closer in spirit and content to the manga. The original anime was widely screened and very successful in the United States. This later raised controversy over its many similarities with Disney's work *The Lion King*.

There are many articles tracing the similarities between the two, but perhaps the real spirit of Tezuka's work, the true difference, is best illustrated by one of his final panels. This shows two tiny figures on the vast African plains, Higeoyaji with the skin of the Jungle Emperor under his arm and Rene padding beside him, while the skyline is dominated by a huge white cloud shaped like a roaring lion. The Disney movie shows a world of animals behaving like humans, but not coexisting with them. Tezuka shows two creatures alien to each other but united by a set of shared values, and by love of one individual whose idealism and self-sacrifice transcended the boundaries of species. Both stories are fantasies, but one is a fantasy of more generous dimensions. The theme of Tezuka's tale is that nature, in its vastness, finally envelops everything, but that in nature, the capacity for love and generosity is ever-present.

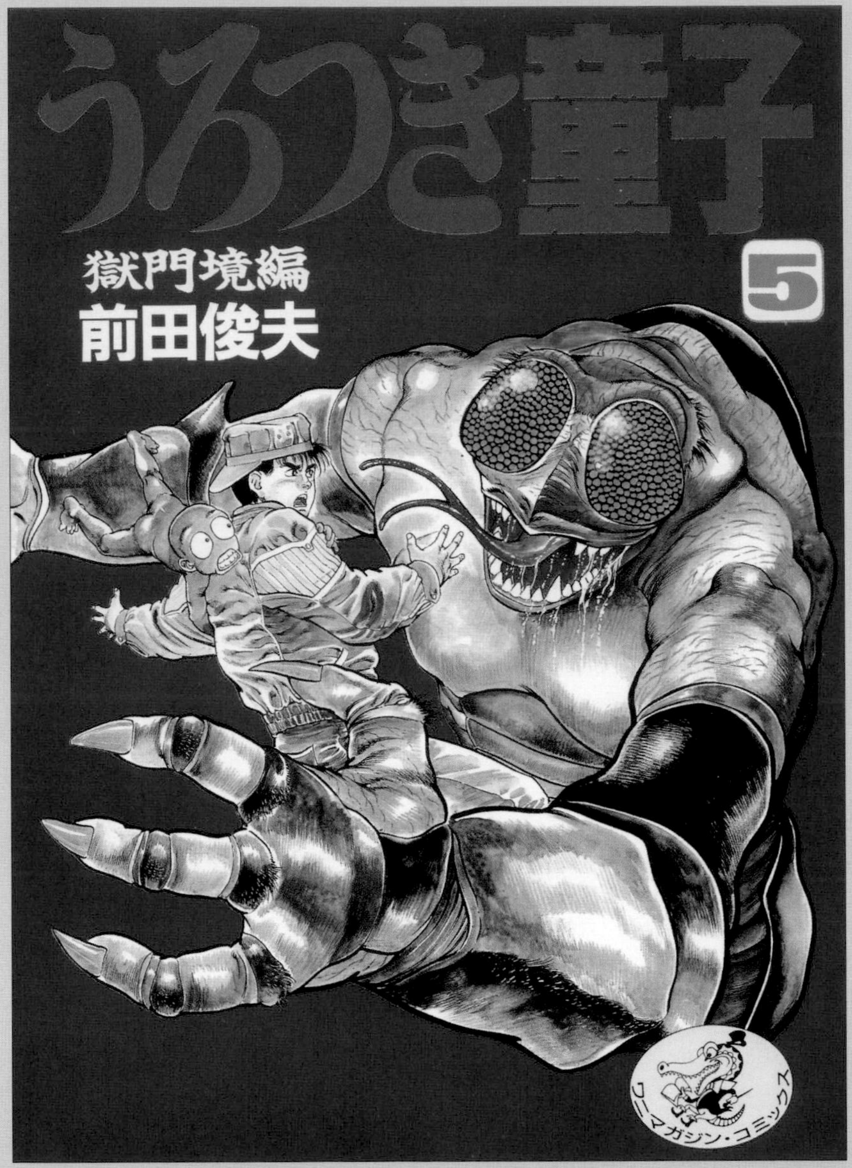
うしおととら
うろつき童子
獄門境編
前田俊夫
5
ワニマガジン・コミックス

(Penguin no Osama), where the human in need of an animal friend is a teenage boy.

MEPHIST [1988]

The beautiful young sorceress from Osamu Tezuka's uncompleted manga *Neo Faust* also appears in the form of a large black dog. She persuades Prof. Ichinoseki to sell his soul to the devil instead of committing suicide, and the professor, despairing of ever finding the secret of life after fifty years of hard study, agrees, providing he can have a new life long enough to enable him to complete his work. Whisking him back twelve years to 1958, Mephist remakes him as a handsome young man. Daiichi has no memory of his past or his promise. He is adopted by a rich man dying of stomach cancer. When he inherits his fortune, Daiichi sets up a laboratory that will create living things for his own dark purpose. Crashing *Faust* into *Frankenstein*, the manga was never completed owing to Tezuka's own death from stomach cancer in 1989.

MICHAEL [1984]

In 1984, Kodansha's *Comic Morning* magazine began a new manga by Makoto Kobayashi. *What's Michael?* starred a fat, lazy ginger feline living in Japan with a well-meaning but very stupid human couple who fondly imagine they own him. Michael has a rich fantasy life and time to indulge it—he dreams of being Michael Jackson, a nightclub gigolo, or a corporate megastar—but his everyday world is full of humor and incident, from his hopeless fights with local bad cat Nyazilla (a tortoiseshell monster named for Godzilla), to scrounging food in shops and playing with the local children. Catlovers all over Japan warmed to the series, which was later released on video and TV. Toren Smith, founder of American manga translators Studio Proteus, cites it as one of his favorite manga; it's available in the United States from Dark Horse Comics.

Left: A makemono from Urotsukidoji—not a tentacle in sight, but still a nasty creature.

MISTER PEN-PEN [1985]

Mister Pen-Pen is the prince of Penguin Land, always formally good-mannered if a little zany, and always beautifully turned out in top hat and tie. He first appeared in Shogakukan's *Second Grader* magazine, in a gentle adventure by Mayumi Muroyama. One morning, he knocks on the door of a typical little Japanese girl named Mika, and he and his penguin pals inject their wacky magic into her everyday world of home and at school. His gentle influence was far more enduring than expected—Hideaki Anno, creator of TV landmark *Evangelion*, paid tribute by casting a new, genetically engineered Mr. Pen-Pen in a similar role in his angst-ridden Armageddon epic.

ICHIGO MOMOMIYA

[1997]

Chirpy, outgoing teenager Ichigo is crazy about cute classmate Masaya Aoyama, but her life changes when a weird incident merges her DNA with that of a wildcat. She's one of five girls with the same problem, and they learn that parasitic aliens are trying to attack Earth through its animals. Now she can transform into a cat! As MewMew, Ichigo finds the other four girls (who can transform into a bird, a monkey, a wolf, and a sea creature) and the team sets up HQ in Café MewMew. The setup will be familiar to fans of Japan's live-action team (*sentai*) shows. *Tokyo MewMew* was drawn by Mia Ikuma and written by *Dragonball Z* and *Digimon* scriptwriter Reiko Yoshida for *Nakayoshi* magazine, in English from Tokyopop.

MONGREL BOW-WOW

[1992]

Mongrel Bow-Wow is a stray who is taken in by a cute little girl. In his new home, he fights local cats, scrounges food, and goes to various festivals. The simple storylines are aimed at small children, featuring the basic rhythms of Japanese life and the toddlers' obsession with food and repetition in a way familiar to Teletubbies fans. Terry Yamamoto's manga *Modern Dog Tales Bow-Wow (Heisei Inu Monogatari Bow Wow)* ran in *Big Comic Superior* for just longer than three years, long enough to generate a TV series and movie spin-off.

NAO [1996]

Nao is a human-cat hybrid girl, born on an island where mysterious experiments had taken place during the war. Poisonous gases tested on cats caused them to mutate and the half-human, half-animal hybrids are the result. Two children named Souta and Mari notice a number of dead cats floating from the island to Souta's shoreline home, and when they go to investigate they meet Nao and take her back for a visit. She tells them that when human-cats die, they revert to cat form. Disguised in Mari's clothes and with a hairband hiding her ears, she is nevertheless found out by some local boys. Souta and Mari rescue her from a beating and take her home, but an earthquake cracks open an underground storage container of gas, and the escaping gas begins to kill the inhabitants. Nao urges Souta and Mari to leave, but refuses to come with them. Days later, the friends find a dying cat wrapped in Mari's clothing in a boat on the beach. It's Nao. Saved by Souta's father, she lives the rest of her life as a cat with her friend Mari. *Child's Toy* creator Miho Obana's manga *Island of Cats (Neko no Shima)* appeared in *Ribon Mascot* magazine.

NORAKURO [1931]

A pre-war manga hero revived by the nostalgia boom of the late 1960s, Norakuro (Black Stray) is the hero of Shiho Tagawa's so-titled manga first published in *Shonen Club* magazine in 1931, where Norakuro, a dog, fights a gang of oppressive monkeys who are bullying the local animals. He was presented as the archetypal little guy standing up for what was right in a bureaucratic and unjust world, which made him an ideal propaganda tool during World War II. He made his big screen debut in a military promotional movie which uses the "it was all just a dream" motif, later resurrected in *Dallas* and other screen potboilers, for a tale of plucky little Japanese animals joining the army. The manga was revived in *Comic Bon-Bon* for the centenary of the Meiji Restoration in 1968, and ran for another decade before transferring to *Comic Morning* to promote a new animation starring the original Norakuro's grandson. By this time Norakuro bore more resemblance to a man in an animal costume than a dog, but the military games motif was still strong, probably accounting for the character's popularity with small boys.

NORIKO [1984]

Noriko thinks she's just an ordinary teenage girl with a crush on classmate Shinya, but she has a strange mark on her left arm and her eyes turn purple in the dark. She's a human-leopard hybrid, and when her transformation is triggered by her science teacher Ms. Sonehara her life is wrecked. Another hybrid, black panther Mitsugu, stalks her and wants her for his mate, threatening to kill her beloved Shinya. Noriko wants a normal life with Shinya but finally realizes that this is impossible, goes to live with Mitsugu, and in despair attempts suicide. Saved by Ms. Sonehara, she finds she is pregnant with Mitsugu's child. Her former teacher wants to use the baby in her research and kill its father. Noriko tries to kill her to protect the child, and Mitsugu sacrifices himself to save them both. Shinya helps her and the baby to escape, but Ms. Sonehara pursues them and Noriko dives into the sea with her to save her daughter Asayi. More than sixteen years later, mother and daughter are finally reunited and Asayi starts a new life in the United States. Chie Shinohara's *Purple Eyes in the Dark (Yami no Purple Eye)* was published in *Comic Margaret*.

NUKUNUKU [1993]

Nukunuku, whose name means "snuggly-wuggly," is a schoolgirl-shaped android of amazing strength with the brain of a dead cat. Created by a husband out to keep their son away from his business-tycoon wife, it transpires that she is more loving and caring than either of his parents, whose feelings for him don't go far enough to stop their constant squabbling over poor trophy child Ryunosuke. Created by Yuzo Takada for *Action* magazine, *All-Purpose Cultural Catgirl NukuNuku (Banno*

BIG SHINY ROBOTS KICK ASS

ONE WAY OF HELPING the little guy have an even chance in a big world is by giving him a great, big, shiny machine. They don't come much bigger than in Japan's giant robot manga.

Robots made their way into manga during World War II. They were already making waves in Western science fiction, and as Japan absorbed the lessons of Western technology it became obvious that there were practical advantages to robots. But it was the romance of the robot that ensured its place in manga. Tezuka presented the robot as gentle and playful in *Astro Boy*; but there was another side to the little robot. A really strong robot could be a powerful weapon, used to fight evil dictators, crime lords, or invaders.

Mitsuteru Yokoyama, a Tezuka fan, dreamed up *Gigantor (Tetsujin 28-go)* in 1958, fueled by childhood memories of American B29 bombers. Sweet-faced Mitchy of *Metropolis* and Astro Boy were a million miles from the powerful images of self-assertion and dominance created by these metal monsters, but the fundamental difference was that both Mitchy and Astro could aspire to personhood. Gigantor is not a being with a will of his own; he is pure machine, doing the bidding of whoever holds his control box. The bad guys have giant robots too, and the forces of good only stay on top because they have a better robot than the forces of evil. The good guys win because they're more intelligent, but only if they use their intelligence to make bigger weapons.

Avowedly antiwar and proscience, Tezuka saw technology as a tool for progress, not an opportunity for macho posturing. He contributed to the giant fighting-machine myth in 1963 with *Big X*, and in 1965 with *Ambassador Magma*, but he wasn't interested in the romance of heavy weaponry. It took Go Nagai's unique vision to move the robot into the pantheon of Japanese fantasy. In 1972 *Mazinger Z* rewrote the Christmas wish lists of generations of boys. A giant robot, equipped with arcanely named technological gadgets, became the ultimate toy.

Nagai was the first writer to understand that what young readers wanted was a special bond with their robot, in which their unique qualities could fulfil its potential. *Mazinger Z* sets up a mystic union between the robot and its pilot, who becomes one with the machine. Instead of the robot being no more than a big suit of armor to hide inside, it was an extension of the operator's own body and spirit. Pilot Tommy Davies (Koji Kabuto) is the brain, heart, and soul of Mazinger Z, turning the robot from a mere machine into a character.

Nagai also created the concept of the combining or transforming robot. One robot could take different forms, or could combine with other robots to form a bigger, more powerful machine. The story possibilities were endless, and so were the merchandizing

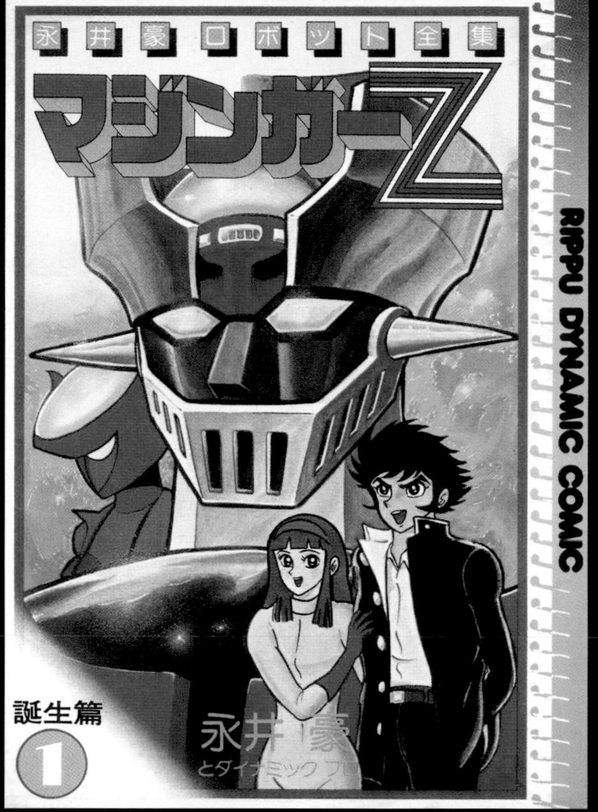

Tommy (Koji) and his girlfriend Sayaka with Mazinger Z and girl robot Aphrodite-A looking coyly over his shoulder.

opportunities. Toy companies all over Japan leapt on the idea, and anime series became half-hour TV commercials for the latest robot toys. The giant robot craze continued in manga, but it was on TV that it took its ultimate form in Yoshiyuki Tomino's *Mobile Suit Gundam*.

Gundam's robots were just machines. An older fan base was growing, ready to move away from magic and towards advanced technology. If inborn, destined talents are needed to pilot a giant robot, readers will turn away from the genre as they outgrow their hope that they have hidden magical capabilities. If all you need is to study, work, and learn the skill, then being a giant robot pilot is within everyone's grasp. You don't have to outgrow the fantasy, any more than you outgrow driving a car. It could be you in that cockpit. Masami Yuki's *Mobile Police Patlabor* takes this premise to its logical conclusion. In a world where more and more robots are being used in everyday work, they'll be used for ordinary urban crime. Police robots are just patrol cars with legs instead of wheels. Yet, despite Yuki's relentless focus on the everyday aspects of police work, the romance and the danger of the giant robot shines through.

One of the outstanding features of Japanese giant robot stories is the extent to which they show collateral damage. A robot battle is always destructive, and often leads to death. The level to which manga acknowledges the inevitability of death, and the extent to which conflict makes death more likely, is one of the attractions of the medium for many Western fans, giving the best examples a resonance not always found in our own mass entertainment.

Flying from fantasy into reality and back again, the giant robot has acquired a massive following. Manga creators, fans and toy manufacturers all seem unlikely to lose interest in this genre just yet.

Bunka Neko Musume) is energetic, noisy, greedy, and inclined to snooze, but utterly devoted to her "little brother," and eventually manages to bring the fractured family back together.

NYAKO [1990]

Garo magazine's *Nekojiru Noodles (Nekojiru Udon)* by Nekojiru, who committed suicide in 1998 at the age of twenty-nine, is a strangely surreal manga full of tales of anthropomorphic cats in a dark world. Nyako is the mother cat of the first story, who is so disturbed by her kitten's wailing that she asks the owner of a nearby noodle shop to castrate him; when he dies, she is devastated. An animated film, *Cat Soup (Nekojiro-so)* was made after the artist's death, based on the manga and featuring brother and sister cats Nyata and Nyako and their own struggles with death.

OYOYO [1983]

Fat, bad-tempered cat Oyoyo charms his idiotic human family while fighting ongoing battles with other neighborhood cats. Arguably the most important character in Misako Ishikawa's manga *Mr. Happy (Shiawase-San)*, still untranslated into English, Oyoyo first appeared in the girls' manga magazine *Shojo*, then moved on to *Ciao*. He got his own animated TV series *Oyoneko Bunichan (Oyo my Huggable Cat)* in 1984,

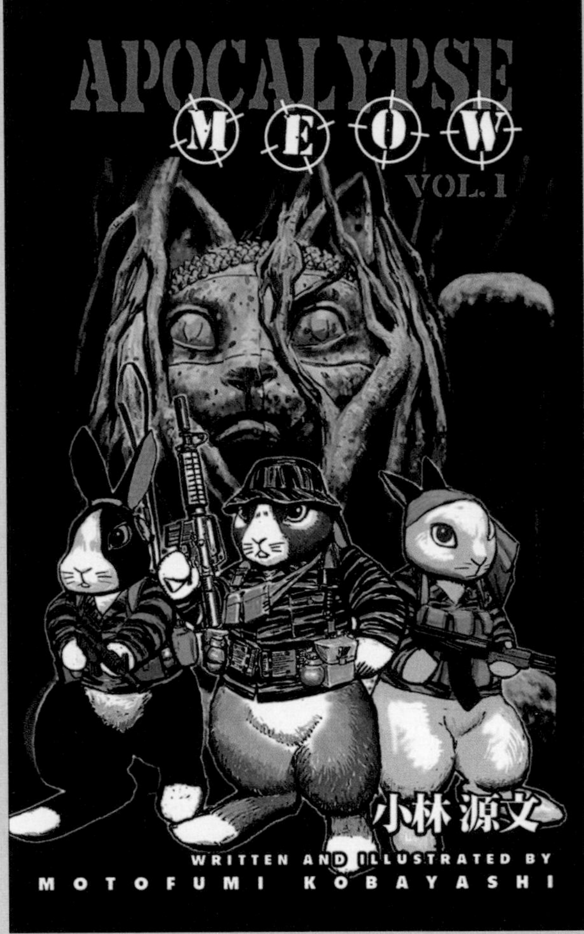

These rabbits aren't chicken as they re-fight the Vietnam War commando-style.

but by then Makoto Kobayashi's *Michael* (see earlier entry) had stolen his thunder as manga's top cat.

"PERKY" PERKINS [2003]

Motofumi Kobayashi's *Apocalypse Meow! (Cat Shit One)* replays the Vietnam War through the eyes of sergeant "Perky" Perkins and his unit of commando rabbits. He and his comrades Rats and Bota fight, live, and talk exactly like American GIs in this *Combat* magazine story, whose only difference from other war comics is that all the Americans are rabbits, the Vietnamese are cats, the Chinese are pandas, the Russians are bears, and the French are pigs. When Kobayashi drew *Psychonaut* for *Marvel Comics* he was the first manga artist to produce a book for the mainstream U.S. market.

PERO [1969]

The hero of an early Hayao Miyazaki manga version of *Puss In Boots*, published in *Chuunichi Sunday News* to promote Toei Doga's movie of the same name, Pero was a gallant and clever talking cat in top-boots and a big feathered hat, whose cunning helped his young master defeat an ogre and win a princess. Named for the author of the original French fairytale, Charles Perrault, Pero was so popular that he went on to become Toei's studio mascot.

PHOENIX [1954]

The linking character of Osamu Tezuka's self-described "life's work," *Phoenix (Hi no Tori* a.k.a. *Firebird)*, the Phoenix embodies the principle of life eternally renewing itself from the ashes. Appearing as a beautiful bird, she can also take human form. Her blood can give 3,000 years of life and she is the target of evil men and women throughout history, observing all the follies of mankind. Starting off in *Manga*

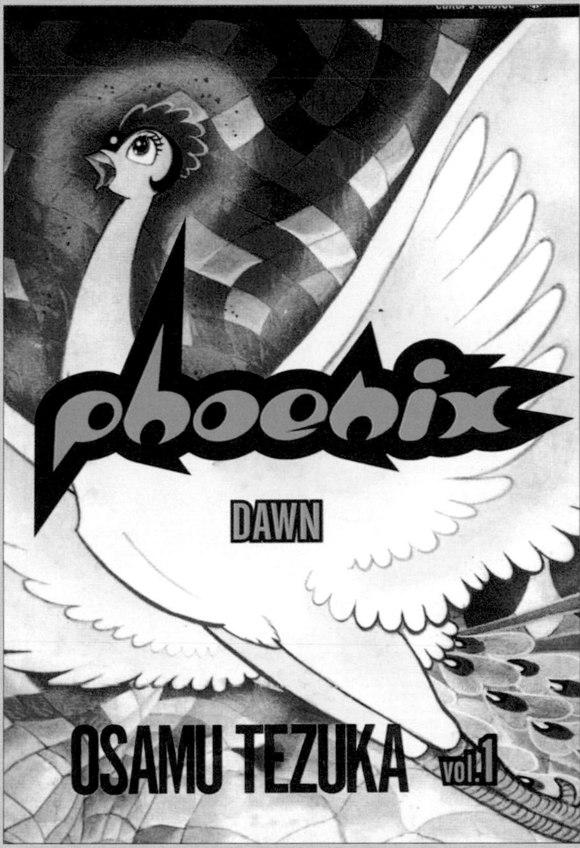

The eternal Phoenix, reborn from flames throughout history in Tezuka's epic story.

Shonen, her story appeared up to 1988 in several different versions, in *Shojo Club*, *COM*, and Kadokawa's *Wild Age*. It was collected into volumes by Tezuka Productions, but was never completed. At the beginning of the saga the Phoenix gives life to two children who save her egg from destruction, and they become the founding gods of Japan. The series tells the stories of those who come into contact with the Phoenix right into the thirty-fifth century, interweaving tales of early Japan, the present, the future, and the conflict between humanity's urge to extinction and the life-affirming beliefs of Buddhism. At the core of the story is the principle that life is a learning process, and we die and are reborn until we achieve enlightenment. The Phoenix herself is eternal, yet gives equal respect to all life, however short. Some of the human characters go through many lives and many encounters with the Phoenix before they learn that all life is precious.

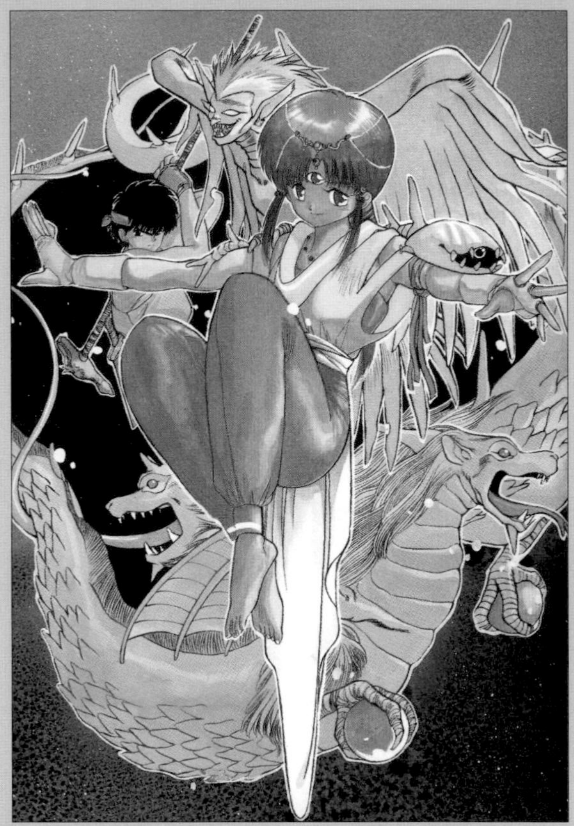

Takuji in both his forms, with his young mistress Pai.

PIKACHU [1996]

The cute yellow icon immortalized in multiple formats all over the world, from trading cards to plush toys to origami, started life as a Nintendo game character before his manga debut. Pikachu is an "electric mouse" Pokèmon, which as any five-year-old can tell you is short for Pocket Monster. He is the devoted companion of young Pokèmon trainer Ash (Satoshi in the Japanese version) and travels the world with him and his friends entering Pokèmon tournaments, where trainers pit their Pokèmon against each other for the glory of being Number One Pokèmon trainer.

The Pokèmon phenomenon evolved from the hugely popular Tamagotchi. The idea of a virtual pet, small enough to carry in your pocket and requiring no input but your time and care, had a huge appeal to Japanese children and soon spread worldwide. Pokèmons combine the low-maintenance appeal of Tamagotchi with the vital boy-toy elements of collection, competition, and constant change. Pokèmons have to be captured and tamed by their trainers, and some are much rarer and harder to tame than others. They are very portable—once lured into their tennis-ball-sized Pokeballs they can be hung from a belt or stashed in a pocket. They can fight other Pokèmon, and best of all, they can evolve and learn. The Pokeverse is a small boy's dream world: Pokèmon trainers don't have to go to school, there are no mothers around to nag about bedtime and washing, but there are friends around every corner, and a big sister or brother figure always materializes to provide a meal, a bed, and any other help that's needed.

There are more than fifty volumes of Pokèmon manga by many different artists and writers; the first four were written and drawn by Toshihiro Ono, but since they are drawn to style sheets laid out by rights holders Nintendo, and aimed at an audience that likes its heroes to look familiar, stylistic variations are very minor. The collected volumes, along with activity books, board books, storybooks, and fold-your-own origami kits, are available in English from Viz Communications in the U.S.

PYONYOSHI [1970]

The title character of Yasumi Yoshizawa's 1970 manga *The Gutsy Frog (Dokonju Gaeru)*, first published in *Shonen Jump* magazine, is remarkably forgiving considering he's squashed flat by a little boy who falls on top of him. Being a magic frog, he survives, stuck flat to the front of little Hiroshi's sweatshirt, from where he comments on the clumsy, noisy kid's every action. With a friend who never leaves his side except on laundry day, Hiroshi has a string of humorous adventures.

GENMA SAOTOME [1988]

The father of Rumiko Takahashi's gender-challenged martial artist Ranma in *Ranma (Ranma Nibbunnoichi)* is a stoic martial artist who takes his son to China to train. He is unfortunate enough to fall into a magic pool, and now turns into a giant panda whenever doused in cold water. Heading back to Japan to try to get Ranma married off as previously arranged to his old friend Tendo's daughter, he finds his affliction is perfectly acceptable in the social world of the small town where they live—half the locals are also martial artists and most of them have a comical animal transformation problem, too.

TAKUJI [1988]

Most of the time, Takuji ("man-bird") looks like an ornate wooden staff. He belongs to Pai, heroine of Yuzo Takada's *3x3 Eyes (Sazan Eyes)* and when she needs his help he transforms into a huge flying dragonlike creature with formidable fighting powers. Growing to dimensions of 65 feet long and 26 feet high in his full form, he hatched from an egg in Konron; he can also appear small enough to perch on a human hand.

UNICO [1976]

Star of Osamu Tezuka's manga of the same name, Unico is a little unicorn with the magical power to bring happiness to all around him. Born on Olympus, he has a special link to the goddess Psyche, and when she incurs the jealousy of Venus for her beauty, Venus decides to get at her by exiling Unico. She commands Zephyrus, the West Wind, to take him to a desolate place on Earth and abandon him. The West Wind must obey, but is sorry for the little unicorn, whose lovable nature and gift of bringing happiness make him popular with everyone but Venus. Unico quickly makes friends and changes the lives of those around him for the better; when she hears of this, the jealous Venus demands that the West Wind moves Unico somewhere else in time and space. Every time he is picked up by the wind and deposited somewhere new, Unico loses his memory of all the happy times and friends he made before and must start again. He goes through hardships and danger, and sees the sad and terrible things humans do to themselves and the natural world, yet he never loses his loving, trusting nature. With settings ranging from industrial, polluted, modern Europe to a medieval castle, imperial Russia

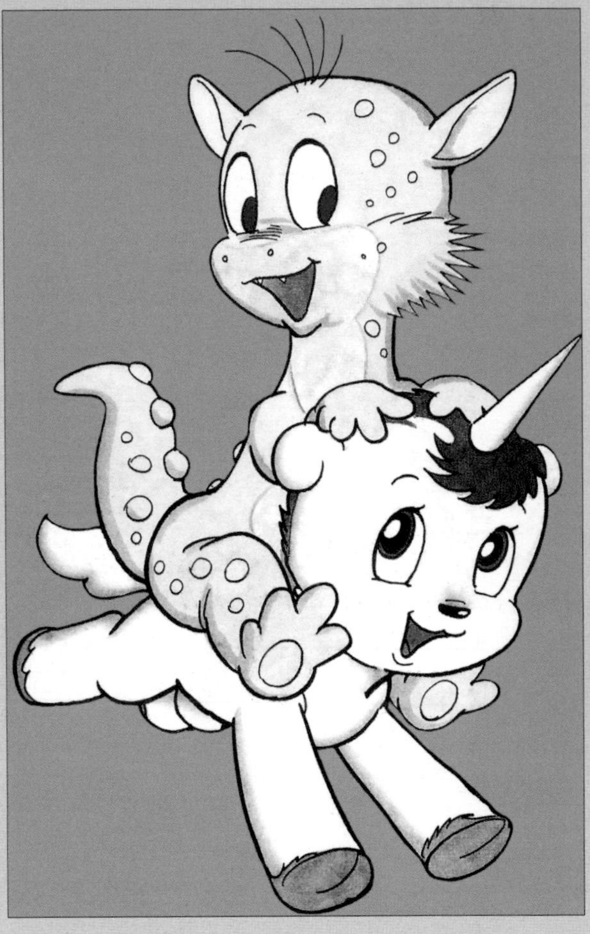

Unico only wants to have fun and help others, but a jealous goddess pursues him through the world.

to poverty-stricken India, the manga's mix of adventure and charm made it a hit with young girl readers of Sanrio's magazine *Ririka* where it first appeared. Episodes were colored and laid out to bleed off the pages, an unusual step at the time. It was reprinted in Shogakukan's *Shogakusei (First-Grade Student) Comics*, and later by Scholar.

WANSA [1971]

Wansa is a cute puppy with a curling, fluffy tail. He is lured away from his mother and sold for 10 yen, but escapes on the way to his new owners. He wanders until he reaches a street corner in a rundown factory district, and falls in with a group of older stray dogs who teach him how to live wild. He is determined to find his mother again. Hiding in a factory, he is befriended by the elderly cleaner, who quits his job rather than kill the pup and takes him home. Osamu Tezuka's manga *Wansa-kun* ran in his own *Tezuka Magazine Leo* but was never completed due to corporate problems. Wansa was originally created as the mascot for Sanwa Bank, and his name is an anagram of theirs.

WEASEL SPIRITS [1990]

Japanese folklore says that the small, almost bloodless cuts that can appear in a sudden eddy of wind are caused by three weasel spirit siblings. One forms little whirlwinds to disorient the target, one makes the cut, and the third puts on a magic salve. In Kazuhiro Fujita's *Ushio and Tora*, weasel whirlwind Raishin and his little sister Kagari attack hero Ushio while he's wandering with his companion Tora in search of his mother. They really want to ask for his help, but they need to see his skill with the monster-slaying Spear of Beasts first. Their brother Juro, the cutter of the trio, has started a killing spree. The constant pressure of humans on the natural habitat of weasels and spirits alike has driven him insane, and he is seeking revenge for his family being driven from everywhere they settle. Raishin and Kagari don't want to kill humans, even to save their own lives, but aren't strong enough to stop Juro. Ushio and Tora manage it.

THE ZOIDS [1982]

Created as a toy line and graduating to an animated TV show, the Zoids also have a spin-off manga, serialized in *Corocoro Comic* in the late 1990s. Tomy designed the toys as a kind of bestial meccano, with different creatures, from gorillas and stingrays to dinosaurs, that could be put together from various parts and moved by motors or clockwork. The name derives from a combination of the Japanese word for beast—*ju*—and the ending of android. For ease of pronunciation by English speakers, *ju-oid* became Zoid.

Teams

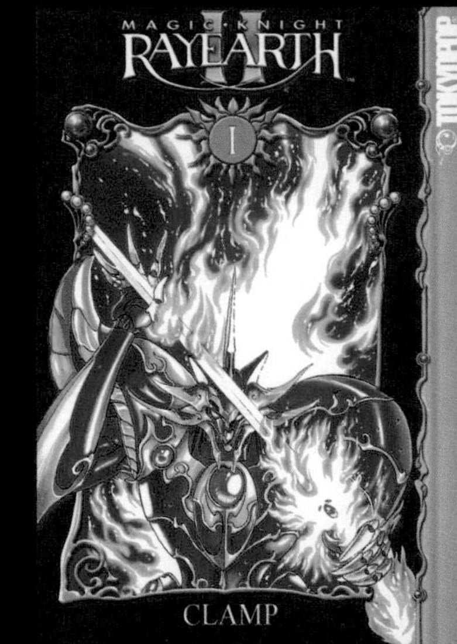

Rune God: Hikaru's Fire Mashi

The team is a vital part of Japanese society, so it's no surprise that manga uses the concept as a base for many stories. *Sentai* shows, with their color-coded fighters in bright uniforms, give us one kind of team; buddy stories provide another. At school, at work, even in the family, it's the links between different people working together that make it possible for them to achieve their goal. That goal can be serious—saving the Earth or winning the tournament, for instance—or very, very silly; what matters is the commitment of the team members and their support for each other. Go teams!

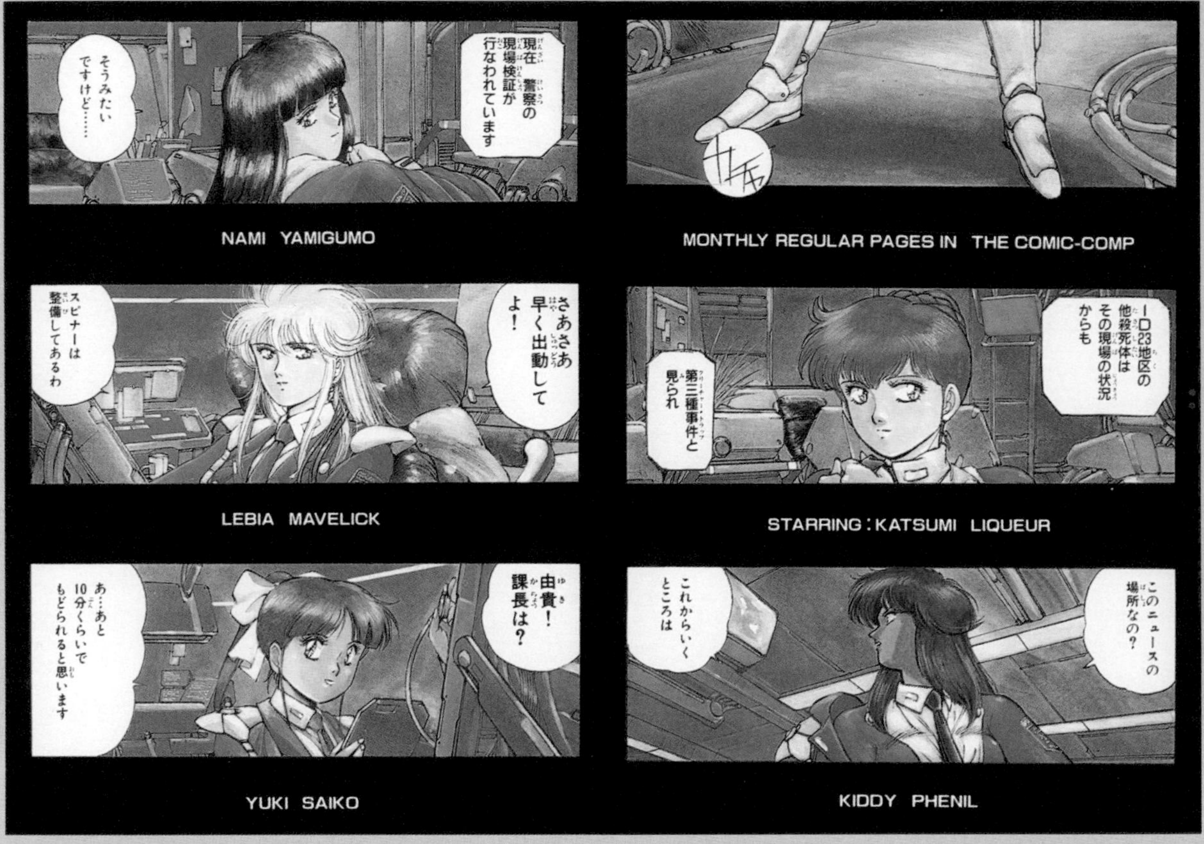

A.M.P.D. [1988]

The A.M.P.D. fighting team getting ready for action. Note the use of English captions, an exotic, edgy element to Japanese graphic designers.

The magnificently named Attacked Mystification Police Department is an elite all-female squad formed in 2023 to combat the rise of demon incursion in twenty-first century Tokyo, in Kia Asamiya's manga *Silent Moebius*. Published in *Comp* and available in English from Viz, the manga is drenched in the cyber-noir vision of its principal inspiration—*Blade Runner* viewed as fantasy rather than science fiction. The AMPD pilots fly spinner vehicles, exactly like those in the film, through a polluted, acid-rain-drenched city. Their foes are the Lucifer Hawks, mighty entities out to dominate mankind and take over the world. Enigmatic leader Rally Cheyenne is part Lucifer Hawk herself. Her sister Rosa joined the other side of their heritage, and in the end the two meet in a titanic fight which Rally wins. The rest of the AMPD are Lebia Maverick, born in Los Angeles, who can send her consciousness into any computer and keeps half of it in storage in an orbital satellite; hereditary Shinto priestess Nami Yamigumo, possessor of a mystic dagger and inheritor of the White Tiger Sword; superstrong Australian Kiddy Phenil, a police officer mortally wounded in the line of duty and rebuilt as a cyborg; Japanese teen psychic Yuki Saiko; and Hawaiian Katsumi Liquer, reluctant mage and the only person who can wield the ultimate weapon against the Lucifer Hawks.

ANGELS [2001]

The Angels are a troupe of cute young women charged to protect Prince Shiva, sole survivor of the royal family after a coup d'etat. Millefeuille, Mint, Ranfa, Vanilla, and Forte are the five members of the group, who pilot a craft known as Emblem Frame and are led by Takuto Meyer. Artist Kanan delivers *Galaxy Angel*, a cute and wacky package featuring staple manga characters (such as space whales and characters named for food) and fan service (bikini basketball and a dominatrix-lite main character), under the supervision of Ryu Mizuno for Kadokawa. Priceless quote from the Broccoli Books translation: "You're a lucky young lady. One doesn't win the all-you-can-eat space buffet every day."

BATS & TERRY [1985]

Members of the same baseball team, best buddies Bats and Terry appeared in Yasuichi Oshima's manga for *Shonen Magazine*. Happy-go-lucky guys with an eye for a pretty girl, always willing to have a laugh, a drink, or a fight, they portrayed the ultimate good-life fantasy for many young Japanese in the 1980s—no exam hell, no tedious office job, just ballgames, pretty girls, cars, and a friend to share the good times.

BRONZE SAINTS [1986]

Masmai Kurumada's *Saint Seiya (Seitoshi Seiya)* ran until 1991 in *Shonen Jump* and in collected volumes that appeared up until 1997. The epic story of a group of young friends who are reincarnations of the defenders of the goddess Athena, the manga sprawls across continents and mythologies. Athena, goddess of wisdom and of battle, returns to Earth every 300 years, and she has created an order of knights to keep the world from harm. The warriors wear "cloths" or magic armors of different metals, based on constellations. The Bronze Saints—Andromeda Shun, Cygnus Hyoga, Draco Shiryu, Phoenix Ikki, and their young leader Pegasus Seiya—defend the current incarnation of the goddess, Saori Kido, from assaults on her power by the other gods. The manga and its animated version are loved by millions of fans worldwide for complex and angst-laden relationships punctuated by slam-bang fighting action.

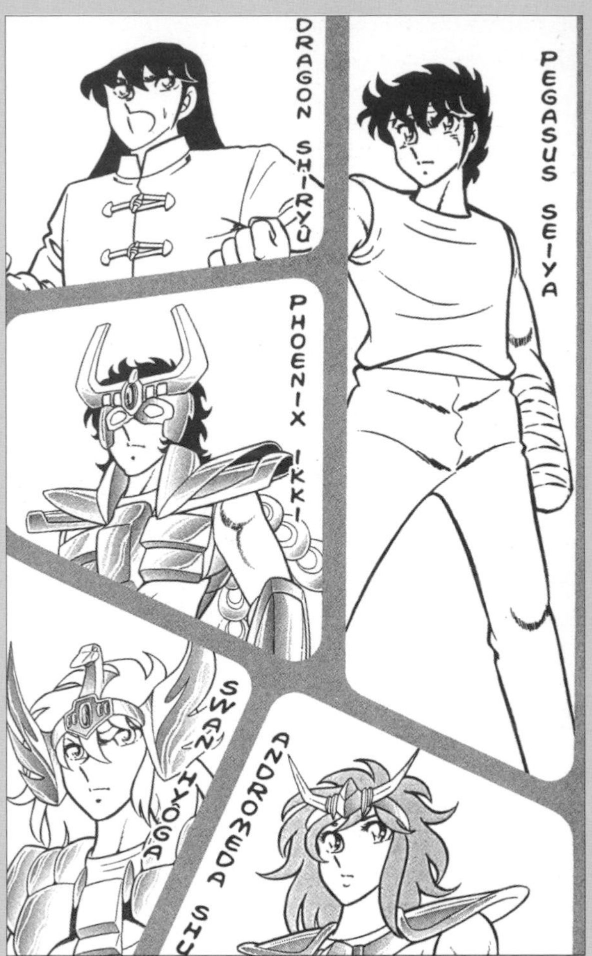

The Bronze Saints fight the gods of many lands to defend Athena, reborn as a mortal girl.

CIPHER & SIVA [1985]

The twin heroes of Minako Narita's manga *Cipher*, first seen in *Hana to Yume*, are the closest of friends as well as being identical. Attending college in New York, they often confuse people by pretending to be each other. Cipher is an art student, Siva is a movie star. Narita made her debut as a manga professional in 1977, aged just seventeen.

ELEMENTARY SCHOOL 9 MONITORS [1999]

It is 2015. Aliens are invading the Earth, and everyone is involved in the struggle to defend the human race—even elementary school children. Hitoshi Tomizawa's *Young Champion* manga *Alien 9* stars three twelve-year-old class representatives from Elementary School 9—Yuri Otani, Kumi Kawamura, and Kasumi Tomomi—whose task is to communicate telepathically with friendly aliens, the Borg, and ward off hostile aliens using rollerblades, a net, and a strange heavy pistol. Yuri, however, doesn't like communicating with the Borg—you have to wear them on your head! She's also shy and unassuming, hardly the best choice as a defender of earth. Helped by the energetic Kasumi and the intelligent, responsible Kumi, and with the constant support of her friend Miya, she does her best for her team, led by teacher Megumi Hisakawa. The manga is out in English from CPM.

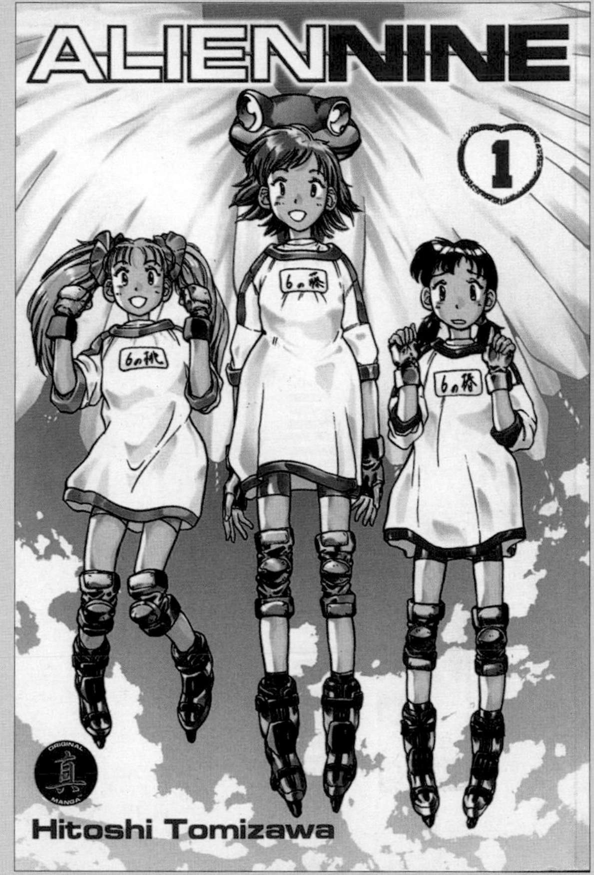

Yuri, center and wearing her Borg headgear, with her friends Kasumi and Kumi.

ELEVEN [1975]

For centuries, mankind has been expanding into space. Ten students of the elite Cosmo Academy are sent on a training exercise on the spaceship *Esperanza*. They can stop or contact base at any time, but then they will all fail. When they realize there are eleven people onboard, they have no way to tell which is the impostor. There are four Terrans in the group from various Earth-colonized worlds: hunter Amazon Carnais, opportunist Chako Kacka, quiet Dolph Tasta, and telepath Tadatos Lane. King Mayan Batesca and nobleman Doricas Soldan IV are from the Savan system, as is empath Toto Ne. Reptilian Vidmenir Knume is from Vidknu, Glenn Groff from Seguran, Ganigas Gagtos from Ganga, and Frobeireichi Frol from Vene. The group is torn by distrust and suspicion, but unwilling to fail the test, so they try to solve the mystery. In the end, the eleventh passenger has a motive none of them anticipated. Moto Hagio's science fiction classic *They Were Eleven (Junichinin Iru)* appeared in *Bessatsu Shojo* magazine when Hagio was just twenty-six and already an established star. She is considered by many the female equivalent of Osamu Tezuka, and was at the forefront of a group of gifted woman manga artists born in 1949 who brought a new depth and daring to the field of *shojo* manga. The manga is available in English from Viz.

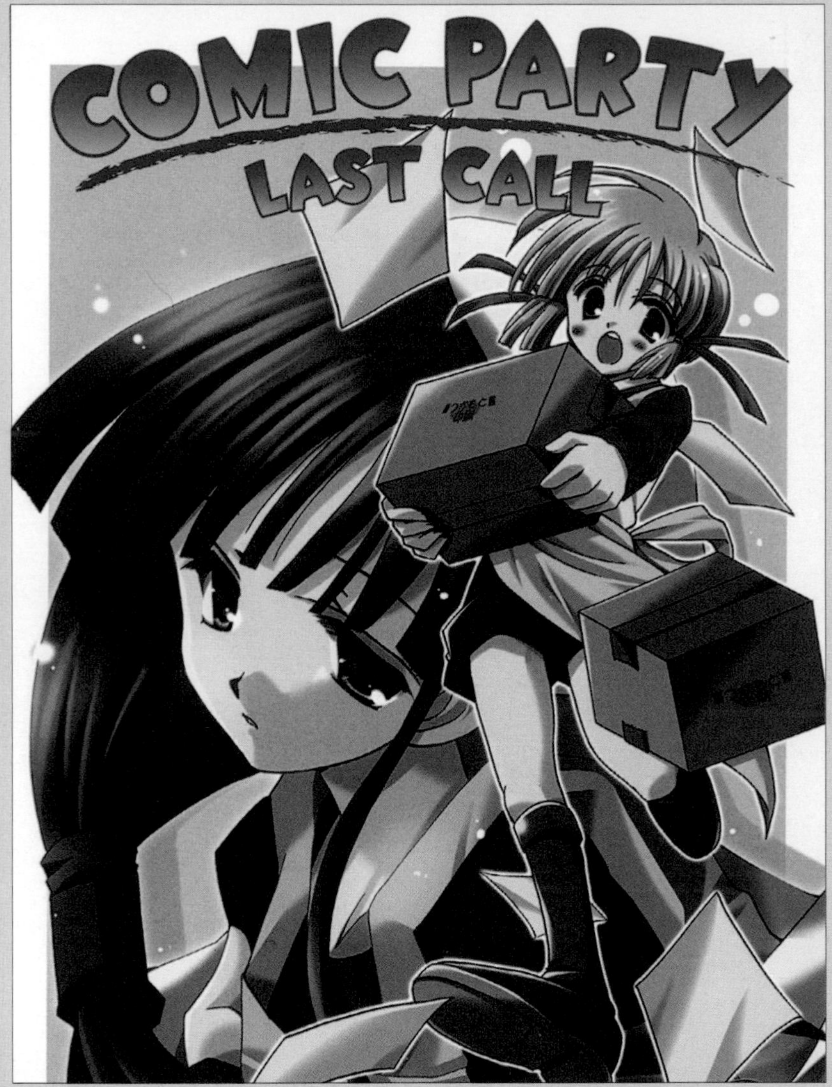

It's hard work making your name in the Japanese fanzine world! Young fans' dreams come true at *Comic Party*.

FANZINE GROUP [2001]

A *dojinshi* is a circle of friends cooperating to produce manga—a fanzine group. There are thousands of such amateur circles all over Japan; a few make the big time as pros. Aquaplus made a hit game, *Comic Party*, based on the trials and tribulations of Kazuki and his friends as they struggle to create a hit manga that will win them admiration, money, and possibly even a pro publisher at the massive Comic Party gathering, where fanzine authors from all over Japan compete for fan attention. The game generated a manga of the same name from Ozora Publishing, containing stories themed around Aquaplus' characters by other artists, and now CPM Manga has published it in English.

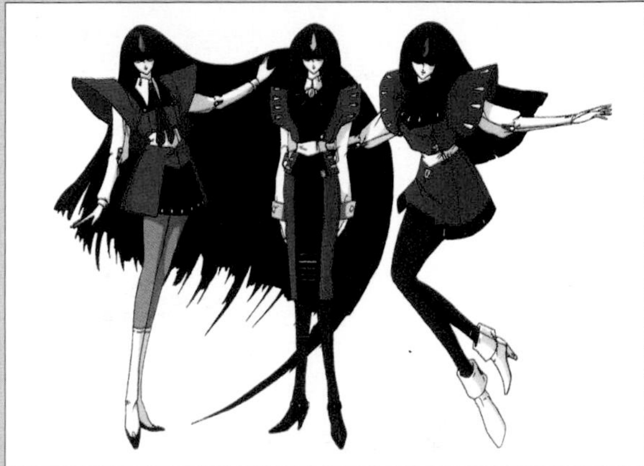

Atropos, Lachesis and Clotho, three sisters created as weapons systems but destined to change the fate of their galaxy.

THE FATIMA FATES

[1988]

The three sisters created by meister (genetic engineer) Dr. Chrome Ballanche play a pivotal role in Mamoru Nagano's epic *The Five Star Stories (Five Star Monogatari)*. Fatimas are beautiful, exotic creatures designed to form symbiotic emotional relation-ships with the elite mechwarriors known as headliners, and form part of the operating systems of Mortar Headd mechas. Some are custom-made to order; most, but not all, are female. They are eternally young and beautiful, but normally sterile. Adored and coveted by humans, they can also be treated as mere playthings or puppets (there are fatima brothels where those who have lost their masters are enslaved), and their intense relationships with their headliners are often viewed as a threat by human wives or lovers. They usually consider their creators as their fathers. All should have minds that can be controlled by their headliners; for Ballanche to leave mind control out of his Fatimas is illegal, but he is making a long-term plan to affect the fate of the empire ruled by god-emperor Amaterasu through his creations.

The eldest of the Fates, Atropos, was completed in 2987 and plays little part in the first book of the saga. She resents her life and hates her father for making her a fatima, yet later marries another of his creations. The second, Clotho, was created in 2988 and was

FUTAKO TAMAGAWA HIGH SCHOOL BASEBALL TEAM [1998]

JAPAN HAS AN ongoing love affair with baseball, chronicled in a huge number of manga. Professional teams are featured heavily but, high-school baseball is a major theme, sustained by the annual ritual of the Koshien high school baseball tournament. Koshien is the goal for which small provincial teams train year in and year out, a ferociously competitive national obsession culminating every summer in a high-profile televised final with heroic status for the winners, a real-world event that has been used in many manga as the metaphor for the hero's journey of self-discovery. Koshien isn't just a high-status tournament; winning brings prestige but there are life-transforming chances, like scholarships and jobs, to be had by the winners. It is the goal of rookie teacher Koichi Kawato in his quest to transform his team of rookie no-hopers, the worst class in the school, from a bunch of life's losers to people with a sense of pride in themselves and a reason to get out of bed in the morning. First, though, he has to put a team together.

Borrowing inspiration from a number of recent successes, especially the previous year's *GTO*, Masanori Morita uses a semi-realistic art style to draw his young male readers into the world of his third manga *Rookies*, published by Shueisha. Koichi is not a conventional authority figure, but a cool young guy whose style and outlook on life is far closer to the kids he wants to inspire than that of most of their well-meaning but stuffy professors. He joins Tamagawa to take charge of first-year class B, the bad boys and no-hopers nobody else at the school can cope with. Head teacher Murayama is looking for a tough guy to sort out the tough guys, and has chosen Kawato with this in mind.

The young man himself, however, has a past to live down and a need to redeem himself. This is his second school placement; in his first, he seriously injured a pupil. One of his new charges, tough guy Aniya, hears about his past and spreads the word around the classroom, creating a stand-off atmosphere as Class 1B decide they're not going to be intimidated by some tough-guy teacher who thinks his hard-man image will fool them. This confrontation gives Kawato's master plan a rocky start. The school baseball team was disbanded after one of the many fights at their games got completely out of hand; he means to revive it, with himself as the coach. He gets the idea from one of his less difficult pupils, Mikoshiba, a dreamy youngster whose secret ambition is to play for a top team; surprised but happy to find at least some ambition in the class, he promises the boy

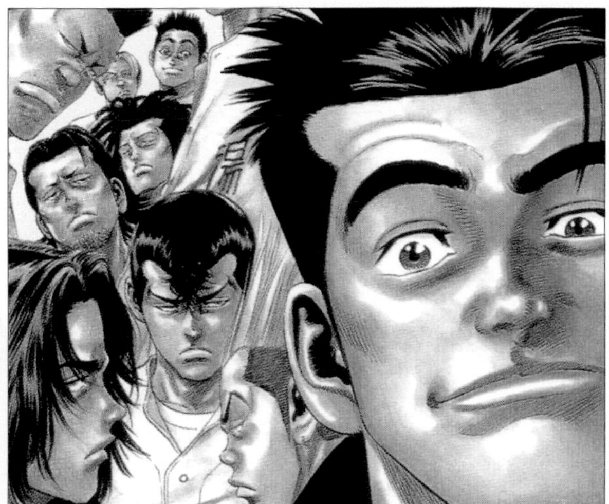

Kawato and his class have a lot to prove in *Rookies*.

he'll get a team going somehow. He tries to sell the class on the importance of dreams, of a goal in life, but they're too wary to trust a teacher, especially one with Kawato's record at this early stage in his career. Realizing that he too has to change, he tells them the truth about his past, but he gets no takers apart from Mikoshiba. His only other support comes from Toko Yagi, one of the girls in his class, and Aniya's girlfriend.

The teacher starts training, even though he only has two team members. Murayama wants to shut the club down again because of lack of interest, but Kawato persuades him to give it a little more time. Other pupils begin to trickle in to practice—lesser bad boys Wakana, Okada, Hiyama, and Yufune, along with several pupils whose school record is more normal. But with two weeks before the first game of the season, Kawato still has only six he can rely on. He finds out that Aniya used to be a good player, but gave up after being made a complete fool of by a pitcher. Kawato tries to persuade him not to be such a coward, and finally loses his temper completely, deciding afterwards to give up on the club and let them find another coach, or fold. Then, next day, Aniya turns up for practice.

At last Kawato has a team. Now all he has to do is get them from rookie status to Koshien competition level. Despite various arguments within the group and difficulties outside, the boys begin to show a will to win and a pride in their team that gives Kawato new hope. The rest of the class slowly get behind them, led by Toko who even makes up team uniforms for their first game. Yet the problems of setting up the team are nothing compared to the problems Kawato and his protégés will face in achieving their goal.

Born in 1966, Morita started his career at the age of seventeen, when his story *It's Late!* caught the attention of manga veteran Tetsuo *Fist of the North Star* Hara. He gave the young artist a job as his assistant, and four years later Morita made his professional debut in *Shonen Jump* with *No-Good Blues (Rokudenashi Blues)* which ran for eight years. He specializes in high-school bad boy stories, and is a baseball fan. Despite Rookies' superficial similarity to *GTO*, it's primarily about the making of a team, with Kawato's own development incidental to theirs.

programmed to fear Mortar Headds and hate fighting. Her destiny is to love King Colus III, whose descendant will overthrow Amaterasu's empire with her help in 4100. The youngest, Lachesis, has a forbidden double epsilon genetic code which makes her part human and part fatima, with powers beyond any other fatima. All the Fatima Fates have human DNA from Deimos Hierarchy, a great warrior, but only Lachesis shares DNA with Amaterasu, making her the only female who can bear him children, and also part god in her own right. Their son Kallen is born in 7779. The Fates also have an older "brother" Ballanche fatima, Uppandora, who serves as Amaterasu's double during his secret abdication, and eventually marries Atropos; and an older "sister," Queen, mother of the headliner Douglas Kaine. Another Ballanche fatima, Auxo, is Kaine's partner in his Knight of Chrome. The manga appeared in *Newtype* and is available in English from Nagano's own Toys Press.

THE GIANTS [1966]

Baseball is a big hit in Japan, with its own genre of manga. Noboru Kawasaki and Ikki Kajiwara's *Star of the Giants (Kyojin no Hoshi)* first appeared in *Shonen Magazine*. The title is a play on the name of the young star, Hyuma Hoshi, whose family name means star in Japanese. Hyuma's father was a famous base-ball player, and when the boy is signed by the Giants, dad and all his old pals join forces to make sure Hyuma achieves his full potential as a baseball superstar. Their training techniques are a little far-fetched at times, but the manga shows all the mundane aspects of baseball, as well as the struggles of a young player's life, including training so tough it causes permanent physical damage, and the determination to play through the pain barrier and win for the team at all costs. It was a huge hit—so much so that it became the first sports manga to be animated.

THE INACHU PING PONG CLUB [1993]

A high-school ping pong club is so hopeless that it risks losing its homeroom to other, more successful sports clubs. The team members are the earnest, gung-ho captain Takeda, the school dreamboat Kinoshita, irreverent troublemaker Maeno, breast-obsessed Izawa, and Tanabe, who has a serious body odor problem. Their coach is the weakest and least respected of all the school's staff and a pushover for other coaches, especially the girls' table-tennis club coach who has his eyes on the boys' clubroom for his successful squad. Minoru Furuya's *Young Magazine* manga *Let's Go! Inachu Ping Pong Club (Ike! Inachu Takkyu-bu)* is a slice-of-life story chronicling the teenage deadbeats' dreams, fantasies, and hopeless aspirations (mostly about having sex with cute girls) and the reality (mostly about getting through every day unscathed, and trying to have fun while doing as little work as possible). Its fantastical comedy and its frequent mooning, farting, and penis gags will offend some readers, but it's a very human story. Redefining the term "loser" from insult to lifestyle, the manga ran until 1997, with thirteen collected volumes, but should not be confused with Taiyo Matsumoto's shorter manga *Ping Pong*.

THE JAPAN YOUTH SOCCER TEAM [1980]

Soccer didn't arrive in Japan with the 2002 World Cup; it had a small but loyal Japanese following long before then. Yuichi Takahashi's manga *Captain Tsubasa* chronicled the triumphs and disasters of young Japanese player Tsubasa Ozora in *Weekly Shonen Jump*. When he moves to a new town and joins the local team, they don't even have a place to train, but gradually they work together to succeed, and former Brazilian ace Roberto Hongo takes Tsubasa under his wing. The young player helps the team win local contests, then works his way up through the various levels of his sport until he faces the best in the world with the Japanese national squad. His rivalries with ace goalie Genzo Wakabayashi and forward Kojiro Hyuga, and his friendships with midfielder Taro Misaki, defender Ryo Ishizaki, and eventually with Hyuga, continue through the long-running manga series, as the players join various teams in and outside Japan and come together for international games as the Japan Youth Team. His wanna-be girlfriend Sanae Nakazawa is one of the most vocal fans throughout his career. Taro Misaki got his own manga *I'm Taro Misaki (Boku wa Misaki Taro)* from Takahashi in 1987.

THE JUNIOR DETECTIVE LEAGUE a.k.a. JUVENILE DETECTIVES CLUB [1996]

Despite the frustrations of being an adult in an child's body, Jimmy Kudo (Shinichi Kudo/Conan Edogawa) rediscovers the joys of childhood when he teams up with three fellow first-grade students, George (Genta), Mitch (Mitsuhiko), and cute girl Amy (Ayumi) to form the Junior Detective League in Gosho Aoyama's manga *Case Closed (Meitantei Conan* a.k.a. *Detective Conan)*. Big, loud-mouthed George is the self-proclaimed leader, but he has a heart as big as his appetite, and he is very protective of Amy. Mitch is very like Jimmy, a bright boy who feels that the rational approach is important in good detective work, but his detachment goes out the window where Amy is concerned and he would do anything to protect her. Amy feels she and Jimmy are destined to fall in love, much to his discomfort. The gang later acquires a fifth member, Ai Haibara, who is another young adult reverted back to childhood and the inventor of the drug that shrank teenage Jimmy. The club is named after a creation of Japan's great real-life detective writer Ranpo Edogawa.

KAGURA SECURITY COMPANY [1995]

The city of Ayagane is plagued by bio-magnetic beings called Phantom Cats, led by the mysterious Black Cat. They can take the form of either cats or humans and cause chaos while carrying out their various nefarious plans. Luckily Yuka Kikushima's Kagura Security Company is on hand to disperse the threat to mankind helped by the latest computer technology—as long as they get paid, that is. Yoichi Taba is the sole guy in the team. Maki Umezaki has gangster fantasies and is gun crazy. Takami Sakuragi is an ace rollerblader with violent tendencies that belie her sweet appearance. Eiko Rando is a computer geek. Yu Himehagi is a former racer and still a speed freak. Akihiro Ito's manga in *Young King* magazine nods to *Reservoir Dogs* (in the design of the villain, who also shows up in his manga *Lawman*) and Hong Kong action flicks, *The X Files* and *Scooby-Doo*, and is in English from CPM Manga.

THE KASUGI SISTERS a.k.a. CAT'S EYE [1981]

Cat's Eye was Tsukasa Hojo's first big hit, appearing in *Shonen Jump* the year after his pro debut. The manga is set in real time—an early frame shows the date 1981 on a newspaper. Three Japanese sisters, Ai, Hitomi, and Rui, are trying to track down their father, Michael Heinz, a German painter and art collector who disappeared under mysterious circumstances. His daughters steal artwork connected with him from museums and galleries to try to gather clues. To make a living, and as a front for their gang, they hide in plain sight, running a coffee shop called Cat's Eye right in front of police headquarters. Middle sister Hitomi is even engaged to a detective, eager young Toshio Utsumi, whose main ambition is to crack the case of the Cat's Eye gang. The family's links to the police cause some hair-raising moments, but somehow the flat-footed cops never quite make the connection, even though every crime of the notorious gang is announced with a Cat's Eye business card. The mystery is never finally solved, either in the manga or the animated version.

THE KILLER COMMANDOS [1988]

A team of disaffected teenagers playing bike games in a rough and ready stadium on the terraformed and settled planet Venus is drawn into adult life when their country is invaded by another Venusian state. Hiro Seno, the star biker, comes of age as he outgrows his apathy and discovers that, like it or not, in wartime it's hard to stay disengaged from life, love, and politics. Miranda, the team's leader, and his other friends stick by him through the transition to

Right: Like *Rollerball*, but rougher—Venusian track ace Hiro Seno.

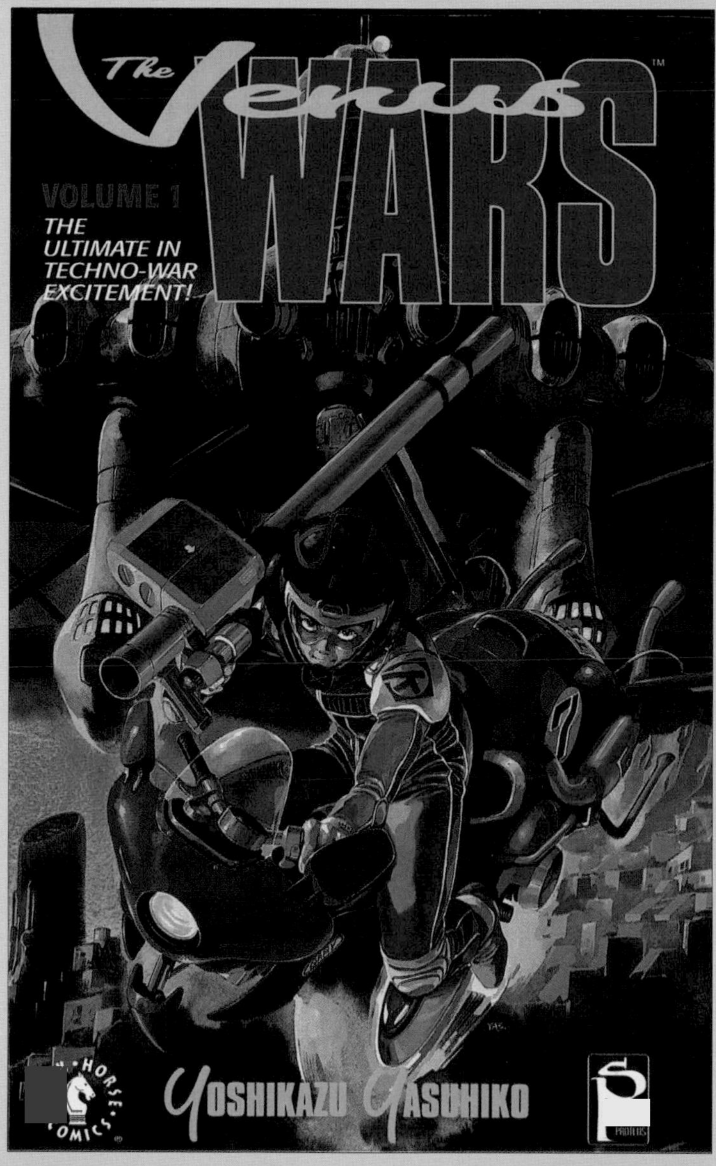
The Venus WARS™
VOLUME 1
THE ULTIMATE IN TECHNO-WAR EXCITEMENT!
YOSHIKAZU YASUHIKO
PROTEUS

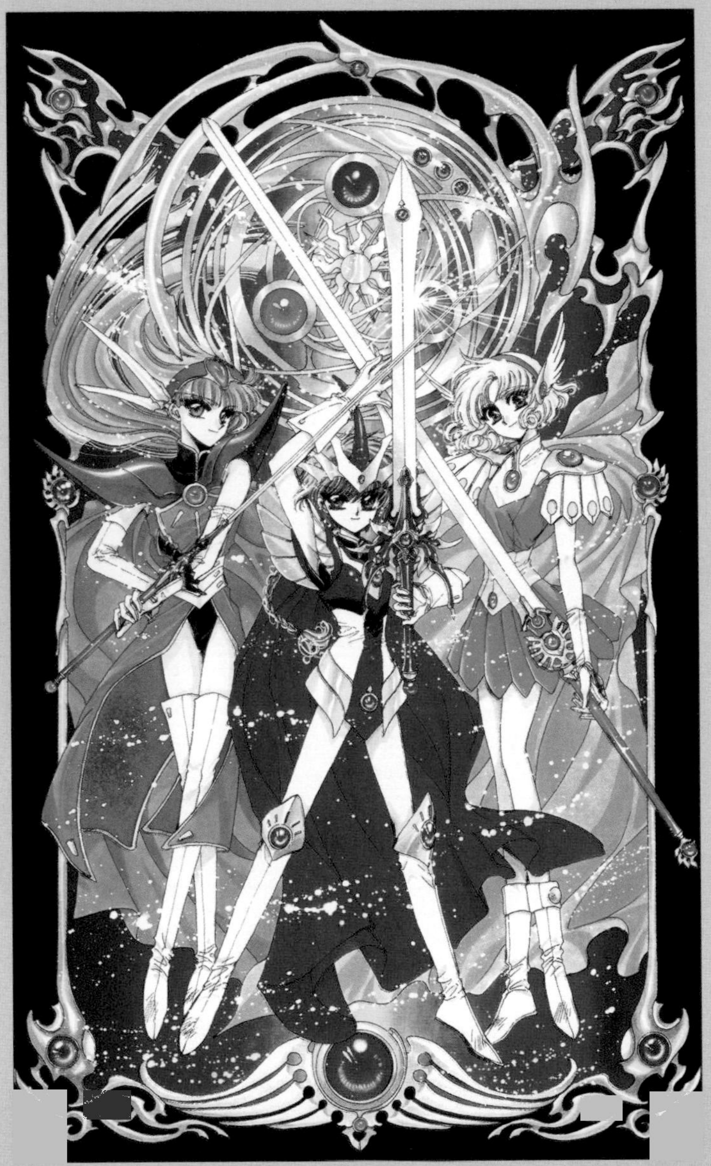

adulthood. Yoshikazu Yasuhiko's manga *Venus Wars (Venus Senki)* was one of the early wave of translations from Dark Horse Comics in 1993.

PRINCESS LORI AND PRINCE MATTHEW

Tomoko Taniguchi's 1994 manga *Princess Prince* is one of several inversions of the classic trope of a girl pretending to be a boy. Twin brothers Matthew and Lawrence can't both inherit their father's crown, and two princes might lead to warring factions; so Lori becomes a princess. He is so successful that his own nature and character are in danger of being submerged in the masquerade. Instead of learning fighting arts and how to behave appropriately as a young nobleman, the prince has to give a performance of femininity as convincing as that of the actors who play women's roles in traditional Japanese theatre.

THE MAGIC KNIGHTS

[1993]

Hikaru Shido, Umi Ryusaki, and Fu Hoji are on a junior high-school field trip to Tokyo Tower when they are drawn into another dimension by the wizard Clef. They are Magic Knights and they must call on powers they never knew they possessed to save a kingdom and its princess. Their names hint at their magic skills. Fu (Japanese for wind) practices wind magic, Hikaru practices fire magic, and Umi's powers come from water. They have giant magical armors, which magnify their powers and are also living creatures, and they are helped by a cute rabbit-like creature called Mokona. In the course of the story they all find love and become firm friends. *Magic Knight Rayearth (Maho Kishi Rayearth)* by CLAMP was serialized in *Nakayoshi* magazine and ran until 1995. It's available in English from Mixx Entertainment.

Left, Hikaru (in red), Fu, and Umi in fighting form, ready to save the world.

THE MIRAGE KNIGHTS

[1988]

The First Easter Mirage Corps, or Mirage Knights, is the elite force serving Emperor Amaterasu in Mamoru Nagano's *The Five Star Stories*. They are all headliners, that is, warriors capable of piloting one of the gigantic Mortar Headd mecha in combat and of forming a mental union with one of the exotic creatures known as fatimas. Some go beyond this level of skill to become Knight Masters. Most are loyal to Amaterasu, but some serve out of pure self-interest and some will be involved in his eventual downfall. Typically, headliners have more cunning and courage than raw brainpower—they are highly intelligent by normal human standards but lack the gifts of advanced mathematics and physics needed to be meisters—makers and maintainers of the machines they operate—or the skills in biogenetics needed to be meights, creators of the Fatimas. In the year 2810, the corps began with eight knights, including Deimos Heirarchy, Dougran Ruth, Bubus Codante, and Paratoku Chrysalis. By 2989, with the growth of the empire, the older generation has mostly retired and the number expands to thirty-six in the higher-ranked Orange Right hierarchy, while the Green Left hierarchy embraces lesser headliners. Amaterasu and Douglas Kaine are members of both. Another notable knight is Lie Ex, owner of one of the few male fatimas; she is desired by the emperor owing to her resemblance to his mother, whose descendant will destroy Amaterasu's palace on his orders in 4099. Other important Mirage Knights include Suoad Graphite New, master of the energy blades endearingly known as spuds; Poesche Nomien, the beam lance specialist; and the Fatima Tower, who serves as a knight in her own right.

NISHIKO HIGH SCHOOL BASEBALL TEAM [2000]

Nishiko's baseball team doesn't have much to be proud of. Their summer 1999 game against LP High resulted in the highest scoring difference ever recorded, and it wasn't in their favor. They didn't get a single run, probably because ace pitcher Hiroaki Oe was the only player on Nishiko's team who actually knew anything about baseball. Despite this, the following year, Hiroaki's sister Yuki, the team manager, is determined to recruit a new team that can compete in Japan's prestigious Koshien school baseball championship. The pair has an ulterior motive. Their father, once a champion high school player, vanished when his debts got out of hand, and they hope that the publicity brought by success in the championship might encourage him to get in touch again. To begin with, Yuki's managing a team of two—her brother the captain, and her cat, Vice Captain. Then she meets weird but sexy transfer student Iria Nanjo, who saves Vice Captain after he's hurt in a car accident. She falls for him and cons him into joining the team. The addition of three hulking guys from the school tea club, one of Hiroaki's fans, and a set of triplets, gives her the nine players she needs to field a team. All they have to do is not get laughed off the field, win games, and avoid getting expelled. Kei Yasunaga, creator of *Zig x Zag* for *Bessatsu Friend*, could have made a serious romantic drama out of this material, but the comic potential of the story wins out and its two volumes get progressively wackier.

THE OFFICE LADIES [1990]

Risu Akidzuki's manga *The Theory of Evolution of the Office Lady (OL Shinkaron)* from *Comic*

Morning is the Dilbert of Japan. A four-panel gag manga, it pokes fun at the life of the female office worker—Office Lady, or OL, as she is known in Japan—and her boss. Meet Emi-chan, Suzuko-chan, Keiko-chan, Ai-chan, Minako-chan, the boss and his wife, and male colleague Tanaka-kun, as they try to support the company loyally despite its arcane idiocies and get through the many ridiculous situations of the working day. Although you need to understand Japanese society to get the full impact of the humor, many of the strips can be enjoyed without any background in Japan's social and business etiquette. Naturally, a wave of OL office-based merchandise—mouse mats, pencil holders, stationery, and the like—was available to adorn desks throughout Japan.

SABU & ICHI [1968]

Young detective Sabu works the mean streets of eighteenth-century Edo, as Tokyo was then known. His boss is crippled by rheumatism and spends much of his time in bed, but he has unexpected help in the form of Ichi, an elderly blind man working as a masseur, whose unthreatening exterior hides surprising talents. Shotaro Ishimori was just thirty when he published *Sabu & Ichi Investigate (Sabu to Ichi Torimono Hikae)* in *Big Comic*, where it ran until 1972. His longest work was also historical—Chuokoronsha published his forty-eight-volume, 10,800-page history of Japan, *Manga Nihon No Rekishi*, in 1989.

THE SAILOR SCOUTS a.k.a. SAILOR SENSHI [1992]

Serena (*Usagi Tsukino*, or "moon bunny") is basically a cheerful, normal teenager, but she's very clumsy and a terrible crybaby. Then she meets a talking cat named Luna, and learns that she is the reincarnation of Moon Princess Serenity, beloved of Prince Endymion, and fated to save the world from evil through the power of love. She receives magical gifts to help her transform, including a tiara and a wand, and when she says a magic word she becomes Sailor Moon, leader of the Sailor Scouts (*Sailor Senshi* a.k.a. *Sailor Warriors*).

Initially the team consists of five girls, each with the powers of a different planet. Amy (Ami) is Sailor Mercury, Mina (Minako) is Sailor Venus, Raye (Rei) is Sailor Mars, and Lita (Makoto) is Sailor Jupiter. They fight the evil Queen Beryl and her minions, helped by Endymion's reincarnation, the dashing Tuxedo Mask (Tuxedo Kamen). The heroines of Naoko Takeuchi's *Sailor Moon (Bishojo Senshi Sailor Moon*, a.k.a. *Pretty Soldier Sailor Moon*) made their debut in *Nakayoshi* magazine, but spun off an earlier manga *Codename Sailor V* in *Run-Run* in 1991. Their adventures, out in English from Mixx Entertainment, introduced a generation of little girls to the joys of anime, manga, and merchandising, both in their home country and in the English-speaking world.

THE WACKY WORLD OF AKIRA TORIYAMA

BORN IN 1955 on the outskirts of Nagoya, the man who created *Dragonball* is one of the most successful manga artists and writers in Japan today.

Toriyama's work is stuffed with slapstick, puns, and satire, and although it can be extremely violent it has an absence of malice that gives it an aura of childlike innocence. Addicted to basic toilet humor as well as visual and verbal gags, Toriyama loves to send up pop culture and mass media, perhaps because of his past as an advertising man. Toriyama means bird mountain, and his company is Bird Studios.

He started out as most children do, copying favorite cartoon characters. He watched anime eagerly, citing Disney's *101 Dalmatians* and Osamu Tezuka's *Astro Boy* as favorites, and got into reading manga when he was ten years old. After graduating high school in 1974 he worked in an ad agency, but got bored and quit after three years, determined to make it in the manga world.

A year later he was in Tokyo, working with manga publisher Shueisha. His first series *Wonder Island* appeared in *Shonen Jump* in 1978, with modest success, and was followed by two more minor works. In 1980 his new series *Dr. Slump* hit the big time, again in *Shonen Jump*. The crazy world of genius inventor and inveterate lecher Senbe Norimaki and his friends in Penguin Village brought Toriyama huge success, selling thirty-five million copies in Japan alone. In a twist on the *Weird Science* premise, the doctor decides to create the perfect woman from porn magazines and pop star photos but instead gets a cute, bespectacled elementary schoolgirl with an inquisitive nature, superhuman strength, and lung power to match. Arale-chan gets him into a succession of crazy adventures involving his many inventions—time machines, cloning devices, x-ray specs, and many other weapons of mass hysteria. The manga ended in 1984, with eighteen collected volumes. It was animated in 1980 and the TV series ran for more than 250 episodes. At its peak, it scored a top rating of 36.9 percent—more than a third of the national audience. Four movies followed.

By 1984 Toriyama was ready to leave Penguin Island and wanted a project with Oriental, rather than Western, roots. Taking elements from the classic *Journey to the West* and looking back to his early Jackie Chan homage strip *Dragon Boy*, he created *Dragonball*, which started publication in *Shonen Jump* as *Dr. Slump* was ending, to even greater success. Martial artist Son Goku sets out to help Bulma find the seven magical

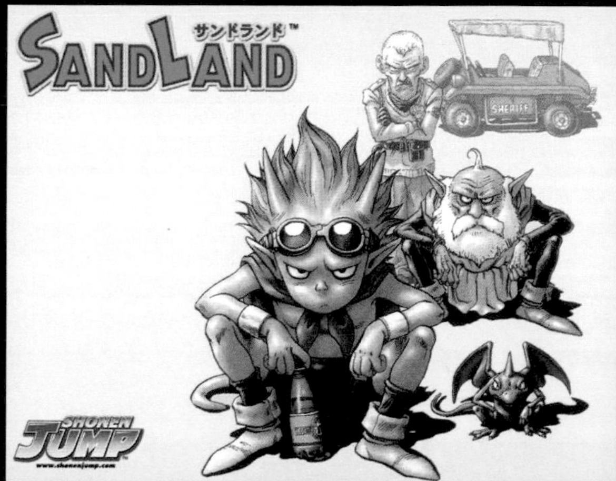

Rao and Beelzebub (front) saving the magical world of Sandland.

Dragonballs, which can grant any wish. Along the way he meets many allies and adversaries and fights epic battles, sometimes running to more than 100 pages. Toriyama's pacing, choreography and knockabout comedy made the series a huge hit. The collected volumes of *Dragonball* have been translated into many languages. Some fans claim the manga has outsold the Bible.

Dragonball was animated in 1986. Two further TV series, *Dragonball Z* and *Dragonball Z GT*, and fourteen movies followed. Toriyama was still producing new episodes of the manga for *Shonen Jump* every week, but this ended in 1995. In a published statement, he told his readers he was too exhausted to go on creating a new episode every week for yet another tournament story arc. He wanted to spend more time with his wife, son, and daughter, and indulge his fondness for military modeling, country walks, and video games.

After a two-year break, he returned to *Shonen Jump* with *Cowa!* The title is a play on *kowai* (frightening) but the series stays in slapstick territory. In a community of monsters, a deadly disease is decimating them. Paifu, the rowdy son of a vampire, and Jose, a ghost, volunteer to go to a distant land seeking a cure from a witch. The story was collected in one volume in 1998, and followed in 1999 by another single-volume story, *Kajika*, about a young boy cursed by a fox he killed. He will wear a fox's ears and tail until he has saved the lives of a thousand creatures. In 2001 he produced another short manga, *Sandland*, set in a barren post-apocalyptic future where water is scarce and human Rao and demon prince Beelzebub band together to seek it.

Now approaching his fiftieth birthday, Toriyama seems content to produce short manga, work in other media, and enjoy his success. He has designed video games for Nintendo and Sony, and worked in anime. There is no sign of any publication of his earlier works in English. Shueisha have published a volume of his illustrations, *Akira Toriyama: The World*, and his book on drawing manga, as well as three volumes of his earlier short works, containing recognizable prototypes of the *Dragonball* cast, under the title *Toriyama Akira Marusaku Gekijo*.

SHOHOKU HIGH SCHOOL BASKETBALL TEAM [1990]

Senior transfer student Sakuragi Hanamichi only joins the Shohoku basketball team to try to impress the girl he's fallen for. Haruko Aragi's brother Takenori is captain of the team and her current boyfriend Kaede Ryukawa is also a basketball star. Sakuragi has red hair and a temper to match, but his attitude problem is outweighed by the fact that he's tall, fast, and determined—good qualities to have in a basketball team. To start with, he just wants to use his height to slam-dunk, but he gradually learns skill and teamwork. As he gets to know his teammates he learns to respect them and the game, and what was just a ploy to get closer to Haruko turns into real passion as he becomes part of Shohoku's success. Takehiko Inoue's manga *Slam Dunk* depicts basketball with cinematic pace and realism and was one of *Shonen Jump*'s big hits of the 1990s. It's available in English from Gutsoon Entertainment.

THE SLAYERS [1989]

Teenage sorceress Lina Inverse wants the magic artifact known as the Sword of Light. She links up with its current wielder, sweet but dim fighter Gourry Gabriev, and the pair roam a fantasy universe meeting and parting with various adversaries and allies, seeking treasure and adventure, and finding a huge range of breast jokes—mostly about Lina's lack of them, and the excessive endowment of her old mentor and traveling companion sorceress Naga the Serpent—in a manner reminiscent of a very long game of *Dungeons and Dragons*. The manga *Slayers* spun off Hajime Kanzaka's short stories for *Dragon* magazine, illustrated by Rui Araizumi. There are also novels (still untranslated from Japanese) and animation.

SORCEROR HUNTERS [1993]

The Sorceror Hunters (Bakuretsu Hunter) are a team of five working for the mystic Big Mama in Satoru Akahori's *Gao* manga of the same name. Two brothers, two sisters, and one beefcake trek around the Spooner Continent defending the poor and weak from power-crazed, exploitative sorcerers. Tira Misu and her sister Chocolate both look reasonably sweet and demure until they take on their magic persona, when they turn into two of the most terrifyingly beautiful women you can imagine; they are both deeply in love with the same man, but they love each other too much for it to be a problem, especially since said man is their companion Carrot Glace, a teen lecher chasing every girl he sees. His younger brother, a quiet and beautiful mage called Marron, is the love object of hunky Gateau Mocha. Between them they also have to control

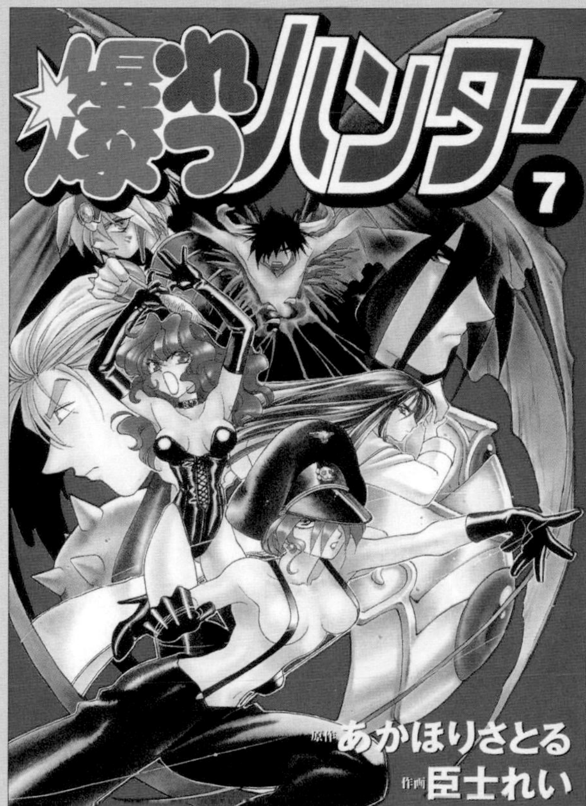

The Sorceror Hunters: Are they trying to keep the world safe with teenage lecher Carrot, or from him?

Carrot's tendency to turn into a huge monster when any of them is threatened. In the end, this transformation is key to resolving the ongoing conflict between rogue sorcerers and Big Mama's faction. *The Sorceror Hunters* is out in English from Tokyopop.

TEAM RACER a.k.a. TEAM MIFUNE [1965]

The Racer (Mifune) family have their own team (Team Mifune) and compete around the world in Tatsuo Yoshida's manga *Speed Racer (Mach Go-Go-Go!)*. Teenager Speed (Go Mifune) drives the Mach 5, an advanced race car designed by his father, retired race driver Pops Racer (Mifune). His mother (Aya) and his girlfriend Trixie (Michi) also work for the team, and his kid brother Spridle and pet chimp Chim-Chim (Kuo and Senpei) tag along, too. Speed's main rival is the mysterious Racer X (Masked Racer). Unknown to Speed this incredibly skilled and brave driver is his own brother, Rex Racer (Kenichi Mifune), who is working undercover as an agent for Interpol (the Japanese government), and had to cut himself off from his family because of the risks involved in his work. Rex keeps an eye on his kid brother and makes sure that rival racers who attempt to throw a monkey wrench in the Mach 5's works are foiled.

Published in Japan by Sun Comics, the manga also spun off an animated TV series which proved very popular in the United States, although the violence of the original had to be toned down considerably for American audiences. Many of *Speed Racer*'s original American fans were completely unaware that their favorite cartoon originated in Japan.

SPECIAL VEHICLE SECTION 2, TOKYO POLICE [1988]

AT THE END of the twentieth century, rising sea levels have led to a massive building program in Japan, triggering the development of heavy construction robots called "labors." These create new opportunities for crime, and the Tokyo police set up a special division to deal with the problem. The Patrol Labor division has its own robots, known as Patlabors, and the two Special Vehicle Sections have to deal with their role as crime-fighters as well as all the trials and tribulations of life as public servants. Budget cuts, bureaucratic idiocy, fraud, political interference, and the ever-present Joe Public with his endless supply of wrenches ready to throw into works, form the background for a story that integrates science fiction effortlessly into modern society by treating robots as if they were patrol cars.

Masami Yuki's *Shonen Sunday* manga *Mobile Police Patlabor (Kido Keisatsu Patlabor)* largely ignores the more efficient Special Vehicle Section 1 in favor of the goofs and misfits of SVS 2. Led by enigmatic Captain Keiichi Goto, the team consists of a bunch of misfits, mavericks, and downright lunatics, alongside some of the finest officers ever to don a uniform. It's impossible to tell which is which. Chain-smoking, hard-drinking Goto is a classic case of a man far too clever for his superiors' liking, shunted into a dead-end job in a deadbeat team. He detests confrontation and actively tries to avoid fighting, but he's sharp as a razor—in fact, that was his old nickname back when he was a detective. As a father figure Goto is interesting, a mentor who would rather sit back and drop the odd hint than step in with guidance, but solidly committed to his team. His number two in the manga, Kumagumi, is a capable, dependable young woman who is determined to ensure her division does well; like a typical Japanese mother, she'll make sure the kids achieve.

The division's two pilots are both, in their different ways, manic-obsessives. Country girl Noa Izumi, daughter of a Hokkaido brewer, has fallen in love with the idea of the labor, and when she gets her own Ingram patlabor she bonds with it to a degree that would be ridiculous if it weren't so touchingly sincere. The other pilot, Isao Ota, is a samurai wannabe more right-wing than Yukio Mishima, a sexist pig whose favorite pastime is gun practice with his Ingram's massive cannon. Ota is a figure of fun in the manga, but he is also lonely, a man out of his era and afraid of the changing world. Yuki writes sensitively, giving him his moments of dignity.

Asuma Shinohara is a rich kid who joined the police just to annoy his father. Unfortunately his family owns the corporation that supplies police labors, so it's impossible for him to escape his background. He's as arrogant as he is clever, but in the role of "backup" controller to Noa, the "forward" or pilot, he becomes close to her, and the spoiled, disaffected young man is gradually brought into the real world by romance. Ota's backup is the gentle, henpecked Mikami Shinshi, who is hardly used in the manga. Newly married to the feisty Tamiko, he has a real talent for computers, but few other distinguishing features except for a tendency to rage when drunk.

Hiromi Yamazaki, a gentle giant too big to fit into a labor cockpit or drive one of the little backup cars, is a country boy who says very little but is a rock in a crisis. He's from a fishing community, but suffers from terrible seasickness, which meant he had problems getting a job at home and had to come to the city. His part is written like a woman's, providing a kind-hearted and supportive sounding board to the rest of the team. This oddball family finds its grandfather figure in old man Sakaki, the maintenance crew chief. His fearsome temper and sharp tongue are feared across the base, but his human side emerges in his love of his sports car and penchant for flashy driving gear.

Patlabor was immensely successful in Japan in manga and animated form. It's a joy to look at in both formats, but it is above all else a writer's show—funny, clever, and humane. Any reader visiting the Tokyo headquarters of Special Vehicle Section 2 is guaranteed an interesting time.

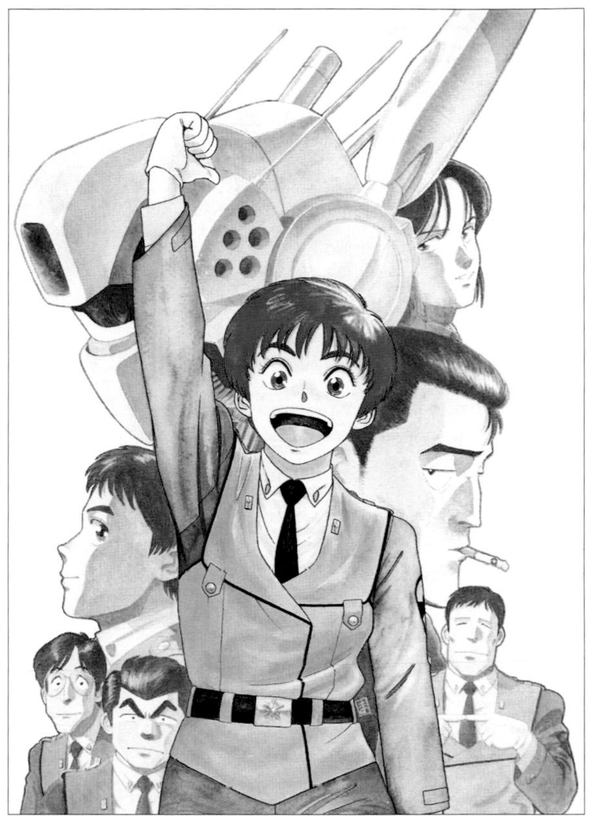

Perky Noa, center, with Shinshi, Asuma, and Ota left, Goto and Yamazaki, right, back Kumagami.

TOKYO METS BASEBALL TEAM [1977]

Teenage Yuki Mizuhara is a southpaw pitcher of outstanding ability, but when spotted by a Tokyo Mets talent scout and signed for the team, Yuki is forced to reveal that he is really a she. Yuki has a hard time convincing her teammates that she is up to the task of representing one of Japan's proudest baseball teams, but she proves that her determination is as strong as her talent, and helps them win against their longtime rivals, the Hanshin Tigers. Shinji Mizushima's manga *Song of the Baseball Enthusiast (Yakyukyu no Uta)* was not his only successful baseball story. The following year, 1978, his manga *Dokaben*, the story of a high-school team's journey to the annual Koshien tournament, propelled him into the list of the highest income earners in Japan by selling more than twenty-five million copies in paperback since its publication in 1972.

TOKYO POLICEWOMAN DUO

Miyuki and Natsumi are partners on Tokyo's police force in the manga *You're Under Arrest! (Taiho Shichauzo)* by Kosuke Fujishima. Gentle, reserved Miyuki is an ace driver and sweet on Officer Ken Nakajima; Natsumi is a hot-headed, impulsive, disorganized motorbike cop. The manga switches between car chases and police work with almost no jeopardy involved, flirting at the police station, and girly loyalties and confidences. Fujishima's almost supernaturally pretty artwork made it a hit and spun off animation and audio dramas, one of which gives the girls the title "Tokyo Policewoman Duo" when they record a rap song.

UNITED NETWORK COMMAND FOR LAW AND ENFORCEMENT

[1966]

The 1960s TV series *The Man from U.N.C.L.E.* was such a huge hit in Japan that it had its own manga spin off from Akita Shoten, successful enough to be collected into three volumes in and reprinted for several years thereafter. Entitled *0011 Napoleon Solo*, the manga by Takao Saito was obviously created using visual reference material from the original show, in which ace agent Solo and his sidekick Illya Kuryakin fight the agents of evil under the direction of avuncular Englishman Alexander Waverley, head of U.N.C.L.E. Apart from getting Solo's badge number—11—right, Saito made him dark-haired and Illya blond. There, however, the resemblance ends. Neither looks very like the actors who played the TV roles, Robert Vaughn and David McCallum, and Waverly, played by the refined, frail-looking,

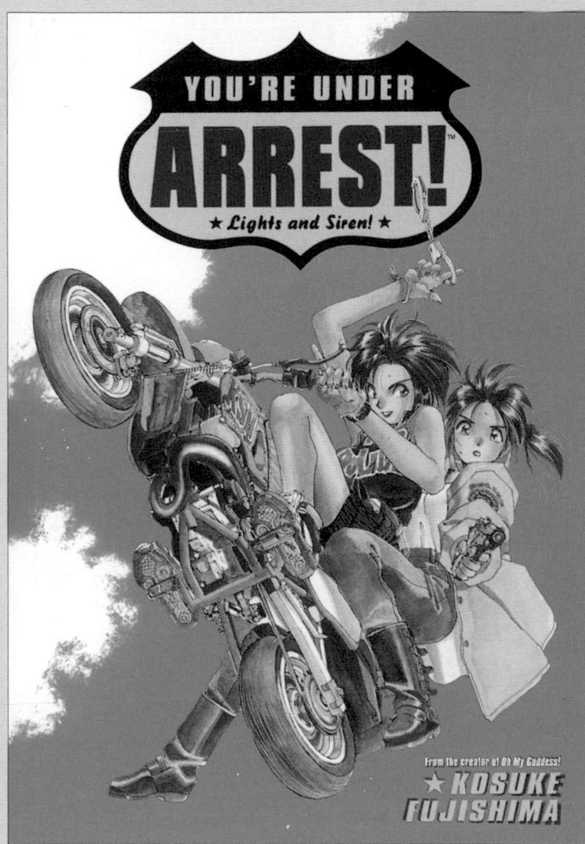

Natsumi drives and Miyuki rides pillion on this stunning Fujishima cover.

and elderly Leo G. Carroll, becomes a burly, dynamic figure. There is also no mention of U.N.C.L.E.'s arch-nemesis, the evil organization T.H.R.U.S.H. The stories focus on attempts to take over the world by unconnected gangs, criminal masterminds, and international spies, all foiled by the intrepid agents. MGM's copyright credit is prominently featured, with photos of the actors on the flaps and the series' official logo on the covers. Saito, now famous as the creator of assassin *Golgo 13*, was working on boys' science fiction and adventure series at the time. His U.N.C.L.E. manga is credited by critic and historian Fred Patten with sparking his interest in Japanese comics and animation, which led to the formation of the first American fan group; so it can be claimed that American manga fandom owes its existence to Saito and *The Man from U.N.C.L.E.*.

USHIO AND TORA [1990]

Ushio Aotsuki is a temple child. His family is the hereditary guardian of the Fugen-In temple, and he has chores to do around the shrine after school and on weekends under the watchful eye of his father. Like most teenage boys, he finds helping out with the family business a bore. Then one day he goes somewhere he shouldn't, and pulls out a stick embedded in a wall. It's the ancestral Spear of Beasts, and Ushio accidentally unleashes the spirit it pinned in the shrine—a huge, tiger-striped, long-maned, glowing-eyed demon named Nagatobimaru, Long-Flyer, also known as Raiju, or Thunder-Beast. The demon can fly, become invisible, shoot lightning out of his mane, and breathe fire. He's immensely strong, with big teeth and claws and a bad temper. His first project in his new, free life is to eat his liberator, descendant of the family who imprisoned him, but when

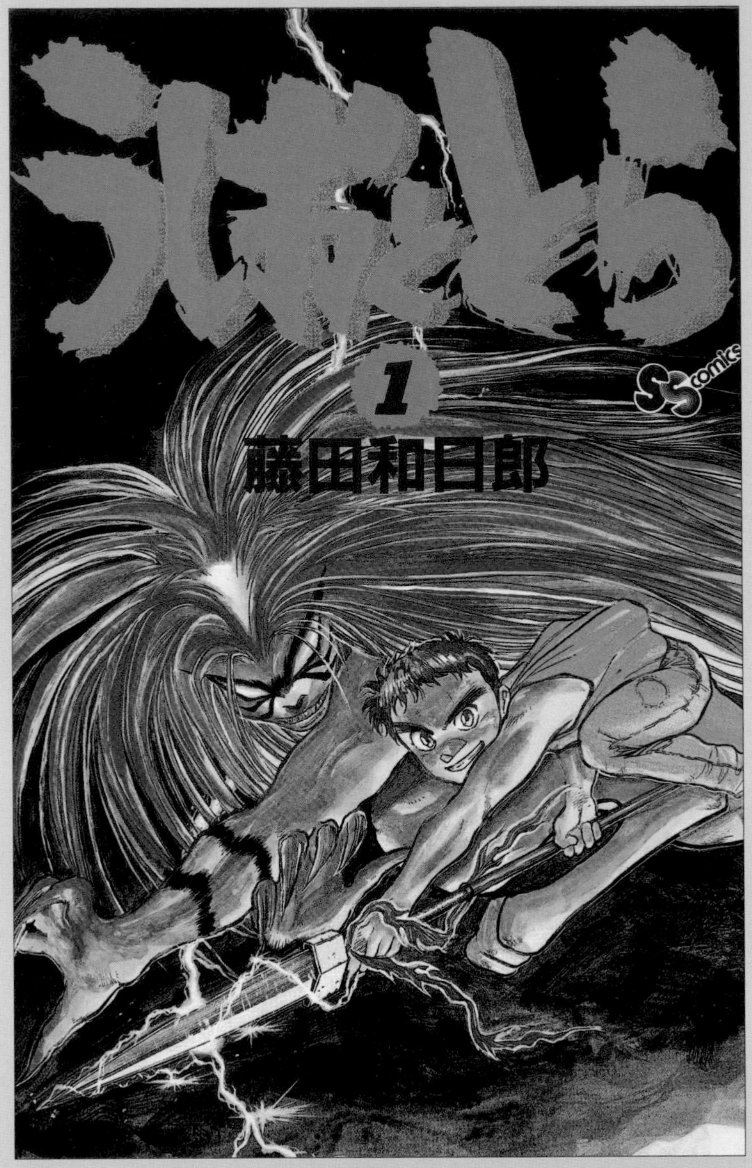
うしおととら
1
SS comics
藤田和日郎

Ushio holds the ancestral Spear of Beasts, a change comes over him, too. His hair grows long and wild and he becomes a man-beast, match for any demon—even the ferocious being he names Tora (Japanese for tiger). The spear was made in China 2,000 years ago to destroy monsters; it feeds off human life energy. Grasping the spear, Ushio can see all the other demons in the world, and he sets out to defend his friends and community from the dangers of the spirit world. At first Tora looks for every chance to eat him, but over time the pair form an unlikely but powerful bond of friendship that makes them a formidable ghost-busting duo. Finally Tora joins Ushio on a quest to find his mother, presumed dead for many years. Kazuhiro Fujita's manga *Ushio & Tora* appeared in *Shonen Sunday* magazine.

THE X-MEN [1963]

The original comic concept, created by Stan Lee and Jack Kirby, was a team of super-powered mutants using their talents to help a world that feared and hated them. In 1996 the team was drawn for Marvel's Japanese market by a roster of artists including Hiroshi Higuchi, Rei Nakahara, Yukikaze Amagi, and Koji Yasue. Imported into the United States in 1998 as *X-Men: The Manga*, the comic was directly based on the U.S. animated TV series, and featured the "classic X-Men" cast of Prof. Xavier,

Left: Unlikely buddies—Ushio with the Spear of Beasts and his new friend Tora.

Wolverine, Cyclops, Storm, Jean Grey, Gambit, Rogue, Beast, and rivals such as Magneto, Juggernaut, and even Morph, who never appeared in the American comic but came exclusively from the animated series. There was even an entire chapter done in squashed-down "super deformed" style by Warrior Ohashi, a pseudonym for an artist who has never owned up. The twelve-volume *X-Men* manga was a failure in Japan and in the U.S., but the mutant superhero team got the manga treatment again when Kia Asamiya produced the art for Marvel's *Uncanny X-Men* issue # 416–420. He also redesigned their costumes and recast their faces in his own mold, annoying some long-time fans. Chuck Austen's story was collected as *Uncanny X-Men 2: Dominant Species*, published by Panini Publishing in 2003. Warren Worthington III, a.k.a. Angel, is going through a stressful time in the family business and in his love life. He and new mutant Paige Guthrie, a.k.a. Husk, run into a group of werewolves under Maximus Lobo, on Warren's payroll but definitely not working to the Worthington corporate objectives. They survive the encounter alive, and with physical changes—both can now heal rapidly, and Warren can use his blood to heal others. Old foe Juggernaut is dealing with issues from his childhood relationship with his father which change his views about the course his life should take, and he joins and finally saves the team. Asamiya has also produced cover art for other *X-Men* titles, as well as creating a manga version of his personal favorite, American comic *Batman*.

Chapter 8

Historical, Mythical, & Literary Heroes & Villains

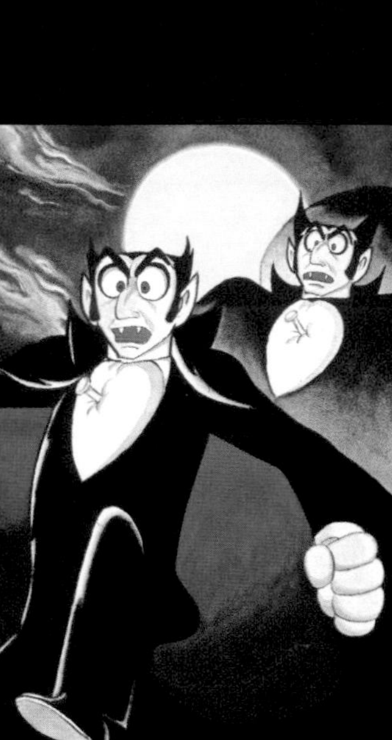

Manga creators search the whole world for inspiration. Japanese history and folklore are just as rich a source for them as European myths were for Stan Lee and Jack Kirby, but they also borrow from the history and legends of other nations, as well as contemporary music, film, and current affairs. Sometimes the characters are rendered with respect for literary or historical accuracy, but just as often they are warped into entirely different forms.

NOTE: The dates after the character names in this section are the confirmed or most likely dates of birth and death for historical figures. For fictional figures, the dates given are of first known publication or circulation of their legend. For consistency, all dates are in the Western Christian system, A.D. or B.C.

ARABIAN NIGHTS

[Pre-eighteenth century]

The beautiful Scheherezade told an enthralling tale to her sultan every night, always ending on a cliff-hanger so he would spare her life until he heard what happened next, thus foreshadowing the modern soap opera. The original Eastern folktales in the *Thousand and One Nights* are very old, but a number were added to the collection in the early 1700s, including the tales of Aladdin, Ali Baba, and Sinbad. Osamu Tezuka included Aladdin (and Ali Baba) in his 1951 manga adaptation of the Arabian Nights, later animated for the big screen. Monkey Punch has also made a manga adaptation of the *Thousand and One Nights.*

MARIE ANTOINETTE

[A.D. 1755-1793]

The French queen who died on the guillotine is a central character in *Rose of Versailles* by Ryoko Ikeda. Born Marie Antoinette Josephe Jeanne of Austria-Lorraine, she was the eleventh child of Maria Theresa, empress of Austria, and Ikeda's manga presents her as a capricious and over-indulged child, but one who is deeply conscious of her duty to her mother and her people, with great pride, intelligence, and loyalty to those she loves. In the manga, as in history, she is ignorant of the lives of the common people and does not understand the inevitability of revolution until it is too late. Her lover, Swedish nobleman Hans Axel von Fersen, whom she met at a ball in Paris in 1774, is based on one of her real admirers. In the manga he dies tragically, but in real life he returned to Sweden after an unsuccessful attempt to rescue his beloved queen's family from the guillotine, and died in 1810.

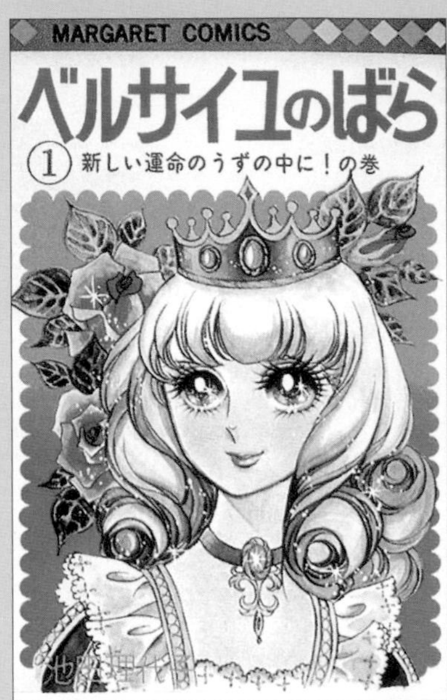

A classic shojo cover for *Rose of Versailles*—Marie Antoinette, Crown Princess of France.

LUDWIG VAN BEETHOVEN [A.D. 1770–1827]

Beethoven is a central figure in Osamu Tezuka's unfinished 1987 manga *Ludwig B*, a psychological drama of love, hate, and obsession. It uses the composer's life as a framework for the tale of nobleman Franz Kreuszstein, who is frightened in childhood by a peacock named Ludwig and grows up hating everything connected with the name and everyone who bears it. Twelve years older than Beethoven, Franz directly causes his childhood deafness, and yet Tezuka's plans for the manga made Franz the person who understood his music best. A classical music lover and pianist himself, Tezuka intended that the manga should end with Ludwig's pure music reaching Franz's heart and silencing the harsh screams that had so terrified him as a child. The great composer's life was also retold for children in a 1984 manga by Teruyaki Noda, published in hardback by Shueisha as part of a series of lives of prominent figures.

NAPOLEON BONAPARTE [A.D. 1769–1821]

The short but dynamic military genius who became emperor of France and conquered much of Europe appears in Ryoko Ikeda's manga *The Glory of Napoleon—Eroica (Eiko no Napoleon—Eroica)*, alongside several of the supporting characters from her earlier *Rose of Versailles*. Napoleon's fabled treasure map turns up as a plot device in *Age of Adventure*, Osamu Tezuka's 1951 tale of a nineteenth-century Japanese envoy adventuring through the American West.

BUDDHA [Sixth century B.C.]

Born Prince Siddhartha in India, the great spiritual teacher started life in a wealthy and privileged family before beginning his journey towards enlightenment at the age of twenty-nine, when he left his wife and family and gave up everything to become a monk. He went on to give teachings which are still followed all over the world. Buddhism is one of the two major belief systems in Japan. Osamu Tezuka told his story in manga form between 1972 to 1983 in three magazines—*Kibo-no-tomo, Shonen World*, and *Comic Tom.*

CATHERINE THE GREAT [A.D. 1729–1796]

Ryoko Ikeda, doyenne of historical manga, told the story of the Russian empress in her manga *Empress Catherine (Jotei Ekaterina)*. Published in 1972 and collected in five volumes, it tells the story of Catherine the Great, empress of Russia, hence the Russian spelling of her name in the original title. It is based on French historian Henri Troyat's renowned life of Catherine.

CINDERELLA [A.D. 1697]

Cinderella made her debut in a collection of French fairy stories by Charles Perrault, already part of folklore in the year they were published. The rags-to-riches heroine of Perrault's fairy tale has inspired many manga. Junko Mizuno, whose cute fantasy girls are available on everything from websites to stationery, produced a version of the legend with a Goth-girl twist in 2002; *Junko Mizuno's Cinderalla*, starring a zombie prince and a girl whose father runs a fast food joint, is available from Viz. Yuki Kawachi's manga *7200 Romance (7200 byo no Romance)* covers the same ground from a slightly different angle—that of the ugly sister.

Plain, unpopular Seiko buys a pair of glass slippers and finds they transform her into a daring, popular party girl with a talent for music. She is spotted and starts a successful career as a singer, changing her name to Seiya. As Seiya she has the courage to get closer to her classmate Iguchi, who has always defended her from bullies and been kind to her even when she was rude to him; when she tells him how she feels, he tells her he is in love with someone else, whom he has been protecting for some time. Realizing that the handsome prince really loves the plain, ordinary girl she was, Seiko breaks the glass slippers, ends Seiya's career and lives happily ever after, just as every fairytale heroine should.

CLEOPATRA [68–30 B.C.]

Cleopatra, whose Egyptian crown name Netjeretmerites is rarely used, was the seventh Cleopatra of her dynasty, and first became co-ruler of Egypt with her father at the age of seventeen. When he died, she and her younger brother became co-rulers before she famously seduced Julius Caesar, and with his support gained sole power. Several years after Caesar's death she and his lieutenant Mark Antony had a love affair so notorious that it has reverberated through history into legend, inspiring both a play by Shakespeare and an epic movie, as well as countless novels and even manga and anime appearances. She and Antony had three children and tried to take over the Roman world before being defeated by Caesar's nephew Octavian. The cause of their deaths is generally accepted as Anthony's battle wounds and Cleopatra's suicide. None of their children seem to have survived for very long. The great queen appears in *Time Traveller Ai* by Ai Ijima and Takeshi Takebayashi, out in English from CPM.

DRACULA [A.D. 1897]

Bram Stoker's Transylvanian vampire and the novel that bears his name inspired Osamu Tezuka to showcase him and his sweet daughter Chocula in *Don Dracula*. (American breakfast cereal Count Chocula has no connection with Tezuka's work.) The vampire, now an earl, has moved from Transylvania to a

Western-style house in a corner plot in a Tokyo suburb with Chocula, who goes to the local junior high school, and his faithful servant Igor. In modern Japan, where no one really believes in vampires, he causes all manner of comical commotions. These are made even sillier by his old enemy Prof. Van Hellsing, who tails him relentlessly. Hellsing is played by one of Tezuka's stock characters, mad scientist Dr. Fooler, an unruly, attention-seeking yet winningly childlike character with a screen persona not unlike that of Danny De Vito, who first appeared in *The Secret Base of Shari River* in 1948. The Dracula legend has inspired other manga, including Kota Hirano's 2002 hit *Hellsing*.

ALBERT EINSTEIN

[A.D. 1879–1955]

Scientific genius Albert Einstein has a vital role in Saki Hiwatari's *Global Garden*. The great scientist is dying, plagued by guilt over his role in providing the science for the atomic bomb. Then he has a dream of a beautiful future for earth, with humanism and ecology linked to create a green paradise, the world a "global garden" guided by a girl with a gentle smile. He confides this dream and his hopes for its realization to two little boys with strange powers, Hikaru and Haruhi. He asks them to find the girl and make the dream come true, and gives them a drug to prevent their aging so that they have time to carry out his wish.

HIKARU GENJI

[Twelfth century A.D.]

Hikaru Genji, also known as the Shining Prince, is the hero of *The Tale of Genji*, a story by Japanese court lady Murasaki Shikibu that is widely described as the world's first novel. Of imperial blood, he is handsome, charming, courteous, a great poet and aesthete, and a famous lover. Chikae Ida adapted the legend under the title *The Tale of Genji (Genji Monogatari)*, as did Miyako Maki in 1988. *Asaki Yumemishi* is another version by Waki Yamato, from *Mimi* magazine in 1986. Yun Kouga's 1988 manga *Genji* from *Wings* magazine is not about the Shining Prince, but about the battle between the Genji and Heike families, one of the great epics of Japanese history. Kouga uses the twelfth-century wars as the background for a modern fantasy romance, with sixteen-year-old Katsumi Ebata following his beloved Sakura back and forth in time between modern Shinjuku and the Kamakura era, and standing in for a recently dead Morimoto prince.

GREEK GODS

[Pre-ninth century B.C.]

The children of Zeus and Hera and their fellow deities make many appearances in manga. Venus, Psyche, and Zephyrus are central to the wanderings of Osamu Tezuka's baby unicorn

Unico, and Poseidon is the villain of his *Blue Triton*, persecuting the mermen. *Ryu* magazine's *Arion*, by Yoshikazu Yasuhiko, also features the gods as cruel, venal, and capricious, and focuses on an amoral Apollo, a sadistic Artemis, a gullible Zeus, and a manipulative Hades. Masami Kurumada's *Saint Seiya* spans many mythologies but features reincarnations of Athena and Apollo, as well as seagod Poseidon and Eris, the goddess of discord. A gentler view comes in *Pollon of Olympus* by Hideo Azuma, originally from *100-ten* Comic, about the naughty little daughter of the god Apollo and her adventures with her cherubic friend Eros. Renowned girls' manga artist Machiko Satonaka published a series of manga versions of Greek myths for Chuokuronsha under the title *Manga Greek Myths (Manga Greece Shinwa)*. Manga writers borrow names from many sources and often use them out of context, for example in Yun Kouga's *Zeus*, which does not feature the father of the Gods.

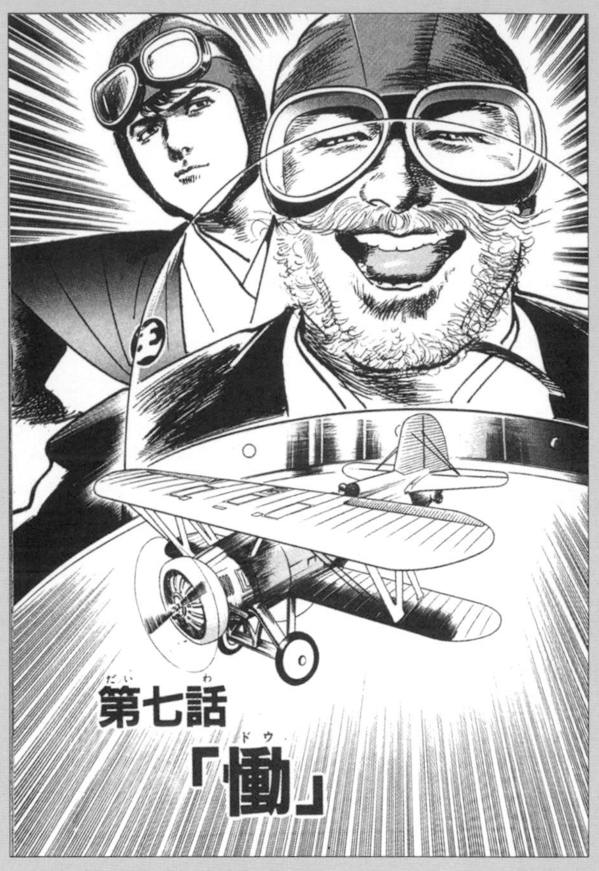

Ernest Hemingway takes Kumomaru on a wild flight across the world of the 1930s.

HANSEL & GRETEL

[A.D. 1812]

The brother and sister, sent into the woods to die by a cruel stepmother, are captured and fattened for eating by a wicked witch, but escape thanks to their ingenuity, courage, and love for each other. First published in a collection of old German folktales by the Brothers Grimm, the adventures of Hansel and Gretel have also inspired an opera and countless pantomimes. *Junko Mizuno's Hansel and Gretel*, a very contemporary twist on the old legend published in 2003, is out in English from Viz. Hansel is a squat little boy who can shatter just about anything with his mouth, so he has a tuna can strapped over it; Gretel is a tall, pink-haired schoolgirl who takes on bullies with her bamboo sword. Their parents run the mountain grocery store, and deal with suppliers like the green girls who grow spinach from their scalps and the 40-foot pig who slices bacon to order off his belly.

ERNEST HEMINGWAY

[A.D. 1899–1961]

Papa Hemingway, as the great American novelist was affectionately known, appears in *Samurai Crusader (Oritsurin Kumomaru no Shugai)*, from writer Hiroi Oji and artist Ryoichi Ikegami, a martial arts fantasy set in Europe, China, and Japan in the 1930s. Hero Kumomaru travels to Europe to seek his fortune, and becomes embroiled in an attempt to prevent a symbolic sword from falling into the hands of corrupt militarists. The manga ran in *Shonen Sunday* from 1991 but was not popular and ended abruptly in 1992. An extract appeared in English in *Manga Vizions* Vol. 2 No. 11 from Viz.

HIMIKO [Third century A.D.]

The semi-legendary empress appears in Chinese chronicles as the "Queen of Wa" and in Osamu Tezuka's *Phoenix: Dawn* as queen of the Yamatai (an aboriginal Japanese people), who orders one of her retainers to capture the Phoenix for her. Tezuka's self-described life's work, the Phoenix saga was started in 1954 in

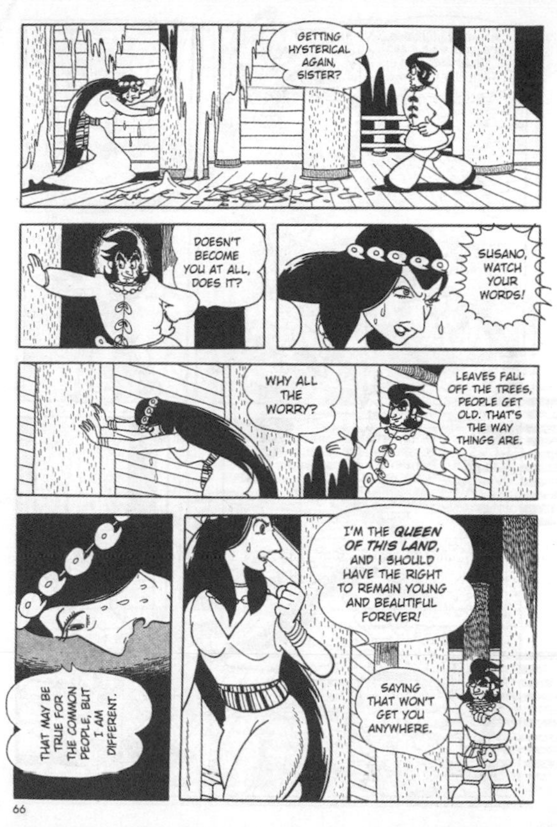

Tezuka's take on the semi-legendary Queen Himiko: absolute power corrupts most humans.

Manga Shonen with this chapter set in primitive Japan, and never completed. Other real characters from Japanese history also crop up in the cycle, including Genji clan leader Yoshitsune. Kamui Furjiwara's 1993 manga *Raika* shows Himiko as a charismatic shaman-queen ruling the population of the land of Yamatai. Himiko appears in other manga, sometimes as a sorceress, but always as a tough, powerful woman.

ADOLF HITLER

[A.D. 1889–1945]

The Nazi leader is one of the three protagonists of Osamu Tezuka's great work *Adolf: A Tale of the Twentieth Century*, completed in 1986 and published in translation in 1995 by Viz's Cadence Books imprint. The story of World War II is told through the eyes of the three Adolfs—the others being Adolf Kaufman, a half-German, half-Japanese boy growing up in Germany, and his friend Adolf Kamil, a German Jew living in Japan. The plot revolves around the loss of a secret document that proves Hitler's Jewish heritage; Japanese reporter Sohei Toge is caught up in the plot when he tries to find the truth behind his brother's brutal murder at the hands of the Gestapo. With the Japanese secret police on his tail, his only hope is Adolf Kaufman's mother Yukie, the widow of a high-ranking Nazi officer. Meanwhile, at his elite school, her son is being taught by the Hitler Youth Movement to hate his old friend Kamil. He is torn between his sympathy for his old friend's people and the need to survive—as someone who is only half Aryan, he has to prove himself to his schoolmates. The pressures of society and war drive the friends apart, but they are reconciled with the creation of the state of Israel. The events of the war are presented from a Japanese perspective, but completely devoid of partisanship or militarism. In an interesting twist, Hitler is portrayed as being executed because of his Jewish ancestry and the execution passed off as suicide. Sohei survives the war and tells his story after the death of the last of the Adolfs, Kamil. A more conventional version of Hitler's death is featured in Shigeru Mizuki's manga biography.

SOJUN IKKYU

[A.D. 1394–1481]

Ikkyu, abbot of Kyoto's Daitokuji Temple, a poet, painter, calligrapher, and master of Zen Buddhism, was widely considered a maverick, or even crazy, in his own day. He was frequently in conflict with the Zen establishment. Widely believed to have been the illegitimate son of Emperor Gokomatsu, he began training as a monk at the age of five. For most of his life he wandered Japan, frequenting taverns and brothels and asserting that he could maintain the pure, original spirit of Zen much more effectively by his method of living its principles in the real world than by merely observing

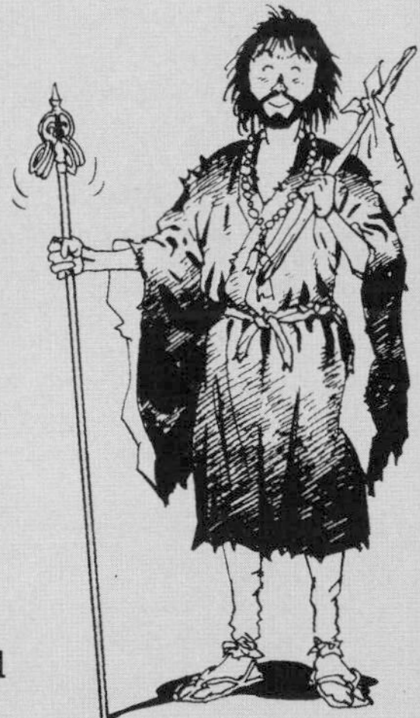

empty religious conventions. *Ikkyu* by Hisashi Sakaguchi is based on his life.

JESUS CHRIST [A.D. 0–33]

Christianity has a longer history in Asia than in the U.S., and the life of its founding figure was given a beautiful and respectful treatment by Yoshikazu Yasuhiko, published as *Jesus* in 2001 by ComicsOne and available as an Adobe download. The story follows the Biblical original closely, but tells the story through the eyes of a young disciple.

JOAN OF ARC

[A.D. c.1412–1431]

Joan, or Jehanne as her own people called her, was a warrior maiden who inspired the French to resist English invasion in the Middle Ages. Initially successful and claiming inspiration from God and the Saints, she was finally captured and handed over to her enemies. Although her date of birth is not certain, she was probably about nineteen when she was burned at the stake in the city of Rouen. She has made several popular appearances in manga. Arina Tanemura's 1998 manga *Kamikaze Kaito Jeanne (Phantom Thief Jeanne)* has the warrior saint reincarnated as sixteen-year-old Japanese high-school girl Maron Kusakabe. She's recruited by trainee angel Finn to help stop Satan from taking over the human race and finally winning his eons-long battle with God. The Prince of Darkness is putting his demonic minions into great paintings, where they lurk waiting to steal the souls of onlookers captivated by the beauty of art. Maron, as the

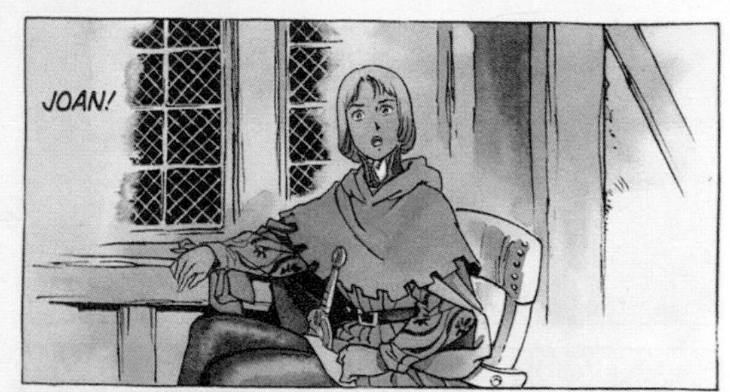

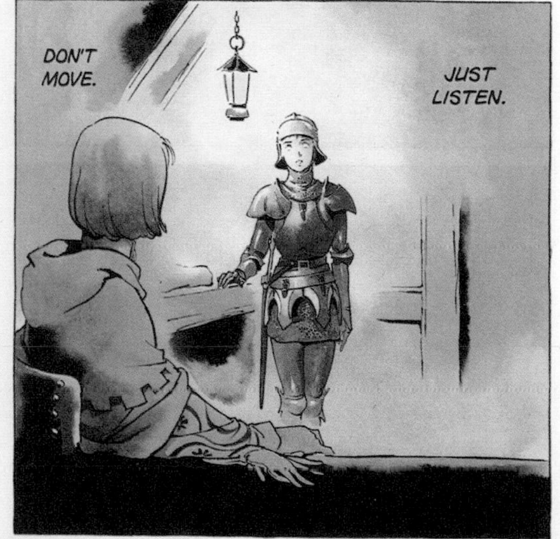

Joan of Arc was a legend in her own lifetime, and Emil is haunted by her presence.

reincarnation of Jeanne, is given the task of stealing the paintings and removing the demons. Finn gives her assignments—and some cool weapons—but he can't help Maron deal with the day-to-day problems of life as a teenage undercover saint. It's not just her ultra-competitive best friend Miyako Todaiji, or the wacky teachers at her school, or her cute new neighbor Chiaki, giving Maron problems; Miyako's dad is the local detective, and he's out to get Jeanne, come what may.

A more serious historical take on La Pucelle, the nickname given Joan by her followers, comes in Yoshikazu Yasuhiko's 1995 manga *Joan*. Interestingly, this book made its English-language debut from ComicsOne in both print and electronic format for Adobe PDF readers. It's also unusual in being created in full color, still a relatively rare step for a manga. Emile, a young girl adopted by Joan's mentor Robert de Baudricourt, is brought up as a boy, Emil, to keep her identity concealed. Emile actually sees Joan once, at her father's castle, as a small girl. Emile is the bastard child of the duke of Lorraine, and after her mother is accused of killing him and is then tortured to death, his retainer Baudricourt brings her up as his son. Tormented by the thought that by helping Joan fulfill her mission he led an innocent girl to her death to serve his king, Baudricourt protects Emil for eleven years, then, the danger over, asks her to live as a girl. Instead, inspired by visions of Joan, Emil decides to stay in men's clothes and follow in Joan's footsteps in trying to help her country stay free. She encounters many of the people who knew Joan: the dukes of Anjou, Alencon, Bourbon, and Burgundy, Joan's loyal captains La Hire and de Xaintrailles, and her old adversary La Tremoille, as well as the son of Joan's king, the Dauphin Louis, a pragmatist who believes that all winners have the favor of God and is opposing his father to win the throne for himself. Emil struggles to understand Joan's vision and avoid her fate.

GENSAI KAWAKAMI

[A.D. 1834–1871]

A master swordsman whose exquisite good looks masked a cold-blooded killer instinct, Kawakami, also known as Hitokiri Gensai, was one of the four great *hitokiri*, or assassins, of the revolutionary groups who brought about the Meiji restoration. He was adopted in childhood and raised to be a Buddhist priest. Short of stature, gentle, and mild-mannered, he could be mistaken for a girl at first glance, but was reputed to be unbeatable in swordplay. He was also a passionate supporter of isolationism, which ran counter to the new government's policies. Once the civil unrest had done its work and the emperor and new government were secure, he was arrested on fabricated charges and executed in 1871. His story is the basis for Nobuhiro Watsuki's manga *Ruro ni Kenshin*, which also features tough guy Sanosuke, who was inspired by the semi-historical Sanosuke Harada, hero of Ryotaro Shiba's novel *Burning Sword*.

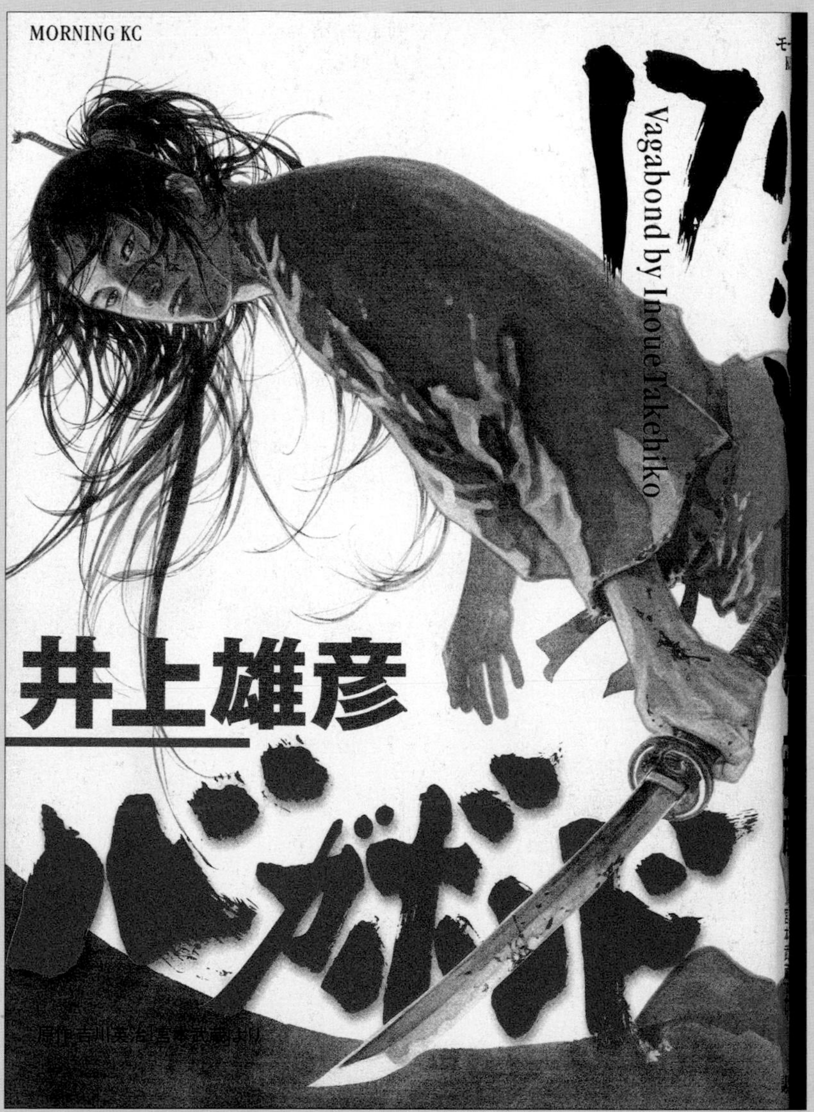

Young Musashi Miyamoto on the road to becoming a legendary sword saint.

LUDWIG II OF BAVARIA [A.D. 1845–1886]

Yo Higuri tells the story of the life and tragic death of Bavaria's legendary Mad King in her 1996 boys' love manga *Ludwig II*. Ludwig came to the throne in 1864 and built several remarkable castles, of which Neuschwanstein is generally recognized as the most beautiful. Other historical characters in the manga include Ludwig's cousin Elizabeth of Bavaria, later empress of Austria, and the opera singer Albert Niman, whom Higuri casts as a magical figure serving as one of the king's lovers and his conscience.

BASHO MATSUO

[A.D. 1644–1694]

The great poet and Zen Buddhist priest, master of Japan's traditional haiku form, makes an appearance at the age of seven under the childhood name of Kinsaku in Jiro Taniguchi and Kan Furuyama's 1992 manga *Samurai Legend*. The manga claims that he was the son of Yozaemon Matsuo of Iga, and that the family had ninja connections. Basho was known as Munefusa Matsuo before he took up his pen name.

MUSASHI MIYAMOTO

[A.D. 1584–1645]

The renowned swordmaster of feudal Japan and author of *The Book of Five Rings* is the hero of Takehiko Inoue's manga *Vagabond*. Adapted from Eiji Yoshikawa's historical novel *Musashi*, it has run in Kodansha's *Morning* magazine since 1998. It opens at the battle of Sekigahara where a young fighter named Takezo has barely escaped alive. A loner all his short life, he decides to keep wandering. His aim is to sharpen his skills and find their limit by challenging swordmasters the length of Japan. As he travels, his reputation as a cold-blooded killer grows, but he begins to change as he acquires a deeper understanding of the value of life through the discipline of studying his chosen skill, and eventually becomes a great master under the name Miyamoto Musashi.

NEFERTITI [c.1300–1336 B.C.]

Possibly the most beautiful woman in the ancient world, the beloved wife of Egypt's heretic pharaoh Akhenaten is also believed by some to have reigned as his co-pharoah and even his successor. She appears in Chie Shinohara's manga *Red River* as Nefertiti, a princess of the Mitanni who has become queen of Egypt. Shinohara makes no attempt to keep within the confines of known history, and uses incidents from other periods and characters in her story. For instance, in the manga a Hittite prince heads for Egypt to marry Nefertiti but the marriage never takes place. This echoes a letter from Nefertiti's daughter, Ankhesenamun, sent to the Hittite king after the death of her husband Tutankhamun, asking him to send one of his sons to marry her. Some historians now believe that this letter may have come from Nefertiti, desperate to have a son after the death of Akhenaten. The prince never arrived, and both Ankhesenamun and Nefertiti disappeared from history with no apparent record of their deaths. Ramses II, also known as the Great, appears in the same manga as Prince Ramses, who helps save the heroine Yuri and falls in love with her, even though he occupies a different era of Egypt's long history. The manga is out in English from Viz. Ankhesenamun makes a starring appearance in *Daughter of the Aton (Aton no Musume)* by the great girls' manga creator Machiko Satonoka. Originally serialized in Kodansha's *Big Gold* magazine, this is the story of the tragic young queen, her husband Tutankhamun, and the religious and political machinations that dominated their lives.

CAPTAIN NEMO [A.D.1870]

Jules Verne's heroic yet misanthropic antihero of *20,000 Leagues Under The Sea* is reborn as a heroic figure fighting impossible odds, but appears in a less serious guise in *The Secret of Comic Blue Water*, the Cyber Comix/Bonita manga spin-off of Gainax's animated TV series *The Secret of Blue Water (Fushigi no Umi no Nadia)*. This Nemo is not even human—he is an Earth-born Atlantean, king of the last surviving city of the former alien empire, which was destroyed in a terrible cataclysm triggered by his former friend Gargoyle. The cause was a political dispute—he wanted Atlanteans to co-exist with the evolving human race as equals, his friend wanted to keep mankind as slaves of Atlantis. His wife and most of his friends died in the aftermath, but his enemy survived and now the two are locked in a deadly struggle. Like Verne's character, he adopted the name Nemo (no-one in Latin) and used Atlantean science and technology to build the super-submarine Nautilus, in which he fights against Gargoyle's far superior force to prevent him dominating the world. In the anime original, he finds his daughter Nadia, who survived the flood and has grown up with no knowledge of her heritage, and his son Neo, who has been turned into a cyborg, a mere puppet of Gargoyle, and realizes that his children are true to his own beliefs before he gives his life to save Nadia's beloved Jean. In the manga his role as strong and silent man of principle is used to comic effect.

ODA NOBUNAGA

[A.D. 1534–1582]

The great shogun has not always been treated sympathetically by manga creators. He is widely credited with supernatural powers, usually malevolent. Ryochi Ikegami and Kazuya Kudo gave him his own title in Shogakukan's

LOUIS DE POINTE DU LAC [1976]

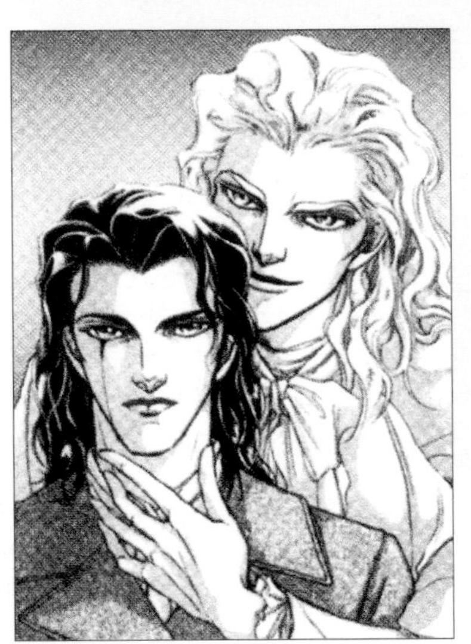

ANNE RICE'S BEAUTIFUL, bored eighteenth-century aristocrat first appeared as the title character of her novel *Interview with a Vampire*, and was immortalized on the big screen by Brad Pitt in the movie version *Interview with the Vampire*. Most Western female viewers seem to agree that Louis the vampire could hardly get much prettier; but then, most haven't seen the manga version. Released under the title *Daybreak's Vampire (Yoake no Vampire)*, Rice's story was drawn and adapted by Udoh Shinohara, whose previous work focused on tales of horror and the occult for women. The success of her 1991 manga *Quart and Half*, about a beautiful young necromancer and his cat, led publishers Tokuma to approach her when they wanted a manga tie-in to the movie's Japanese release in 1995.

Rice's novel gets its title because Louis decides to tell his story to reporter Daniel Molloy. The interview provides the framing device for the film, and Shinohara kept it for the manga. She also keeps the story split into the film's three acts. We see Louis, a Franco-American living the life of a rich plantation owner in New Orleans, killed by the reckless, self-centered but vastly attractive French vampire Lestat de Lioncourt , an escapee from the Old World spreading his ancient infection in the New. Lestat is intelligent, charismatic but shallow, a good-time guy who believes in making the best of the opportunities his new situation has provided. Louis, on the other hand, is a moral young man, and as he realizes that he really does have all the time in the world, he begins to ponder what it means to be a scavenger who lives by stealing the lives of others.

As his protégé becomes less dependent on him and more caught up in dark moral questions, Lestat tries to lure him back by creating a surrogate family with Claudia, daughter of a woman killed by plague. The ancient laws of vampirism say that children should not be made vampires, but Lestat persuades Louis that if the child is left sitting beside the corpse of her dead mother, she too will die. The pair wander the world with their adopted daughter, who resents her perpetual childhood. However much her mind expands, however much she learns and develops, her body can never change,

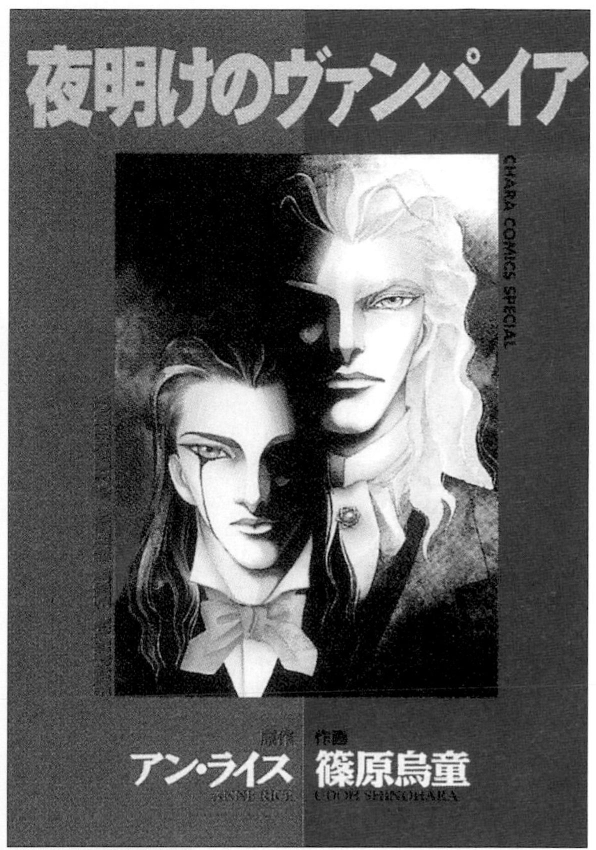

Cover and interior art from Udoh Shinohara's manga: prettier than Brad Pitt?

making her little more than a pretty doll for two spoiled, bored adult men who can't resolve the problems in their own relationship. The vampires of Paris, rigid adherents to vampire law, finally destroy her.

Shinohara made some changes to the film story for the manga version, but she is only restoring the primacy of the original novel as source. Her Louis is cast into despair and made easy prey for Lestat by the death of his younger brother, not the loss of his wife in childbirth, as in the movie. Claudia, beautifully played by Kirsten Dunst at around ten years old in the movie, was just five in the book, and Shinohara's five-year-old Claudia brings even more pathos to her story in consequence. The end of the film, where Molloy finds Lestat hiding in his car, is replaced by his watching Louis walk away as the sun comes up over San Francisco. He muses that this is the last sunrise he will ever see, and as Louis vanishes into the distance we see the marks of a vampire's fangs on Molloy's neck.

Rice once told an interviewer that at one stage in the film's genesis she had considered making Louis a woman, cross-dressing to function as a plantation owner in a world where only men controlled businesses. Cross-dressing is, of course, a staple of the pretty-boy *bishonen* manga genre, but not for the same reasons. Rice was responding to concerns that a Western audience wasn't ready for a mainstream movie with such a powerful homoerotic charge; Shinohara's readers were already lapping it up across a vast range of manga titles. Her manga vampires are androgynous beauties. Louis is dark-haired, a usual feature of the younger, more passive character with whom the reader generally identifies. Lestat is returned to his original glory, depicted as the blond, blue-eyed demon-angel of Rice's text.

1987 *Nobunaga*. He appears in *Samurai Deeper Kyo* by Akimine Kamiyo, along with Shogun Tokugawa Ieyasu. Sanpei Shirato showed Oda's death in his 1959 work *Ninja Bugyeicho/Ninja Chronicles*, which was later literally made into a film by Nagisa Oshima, shooting frames of the manga from various camera angles with voiceovers. Oda uses psychic powers and magic to work his evil ends in Go Nagai's 1992 manga *Black Lion (Kuro no Shishi)* in which he introduces machine guns, lasers, and missiles to sixteenth-century Japan with the help of immortal ninja Ginnai Domu. On a lighter note, he is reincarnated as a modern teenager, along with his wife and his enemy, as the protagonists of psychic love-triangle *Ten yori mo Hoshi yori mo* by Michiyo Akaishi (*Flower Comics*).

NORSE GODS

[Pre-third century A.D.]

The gods of Norse mythology show up in several guises in manga. In Masaki Kurumada's *Saint Seiya* they have a long-running story arc. In a less renowned work, Sakura Kinoshita's 2002 manga *Mythical Detective Loki*, the trickster god and his family—including Thor, Heimdall, and the mighty Odin—have been reincarnated as ordinary Japanese teenagers and have to navigate a series of typical high-school romantic comedy scenarios, solve crime puzzles, and try to work out what sorcery accomplished the transformation. Sister goddesses Skauld, Urd, and Verdandi (or Belldandy, as she is called in the comic) appear in much prettier form in Kosuke Fujishima's *Oh My Goddess! (Aaa Megamisama!)*. Sexy vamp Urd is the goddess of the past, so appropriately is the elder sister; sweet, gentle home-maker Belldandy is goddess of the present; and preteen computer whiz and technofreak Skuld is goddess of the future.

RASKOLNIKOV [A.D. 1866]

A manga based on one of the works of Feyodor Dostoyevsky doesn't sound like the world's most obvious cultural blend, but Osamu Tezuka found the Russian novel *Crime and Punishment* fascinating. He produced a version which is fairly faithful to the original until the conclusion. In St.Petersburg, just before the Revolution, penniless student Raskolnikov claims that geniuses should have the right to do anything they choose, even kill, "as long as it is for the good of the world." He kills a moneylender and steals all her money. The moneylender is an old woman, but that doesn't deter him. Investigator Polifili immediately suspects him because of his published opinions, but at first the murderer feels invincible. Eventually, under pressure of pursuit and guilt, he tells Sonia, a good woman forced into prostitution by poverty, about his sin. Sonia urges him to confess, and accept the consequences with a clear conscience. He goes to the central plaza, kisses the ground, and confesses. However, the revolution has started, there's panic on the streets and nobody notices Raskolnikov, or even hears his confession over the hubbub. The manga ends with his leaving unnoticed amid the chaos around him. Tezuka used many of his favorite characters in the manga. Old Man Mustache can be seen rushing along in the final scene in the square. Duke Red is cast as Polifili, and pirate Buku Bukk as Rugin.

The manga was published in book form by Tokodo in 1953. It was the last work he did for the Osaka publisher who brought him to fame with *New Treasure Island*; he drew much of it while traveling on the train between his home town and Tokyo, while doing more and more work for Tokyo publishers. So his version of *Crime and Punishment* marks the end of an era, as well as the further development of a great storytelling talent.

RICHARD THE LIONHEART [A.D. 1157–1199]

Yasuko Aoike featured England's crusader king as hero of *Richard the Lion-Hearted* in *Princess* magazine. Richard is the ideal hero for a boys' love manga: handsome, homosexual, a noted poet and musician, a great warrior, a king, and a member of one of the most complex and dysfunctional families in English history. She also devoted a *Flower Comics* title to his principal opponent, the chivalrous and cultured Muslim warrior Saladin, *The Day of Saladin (Saladin no Hi)*.

ANASTASIA ROMANOVA [A.D. 1901-1918]

The daughter of the last Tsar of Russia, Grand Duchess Anastasia was shot with her whole family after the Revolution. A woman later claiming to be the grand duchess fought for many years to have her right to the Romanov name—and the remnants of the family fortune—recognized, but died without success. Chiho Saito's short manga *Requiem* tells the story of a young Parisian actor who finds a girl claiming to be Anastasia picking pockets on the streets of Paris, and sets out to help her establish her claim.

RYOMA SAKAMOTO [A.D. 1834–1867]

Ryoma was born into a traditional samurai family, but realized that Japan would never modernize and become a great nation unless the feudal powers of the shogun gave way to imperial rule. One of the pivotal figures in the restoration of the Meiji emperor and the modernization of Japan, he was assassinated at the age of thirty-three, just after achieving the near miracle of a bloodless coup transferring power back to the emperor. Tetsuya Takeda and Yu Koyama's manga *Oi Ryoma!* shows him growing up, completing his training, and leaving his hometown for a life of adventure.

WHAT A MAN'S GOTTA DO

THE UNIVERSE according to Leiji Matsumoto. Born in 1938 in Fukuoka prefecture on the southern island of Kyushu, the artist known as Leiji Matsumoto was a manga professional from the age of fourteen, making his debut in girls' comics. Leiji is a pseudonym; his personal name is Akira. He's married to a fellow manga artist, Miyako Maki.

After half a century, Matsumoto's uniquely personal vision attracts artists young enough to be his grandchildren from all over the world. When cult band Daft Punk wanted to make an animated science fiction movie, they headed for Japan to pitch the concept to Matsumoto in the hope of getting him on board.

Some might think it odd that, with a universe of Western talent to choose from, a young band should pursue a sixty-something Japanese artist with strongly traditional views, but Matsumoto's years of experience as a writer, artist, director, producer, and actor make him a good bet for any movie project. The result was *Interstella 5555*, a movie and album about a band kidnapped from another galaxy by an evil manager, imprisoned on Earth in the shackles of fame.

Some might also wonder why Matsumoto would accept, but his enthusiasm for new projects and new ideas is as great as ever. The man is a sci-fi fan. He has a huge comics collection, widely recognized as one of the most important in Japan, but it's his other collection that holds the key to his unique vision. He collects militaria, especially from World War II, the conflict that dominated his early years. His comics resonate with the tragedy and senseless waste of war, and the male response to a life dominated by conflict is his primary interest.

"Sore ga otoko da" translates roughly as "That's the man," meaning "That's what being a man is all about." In Matsumoto's universe, manhood has its own special meaning. Matsumoto's heroes believe in themselves. They are not afraid of challenge and failure, and they don't whine when everything comes crashing around them. From heroic *Captain Harlock* to the Japanese grunts in the Pacific War tales of *Battlefield (Senjo)*, Matsumoto's heroes are defined by their response to life's challenge. Even failure can be heroic, and few writers have ever been so in love with the heroism of failure as Matsumoto.

Many of his stories concern the boy's journey towards manhood. Man must leave childhood behind and take responsibility for his dreams and ambitions. "If you are a man, sometimes you must go even when you know you will lose. Sometimes you must fight even when you know you will die. That's manhood." So says the romantic pirate-knight Harlock when he joins his young friend Tetsuro to destroy the evil Machine Empire. The soul of engineering genius Tochiro, within the spaceship Arcadia's computer, says something along the same lines when Arcadia

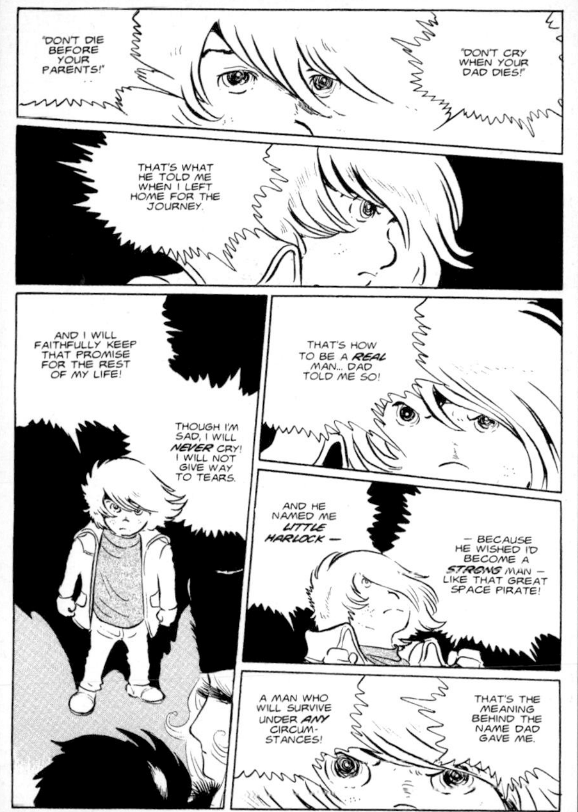

Real men don't cry: A character from *Galaxy Express 999,* encapsulates Matsumo's philosophy.

sets out on a mission against terrible odds to rescue one of its crew. When Harlock rebuffs the alien Mazone Queen, who wants him to betray humankind in exchange for power and her love, he tells her, "You could never understand a real man's heart." Matsumoto says: "My work is drawn from a man's point of view. Women are an eternal mystery to me. We men don't understand women at all—that's why they are so wonderful."

Like many of his contemporaries from the first half of the twentieth century, Matsumoto appears to see men and women in fundamentally different roles. Women are builders, nurturers, peacemakers. Men are the ones who push back the frontiers, fight the invaders, defend what women have built. It could be said that he views women as the stable principle of the universe, creators of life, order, and harmony, while men are constantly moving, both creators and tamers of chaos, ultimately bringers of death. Matsumoto creates mother-queens who inspire and nurture, but kings and statesmen seem to have little place in his universe. Like Rudolf Rassendyl in *The Prisoner of Zenda*, his heroes swashbuckle into town, fight for right and justice, and swashbuckle out again on some new adventure, carrying an image of the beautiful in their hearts and leaving behind a strong, powerful, lonely woman.

Matsumoto views time as a circle, an eternal sphere within which all life and all living beings can meet again and again. This neatly rationalizes many of the apparent contradictions and repetitions in his vast manga universe. The only true constant is man's struggle to define himself and shape his world. The mark of the Matsumoto hero is not how far he succeeds, because in the end time defeats us all. It is how he approaches the final defeat that defines him as a true hero and a true man, until his next incarnation in the circle of time.

He is an important character in George Akiyama's *Big Comic* manga *Drifting Clouds (Ukigumo)*.

TAKEDA SHINGEN

[A.D. 1521–1573]

The great warlord has been portrayed several times in manga, notably by Hiroshi Hirata in *The Warrior*. Born in 1937, Hirata spent some time working in the family business before taking up manga, and became one of the foremost masters of the *jidaimono*, or samurai epic. He was one of Yukio Mishima's favorite artists.

PRINCE SHOTOKU

[Sixth century A.D.]

The prince was an influential figure in spreading and encouraging Chinese culture and Buddhism in early Japan. *Emperor of the Rising Sun (Hizurutokoro no Tenshi)* by Ryoko Yamagishi appeared in LaLa in 1980, and also credited him with supernatural powers and bisexual tastes.

SNOW WHITE [A.D. 1812]

Another tale first published by the Brothers Grimm, the legend of the beautiful princess hidden from her wicked stepmother by seven dwarves was retold by Osamu Tezuka in his 1955 manga *Snow White* in Shueisha's educational magazine *First Grade Book*. Azumi Nakayama also told a Japanese version of the story, under the title *Shirayuki*, in her manga *Angelic Tales*. Japanese teenager Himeno finds she is the Snow Princess, fated to save the world with the help of seven pretty boys, in a modern version by Kaoru Naruse, published in Asuka magazine in 2001 as *Preytia: New Snow White Legend*. The Japanese Snow Goddess Shirayuki appears in many manga including CLAMP's *Snow Goddess Tales (Shirahime-sho)*, and Rumiko Takahashi's *Urusei Yatsura* as alien princess Lum's friend Oyuki.

OSAMU TEZUKA

[A.D. 1928–89]

The "god of manga" used himself in many of his works. Some appearances were as set-dressing, for instance as a painting in a room in *Black Jack* or as one of *Astro Boy*'s doodles. Some were brief Hitchcockian cameos, like his appearance as a passerby in *The Three-Eyed One* in 1975 or as a TV show panelist in 1969's *Land of the Tigermen*. Some were actual roles in the story. He was particularly fond of giving himself roles in *Black Jack* and shows up there over twenty times, often playing a doctor, his other real-life profession. He also played himself as author, artist, or studio boss. In *Vampires* he is the head of animation studio Mushi Productions, who is persuaded to hire werewolf boy Toppei and helps him prevent open warfare between his people and mankind; in *Tales of the Tokiwa Apartment* he tells the true story of his time sharing an apartment block with other young lions of manga. He usually appears as a short, skinny chap in heavy-rimmed glasses, his trademark beret on his head, though he has been seen with black curly hair, something that got him teased in his schooldays.

DR. RYOAN TEZUKA

[A.D. c.1850]

The real-life ancestor of manga artist Osamu Tezuka, young doctor Ryoan is the son of Dr. Ryosen Tezuka, and the pair practice in the Koishikawa district. They use the new Western medicine imported from Holland, and young Tezuka is passionate about science and the benefits of Japan's move into the modern world. In the 1981 manga *Tezuka's Ancestor Dr. Ryoan Tezuka*, he comes into conflict with traditionalist samurai Majiro Ibuya, both over their different beliefs and their love for the beautiful Ozeki. In real life, he was the first army doctor in Japan. His story was animated as *A Tree in the Sun (Hidamari no Ki)*.

IEYASU TOKUGAWA

[A.D. 1543-1616]

The great shogun is a key character in artist Tetsuo Hara and writer Keichiro Ryu's 1990 manga *Keiji of the Flowers (Hana no Keiji)* in *Shonen Jump*. Hero Keiji Maeda is a wacky yet gifted swordsman who meets Tokugawa, and other real people of the day like tea master Rikyu, in the capital during the shogunate of his predecessor Hideyoshi Totomi. The manga brings Hara's ideal of Japanese manhood into the exotic foreign cult of Christianity. Hara and Ryo gave Tokugawa his own title, *Ieyasu Tokugawa Shadow Warrior (Ieyasu Tokugawa Kagemusha)* when Keiji's story ended its three year run. 1961's *Sarutobi Sasuke* by Sanpei Shirato, based on Kazuo Den's novel, reworks the true story of a sixteenth-century ninja serving Tokugawa's opponent Daisuke Sanada, into a fable of a ninja child growing up after the battle of Sekigahara, when Tokugawa became shogun.

ULYSSES [c.750 B.C.]

The wandering prince Ulysses from Homer's epic story of the Trojan War appears in Tezuka's 1956 *Phoenix: Egypt* with Hector and Helen of Troy.

LEONARDO DA VINCI

[A.D. 1452–1519]

The great Italian artist of the Mona Lisa, whose many speculative works included designs for flying machines. He appears in *Time Traveler Ai* by Ai Ijima and Takeshi Takebayashi. Renaissance Italy is a popular setting for girls' manga, one example being Chiho Saito's *Flower Crown Madonna (Kakan no Madonna)* from *Flower Comics* in 1993.

JUBEI YAGYU

[After A.D. 1603]

An historical fgure of the seventeenth century, Jubei was a swordmaster to the Tokugawa shogunate who vanished in mysterious circumstances. Rumored to be a ninja master whose combat skills were matched only by his passion for justice, he occupies a similar place in Japanese folklore to Robin Hood in English legend—the loner who lives outside the law and risks his life to fight injustice or to protect those weaker than himself. He is, of course, irresistible to women of all classes, pickpocket or princess, good or evil. He is known to have lost an eye, but the exact circumstances can't be confirmed, though some legends say he lost it to his father during sword practice.

His life and legendary adventures have inspired many plays, novels, manga, and films. He came from a famous family. His grandfather Mataemon founded the Yagyu sword school and his father Munenori was swordmaster to the first three shoguns of Japan. His brother Matajuro inspired the 1887 Kabuki play *True Tale of Twin Umbrellas*. In 1992, Jiro Taniguchi drew and Kan Furuyama wrote *Samurai Legend (Kaze no Sho)*, originally published in *Young Champion* magazine and now available in English from CPM Manga. Carefully researched by both artist and writer, it is an attempt to set the Jubei legend in an historical context and relate it to the fall of the Bakufu government and the development of modern Japan over two centuries later. Real people,

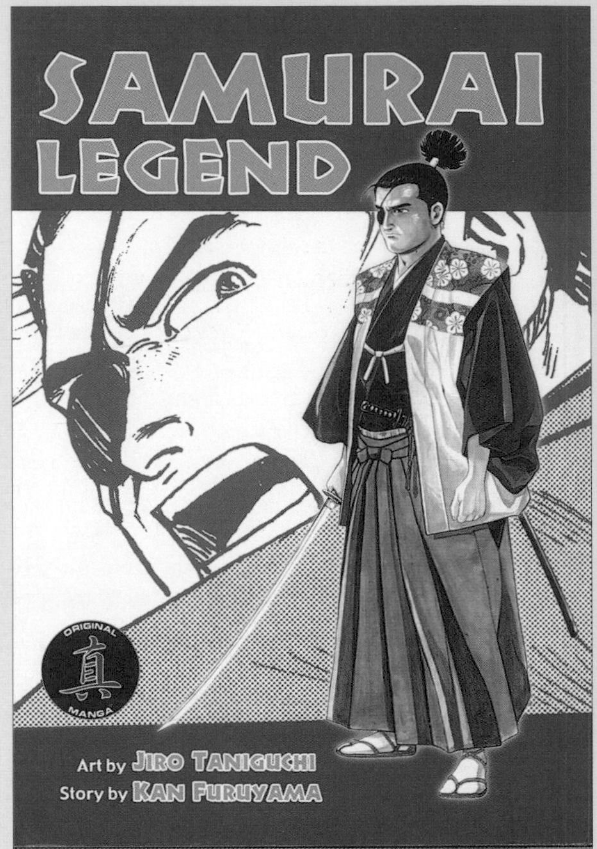

Jubei's legend has inspired many artists, but Taniguchi's version is based on historical research.

real sword schools—like Jubei's Yagyu style and the Jigen style from Satsuma—real costumes, real politics, and real weapons are woven into a convincing backdrop.

A visit from old adversaries to the aging Kaishu Katsu, the government official who oversaw the relatively peaceful surrender of the Bakufu and enabled the Meiji restoration to go ahead without destroying Japan in civil war, forms a framing device for the legend of Jubei and the Yagyu family's secret chronicles, which are said to be the *Kojiki*, the three sacred books of Japan. This ties in neatly with the fact that the *Kojiki* texts were unknown until the mid-Edo period, just after Jubei's time. The villain of the piece is retired emperor Gomino, obsessively dedicated to the destruction of the Tokugawa shogunate and restoration of direct imperial rule. As emperor, he was forced to marry shogun Hidetaka Tokugawa's grand-daughter, and, to ensure that Tokugawa blood would run in the veins of a future emperor, all his other possible heirs were executed. Gomino's attempts to seize power bring Jubei into conflict with both historical figures and invented characters like Yashamaro, a samurai loyal to the old ways who takes Jubei's eye in a thrilling fight. Gomino's daughter, Lady Tsukinowanomiya, who as Empress Myosho was Japan's 109th ruler from her father's retirement when she was seven years old until she abdicated at twenty-one, appears briefly. At the end of the story, in 1650, Jubei dies after killing Yashamaro in a final duel on a riverbank near his home. With his dying breath, he urges his young brother Rokumaru to write a book about the events leading to his death as a companion to his own volume on sword techniques.

PRINCE FELIX YUSSUPOV [A.D. 1887–1967]

The imperial Russian prince, son-in-law of the Tsar's sister, is the basis for the character of Leonid Yussupov in Ryoko Ikeda's *Window of Orpheus (Orpheus no Mado)*, first published in *Margaret* magazine in 1975. The real life Yussupov was one of the murderers of Grigory Efimovich Rasputin, the monk whose influence on the royal family was one of the factors in bringing about the Russian Revolution. After the Revolution he and his wife, Princess Irina, escaped to Paris. In the manga, Leonid shoots himself just before the Revolution in 1917, after the failure of a plot to end the regime of Alexander Kerensky. The historical events and characters are a backdrop for a complex love story. Legend has it that any couple who see each other through the Window of Orpheus in Regensburg, Germany, will be lovers for eternity. A girl disguised as a boy catches sight of two different boys through the window—so who will she love? Music student Julius has been raised as a boy for revenge and to secure an inheritance. The story moves from Germany to Russia as revolution looms. The legend continued in 1998's *Window of Orpheus New Chapter (Orpheus no Mado Gaiden)* in *Young You* magazine with art by Erika Miyamoto.

Bibliography

Lack of space prevents me from listing all the books, magazines and websites I've consulted in writing this book, but here are a few key sources. Apologies to all those I've had to leave out. An ongoing problem with web research is the frequent disappearance of sites, especially fan sites; I strongly recommend a visit to the Anime News Network or Anime Turnpike sites for up-to-date links on Western releases.

Periodicals

Newsweek Japan 18062003
Publishers Weekly 16062004
Ashby, Janet: The Book Report, Japan Times, 14 August 2004
Clements, Jonathan, ed: Manga Max, 1998-2000, Titan Publishing London, UK
West Laurence, Yvan, ed: Animeland, 1992-, Anime Manga Presse, Paris, France

Books

Amano, Masanao: Manga, Taschen, Germany, 2004
National Museum of Modern Art: Osamu Tezuka, NMMA Tokyo, Japan, 1990
Patten, Fred: Watching Anime, Reading Manga, Stone Bridge Press, Berkeley, CA, 2004
Schodt, Frederik L: Manga! Manga! A History of Japanese Comics, Kodansha International, Tokyo, Japan, 1984
Ibid.: Dreamland Japan: Writings on Modern Manga, Stone Bridge Press, Berkeley, CA , 1996

Websites

Asahi Shimbun newspaper website ***www.asahi.com***
Japan Times newspaper website ***www.japantimes.co.jp***
JAPRO website devoted to various Japanese creators ***www.japro.com***
Mainchi Daily News Interactive English language newspaper website ***http://202.221.31.68/news/index.html***
Osamu Tezuka World Official website for his work ***http://en.tezuka.co.jp***
Tokyo Foundation website ***www.tkfd.or.jp/eng***
Youkaimura: excellent Japanese-owned English language guide to Japanese ghosts and goblins ***www.youkaimura.org***

Picture Credits

ADV Manga: 113, 119, 223, 257, 286; *Futabasha*: 257
Antarctic Press: *Akita Shoten*: 176
Bandai, Viz LLC: 142
Comics One Corporation: 204
CPM Press: 75, 297, 342
CMX: 159
Dark Horse: 58, 183
DH Publishing Inc.: 267
Dragon Comics: 97
Dynamic Planning: 1, 19, 29, 31, 167, 199, 241, 249, 250, 276, 285
Flower Comics: 104
Fujiko Pro: 270
Gainax: *Kadokawa, Tokyopop Inc.*: 64; *Viz LLC*: 163
Gao, Kadokawa: 313
Hakusensha Inc., Viz LLC: 145, 151, 190, 218, 238, 245
Kazuhiza Kondon, Media Works, Sotsu Agency/Sunrise, Viz LLC: 148-9
Kodansha Ltd: 196, 272, 328, 331; *Bloomsbury Publishing*: 26; *Dark Horse*: 136, 137, 255, 262, 269, 288, 317; *IG, ITNDDTD*: 38, 39, 265; *Tokyopop Inc.*: 4, 73, 110, 122, 129, 184, 227, 292, 306; *Viz LLC*: 53, 195, 274
Kodokawa: *Antarctic Press*: 2; *Toho, Dark Horse*: 264
Lead Publishing Co.,Ltd., Saito Pro, Viz LLC: 233
MacFarlane: 165
Marvel Comics, Asahi Sonorama: 76, 77
Media Works Inc., CPM Press, Tokyopop Inc.: 298
Mushi: 52
Nibariki Co., Ltf., Viz LLC: 86, 247
Project Gen: 13
Shogakukan, Inc. Viz LLC: 6, 40, 44, 55, 92, 98, 115, 117, 128, 130, 140, 153, 175, 189, 318, 326, 339
Shonen Captain Comics: 83
Shuisha Inc.: *Bird Studios, Viz LLC*: 33, 93, 311; *Project Gen*: 35; *Scholars Press, Viz LLC*: 154; *Viz LLC*: 41, 45, 50, 51, 67, 80, 90, 101, 107, 109, 134, 173, 187, 209, 211, 225, 231, 296, 315, 322
Studio Tron: *CPM Press*: 27, 79; *Viz LLC*: 294
Sunrise/Kodansha Ltd. Viz LLC: 71
Tezuka Productions: 23, 24, 47, 63, 124, 125, 133, 215,224, 236, 237, 278, 279, 287, 290, 320
The Culture Archive: 10, 11
Tokuma Shuten: 169, 334, 335
Tokyopop, Inc.: 216, 260; *Chuokoron-Shinsha, Inc., Tohan Corp*: 179; *Sanama Matoh, Biblos*: 56; *Shizuru Seino, Kadokawa*: 88
Toys Press: 16, 299
Wani Comix: 280
Yoshikazu Yasuhiko, Sotsu Agency: 305, 329

Index